Contents

PART ONE: Historical Perspectives

PART TWO: Theory and Practice

PART THREE: The Wider Context and Links to the Other Conditions

Dedication

This book is dedicated to the memories of Ruth Sanford and Nel Kandell

Ruth Sanford and Nel Kandell each made great contributions in their own ways to the client-centered/person-centered approach world-wide. Ruth was well known for her work with Carl Rogers as well as for her role in the development of a major person-centered training program in the United States. Nel was known for her quiet work with the Carl Rogers' Library and as a member of the Center for Studies of the Person. Ruth's chapter in this book represents more than herself.

Introduction to the Series
Gill Wyatt

The concept for this series grew out of my idea to publish a book of edited papers on congruence and Pete Sanders (of PCCS Books) vision of extending this to Rogers' six conditions. We felt it crucial that all six conditions would need to be addressed in order to avoid repeating a recent pattern of emphasising the significance of what has become 'the three core conditions' i.e. congruence, empathy and unconditional positive regard. The four volumes of *Rogers' Therapeutic Conditions: Evolution, Theory and Practice*, are then,

Vol 1 Congruence (condition three)
Vol 2 Empathy (condition five)
Vol 3 Unconditional Positive Regard (condition four)
Vol 4 Contact and Perception (conditions one and six)

The editors of each of these volumes, where appropriate, have included:
• both previously published papers and newly commissioned work;
• client incongruence as it affected the theme of that volume;
• international contributors;
• the full diversity of person-centred therapy would be represented — client-centred, experiential and process-directed
• an historical review of the conceptualisation and development of the condition;
• research projects and findings;
• at least one contribution in each volume which focuses on the (re)integration of the volume condition with Rogers' other conditions.

The more experience I gain as a psychotherapist and counsellor and the more examination of theory I make, the more I realise the complex and subtle interplay of the six conditions. I used to see congruence, empathy and unconditional positive regard as the therapist conditions; client incongruence as the client's condition; and contact and the client's perception as the conditions of the relationship. It made sense on many levels. Now, however, I see all these conditions as more relational in their nature and more entwined in practice. Others have hypothesised that there may be only one therapeutic condition and that Rogers' conditions are facets of this meta-condition (Bozarth, 1998; Wyatt, 2000; Schmid, 2001, [this series Chapter 14, Vol. 1]). So although this series is in some respect separating the conditions from one another, I want the reader to understand that the spirit of this separation is in the hope that the examination of the separate parts will facilitate a deeper exploration of the inter-relationship of the conditions and how they create a whole.

ROGERS' SIX CONDITIONS

It has been suggested by many writers that Rogers' theoretical statement of 1957

i

The Necessary and Sufficient Conditions of Therapeutic Personality Change was the most critical event in the development of client-centred therapy — and perhaps even for psychotherapy as a whole (Barrett-Lennard 1998). In writing this paper he had set himself the task '. . . to state, in terms which are clearly definable and measurable, the psychological conditions which are both necessary and sufficient to bring about constructive personality change' (Rogers, 1957, p. 95). He hypothesised that no other conditions were necessary, if these six conditions existed and continued over time '. . . this is sufficient. The process of constructive personality change would follow' (ibid.). 'Constructive personality change' meant a change in the personality structure of the individual which would lead to 'greater integration, less internal conflict,' (ibid.) an increase in energy for living and a shift in behaviour away from what is regarded as 'immature' to behaviours regarded as 'mature'. Rogers had successfully delivered to the psychotherapy world a crucial statement that described the basic attitudes and conditions necessary for an effective therapeutic relationship for all theoretical orientation.

In 1959 Rogers published his major theoretical conceptualisation of Client-centred Therapy *'A Theory of Therapy, Personality, and Interpersonal Relationships, as Developed in the Client-Centered Framework'*. Here he writes his theory of therapy and personality change as an 'if-then' statement. If the conditions of the therapeutic process exist then a process is set in motion by these conditions and the result of this process will be 'certain' outcomes in personality and behaviour (Rogers, 1959, p. 212). In an interview with R. T. Hart (1970) Rogers explained that this theory formulation in Koch (1959) was actually written in 1953–54 and so although his 1959 paper was published after his 1957 statement it has to be seen as an antecedent for his 1957 statement. Other sources of this pivotal theoretical exposition can be found in earlier writings (1939, 1942, 1946 and 1951). In the little known 1946 paper Rogers described '. . . six "conditions" of therapist attitude and behaviour which . . . led predictably to a pattern of described qualities of therapy process and outcome.' (Barrett-Lennard, 1998, p. 66). These conditions included creating a warm, safe non-judgmental environment, to 'respond with deep understanding' of the client's emotional experience, 'to set limits on behaviour but not attitudes and feelings', and for the therapist to withhold from '. . . probing, blaming, interpreting, reassuring or persuading.' (Rogers, 1946, quoted in Barrett-Lennard, 1998, p. 66).

Then, in *Client-Centered Therapy* (1951), Rogers developed these precursors of his conditions referring to the importance of warmth (p. 41), therapist attitudes, deep understanding, and respect and acceptance; that these attitudes needed to be deeply and genuinely held by the therapist to be effective; and that the therapist should relate to the client 'in a deeply personal way' (p. 171). Within his personality theory he first coined the term 'congruence' and finally, the forerunner of condition six can be identified by Rogers giving attention to how the client perceives the counsellor (p. 42).

A wealth of research was also being carried out at the Chicago Counseling Center during the 1950s. This included The Parallel Studies Project and the research findings published by Rogers and Dymond (1954). This research revealed a surprisingly regular process during client-centred therapy, raising questions about the requirements for the occurrence of this process. (Barrett-Lennard 2001, personal communication). Looking for an answer to this brought Rogers a step closer to his 'conditions statement'.

Two other factors were part of this evolution. In 1954 Standal published his PhD thesis on *The Need for Positive Regard* in which he developed the idea of unconditional positive regard (UPR). The warmth, acceptance and respect that Rogers had referred to earlier came to fruition in Standal's concept. UPR was the term that Rogers used in his future writings. There was also an elaboration on the idea of the therapist needing to be genuine in his ability to step into the client's frame of reference and to relate 'in a deeply personal way'. Streich and Bown both accentuated the significance of the therapist being a whole person, with Bown advocated therapists allowing their (strong) emotions into the therapeutic relationship (Raskin, 1996), and Seeman wrote about the importance of the 'integration' of the therapist (1951). The therapist's congruence as one of Rogers' conditions was taking form.

Rogers 1957 conditions statement was integrative in the sense that it applied equally to all theoretical applications whereas his 1959 theoretical statement was specifically addressing client-centred therapy. There are some minor differences between Rogers' two theoretical statements of his six conditions. In 1959 he expressed them as follows and I have shown the (later) 1957 wording when different in italics. Before researching this chapter I believed the changes occurred between the 1957 paper and the 1959 paper and that the dates represented the chronological order of writing. Now we need to understand any significance of these changes in reverse. I have been unable to find any discussion of the importance of the changes, whether they were connected to the shift from a client-centred statement to an integrative statement or reflected other developments in Rogers' thinking.

1) That two persons are in *(psychological)* contact
2) That the first person, whom we shall term the client, is in a state of incongruence, being vulnerable, or anxious.
3) That the second person, whom we shall term the therapist, is congruent *(or integrated)* in the relationship.
4) That the therapist is experiencing unconditional positive regard toward the client.
5) That the therapist is experiencing an empathic understanding of the client's internal frame of reference *(and endeavours to communicate this to the client)*.
6) That the client perceives, at least to a minimal degree, conditions 4 and 5, the unconditional positive regard of the therapist for him, and the empathic understanding of the therapist. *(The communication to the client of the therapist's empathic understanding and unconditional positive regard is to a minimal degree achieved)*.

In the late 1950s and 1960s there was a profusion of research studies based on Rogers' Necessary and Sufficient Conditions. Barrett-Lennard developed his Relationship Inventory (BLRI) to measure the presence of the conditions in the therapeutic relationship to facilitate quantitative research. His research in 1962, although criticised later, did imply that the perceived therapist's conditions were 'involved in the generation of the associated change' of the client (Barrett-

Lennard, 1962 p. 31). Rogers, with colleagues, undertook the Wisconsin Project with hospitalised clients who were diagnosed 'schizophrenic '(Rogers, Gendlin, Kiesler and Truax 1967). This was an ambitious research project that failed to produce the hoped for results that unequivocally supported the conditions. Despite this disappointing conclusion, much more work was carried out that continued to explore the link between the therapeutic conditions and personality change for the client. The BLRI continued to be used, as were the rating scales of therapist congruence, empathy and UPR generated by Truax (Truax and Carkhuff, 1967). The results of this research, and later reviews of these studies, produced conflicting conclusions. Truax and Carkhuff (1967), Truax and Mitchell (1971), Patterson (1984), Gurman (1977) Stubbs and Bozarth (1994) reported evidence ranging from 'significant' to 'overwhelming' in support of the relationship between client-perceived therapist conditions and client outcome. On the other hand Mitchell, Bozarth and Krauft (1977), Parloff, Waskow and Wolfe (1978), Lambert, DeJulio and Stein (1978), Watson (1984) Beutler, Crago and Arizmendi (1986) and Cramer (1990) concluded that none of the studies had been designed, (a) to deal with the complexity of all of the therapeutic conditions in determining outcome; (b) to deal with the relational nature of these conditions; (c) to address sampling difficulties or (d) to utilise accurate enough measures. These findings suggested that Rogers' therapeutic conditions had not been tested rigorously enough. Whether this is true or not, there does seem to be overwhelming evidence from this time (1950s and 1960s), and more recent reviews, which support the hypothesis that the client-counsellor relationship and client variables (factors unique to each client and their environment) are the major determinants in client outcome rather than therapist-employed techniques or the particular theoretical orientation of the therapist (Duncan and Moynihan 1994, Bozarth, Zimring, and Tausch in press).

Rogers moved to La Jolla in 1963 and established the Center for Studies of the Person in 1968. His focus during these 'California years' moved strongly away from clinical work, as he became fascinated with groups in general and the encounter movement in particular. He increasingly turned to the application of the client-centred philosophy beyond the therapeutic relationship — including education, facilitation of client-centred therapists, large groups and international cultural conflicts. He was not to return to his earlier clinical focus and so he made no further major theoretical additions to his 1957 and 1959 conditions statements

The one notable exception was a paper written by Rogers and Sanford published in 1984. In this paper the first condition concerning 'psychological' contact is dropped. The condition related to the therapist's congruence is expanded to include the therapist's communication and the last condition is extended from the therapist's empathy and UPR, to now include the therapist's 'realness' needing to be perceived minimally by the client (Rogers and Sanford 1984, p. 1382–83). Again I have been unable to trace the significance of what would appear to be a major shift from his 1957/1959 conditions statement.

There have been three developments arising from Rogers clinical research and theoretical writings: (a) Gendlin, drawing from European existential philosophy, emphasised the significance of the experiential process of the client and developed 'focusing' (and subsequent evolution into experiential psychotherapy); (b) Wexler and Rice, using cognitive learning psychology, concentrated on the client's style of information processing (developing into process-directed therapy); and (c) Truax and Carkhuff's elaboration of a skills based eclectic model of the helping relationship.

The impact of Rogers' therapeutic conditions on psychotherapy, counselling and the helping professions has been immense. Even though the mainstream psychotherapy world challenged his findings, they also publicly awarded him honours and validation during the 1950s and early 1960s. Since then there has been a decline in the appreciation of his work, particularly in the United States. This is despite the fact that most, if not all, theoretical orientations acknowledge the significance of the therapeutic relationship and the importance, particularly of empathy. Psychotherapy research over the last 10 years has been specificity-based — defining specific treatments for specific psychological problems. This, along with the ill-informed criticism that client-centred and experiential psychotherapies lack depth of theory and cannot be applied to 'disturbed' clients, has meant that Rogers and his conditions are seldom acknowledged. Furthermore, client-centred and experiential psychotherapies are often misrepresented and dismissed as valid theoretical orientations.

Over the last ten years there has been renewed interest in person-centred therapy, particularly in Britain and Europe where numerous successful training programmes for person-centred counselling and psychotherapy have been developed. There has been renewed interest in research by, among others, Tausch et al., Greenberg, Lietaer, McLeod and there has been the theoretical contributions of Prouty, (Pre-therapy), Warner (Fragile Process) and Mearns (Working at Relational Depth and Configurations of Self). These contributions may help to elevate the standing of person-centred therapy. This series is another endeavour to extend the theoretical and clinical standing of person-centred therapy so that it can take its rightful place within psychotherapy, counselling and related mental health professions.

REFERENCES

Barrett-Lennard, G.T. (1998). *Carl Rogers' Helping System: Journey and Substance*. London: Sage.

Barrett-Lennard, G. T. (1962). Dimensions of therapist response as casual factors in therapeutic change. *Psychological Monographs*, 76(43), whole 562.

Beutler, L. E., Crago, M. and Arizmendi, T. G. (1986). Research on therapist variables in psychotherapy. In S. L. Garfield and A. E. Bergin (Eds.), *Handbook of psychotherapy and behavior change*. New York : Wiley, 3rd ed. pp. 257–310.

Bozarth, J.D. (1998). *The Person-Centered Approach: A Revolutionary Paradigm*. Ross-on-Wye: PCCS Books.

Bozarth, J.D., Zimring, F.M. and Tausch, R. (in press). Client-centered therapy: Evolution of a revolution. In D. Cain and J. Seeman (eds) Handbook of Research and Practice in Humanistic Psychotherapies. Washington D.C.: American Psychological Association

Cramer, D. (1990). Towards Assessing the Therapeutic Value of Rogers' Core Conditions. *Counselling Psychology Quarterly*, 3, pp. 57–66.

Duncan, B. L. and Moynihan, D. (1994). Applying outcome research: Intentional utilization of the client's frame of reference. *Psychotherapy* , 31, pp. 294–301.

Gurman, A. S. (1977). The patient's perception of the therapeutic relationship. In A. S. Gurman and A. M. Razin (Eds.), *Effective Psychotherapy: A handbook of research*. New York: Pergamon, pp. 503–43.

Hart, J.T. and Tomlinson, T.M. (1970). New directions in client-centered therapy. Boston: Houghton Mifflin.

Lambert, M. J., DeJulio, S. J. and Stein, D. M. (1978). Therapist interpersonal skills: Process, outcome, methodological considerations, and recommendations for Future Research. *Psychological Bulletin*, 85, pp. 467–89.

Mitchell, K. M., Bozarth, J. D. and Krauft, C. C. (1977). A reappraisal of the therapeutic effectiveness of accurate empathy, non-possessive warmth, and genuineness. In A. S. Gurman and A. M. Razin (Eds.), *Effective psychotherapy: A handbook of research.*. New York : Pergamon , pp. 482–502.

Parloff, M. B., Waskow, I. E. and Wolfe, B. E. (1978). Research on therapist variables in relation to process and outcome. In S. L. Garfield and A. E. Bergin (Eds.), *Handbook of psychotherapy and Behavior Change: An empirical analysis*. New York: John Wiley and Sons, 2nd ed. pp. 233–82.

Patterson, C. H. (1984). Empathy, warmth, and genuineness in psychotherapy: A review of reviews. *Psychotherapy* , 21(4), pp. 431–38.

Schmid, P. F. (2001). Authenticity: The Person as His or Her Own Author. Dialogical and Ethical Perspectives on Therapy as an Encounter Relationship. And Beyond. In G. Wyatt (Ed.), *Rogers' Therapeutic Conditions. Volume 1: Congruence*. Ross-on-Wye: PCCS Books, pp. 213–22.

Standal, S. (1954). The need for positive regard. A contribution to client-centered therapy. Unpublished doctoral dissertation, University of Chicago.

Raskin, N.J. (1996). Person-Centred Psychotherapy. In W. Dryden *Twenty Historical Steps in Developments in Psychotherapy*, London: Sage, pp. 1–28.

Rogers, C.R. (1939). The clinical treatment of the problem child. Boston: Houghton Mifflin.

Rogers, C.R. (1946). Significant aspects of Client-Centered Therapy. *American Psychologist*, 1, pp. 415–22.

Rogers, C.R. (1951). *Client-Centered Therapy*. Boston: Houghton-Mifflin.

Rogers, C.R. (1957). The Necessary and Sufficient Conditions of Therapeutic Change. *Journal of Consulting Psychology*, 21, pp. 95–103.

Rogers, C.R. (1959). A Theory of Therapy, Personality, and Interpersonal Relationships, as Developed in the Client-Centered framework in Koch S. (Ed.), *A Theory of Therapy, Personality and Interpersonal Psychotherapy*. New York: McGraw Hill, pp. 184–256.

Rogers, C. R. and Dymond, R. F. (1954). *Psychotherapy and personality change*. Chicago: University of Chicago Press .

Rogers, C. R., Gendlin, G. T., Kiesler, D. V. and Truax, C. B. (1967). *The therapeutic relationship and its impact: A study of psychotherapy with schizophrenics*. Madison: University of Wisconsin Press.

Rogers, C.R. and Sanford, R.C. (1984). Client-Centered Psychotherapy. In Kaplan, H.I. and Sadock, B.J. (Eds.) *Comprehensive Textbook of Psychiatry, IV*. Baltimore: Williams and Wilkins Co, pp. 1374–88.

Stubbs, J. P. and Bozarth, J. D. (1994). The dodo bird revisited: A qualitative study of psychotherapy efficacy research. *Journal of Applied and Preventive Psychology* , 3(2), pp. 109–20.

Truax, C. B. and Carkhuff, R. R. (1967). *Toward effective counseling and psychotherapy: Training and practice*. Chicago: Aldine .

Truax, C. B. and Mitchell, K. M. (1971). Research on certain therapist interpersonal skills in relation to process and outcome. In A. E. Bergin and S. L. Garfield (Eds.), *Handbook of Psychotherapy and Behavior Change*. New York: Wiley, pp. 299–344.

Watson, N. (1984). The empirical status of Rogers' hypothesis of the necessary and sufficient conditions for effective psychotherapy. In R. F. Levant, and J. M. Shlien (Eds.), *Client-Centered Therapy and the Person-Centered Approach: New directions in theory, research, and practice* . New York: Praeger, pp. 17–40.

Wyatt, G. (2000). *Presence: Bringing together the core conditions*. Paper presented at ICCCEP Conference in Chicago, USA.

Introduction to Volume 3: UPR

Unconditional Positive Regard in Context

Paul Wilkins and Jerold Bozarth

OUR UNDERSTANDING OF UNCONDITIONAL POSITIVE REGARD

The fourth of Rogers' (1959, p. 213) necessary and sufficient conditions for therapy to occur is 'that the therapist is *experiencing unconditional positive regard* toward the client'. That it is the fourth in the list implies nothing about its importance relevant to the other five conditions. In terms of theory and our own experience, we understand the client's perception of unconditional positive regard (UPR) to be the active facilitator of constructive personality change (the actualising tendency of the client is the actual agent) but there is little or no confirmation of this from research. Indeed, whereas empathy and congruence have been considered separately, in a recent effort to find research studies of UPR (as distinct from studies in which the conditions were considered together), only the study of Kilborn (1996, pp. 14–23) seemed relevant. Why there is a paucity of research into UPR we do not know but we do think there is a fruitful field here for exploration — but see chapter 15 by Jeanne Watson and Patricia Steckley for a more complete picture.

We have both asserted that unconditional positive regard is the curative factor in person-centred therapy (see Bozarth, 1998, p. 82; Bozarth in this volume; Wilkins in this volume); we also believe that Rogers' theoretical statements support this view (see Bozarth, 1998, p. 45). Rogers suggests that the effectiveness of the therapist's unconditional positive regard is dependent upon being perceived by the client to at least a minimal degree. It is in combination that the conditions are necessary and sufficient, exclude any and the proposition falls. It is axiomatic that it is not the so-called core conditions of congruence, unconditional positive regard and empathy which make for successful therapy (see Tudor, 2000, pp. 33–7), still less any one of them, but the six together. This is of great importance when any evaluation of person-centred therapy is attempted. That said, in this series tradition and precedence are followed in that the six conditions are teased apart and considered separately. And this is a useful thing to do because the whole may be understood by deliberation on its parts. We and our fellow contributors offer here different and differing views of UPR, what it means, how the concept arose, what is known about it from practice and research, how it fits in with other systems of philosophy and so on. In our various ways we, the chapter writers, have thought a great deal about UPR. The writing presented here draws on many years of practice in many different settings and nations (including Austria, Belgium, Brazil, Canada, Japan, the UK and the USA).

This book then comprises chapters gathered together under the headings of 'historical perspectives', 'theory and practice' and 'the wider context'. They are written from a variety of perspectives within the broad person-centred tradition. The chapters range from a brief experiential statement in the form of a poem by Armin Klein and a brief comment from Gerald Bauman from the perspective of a client-centred therapist to a review of formal research by Jeanne Watson and Patricia Steckley. The classic client-centred position is reflected (for example) by Barbara Brodley and Carolyn Schneider who draw directly on practice to explain how UPR may be communicated in verbal behaviours. Mary Hendricks, James Iberg and Germain Lietaer offer a different perspective; that of experiential psychotherapy with its emphasis on focusing and 'process'. Mary Hendricks draws on her own practice to consider an experiential version of UPR, James Iberg discusses the constituent activities of UPR and Germain Lietaer writes about unconditional positive regard as a multidimensional concept and considers the implications of this view. Some of the other chapters also represent an attempt to understand unconditional positive regard in terms of person-centred theory and/or practical experience. Paul Wilkins' chapter falls into that category as does Jerold Bozarth's 'reconceptualization' chapter and Elizabeth Freire's chapter about UPR as the distinctive feature of client-centred therapy. Garry Prouty's consideration of the importance of UPR in the practice of Pre-therapy also fits into this category. Judy Moore and Toru Kuno both consider the relationship between the person-centred concept of UPR and aspects of Japanese philosophy or religion and Peter Schmid offers an erudite chapter interweaving the concept of UPR with others from the European philosophical tradition. Other contributors write of the 'historical' role and evolution of unconditional positive regard, thus Kathy Moon, Bert Rice and Carolyn Schneider re-evaluate and represent the important early work of Standal. Jerold Bozarth presents an historical perspective of UPR. Perhaps Ruth Sanford's paper 'A Misunderstood Way of Being' (written in 1984) bridges the gap between 'historical perspectives' and 'theory and practice'. As a review of UPR research, the paper by Jeanne Watson and Patricia Steckley is unique.

Collectively, these contributions offer the reader insight into the variety of thought which theorists and practitioners who label themselves as 'person-centred' have about unconditional positive regard. We do not claim 'completeness', there are other views or variations and our approach continues to evolve but we do claim to be inclusive of the range of opinion. As well as the views expressed in the chapters themselves, we have taken the opportunity to cover two other areas in the introduction. These are the role of 'client incongruence' in the demonstration and perception of unconditional positive regard and how that condition is seen from the perspectives of practitioners of other forms of therapy.

UNCONDITIONAL POSITIVE REGARD AND CLIENT INCONGRUENCE

Human beings have a great need for positive regard. It is fundamental to psychological survival, so much so, that experience can be distorted or denied to maintain the self-concept. As Thorne (1992, p. 31) records, the quest for positive regard can lead to the development over time of 'a marked discrepancy between the self as perceived and the actual experience of the total organism'. This leads to that gulf between self and experience which, in person-centred terms, is called incongruence. Client incongruence is necessary (condition two) for constructive personality change to occur, indeed person-centred therapy is about increasing (or bringing about) harmony between the self and experience, the inner world and the outer such that they are in accord and situations evaluated and choices made in line with a personal valuing system rather than an introjected one.

Why is unconditional positive regard a necessary condition for such changes? Because when this attitude of the therapist is perceived by the client its major effect is assumed to be to counter conditions of worth. Freedom from conditions of worth ideally leads to the state of being fully functioning and is therefore a desirable outcome of therapy — or indeed of personal growth processes of any kind. Conditions of worth result when the positive regard of a significant other is *conditional*. They lead to an evaluating of experience with reference to external factors rather than to the maintenance or enhancement of the organism. Because a condition of worth disturbs the individual's internal valuing process it prevents free and full functioning (see Rogers, 1959, pp. 209–10). This, by definition, results in incongruence. Thus, incongruence can be viewed as arising from a lack of (or insufficient) unconditional positive regard. Similarly, the 'corrective' for incongruence becomes the consistent perception of unconditional positive regard from a significant other. In the context of therapy, this significant other is the person in the role of the therapist. Rogers (1959, p. 215) offers evidence in support of this hypothesis, recording that Seeman 'found that an increase in the counselor's liking for the client during therapy was significantly associated with therapeutic success' and that he and Lipkin (in a separate study) 'found that clients who felt themselves to be liked by the therapist tended to be more successful'.

The second of Rogers' necessary and sufficient conditions requires that the person in the role of the client is in a state of incongruence being *vulnerable or anxious*. Vulnerability and anxiety (see Rogers, 1959, pp. 203–4 for an explanation of these terms) imply the existence of conditions of worth and are therefore counteracted by the UPR of the therapist. Rogers (1959, p. 209) states that the positive regard of others results in positive self-regard — 'a positive attitude toward self which is no longer directly dependent on the attitudes of others'. When the locus of evaluation has become internalised and 'no self-experience can be discriminated as more or less worthy of positive regard than any other' an individual is experiencing unconditional positive self-regard and is thus no longer incongruent.

Vulnerability and anxiety are not causes of incongruence but products of it. This raises the question as to whether it is possible to be incongruent without being vulnerable or anxious and therefore that therapeutic interventions are contra-indicated. Barrett-Lennard (1998, p. 79) states 'some degree of vulnerability and anxiety seems bound to apply to anyone voluntarily in therapy and, perhaps, to most people'. If we allow of Barrett-Lennard's implication that anyone putting themselves forward in the client role is, at least to some degree, experiencing incongruence and even that this is a common state, does this necessarily mean that everyone will benefit from person-centred therapy? Perhaps not. Although unperceived incongruence exposes an individual to *potential* vulnerability and anxiety, it seems that Rogers' proposition requires that incongruence per se is not a necessary condition for therapy but that its emergence as vulnerability or anxiety is. Although Rogers (1959, p. 215) reports that there had been little research on condition two [and writing 39 years later, Barrett-Lennard (1998, p. 79) also comments on the lack of research into this condition], he cites a study by Gallagher as indicating 'that less anxious clients tend never to become involved in therapy, but drop out'. Whether these less anxious clients are actually more congruent and therefore less in need of unconditional positive regard from another, or unaware of their incongruence is hard to know. But perhaps it is irrelevant. Does condition two imply that therapy will only be successful if, in some way and on some level, the person in the client role is sufficiently aware of and troubled by incongruence to persist in the endeavour? Almost certainly.

No discussion of UPR and client incongruence would be complete without at least indicating the work of Speierer (1990, 1996) who proposes a 'differential incongruence model' which he sees as offering (1996, p. 299) a 'theory of disorder on the basis of the incongruence-paradigm'. Speierer hypothesises incongruence as having different origins rather than originating simply from conditions of worth. Other sources (p. 299) are 'a non-socially caused bio-neuropsychological inability to reach congruence' and 'social and non-social life-changing events'. He further postulates (p. 300) that 'neurotic disorders, personality disorders and psychotic disorders differ from each other in the presence or absence of conscious incongruence'. In Speierer's model (which diverges from classic client-centred theory), the sources of client incongruence dictate appropriate therapy options. These options (p. 299) 'go beyond the three basic variables or therapeutic attitudes'. It seems that Speierer does not see incongruence as arising solely from conditional positive regard and, in his thinking, unconditional positive regard becomes less than central to effecting therapeutic change.

In the first book in this series, which addresses congruence, Bozarth (2001, pp. 184–99) suggests that in client-centred therapy congruence cannot exist without the integral relationship with empathic understanding and unconditional positive regard. He goes so far as to suggest that client-centred therapy is threatened as a viable theory if this relationship is not understood. Bozarth (2001, p. 185) proposes the definition:

> Congruence is the manifestation of unconditional positive self-regard (UPSR) and can be identified as the therapist's presence in client-centred therapy. Unconditional positive regard towards and empathic understanding of the client's frame of reference characterize this presence.

Bozarth's position has little room for arguments outside of Rogers' basic premises since he takes the view that such arguments are referring to a theory different from classic client-centred theory. Bozarth argues that UPR is the curative factor in client-centred theory and that this can be no other way given Rogers' 'theory of pathology'. See his chapters (3 and 14) in this volume for an expansion of this argument.

UNCONDITIONAL POSITIVE REGARD FROM OTHER PERSPECTIVES

The chapters in this book are representative of several person-centred perspectives on UPR (including some of our internal controversies). However, what is less obvious from our accounts is the understanding of UPR from other perspectives. Even though Patterson (1984, p. 437) asserts that 'the evidence for the necessity, if not the sufficiency, of the therapist conditions of accurate empathy, respect, or warmth, and therapeutic genuineness is incontrovertible', the proposition that Rogers' conditions are 'necessary and sufficient' is often dismissed by therapists of other orientations (see for example Lazarus, 1993, pp. 404–7) who may argue that while they are necessary in the forming of a therapeutic relationship, these conditions are not sufficient to engender change. Some of the controversy surrounding the sufficiency of Rogers' conditions can be found in Lazarus and Lazarus (1991) and Bozarth's (1991) rejoinder to it and Patterson (1969, 1984, 1985) has repeatedly responded to the conclusion that the conditions are not sufficient to engender change.

Implicit in these doubts of the proposition of the necessary and sufficient conditions are doubts about UPR although 'acceptance' is widely held to be a desirable therapist quality. There are even arguments that the core conditions (severally or together) may be counter-therapeutic. Often, while broad agreement with person-centred theory is indicated, so are reservations, refinements or differences. For example, Dryden (1990, pp. 17–18) records that rational-emotive behaviour therapists agree with the need for the core conditions 'particularly the importance of unconditional acceptance and genuineness' (the latter is a synonym for congruence). However, rational emotive behaviour therapists are critical of offering clients 'undue counsellor warmth' (warmth is one of Rogers' synonyms for unconditional positive regard). This, Dryden (p. 18) goes on, is because:

> First, counsellor warmth may unwittingly reinforce clients' dire need for love and approval — an irrational belief which is believed to lie at the core of much psychological disturbance. Secondly, counsellor warmth may also reinforce the philosophy of low frustration tolerance that many clients have.

Even though Dryden acknowledges the place of the Rogers' conditions, he reaches an opposite conclusion as to the effect of 'warmth' as that presented in person-centred theory. As Rogers (1959, p. 230) points out in his section on re-integration, it is the communicated unconditional positive regard of 'a significant other' which facilitates a decrease in conditions of worth and an increase in unconditional self-regard. This must result in an increasing internalisation of the locus of evaluation and thus a decreasing need for 'approval'.

In other orientations too there are differences from the person-centred position. For example, from the point of view of psychosynthesis, Whitmore (1991, p. 22) indicates the agreement between Rogers and Assagioli as to the importance of the relationship in the counselling process but her list of 'counsellor attitudes' (pp. 26–34) includes not only acceptance (which, p. 26, 'is similar to Rogers' concept of unconditional positive regard') but also 'knowing and understanding', 'confirming', 'non-attachment to outcome', 'stimulating' and 'connecting'. It is probably only non-attachment to outcome which is also shared with person-centred counsellors who might find some of the other attitudes contrary to an attitude of unconditional positive regard because they imply approval. Sometimes the same terms are used by therapists of other orientations but the meaning or understanding of the effects of a condition or attitude is different. For example, Jacobs (1988, p. 13) records that a psychodynamic counsellor would expect 'unconditional regard' to encourage positive transference. References to the need for 'acceptance' are relatively common from therapists of other orientations but if acceptance is an accurate synonym for UPR, why not use the simpler term? (See Paul Wilkins [Chapter 5] for an exploration of this argument.) We are not convinced that the term 'acceptance' as used by therapists of other orientations is necessarily the same as the person-centred concept of unconditional positive regard. What is also widely doubted is a therapist's ability to offer unconditional positive regard. This is questioned from both within and without the approach.

HOW CAN ANYONE *GUARANTEE* UNCONDITIONAL POSITIVE REGARD?

The unconditional positive regard of the counsellor for the client is a *necessary* condition for constructive change. Indeed Bozarth (1998, pp. 83–8 and in this volume) concludes that UPR is *the* necessary and sufficient condition for constructive change as presented in Rogers' theory of therapy. However, the world is full of hostile, reprehensible, malefic individuals. How can they possibly be acceptable to anybody? Not unreasonably and leaving aside the important matter of definition, Masson (1992, p. 234) asks, 'faced with a brutal rapist who murders children, why should any therapist have unconditional regard for him?' (Masson omits 'positive'). There is no reason at all why any therapist *should* but the therapeutic endeavour will be pointless without it. While therapists may be limited by their ability to offer unconditional positive regard, this in no way implies that person-centred therapy is similarly limited. Theory asserts that *if* (for example) a paedophile consistently experiences the six conditions, then therapeutic change *will* occur. Of course it may be that this is a big 'if'. But what is important is that it is realised that the limitation is in the practitioner, not the theory. This does, of course, raise the question of whether, given the nature of people (not excepting counsellors and psychotherapists) as, often and at least to some extent, prejudiced, fearful beings, the theory can ever be put to the test. Luckily, although we share the tendency to be unaccepting of some things, these are not necessarily the same things and we may therefore be appropriate therapists for different clients. Also, as implied earlier, theorists and practitioners of other orientations often miss the point of Rogers' conceptualisation of UPR. The most parsimonious definition of Rogers' is that of the acceptance of every momentary experience of the client. The good, bad and indifferent momentary experiences are accepted with equality.

Masson is not alone in questioning the achievability of unconditional positive regard. Even Rogers stated that to hold someone in unconditional positive regard is 'sometimes very difficult' (Rogers quoted in Hobbs, 1987, p. 20). Lietaer (1984) examines the controversy which surrounds unconditional positive regard stating (p. 41) 'unconditional positive regard is probably one of the most questioned concepts in client-centered therapy'. He considers that unconditionality has its problems (1984, p. 41). These Lietaer lists as:

(1) There is a potential conflict between genuineness or congruence on the one hand, and unconditionality on the other; (2) It is a rare person and a rare time in which the constancy of acceptance can be provided by any therapist for any client. Thus, while unconditionality is not impossible, it is improbable; (3) Unconditionality calls upon the therapist for a devoted self-effacing that often leads to a compensatory reaction in which confrontation becomes a form of self-assertion.

Lietaer sees that these questions and difficulties arose as the client-centred therapy became more relationship-centred with a resulting increased prominence given to the therapist's congruence ('which implies among other things feedback and confrontation'). Bozarth (1998, p. 85) believes Lietaer to be in error, he expresses the view that 'client-centred' and 'relationship-centred' are not differently defined and that Lietaer's 'behavioral definition of genuineness as involving feedback and confrontation' leads to a shift in emphasis from trusting the client's experience towards trusting the 'expertise' of the therapist. In Bozarth's view, Lietaer's position is predicated upon the assumptions of Gendlin's experiential therapy rather than upon the theory of Rogers.

THIS BOOK IN SUMMARY

Our introduction and the following chapters indicate something of the complexity of unconditional positive regard and (explicitly and implicitly) some of the controversies which surround that concept. We believe that many of the differences and similarities of various perspectives on unconditional positive regard in Rogers' theory of therapy are identified in this book. The contributions of the editors and other authors from their various and varying perspectives add richness to the fundamental concept of UPR. In the chapters, readers will find ideas and comments about the relationship between UPR and the other conditions both from a theoretical perspective and in practice, explanations of its relative importance, notions as to how a client's perception of the therapist's UPR may be facilitated and much, much more. You may not agree with everything you read here but we hope that you are stimulated to reconsider your own ideas about UPR and to enhance your practice as a result.

REFERENCES

Barrett-Lennard, G. T. (1998). *Carl Rogers' Helping System: Journey and Substance*. London: Sage.

Bozarth, J. D. (1991). Rejoinder: perplexing perceptual ploys. *Journal of Counseling and Development*, 69, (5), pp. 466–8.

Bozarth, J. D. (1998). *Person-Centered Therapy: a Revolutionary Paradigm*. Ross-on-Wye: PCCS Books.

Bozarth, J. D. (2001). Congruence: a special way of being. In G. Wyatt (Ed.) *Rogers' Therapeutic Conditions: Evolution, Theory and Practice. Volume I: Congruence*. Ross-on-Wye: PCCS Books, pp. 184–99.

Dryden, W. (1990). *Rational-Emotive Counselling in Action.* London: Sage.

Hobbs, T. (1987). The Rogers' interview. *Counselling Psychology Review,* 4 , (4), pp. 19–27.

Jacobs, M. (1988). *Psychodynamic Counselling in Action.* London: Sage.

Kilborn, M. (1996). The quality of acceptance. *Person-Centred Practice,* 4, (1), pp. 14–23.

Lazarus, A. A. (1993). Tailoring the therapeutic relationship or being an authentic chameleon. *Psychotherapy,* 30, (3), pp. 404–7.

Lazarus, A. A. and Lazarus, C. N. (1991). Let us not forsake the individual nor ignore the data: a response to Bozarth. *Journal of Counseling Development,* 69, (5), pp. 463–5.

Lietaer, G. (1984). Unconditional positive regard: a controversial basic attitude in client-centered therapy. In R. F. Levant and J. M. Shlien (Eds.) *Client-Centered Therapy and the Person-Centred Approach: New Directions in Theory, Research and Practice.* New York: Praeger, pp. 41–58.

Masson, J. (1992). *Against Therapy.* London: Fontana.

Patterson, C. H. (1969). Necessary and sufficient conditions for psychotherapy. *The Counseling Psychologist,* 1, (2), pp. 8–26.

Patterson, C. H. (1984). Empathy, warmth, and genuineness in psychotherapy: a review of reviews. *Psychotherapy,* 21, pp. 431–8.

Patterson, C. H. (1985). *The Therapeutic Relationship: Foundations for an Eclectic Psychotherapy.* Monterey, CA: Brooks/Cole.

Rogers, C. R. (1959). A theory of therapy, personality, and interpersonal relationships, as developed in the client-centered framework. In S. Koch (Ed.) *Psychology: A Study of a Science Vol. 3. Formulations of the Person and the Social Context.* New York: McGraw-Hill, pp. 184–256.

Speierer, G.-W. (1990). Towards a specific illness concept of client-centered therapy. In G. Lietaer, J. Rombauts and R. van Balen (Eds.) *Client-Centered and Experiential Psychotherapy in the Nineties.* Leuven: Leuven University Press, pp. 337–60.

Speierer, G.-W. (1996). Client-centered psychotherapy according to the differential incongruence model (DIM). In R. Hutterer, G. Pawlowsky, P. F. Schmid and R. Stipsits (Eds.) *Client-Centered and Experiential Psychotherapy: A Paradigm in Motion.* Frankfurt-am-Main: Peter Lang.

Thorne, B. (1992). *Carl Rogers.* London: Sage.

Tudor, K. (2000). The case of the lost conditions. *Counselling,* 11, (1), pp. 33–7.

Whitmore, D. (1991), *Psychosynthesis Counselling in Action.* London: Sage.

1   # Unconditional Positive Regard
Deep Openness
Armin Klein

When people come to me asking for help
     With their confusion about themselves, about their lives,
I offer to try to facilitate their own growth process,
     Their own self-explorations.

I try to open myself, empty myself of any thinking about them,
     Before I meet them. That is very difficult for me.
My cultural conditioning has always been to think, to problem-solve,
     What knowledge, what identities will provide understanding?
At first, my openness — when I can reach it — feels small and guarded,
     Scared as I am about new interactions and scared as I am, especially,
About facing the unknown — without structures.
     As I try to open, I cannot fool myself that there is any place
To which I am going other than to the unknown and to the unpredictable.
     So I am fearful, though I have grown comfortable with my fears,
Excited about the growth they promise me.

When we meet, I begin to relax as I begin to sense, experience,
     Something more of the person, the individual being,
Some comes from our talk.
     More sensing of their being comes from our non-verbal communication,
The moments and the ways in which we each smile, we cry, we laugh, and we frown.
     We touch each other powerfully in those moments — without words.
We facilitate each other — and my openness grows.
     My mind empties itself of my cultural conditioning and all of its structures.
          My understanding becomes less problem-solving.
               I experience it, and myself, as more deeply empathic.
          My empathy comes more from my inner self, what I like to call my heart.
               I experience myself as more deeply genuine.
     When I become very open, or very 'empty'— to the extent that I can —
     My interest simply, and apparently naturally, deepens and changes.
My interest becomes very loving — without any apparent motivation.

UNCONDITIONAL POSITIVE REGARD

I experience my positive regard as unconditional.
I feel myself moving into, and being in, an altered state of consciousness.

• •
• •

I love this process of opening, emptying, that has developed for me in my work.
It has enriched and changed my work, which I love.
This process, however, has also changed my life.
It has become a wishful model for all my relationships and my self-explorations,
Although the framework of non-therapy relationships is markedly different.

In psychotherapy, I am devoted to the explorations of the other person.
I am always surprised at the unexpected gifts I receive from their explorations.
In my friendships, the structure jumps over all the possibilities.
The responsibilities are more in the background, and they are more shared.
I am still, however, always trying to be more open and more empty of culture.
When I succeed I feel, here also, very loving.
I experience my positive regard as unconditional.

This model has become my vision of how, with many ups and downs,
I am trying to live. The ups are joyful.
I sense the deepening of my openness and my cultural emptiness as
Being at the core of the successes and joy
That I have in my work and in my friendships.
When I am less open, closing a little or closing a lot,
I diminish my genuineness,
The people who work with me in psychotherapy are very forgiving.
My friends are also very forgiving.
I am very grateful and encouraged that both groups of people
Recognize and treasure my struggle to be deeply open with them and myself.

Reaching for the place of deeper, loving openness brings me
To Unconditional Positive Regard.

2   Unconditional Positive Regard

Gerald Bauman

When Jerold invited me and Armin to write a chapter on UPR by a couple of 'Old-Timer Rogerians' (OTRs), I felt more than usually shy. While Armin *is*, in fact, an authentic OTR, I can legitimately claim only to be an OT (I'm over 70) and an R, but not an OTR — my early training was in psychoanalysis. I came to Rogers only after many soul-searching years of psychotherapy practice in which I tried to come to some understanding of what I was trying to do and, if it was effective, why?

I've had no formal training in Client-Centered Therapy, and I have no 'old-timer's' view of UPR. In fact, I don't think much about the three conditions when I'm doing therapy. Yet, I count myself very much a Rogerian; in fact, a fairly orthodox one.

So when Armin and Jerold 'leaned' on me to join Armin in writing something, my first response was a kind of review/appreciation of Armin's poem (see below). They then asked for a more revealing statement of my own therapeutic view.

So here's how I think about the role of positive regard in therapy.

I see psychotherapy as an interpersonal transaction governed by two overarching motives, the need to know and the need to be known. While these needs operate continuously in both therapist and client, the therapeutic effect occurs when the client's need to be known is satisfied by effective 'knowing' on the therapist's part; i.e. by the therapist's more or less accurate empathic understanding and its communication to the client.

Perhaps the most powerful growthful moment in therapy occurs when the client experiences new clarity of a heretofore unavailable aspect of his/her experience arising from the therapist's communication of empathic understanding, *followed by the client's experience of no reduction in the therapist's need or willingness to know the client.*

This experience of *uninterrupted* therapist's acceptance (positive regard) confounds the client's expectation of disapproval and helps to generate in the client a further sense of the unconditionality of the therapist's positive regard.

REACTIONS TO ARMIN KLEIN'S POEM

On the very rare occasions that those of us who are lucky enough to do excellent psychotherapy for even a part of a session, I believe that we go through the inner development depicted in Armin's poem, typically with only minimal awareness. He describes the following development:

First, he 'tries to open myself, to empty myself . . .'. Armin alludes to the difficulty very often in achieving 'openness', and that often the other person (the client) offers crucial help, as he and the client 'touch' each other, leading to the growth of Armin's openness. (It's tempting to contrast Armin's 'openness' with Freud's 'blank screen'.) As this process deepens, his regard for the client becomes more and more unconditional, and then Armin notices, as though in passing, that he is becoming increasingly congruent and empathic — Rogers' three 'conditions' emerge, effortlessly, requiring no 'decision' to offer them! Armin thus may be seen as arguing that UPR is the primary condition, which makes the other two more or less inevitable.

Thinking of my own efforts to become 'open', I recognize the value, prior to a therapy session, of a brief nap, and sometimes by practicing meditation. I also sometimes experience the client's attention to me as facilitating reduction of my anxiety; it seems to reassure me that I am not alone, and frees me to remain 'open'.

In thinking about the therapeutic effect of UPR, I see that the client's benefit from empathic contact and clarification depends heavily on the client's perception of its accuracy, or at least it depends on the client's sense that the therapist is genuinely seeking contact. In addition, I think that therapeutic effect depends on the client's perception that the therapist's desire for further empathic exchange is undiminished, that is, that there's been no 'post-empathic' reduction in positive regard.

3 Client-centered Unconditional Positive Regard: A historical perspective

Jerold D. Bozarth

Unconditional Positive Regard (UPR) evolved from Rogers' postulate of an 'accepting therapeutic atmosphere' to become the curative variable in client-centered therapy. Rogers defined UPR as the extent to which the therapist is ' . . . experiencing a warm acceptance of each aspect of the client's experience being a part of the client . . . ' (Rogers, 1957, cited in Kirschenbaum and Henderson, 1989, p. 225). Rogers extended this definition and repeats it in one of his last written articles:

> When the therapist is experiencing a positive, nonjudgmental, accepting attitude toward whatever the client is at that moment, therapeutic movement or change is more likely. Acceptance involves the therapist's willingness for the client to be whatever immediate feeling is going on — confusion, resentment, fear, anger, courage, love, or pride. It is a nonpossessive caring. When the therapist prizes the client in a total rather than a conditional way, forward movement is likely (Rogers, 1986, p. 199).

The identification of unconditional positive regard nudged client-centered theory from the ambivalence between a self or organismic theory to primarily that of an organismic theory. Rogers' theory of pathology shifted from the reorganization of self to that of UPR as the central aspect of the theory (Rogers, 1951, 1959). This evolutionary development was a radical shift that clarified and concretized client-centered therapy as a way of being for the therapist rather than as a method of doing therapy. Therapist attitudes rather than therapist method or goals became the central axiom of client-centered therapy.

EARLY HISTORY (1940–51)

Raskin's history of nondirective theory identifies Rogers' early contributions and reveals the evolutionary direction of the theory (Raskin, 1948). Central to Rogers' contributions was the concept of 'acceptance' of the client. Freud, Rank, Allen, and Taft were forerunners of Rogers who emphasized the strength of the client and the acceptance of momentary feelings as critical therapeutic variables. However, they believed that it was the expert therapist who directed the client towards personal growth. Freud, for example, accepted the client's feelings but believed that it was the therapist who had to identify the origins of the feelings.

Rank's acceptance was curtailed by the need for the therapist to help the client discover the purpose of certain feelings (Raskin, 1948, p. 104). Rogers' acceptance was a 'nondirective acceptance'. It was this nondirective acceptance that ' . . . steadily deepened into a condition that people in mental turmoil need no more than to be accepted as they are' (Raskin, 1948, p. 105). Herein, 'the client's concept of self . . . [was] . . . believed to be the most central factor in his adjustment and perhaps the best measure of his progress in therapy' (Raskin, 1948, p. 105). Raskin suggests that most of the significant changes in client-centered therapy that occurred between 1943 and 1948 focused on the client's internal frame of reference. Raskin suggested that the term 'client-centered therapy' as it replaced 'nondirective therapy' reflected this broader focus on the client's frame of reference. This change was characterized by a ' . . . de-emphasis on nondirective *techniques*, together with an increased appreciation of the importance of a nondirective *attitude*' (Raskin, 1948, p. 106).

The role of the self-concept took on increased importance as a central aspect of the theory. The concept of self became central to the internal frame of reference ' . . . for understanding personality and the changes in personality which occur in therapy' (Raskin, 1948, p. 106). At least one dissertation at the University of Chicago advanced hypotheses concerning the self for client-centered theory (Raimy, 1943). Also, Rogers and others added to the increased role of self in the theory (Lecky, 1945; Rogers, 1940; Snygg and Combs, 1949). Even earlier, Rogers identified self-recognition as being central to the theory:

> In the rapport situation, where he is accepted rather than criticized, the individual is free to see himself without defensiveness, and gradually to recognize and admit his real self with its childish patterns, its aggressive feelings, and its ambivalences, as well as its mature impulses, and rationalized exterior (Rogers, 1940, p. 162).

The crux of counseling was defined by the extent to which the client could examine her self-concept and accept those parts of self that were denied and distorted. As hypothesized in one dissertation: 'In counseling, the counselor tries to create a permissive atmosphere in which the client can drop his guard and look at the parts of the self-concept which are causing difficulty' (Raimy, 1943, cited in Raskin, 1948, p. 107). The emphasis of the self was evident in Rogers' early reference to 'Client-Centered Therapy' (Rogers, 1951). Specifically, nondirective acceptance, 'the permissive atmosphere', of the momentary experiences of the self freed the individual to accept her 'real self' and to examine the difficult areas of the self-concept. This *attitude* of nondirective acceptance by the therapist was the forerunner of unconditional positive regard. The evolving development of the concept of UPR eventually took on a more central role in client-centered therapy.

TRANSITION (1951–57)

The transition of the theory from examination of self to the experiencing of UPR continued with various tributaries that included empirical research on specific responses of therapists, attention to emotional expressions of clients, the process of self-concept development, and the development of Regard (Bozarth, Zimring and Tausch, 2001).

Rogers continued to develop his theory from the middle 1940s to the middle 1950s. In 1947, he presented a talk to the American Psychological Association which was the predecessor to his chapter on personality and behavior in his book, *Client-Centered Therapy* (Rogers, 1951). Several of the propositions in Rogers' chapter referred to the increasing phenomenological and organismic foundations of the theory. Rogers set forth the attitude and orientation of the client-centered therapist (Rogers, 1951, pp. 19–64). He also delineated a theory of personality and behavior that laid the groundwork for further theoretical direction (Rogers, 1951, pp. 481–533). This orientation offered a context for the eventual identification of unconditional positive regard as the 'curative' factor in client-centered therapy.

The essence of Rogers' chapter on personality and behavior is found in a series of nineteen propositions (Rogers, 1951, pp. 483–524). A general idea of these propositions can be reflected by several broad categories of reference. Four of the propositions relate to phenomenological statements (I, II, III, V), one proposition relates to organismic experience (IV), five relate to a relationship between phenomenological and organismic (VI, VII, VIII, IX, X), two relate to self (XI, XII), and seven relate to 'experience and self' (XIII, XIV, XV, XVI, XVII, XVIII, IX).

The eighteenth proposition refers to the organismic foundation of the theory. Similarly, the nineteenth proposition refers to acceptance of organismic experiences into the structure of self resulting in the replacement of an individual's valuing system. These two propositions are stated as follows:

> XVIII When the individual perceives and accepts into one consistent and integrated system all his sensory and visceral experiences, then he is necessarily more understanding of others and is more accepting of others as separate individuals (p. 520).

And

> XIX As the individual perceives and accepts into his self-structure more of his organismic experiences, he finds that he is replacing his present value system — based so largely upon introjections which have been distortedly symbolized — with a continuing organismic valuing process (p. 522).

My interpretation is that client-centered theory had taken on increasing organismic underpinnings, perhaps shifting towards or even becoming an organismic theory at this time. Nat Raskin considers the 1951 statement to be strongly organismic, and also still replete in the centrality of the self-concept (Raskin, Personal Communication, February, 2001). Much of the substance of the nineteen propositions supports Raskin's belief.

Rogers wrote an unpublished discussion paper at the University of Chicago in 1953 which was an early draft of his most formal theory statement (Rogers, 1959). A dissertation at the University of Chicago greatly influenced Rogers' theoretical statement (Moon, Rice and Schneider, see chapter 4 in this book; Standal, 1954). Standal's dissertation summarized and expanded the discussions of client-centered theory at the University of Chicago and was the first formal public reference to the term 'Unconditional Positive Regard'. At least part of

Standal's theoretical discourse was stimulated by the discussions and contributions of students and staff at the University of Chicago. There were many contributing individuals. Among them, Oliver Bown stimulated discussion regarding the emotional level of the therapeutic interaction as a primary ' . . . effective ingredient in therapeutic growth' (Bown, cited in Rogers, 1951, p. 160). Rogers cites Oliver Bown as a major contributor to the emphasis of the ' . . . deep and significant relationship, to which the client can bring everything that he emotionally is, and to which he is met by the therapist's feelings' (Rogers, 1951, p. 160). In fact, Bown's stimulation of the idea of 'love' and emotional involvement of the therapist was a major stimulant in the staff discussions at that time (Shlien, personal communication, February, 2001). Bown's major assertions were that: (1) the therapist can allow strong feelings of self to enter the therapeutic relationship, and that is important for the client, (2) a very basic need of the therapist to express his fundamental penetrating warmth *must* be satisfied if the relationship is to be healthy and legitimate, and (3) the therapeutic relationship 'at this emotional level, rather than interaction at an intellectual cognitive level, regardless of the content concerned, is the effective ingredient in therapeutic growth' (Rogers, 1951, p. 160). Bown placed 'love' at the forefront of his considerations; love was what the therapist offered the client. It would be experienced subjectively 'out of the range of a recording machine' (p. 161). The condition of love would be communicated, 'primarily, at subverbal, subliminal or subconscious levels' (p. 161). The therapist can only attempt to bring such communications to the level of words. He touches upon the importance of the therapist's understanding:

> It seems to me that we can love a person only to the extent that we are not threatened by him (the client); we can love him only if his reactions to us, or to those things which affect us, are understandable to us and are clearly related to those basic motivations within us all which tend to bring us closer to compatible and meaningful relationships with other people and with the world (p. 161).

John Shlien (personal communication, March 2001), who participated in these interactions at the University of Chicago, suggested the importance of Bown's role in the University of Chicago Counseling Center staff discussions. Rogers quoted much of Bown's memo cited above and identified these ideas as 'a stimulating formulation of therapy, which is, in some significant ways, at variance with the previous descriptions' (p. 172). The hypotheses suggested to Rogers the emphasis of 'direct experiencing in the relationship' (p. 172). Rogers elaborates:

> The process of therapy is, by these hypotheses, seen as being synonymous with the experiential relationship between client and therapist. Therapy consists in experiencing the self in a wide range of ways in an emotionally meaningful relationship with the therapist. The words — of either client or counselor — are seen as having minimal importance compared with the present emotional relationship which exists between the two (p. 172).

As early as his 1955 recorded sessions of Miss Mun, Rogers stated that in general terms ' . . . that what the individual experiences in therapy is the experience of being loved' (Rogers, 1955, transcript, in Rogers and Segal, 1955). Perhaps, the term 'love' was too value-laden for Rogers' scientific bent. For whatever reasons, Standal's (1954) dissertation became the referent for the crux of client-centered theory, and the term 'unconditional positive regard' communicated a slightly different conception on the notion of 'love'. 'Unconditional Positive Regard' was to become the central notion of Rogers' theory. Years later, C. H. Patterson suggests the parallel of the facilitative conditions, including UPR, with the Greek term for love, 'agape' (Patterson, 2000, p. 131; Patterson and Hidore, 1997, p. 91).

THE FACILITATIVE ATMOSPHERE: ATTITUDES AS THE CONTEXT

Armin Klein who interned at the Chicago Counseling Center in 1950–51 describes Rogers as the individual who set the course for the atmosphere of the center:

> In his reserved manner, Carl was very warm and extremely encouraging. I witnessed his growth, both theoretically and personally, toward ever more emphasis on the importance of the personal relationship and personal interaction between psychotherapist and client (Klein, 2000, pp. 67–8).

Klein further comments in relation to the new formulation presented by Rogers which identified 'the necessary and sufficient conditions of therapeutic personality change' (Rogers, 1957). He comments as follows:

> Attitudes, which imply levels of thinking, conscious or not, were replaced by deep conditions of the therapist's being. This was a major contribution which not only became the touchstone and identifying concepts of the person-centered approach, but was a serious, stimulating, and challenging attempt to isolate what might be what really works in any successful psychotherapy, regardless of schools of therapy and their differences in overt behaviors (p. 68).

Klein's experience with Rogers and the milieu of the University of Chicago Counseling Center provided him with an experiential understanding and astute observation of Rogers' most formal theoretical statement nearly a decade later (Rogers, 1959). The attitudes had evolved to ' ... deep conditions of the therapist's being'.

Barbara Brodley reports her experience of the importance of the therapist's attitudes as early as 1953 when she was an undergraduate student at the University of Chicago and associated with the University of Chicago Counseling Center. (Brodley, Personal Communication, February, 2001). The attitudes were part of the milieu of client-centered practice. They were present at this time even though not yet identified with the particular terminology of Rogers' axiom of the necessary and sufficient conditions.

THE ADVENT OF 'UNCONDITIONAL POSITIVE REGARD' (1954–59)

The evolution of Client-Centered Therapy is clear. Rogers increasingly trusted the organismic tendency of the human being towards constructive growth. The client was enabled to experience his feelings ' . . . because another person has been able to adopt his frame of reference, to perceive with him, yet to perceive with acceptance and respect' (Rogers, 1951, p. 41). It was the respect and acceptance of the client's most horrific aspect of himself that facilitated the client's self-respect and self-acceptance. It was not the client's experience of being understood that was the 'curative' factor. It was the client's experience of being accepted and respected by someone who understood her true frame of reference. In the discussions stimulated by Bown, it was the therapist's understanding that enabled the therapist to be able to 'love' the client. This is an important distinction for understanding client-centered theory because it is the forerunner of UPR as the underpinnings of the theory. Shortly, client-centered therapy embraced the terminology, 'Unconditional Positive Regard'. The specific term resonated from Standal's dissertation which was heavily referenced in Rogers' formal theory statement (Moon et al., see chapter 4 in this book; Rogers, 1959; Standal, 1954). It was in the 'integration' statement of the necessary and sufficient conditions where Rogers first formally referred to UPR (Rogers, 1957). However, it appears as though Rogers (1959) wrote his theory statement concomitant with the 1957 integration statement. Unconditional positive regard was identified as one of the therapist's conditions to be related to constructive personality change regardless of the therapeutic orientation of the therapist but as a central axiom for client-centered therapy. If the therapist could *experience* UPR towards the client as well as *experience* empathic understanding of the client's frame of reference, the client would move towards constructive personality change. The therapist's role was no longer that of endeavoring to understand the client's world with acceptance and respect. It had become that of the *therapist's experience* of UPR towards the client and empathic understanding of the client's frame of reference. In fact, UPR had become the central pathological deterrent by the time of Rogers' primary theory statement (Rogers, 1959).

THE CENTRALITY OF UNCONDITIONAL POSITIVE REGARD

The question at this point is: 'Does the adaptation of the term "unconditional positive regard" affect the thrust of client-centered therapy?' To answer this question, an examination of the treatment rationale for client-centered therapy can be identified in relation to the first full statement of the theory (Rogers, 1951). The client is helped by the freedom from threat, every exposed aspect of self is accepted equally by the therapist. The client discovers complex and contradictory experiences to his perception of himself. He moves toward assimilation of contradictory experience and alters them into new and revised patterns (Rogers, 1951, pp. 192–3). The reorganization of self occurs because (1) '. . . the previously denied perceptions of self are as much valued by the therapist as the rigidly structured aspects', and (2) ' . . . the therapist's attitude of calm acceptance . . .' directed ' . . . toward the client's newly discovered aspects of experience' (Rogers, 1951, p. 194). The therapist provides a sense of safety. In 1951, the therapist's role was to help the client to pave the way for acceptance of more clearly perceived elements of self (Rogers, 1951, p. 41). The client could experience himself in a new way because ' . . . another person has been able to adopt his frame of reference, to perceive with him, yet to perceive with acceptance and respect' (p.

41). In 1951, the focus of the therapist was on the adaptation of the client's frame of reference. Nondirective acceptance through emphasis of techniques had evolved to the nondirective attitude. Without the nondirective attitude, the counselor would likely be inaccurate with 'reflection of feeling' type responses as well as more prone to utilizing various directive techniques (Raskin, 1948, p. 106). One of the earliest allusions to the meaning of the therapist's 'way of being' in client-centered therapy was captured in Raskin's history of nondirectivity (Raskin, 1948). In Raskin's words:

> As the counselor learns, through increased experience, that clients can progress when they are not guided, he comes to have a more genuine nondirective attitude. He then is better able to concentrate on understanding the way things appear to his clients, and to forget the employment of techniques (p. 106).

The shift from 'nondirective techniques' to a 'nondirective attitude' has been lost to some extent by Rogers' shift of 'Nondirective Therapy' to 'Client-Centered Therapy' (Rogers, 1951). The fact that he used the terms interchangeably without discarding nondirectivity has been ignored in most and misstated in much of the literature (Bozarth, 2000; in press).

The transition to the centrality of UPR was in play as early as 1948 but still, in 1951, treatment was centered on ' . . . endeavoring to understand' (Rogers, 1951, p. 40). The treatment rationale was that of understanding the client's perceptual world. Unconditional positive regard did not enter the developmental course as an organismic thrust until a few years later.

In 1959, the theory focused on the therapist's unconditional positive regard as the correction for the client's conditional regard introjected by parents and society. The concept of the self was still prevalent in the theory but no longer the central reference. Self, self-structure, and ideal-self are minimally discussed in Rogers' major theoretical statement (Rogers, 1959). Later, Rogers' discussion of the 'self' is found only in periphery references. The 'necessary and sufficient' therapist conditions of congruence, unconditional positive regard, and empathic understanding of the client's frame of reference became the central instructional axiom for client-centered therapy (Rogers, 1959).

Unconditional Positive Regard became the curative factor in Client-Centered Therapy. To reiterate, it can be no other way since conditionality is the bedrock of Rogers' 'Theory of Pathology' (Bozarth, 1998, p. 83). However, the centrality of UPR is complex in theory and practice.

COMPLEXITY OF THE POSTULATE OF 'THE NECESSARY AND SUFFICIENT CONDITIONS'

The importance of UPR must be related to the postulate of the necessary and sufficient conditions. The fundamental therapeutic axiom of Client-Centered Therapy is that of the necessary and sufficient conditions (Rogers, 1959). When these conditions exist in the relationship, constructive personality change ensues. The therapists' conditions in this axiom are that the therapist is congruent in the relationship and experiences UPR towards and EU of the client's frame of reference. The crux of the theory, however, is not only embedded in the 'theory' of pathology that consists of introjected conditional positive regard, but also the 'curative' feature is clearly defined in the process of therapy as UPR (Rogers, 1959, pp. 187–9). Although the therapist's experience of empathic understanding of the client's frame of reference is one of the therapist's therapeutic conditions, Rogers' theory does not include this concept either in his discussion of 'the process of therapy', 'outcomes in personality and behavior', or in 'A Theory of Personality'. He has minimal reference to empathic understanding in his discussions of the 'theory of the fully functioning person', 'a theory of interpersonal relationship', or 'Theories of Application' (Rogers, 1959). This is somewhat disturbing since EU is clearly a major therapist condition in the axiom of client-centered therapy; i.e. 'the necessary and sufficient conditions', condition 5 (Rogers, 1959). Previously, I have speculated that the conditions are integrally related to each other in an interacting process (Bozarth, 1996, 1998, pp. 43–9, also see chapter 14 in this book). Further, I have speculated that at a higher level of abstraction that the conditions are one condition (Bozarth, 1997, 1998, pp. 51–67, 2001a). The underlying assumption of both of these speculations is that UPR is the 'curative' factor in client-centered therapy. In the first speculation, 'A reconceptualization of the necessary and sufficient conditions for therapeutic personality change', the conditions were interpreted from Rogers' 1959 statement to be related in the following way:

> Genuineness is a therapist trait that must exist . . . that enables the therapist to be more able to experience empathic understanding unconditional positive regard towards the client . . .
>
> Empathy is also contextual. Empathy is the 'vessel' by which the therapist communicates unconditional positive regard in the most pure way . . .
>
> Unconditional Positive Regard is the primary theoretical condition of client change in person-centered therapy (Bozarth, 1996, 1998, pp. 51–7).

I have also suggested that there is a 'conditions loop' among the conditions that functionally make them one condition (Bozarth, 1997 1998, pp. 80–2; 2001). The inescapable conclusion of my reviews is that UPR is the crux of Rogers' theory. It is the client's experience of UPR that promotes the actualizing process. This is, however, a somewhat contentious conclusion. Mearns suggests that the United States focuses on Empathic Understanding, and that England focuses on Congruence as the most important elements of client-centered theory (Mearns, 1994). Japan focuses on Unconditional Positive Regard as the most important element (Kuno, see chapter 17 in this book). These differences are, however, superficial when observed from this historical perspective. Unconditional positive regard is the theoretical premise regardless of the varying differences of clinical emphasis.

THE SCIENTIFIC METHOD AND UNCONDITIONAL POSITIVE REGARD

Barrett-Lennard (1962) proposed one of the earliest and the most universal operational definitions of unconditional positive regard. He notes that UPR is '. . .

conceptually and operationally difficult to handle as a single variable' (Barrett-Lennard, 1998, p. 81). Barrett-Lennard, who probably developed the most viable measurement of the therapeutic conditions and is one of the great contributors to scientific investigation of Rogers' theory, clamped the vice of the scientific method on Rogers' therapeutic concepts. He identified two components of UPR; namely, 'level of regard' and 'unconditionality of regard' which Rogers had referred to in his 'Theory of Therapy' article (Rogers, 1959). Barrett-Lennard operationally defined regard as:

> the 'composite "loading" of all the feeling reactions of one person toward another, positive and negative, on a single, abstract dimension' of which the lower extreme presents maximum predominance and intensity of negative-type feeling, not merely a lack of positive feeling' (Barrett-Lennard, 1962a p. 4; Gurman, 1977). (Barrett-Lennard, 1998, p 81)

Unconditionality is operationally defined by Barrett-Lennard as: 'A's attitude does not vary contingently, that is, according to the particular self-revelations, feeling reactions or other expressions of B' (p. 81). This definition is consistent with Rogers' theoretical discourse. However, the scientific method dictates UPR to be defined as a behavioral and verbal response. Thus, the double-edged sword of scientific method research began to direct the meaning of UPR. For example, the research scales were adopted for training purposes (Carkhuff, 1969; Truax and Carkhuff, 1967). Among other things, such research promoted emphasis on empathy and, as such, promoted this condition as the central clinical ingredient of Rogers' theory. Therapist's congruence and unconditional positive regard were accorded less emphasis. Such research initially lent credibility to the understanding of client-centered therapy and verified the effectiveness of the approach (Bozarth, 1998; Bozarth, Zimring and Tausch, 2002). However, the logical positivistic nature of such research misdirects both the simplicity and the complexity of UPR. Rogers' simple definition of UPR as: ' . . . experiencing a warm acceptance of each aspect of the client's experience being a part of the client . . .' integrated as a therapist attitude is enough to enable compatible therapist behaviors. Rogers (1975) rather passively acknowledges this point when he refers to the importance of operational definitions for research but also points out that such definitions are significantly different from the theoretical definitions.

THE CONFOUNDING OF THEORY AND FUNCTION

The historical perspective clarifies the confounding of theory and function. Rogers' theory presents the conditions as the *functional* axiom that must exist for the process of therapy to take place (Rogers, 1959). They are, in essence, instructions to the client-centered therapist as the way to be; that is, the way to be as a client-centered therapist is to *experience* the conditions of UPR towards the client and EU of the client's frame of reference. This way of being is directed towards accepting and respecting the client as she experiences herself at any given moment. This is clear from Raskin's early analysis that the nondirective attitude had ' . . . steadily deepened into a condition that people in mental turmoil need no more than to be accepted as they are' (Raskin, 1948, p. 105). It is further clarified by Rogers that client progress was due to the therapist's acceptance and respect of the person, while the therapist endeavored to understand the client's frame of reference (Rogers, 1951, p. 40). The crux of the theory is remarkably clear and simple as Rogers summarizes in his statement applying the theory of therapy to family life:

The theoretical implications would include these:

1. The greater the degree of *unconditional positive regard* which the parent experiences toward the child:

(a) the fewer the *conditions of worth* in the child.

(b) the more the child will be able to live in terms of a *continuing organismic valuing process*.

(c) the higher the level of *psychological adjustment* of the child (Rogers, 1959, p. 241).

The term 'therapist' can be substituted for 'parent' since Rogers related therapy directly in his statement of family life. He states: '... the theory of the process and outcomes of therapy and the theory of the process and outcomes of an improving relationship apply' (Rogers, 1959, p. 241). In short, the therapeutic impact is due to the '... warm acceptance of each aspect of the client's experience being a part of the client' (Rogers, 1957, cited in Kirschenbaum and Henderson, 1989, pp. 225ff). Theoretically, *unconditional positive regard is the 'curative' factor.* Functionally, congruence and empathic understanding are equally important only because of their integral relationship to UPR.

CONGRUENCE AND UNCONDITIONAL POSITIVE REGARD

Therapist congruence is critical because UPR is begotten by the therapist's unconditional self-regard (USR). As Rogers continued the above quote:

2. The parent experiences such *unconditional positive regard only* to the extent that he experiences unconditional self-regard (Rogers, 1959).

I assert elsewhere that the very *presence* of the client-centered therapist is intended to represent unconditional self-regard in order to beget unconditional positive regard towards the client (Bozarth, 2001b). Therapist congruence is, then, the personal striving of the therapist to experience UPR towards the client.

EMPATHIC UNDERSTANDING AND UNCONDITIONAL POSITIVE REGARD

Empathic understanding of the client's frame of reference is equally important in the triad of interaction that calls for the acceptance of all aspects of the client. It is not, as commonly thought even by client-centered adherents, that the client progresses because of feeling deeply understood by the therapist. Client progress is due to the client's experience of UPR when the therapist experiences UPR towards and empathic understanding of the client's frame of reference. Rogers' statement concerning empathic understanding as the necessary context in which to communicate UPR seems to be the best way to describe the interactive role of

EU with UPR (Rogers, 1959, p. 230).

In his re-evaluation and re-examination of empathy, Rogers (1975) repeated his earlier definition of empathy as a state wherein ' . . . being empathic, is to perceive the internal frame of reference of another with accuracy and with the emotional components and meanings which pertain thereto as if one were the person, but without ever losing the "as if" condition . . . ' (Rogers, 1959, pp. 210–11). He followed the earlier definition with a 'current definition' wherein empathy was considered a process rather than a state. He also considered empathy to include several facets. The way of being empathic would:

> . . . mean entertaining the private perceptual world of the other and becoming thoroughly at home in it . . .
>
> . . . involve being sensitive, moment to moment, to the changing felt meanings which flow in this other person . . . means temporarily living in his/her life, moving about in it delicately without making judgments . . .
>
> . . . include your sensings of his/her world as you look with fresh and unfrightened eyes at elements of which the individual is fearful.
>
> It means frequently checking with him/her as to the accuracy of your sensings, and being guided by the responses you receive (Rogers, 1975, p. 4).

Rogers adds that to be with a person in this way ' . . .means that for the time being you lay aside the views and values you hold for yourself in order to enter another's world without prejudice . . . you lay aside your self . . .' (p. 4).

Freire identifies Rogers' facets as follows: (1) empathic experience, (2) empathic understanding and (3) empathic understanding responses Empathic Experience is identified as the ' . . . experience of entering another's private world without judgments . . .' Referring to her dissertation analysis, Freire (see chapter 12 in this book) also identifies Empathic Understanding and Empathic Understanding Response and relates them to Rogers' re-evaluation of the 'empathic way of being'. She suggests that *empathic understanding* is the knowledge of the meanings and feelings that are being experienced by another individual. *Empathic understanding response is* related to a specific mode of communication within a relationship. She points out that Rogers viewed these three facets as comprising a sole phenomena: the *empathic way of being*. In Rogers' words, empathy as a process is the following:

> entering the private perceptual world of the other and becoming thoroughly at home in it . . . Temporarily living in his/her life, moving about in it delicately without making judgements . . . for the time being you lay aside the views and values you hold for yourself in order to enter another's world without prejudice. In some sense it means that you lay aside your self .. . (Rogers, 1975, p. 4).

Freire elaborates:

> This description leads us inevitably to the conclusion that empathic experience and unconditional positive regard are ultimately the sole and same experience. With unconditional positive regard, the therapist accepts every aspect of the client's experience as she offers her *presence* to the client. With empathic experience, the therapist accepts every aspect of the client's frame of reference as she enters in the client's world. Being *present* with unconditional acceptance

and 'entering in the client's world laying her self aside' are ultimately the same experience. (Freire, in this book)

Freire continues by referring to my investigation of empathy wherein I also conclude that: 'the empathic and unconditional acceptance of the therapist is, in essence, the same experience' (Bozarth, 1997, 1998, p. 58, 2001a, p. 152). Freire adds: '*This experience is the essence of client-centered therapy*'.

The clinical ramification is that the extent of the therapist's experience of unconditional positive regard towards the client leads to client adjustment (Rogers, 1959, p. 241). The degree of therapist unconditional positive SELF REGARD dictates the extent of unconditional positive regard towards the client.

SUMMARY

This historical perspective offers a frame for the development of the concept, Unconditional Positive Regard (UPR) in Rogers' theory of client-centered therapy.

In the 1940s, client-centered therapy was ' . . . steadily deepened into a condition that people in mental turmoil need no more than to be accepted as they are' (Raskin, 1948, p. 105). Herein, 'the client's concept of self . . . was . . . believed to be the most central factor in his adjustment and perhaps the best measure of his progress in therapy' (Raskin, 1948, p. 105).

In 1951, client-centered theory had increasingly taken on organismic underpinnings, perhaps shifting towards or even becoming an organismic theory. Nat Raskin considers the 1951 statement to be strongly organismic, and also still replete in the centrality of the self-concept (Raskin, Personal Communication, February, 2001). Rogers also identified the therapy at this time as that of a ' . . . deep and significant relationship, to which the client can bring everything that he emotionally is, and to which he is met by the therapist's feelings' (Rogers, 1951, p. 160). This statement was, perhaps, reflective of the discussions of staff at the University of Chicago Counseling Center during the late 1940s and early 1950s. Oliver Bown was one of those who stimulated discussion on the experiential relationship of therapist and client with the underlying theme of love (akin to the Greek term, agape).

The focus on 'love' took a slightly different direction with the advent of Standal's (1954) doctoral dissertation. Standal coined the term, Unconditional Positive Regard, a term adopted by Rogers in his most classic statements about Client-Centered Therapy. The formal theoretical delineation of client-centered theory identified UPR as the curative factor for the pathological development of personality (Rogers, 1959). This simply has to be true given Rogers' conceptualization of personal dysfunctions being predicated upon the introjection of conditional positive regard by significant others and by society. Conditional regard is countered by the unconditional positive regard of the therapist.

Recent examinations of the necessary and sufficient conditions suggest that attention to these conditions, as the central axiom of client-centered therapy, have focused more on empathic understanding than on unconditional positive regard and often ignored the interrelationship of the therapist conditions

(Bozarth, 1996, 1997, 1998, 2001a, 2001b). The existence of the therapist conditions as, in essence, being the same condition of unconditional positive regard has had little attention.

Attention towards the clarification of the central notion of unconditional positive regard as the curative factor in client-centered therapy is critically important or the historical foundation of client-centered therapy as an organismic theory will continue to be misdirected.

REFERENCES

Barrett-Lennard, G. T. (1962). Dimensions of therapist response as causal factors in therapeutic change. *Psychological Monographs*, 76 (43. Whole No. 562).

Barrett-Lennard, G. T. (1998). *Carl Rogers' Helping System: Journey and Substance*. London : Sage.

Bozarth, J. D., (1996). A theoretical reconsideration of the necessary and sufficient conditions for therapeutic personality change. *The Person-Centered Journal*, 3,(1), 44–51.

Bozarth, J. D. (1997). Empathy from the framework of client-centered theory and the Rogerian hypothesis. In A. C. Bohart and L. S. Greenberg (Eds.) *Empathy Reconsidered: New Directions in Psychotherapy*. Washington D. C.: American Psychological Association, pp. 81–102.

Bozarth, J. D. (1998). *Person-Centered Therapy: A Revolutionary Paradigm*. Ross-on-Wye: PCCS Books.

Bozarth, J. D. (March, 2000). Non-directiveness in client-centered therapy: A vexed concept. Paper presentation at the *Eastern Psychological Association*, Baltimore, Md.

Bozarth, J. D. (2001a). An addendum to Beyond Reflection: Emergent modes of empathy. In S. Haugh and T. Merry (Eds.) *Rogers' Therapeutic Conditions. Volume 2: Empathy*. Ross-On-Wye: PCCS Books, pp. 144–54.

Bozarth, J. D. (2001b). Congruence: A special way of being. In G. Wyatt (Ed.) *Rogers' Therapeutic Conditions. Volume 1: Congruence*. Ross-On-Wye: PCCS Books, pp. 184–99.

Bozarth, J. D. (in press). Non-directivity in the person-centered approach: Critique of Kahn's critique. *Journal of Humanistic Psychology*.

Bozarth, J. D., Zimring, F. and Tausch, R. (2002). Client-Centered Therapy: Evolution of a revolution. In D. Cain and J. Seeman (Eds.) *Handbook of Humanistic Psychotherapy: Research and Practice*. Washington D. C.: American Psychological Association, pp. 147 –88.

Carkhuff, R. R. (1969). *Helping and Human Relations, Vol. 1*. New York: Holt, Rinehart, and Winston.

Freire, E. (2000). A implementação das atitudes facilitadoras na relação terapêutica centrada no cliente. *Unpublished masters dissertation. Universidade de Campinas*.

Kirschenbaum, H. and Henderson, V.L. (1989). *The Carl Rogers Reader*. Boston: Houghton Mifflin Company.

Klein, A. (2000). *Songs of Living*. New York: Armin Klein Self-Published.

Lecky, P. (1945). *Self-Consistency: A Theory of Personality*. New York: Island Press.

Mearns, D. (1994). *Developing Person-Centred Counselling*. London: Sage.

Patterson, C. H. (2000). *Understanding Psychotherapy: Fifty years of client-centered theory and practice*. Ross-on-Wye: PCCS Books.

Patterson, C. H., and Hidore, S. C. (1997). *Successful Therapy: A Caring, Loving Relationship*. New Jersey: Jason Aronson Inc.

Raimy, V. C. (1943). *The self-concept as a factor in counseling and personality organization*. Ph.D. Thesis, Ohio State University.

Raskin, N. (1948). The development of nondirective therapy. *Journal of Consulting Psychology*, 12, (94), pp. 92–110.

Rogers, C. R. (1940). The process of therapy. *Journal of Counseling Psychology*, 4,(5), pp. 161–4.

Rogers, C. R. (1942). *Counseling and Psychotherapy*. Boston: Houghton Mifflin.

Rogers, C. R. (1951). *Client-Centered Therapy: Its Current Practice, Implications and Theory*. Boston: Houghton Mifflin .

Rogers, C. R. (1957). The necessary and sufficient conditions of therapeutic personality change. *Journal of Consulting Psychology*, 21, (2), pp. 95–103.

Rogers, C. R. (1959). A theory of therapy, personality, and interpersonal relationships as developed in the client-centered framework. In S. Koch (Ed.) *Psychology: A Study of Science: Vol. 3 Formulation of the person and the social context*. New York: McGraw Hill, pp. 184–256.

Rogers, C. R. (1975). Empathic: An unappreciated way of being. *The Counseling Psychologist*, 5, (2), pp. 2–10.

Rogers, C. R., (1986). A client-centered/person-centered approach to therapy. In I. Kutash and A. Wolfe (Eds.) *Psychotherapists' Casebook*. Jossey-Bass, pp. 197–208.

Rogers, C. R. and Segal, R. H. (1955). *Psychotherapy in process: The case of Miss Mun*. Pennsylvania State University Psychological Cinema Register.

Snygg, D. and Combs, A. (1949). *Individual Behavior: a New Frame of Reference for Psychology*. New York: Harper and Brothers.

Standal, S. (1954). The need for positive regard: a contribution to client-centered theory. Unpublished doctoral dissertation, University of Chicago.

Truax, C. B. and Carkhuff, R. R. (1967). *Toward Effective Counseling and Psychotherapy: Training and Practice*. Chicago: Aldine.

4   Stanley W. Standal and the Need for Positive Regard

Kathryn Moon, Bert Rice and Carolyn Schneider

In the 1951 volume, *Client-Centered Therapy*, Rogers included as the last chapter, 'A Theory of Personality and Behavior'. Although this theoretical statement was ground breaking, it was not a completely finished treatise. It had been preceded by an earlier formulation (Rogers, 1947) and it would be followed by later ones (Rogers, 1957, 1959, 1961). In concluding his 1959 formulation, Rogers wrote:

> It is to be hoped that the presentation has made it clear that this is a developing system, in which some of the older portions are being formulated with considerable logical rigor, while newer portions are more informal, and contain some logical and systematic gaps and flaws, and still others (not presented) exist as highly personal and subjective hunches in the minds of members of the client-centered group. It is also to be hoped that it is evident that this is a system which is in a continual state of modification and clarification. Comparison of the theory as given above with the theory of therapy and personality given in *Client-Centered Therapy* in 1951 [Chapters 4 and 11] or with the paper presented to the American Psychological Association in 1947 will show that although the major directions have not markedly changed, there have been many changes in the constructs employed, and far-reaching changes in the organization of the theory (p. 244).

For his 1954 doctoral dissertation at the University of Chicago, Stanley Wallace Standal, a student of Rogers, described 'unresolved problems' in Rogers' 1951 theory statement and wrote a theoretical paper intended to complement and become a part of Rogerian theory. The aim of this chapter is to provide a detailed summary of Standal's dissertation, 'The Need for Positive Regard: A contribution to client-centered theory'.

In illustration of his thesis, Standal introduced several terms, the most famous of which, *unconditional positive regard*, was used foundationally by Rogers, very soon after, as a necessary and sufficient condition for therapeutic personality change (1957).[1] Other client-centered nomenclature introduced by Standal, including *the need for positive regard, the need for self-regard, conditions of worth,*

---

1. According to Godfrey Barrett-Lennard (1998, p. 65), Rogers first used the term 'unconditional positive regard' in a 1956 article, 'Client-centered therapy: a current view'. Barrett-Lennard speculates that the 1956 article was written in 1955 (the year following the December 1954 completion of Standal's dissertation).

regard complex, and *unconditional self-regard* became intrinsic to Rogers' 1959 statement.

Ferdinand van der Veen, who was contemporary with Standal at the University of Chicago Counseling Center, has written:

> UPR [unconditional positive regard] was originally formulated by Stan Standal in his theoretical dissertation at the University of Chicago (about 1954) in which he proposed the whole theory regarding conditions of worth and positive regard and unconditional regard, as a more rigorous statement of Rogers' theory regarding introjected values in personal development and the role of acceptance by the therapist in overcoming the detrimental effects of such incongruent introjects. Rogers preferred Standal's concepts and adopted pretty much his entire formulation into his own theoretical statements (1998).

It is difficult to reconstruct the exact nature and extent of Standal's original contribution to the theory. However, a comparison of the theoretical statement Rogers proposed in 1951, with the necessary and sufficient therapeutic conditions he proposed in 1957 and the theories of personality, therapy and interpersonal relationships he proposed in 1959 and 1961 shows that Standal may have contributed language, definition and even a theoretical explanation for the theories of both personality and therapy. It seems logical to conclude, as well, that Standal's theoretical explanation of the mechanisms of personality growth deepened the use of the term 'congruence' in reference to the intrapsychic relationship within the therapist between awareness and experience (Rogers, 1957). Standal's language dominates many sections of Rogers' principle theory statement (1959) and within that paper, Rogers credits Standal extensively.

ROGERS' 1951 THEORY OF PERSONALITY AND BEHAVIOR

In his 1951 statement, Rogers postulated 19 propositions. These propositions put forth the foundational premise of client-centered theory, the actualizing tendency (proposition IV), and propose that a therapist seeks understanding through the client's frame of reference (proposition VII). The propositions also describe the development of the rudimentary self and personality. Using concepts such as 'organismic valuing process', 'consistency' between self and new experience, 'threat', and the ideas of acceptance and self-acceptance, Rogers hypothesizes a developmental progression of psychological maladjustment and readjustment.

According to the 1951 theory, we humans begin as organisms, neonates, and we only gradually make differentiations by which we become conscious of a '*self,* . . . the awareness of being, of functioning' (Rogers, p. 498). Rogers wrote, 'The very young infant has little uncertainty in valuing' (p. 498); 'Organismic valuing' (p. 498) readily dawns into awareness of likes and dislikes.

> He[2] appears to value those experiences which he perceives as enhancing himself, and to place a negative value on those experiences which seem to threaten himself or which do not maintain or enhance himself (p. 499).

---

2. Since many direct quotations in this chapter are from the 1950s and follow the convention of using male pronouns in universal contexts, at all other junctures, feminine pronouns will be used.

Standal writes:

> . . . although the individual is psychologically adjusted in the neonatal period, it appears that he can become psychologically maladjusted . . . This condition of being adjusted but subject to the possibility of maladjustment I shall arbitrarily call *psychologically adjusted but immature* (p. 3).

In 1951, Rogers described maladjustment as arising from a conflict or inconsistency between a child's self-image as loved or lovable and her perception that some of her satisfying experiences are experienced negatively by those who love her. The child then might deny awareness of positive experiences or distort symbolization of what has occurred.

> The accurate symbolization would be: 'I perceive my parents as experiencing this behavior as unsatisfying to them'. The distorted symbolization, distorted to preserve the threatened concept of self [as lovable], is: 'I perceive this behavior as unsatisfying. .It is in this way . . . parental attitudes are not only introjected, but what is much more important, are experienced not as the attitude of another, but in distorted fashion, *as if* based on the evidence of one's own sensory and visceral equipment (p. 500).

With the first introjection, the child has become psychologically maladjusted, as described in proposition XIV. From then on, as described in proposition XI,

> *As experiences occur in the life of the individual, they are either (a) symbolized, perceived, and organized into some relationship to the self, (b) ignored because there is no perceived relationship to the self-structure, (c) denied symbolization or given a distorted symbolization because the experience is inconsistent with the structure of the self* (p. 503).

Rogers defines 'threat' in proposition XVI:

> *Any experience which is inconsistent with the organization or structure of self may be perceived as a threat, and the more of these perceptions there are, the more rigidly the self-structure is organized to maintain itself* (p. 515).

Or as Standal describes this situation, since a multitude of varied experiences '. . . may also threaten the consistency of the structure of the self by virtue of their being similar to or associated with those involved in the original introjections' (1954, p. 6), all sorts of distorted values can develop exponentially, rendering the self-structure of the individual ever more vulnerable to threat.

Proposition XVII suggests that a person suffering from the psychological tensions and anxieties involved in maintaining a cumbersome and rigid or fragile sense of self can be helped in psychotherapy:

> *Under certain conditions, involving primarily complete absence of any threat to the self-structure, experiences which are inconsistent with it may be perceived, and examined, and the structure of self revised to assimilate and include such experiences* (Rogers, 1951, p. 517).

Rogers offers an explanation of how therapy effects self-change:

> If we try to analyze the elements which make possible this reorganization of

21

the structure of self, there would appear to be two possible factors. One is the self-initiated apprehension of the new material . . . Another factor which may be involved is that the counselor is accepting toward all experiences, all attitudes, all perceptions. This social value may be introjected by the client, and applied to his own experiences (1951, p. 518).

Propositions XVIII and XIX describe an individual who has learned 'a new configuration of self' (p. 520) and attained 'psychological maturity' (Standal, 1954, p. 10):

XVIII *When the individual perceives and accepts into one consistent and integrated system all his sensory and visceral experiences, then he is necessarily more understanding of others and is more accepting of others as separate individuals* (Rogers, 1951, p. 520).

XIX *As the individual perceives and accepts into his self-structure more of his organic experiences, he finds that he is replacing his present value system — based so largely upon introjections which have been distortedly symbolized — with a continuing organismic valuing process* (ibid. p. 522).

Standal notes that there is a similarity between the neonate, the infant who has yet to introject the values of the parent, and the psychologically mature individual. The latter resembles the fully functioning person described by Rogers in 1952. Standal quotes from the 1952 paper:

The person, who hypothetically experienced the maximum gain from therapy, would be completely 'open' to all of his experiences. Every stimulus received by the organism, whether originating within the organism or in the environment, would be freely relayed through the nervous system, without being distorted by any process of defensiveness acting through 'subception'. Each experience would thus be completely available to awareness without distortion (1954, pp. 9–10).

Or, as Rogers (1951) says, the client, gradually:

. . . comes to experience the fact that he is making value judgments, in a way that is new to him, and yet a way that was also known to him in his infancy (pp. 522–3).

STANDAL'S IDENTIFICATION OF 'UNRESOLVED PROBLEMS' IN ROGERS' 1951 STATEMENT

Questioning how psychological maladjustment and readjustment occur and how readjustment is maintained by an individual, Standal discusses three problems he sees in the logical progression of the 1951 statement.

The first problem centers around the question of how an individual becomes maladjusted. Standal describes the postulated Rogerian newborn as 'psychologically adjusted but immature' (p. 3), and vulnerable to maladjustment through the introjection of values as the self develops. But, he argues,

In the explanation of becoming maladjusted, the first introjection cannot be accounted for by the principle of self-consistency since to do so immediately raises the question of how the child can change any existing concept of self. Nor does the child's need to maintain the concept of the self as lovable seem to be an adequate explanation since, in the first place, to explain the first introjection upon this basis requires that the theory explain why the concept of being lovable has such special significance, and in the second place, given the process of organismic valuation, it is difficult to understand how an unqualified concept of the self as lovable could ever develop in the social environment of the average child (p. 18).

The second theoretical problem according to Standal relates to the question of readjustment:

> In its explanation of becoming readjusted, the theory is confronted by the problem of threat and defense. On the one hand, the theory maintains that experiences which are inconsistent with the structure of self arouse a state of threat when they are discriminated and lead to defensive behavior . . . Threatening experiences also are held to be accompanied by anxiety. On the other hand, the theory maintains that under certain conditions experiences which are inconsistent with the structure of self cease to be threatening and can be accurately perceived and symbolized and hence integrated into the self-structure. Although acceptance and understanding appear, from therapeutic observation, to be the conditions which allow for accurate symbolization of threatening experiences, these terms bear no clearly delineated relationship to that part of the theory which maintains that threatening experiences will be avoided. Furthermore, the discomfort which usually accompanies self-exploration in therapy would seem to indicate that it is not the absence of threat which allows the individual to symbolize experiences which ordinarily are threatening, but rather that the individual symbolizes such experiences *in spite of* their threatening nature (pp. 18–19).

The final problem is identified by Standal as *the problem of the irreversibility of psychological maturity* (p. 16). How does the organismic valuing process defend a fully functioning individual but not the neonate from introjection and distorted values?

In answer to the problems he has identified, Standal posits:

> (1) [A]n individual introjects values from others and subsequently must avoid experiences inconsistent with those values in order to avoid frustration of the need for self-regard (that is he becomes maladjusted);
> (2) he eliminates introjected values when through a relationship with another person he learns that he need not hold such values in order to experience a consistently satisfying level of satisfaction of the need for self-regard (that is, he becomes readjusted); and
> (3) he would no longer introject values, nor deny or distort experiences, once it becomes impossible to frustrate the need for self-regard (that is, he becomes psychologically mature) (p. 20).

STANDAL'S FIRST HYPOTHESIZED NEED: THE NEED FOR POSITIVE REGARD

By listening to recordings of sessions and observing how clients responded, Rogers' group of student and staff counselors at the University of Chicago studied the therapy process, gave definition to their experiences of it, and developed theory. From this emerged, according to Standal, a shared view of the factors that define the therapeutic process:

> The client perceives . . . *that some experience discriminable as self . . . is being discriminated by the therapist accurately . . . ; the client further perceives that the attitude of the therapist during his interaction remains positive* (p. 25).

'[I]t would seem,' writes Standal,

> that a basic tenet of client-centered practice could be stated as follows: perception by the client that self-experiences are making a positive difference in the experiential field of the therapist is a necessary, if not a sufficient, cause for psychological readjustment (p. 25).

From that tenet, then, Standal fashions his first hypothesis:

> *With the emergence of awareness of self, there develops in the individual a need to perceive self-experiences as making a positive difference in the experiential fields of others. This need is the need for positive regard* (p. 26).

While the genesis of a need for positive regard does not fall under the purview of his dissertation, Standal does express his opinion that it is 'more reasonable and more fruitful' to regard this need as 'a secondary or learned need' that begins in infancy rather than 'the mature form' of a primary need for affection (p. 28). That is to say, expressions of positive regard, such as smiles and coos, that accompany warm care-giving, become associated with the satisfaction of primary needs for food, warmth and protection while negative expressions, such as scowls and shouts, become associated with primary need frustration.

Standal regards the need for positive regard as *universal* (because all humans, in the early stages of life, depend upon others to take care of their primary needs) and as *persistent* (because of the sheer number of satisfactions of this need, because of their aperiodic pattern, and because of the great variety of reinforcements of this need in each of our lives) (pp. 30–4). In preparation for relating a need for positive regard to personality development, Standal describes three characteristics which he regards as corollaries to the need.

Characteristic 1: The satisfaction or frustration of the need for positive regard depends solely on inferences about the experential [sic] field of another (p. 36).

For example, an individual's need for positive regard on a particular occasion might be satisfied because that person unwittingly put an unduly positive spin on something another said that had been intended as negative. Standal suggests that since inferences are subjective in nature, they are marked by ambiguity (p. 38). Furthermore, in order to infer anything about the experiential field of another,

' . . . there is a necessity for a social being . . . real or imagined' (p. 39). Since both satisfaction and frustration are based upon subjective experience, Standal also reasons that the need for positive regard is satisfied or frustrated completely independently of other needs (pp. 40–1).

Characteristic 2: Any or all self-experiences may become directly connected with the satisfaction or frustration of the need for positive regard (p. 41).

This second characteristic suggests that the need for positive regard is pervasive:
> Positive regard may be given or denied (or — through fantasy mechanisms, projection, misinterpretation, and so on — thought to be given or denied) for aggressiveness or passivity, for dependence or independence, for sexual abstinence or sexual promiscuity, for eating heartily or eating sparingly. There is almost no behavior [or] attitude for which positive regard might not be given or denied, or be thought to be given or denied (p. 44).

Characteristic 3: When an individual discriminates himself as satisfying another's need for positive regard, he necessarily experiences satisfaction of his own need for positive regard (p. 46).

When a parent believes she has met her child's need for positive regard, she becomes cognizant of having made a positive difference in the child's experience. Therefore, the parent experiences satisfaction of her own need for positive regard. Standal believes there is a reciprocal quality to the need for positive regard. He points out that this reciprocity can serve as a motivational force for the psychotherapist and for the parent in their respective realms.

The need for positive regard and its corollary characteristics are adopted in their entirety in Rogers 1959 theory statement (pp. 223–4).

PERSONALITY DEVELOPMENT: HYPOTHESES FOR THE REGARD COMPLEX AND THE NEED FOR POSITIVE SELF-REGARD

Rogers had postulated in 1951 that organismic valuing is the characteristic response of an infant to her environment and that a sense of self as lovable develops and becomes a part of the self-structure. In times of threat to the self-structure, this sense of a lovable self is defended through introjection of the values of significant others. While organismic valuing is considered to be a positive, well-adjusted valuing response, introjection is considered maladjustive. According to Standal, there is a problem with this schema:
> [I]t is inconsistent to posit organismic valuing as characteristic of the neonate and then to assume that the concept of self as lovable will be an emerging core concept in the emerging self-structure . . . [O]rganismic valuing must necessarily lead the individual to a concept of self as only sometimes lovable . . . There is thus no adequate explanation within the theory of why the evaluation placed by others upon his self-experiences should be of greater importance to the individual than his own direct evaluation of those experiences (p. 54).

In trying to provide such an explanation, Standal creates the concept of the *regard complex,* which he defines as

. . . all those self-experiences together with their interrelationships which the individual discriminates as being related to the positive regard of a particular social other (pp. 51–2).

He then posits two more hypotheses, the first of which is:

At the time it is expressed, the positive regard of any social other is communicated to the total regard complex the individual associates with that social other (p. 54).

Under this hypothesis, Standal concludes that each new interaction with a particular person has the potential to undermine the entire history of positive regard already received from that person. A child will refrain from taking a forbidden cookie not so much because of momentary parental disapproval but because of the feeling that all accrued positive regard from the parent will be withdrawn. Rogers followed this formulation in 1959:

d. It [the need for positive regard] is potent, in that the *positive regard* of any social other is communicated to the total *regard complex* which the individual associates with that social other.

   (1) Consequently the expression of positive regard by a significant social other can become more compelling than the *organismic valuing process*, and the individual becomes more adient to the *positive regard* of such others than toward *experiences* which are of positive value in *actualizing* the organism (p. 244).

But there is another question. Why doesn't the child opportunistically perceive what is necessary for parental approval and proceed accordingly, manipulating the parents while maintaining organismic valuing? Why is it necessary to introject parental values as if they were one's own? Standal's third hypothesis responds to these questions:

Positive regard satisfactions or frustrations associated with any particular self-experience or group of self-experiences come to be experienced independently of positive regard transactions with social others. Positive regard experienced in this fashion will be called self-regard (pp. 58–9).

Both the need for positive regard and the need for self-regard develop as learned needs through association with satisfactions. In the case of positive regard, the associations were to self-experiences of positive regard when nurturing needs were satisfied in the company of positive communications from parents. The need for self-regard is learned through association with satisfaction of the need for positive regard. Stimuli which have become associated with the bestowal of positive regard come

   . . . to take on rewarding characteristics so that in effect the individual experiences something similar to positive regard when that self-experience occurs (p. 59).

Or, a stimulus which was previously associated with a self-experience involving withdrawal of positive regard takes on a 'punishing character' (p. 59). The individual eventually begins to experience positively and negatively charged self-experiences of personal regard or the lack thereof, even when the significant social other is uninvolved.

> Although he [the child] may at first only pay lip service to the parents' values, living up to them eventually becomes rewarding in and of itself, while disregarding them leads to painful consequences (anxiety, etc.) even when no one but the individual himself becomes aware of his defection (p. 60).

The child has grown to become her own social other, satisfying or frustrating her own need for positive self-regard. Rogers adopted Standal's formulation in 1959 (p. 224).

CONDITIONS OF WORTH AND THE DEVELOPMENT OF PSYCHOLOGICAL MALADJUSTMENT

Standal's formulation of a need for positive self-regard leads to his concept of 'conditions of worth':

> The self-structure will be said to be constrained or characterized by a *condition of worth* whenever *a self-experience or set of related self-experiences is either avoided or sought because the individual discriminates it as being less or more worthy of self-regard* (p. 62).

Standal then defines psychological maladjustment as the existence within the self of any condition of worth which, through threat of loss of self-regard, blocks a spontaneous organismic valuing response (p. 64).

Since the existence within the self-structure of even a single condition of worth denotes psychological maladjustment, good adjustment is defined as the complete absence of conditions of worth. The well-adjusted individual does not need to seek or avoid any self-experience in order to preserve positive self-regard. In Standal's view,

> [T]he psychologically adjusted individual must have received *unconditional positive regard* for all experiences comprising his self-structure. The positive regard of a significant social other can be said to be unconditional *whenever the individual is unable to discriminate any self-experience in the regard-complex associated with that other as being more or less worthy of positive regard than any other self-experience* (p. 64).

In Rogers' 1951 theory, distortions and denials of self-experience are triggered in defense of consistency within the self-structure. In Standal's revision of the theory, distortions and denials result from the need for positive regard and positive self-regard:

> If the positive regard of significant others is expressed *unconditionally* during the early years of life — that is, in such a way that no self-experience can be discriminated as more or less worthy of positive regard than any other — then the self-regard of the individual will be similarly unconditional ... [S]elf-regard

of this quality is the distinguishing characteristic of the psychologically mature individual . . . (pp. 67–8).

Rogers essentially adopted this formulation in 1959 (p. 224).

Standal's description of the advancement of psychological maladjustment has an exponential feel to it, a sense of glass cracking slowly in myriad crooked directions. In the beginning,

> The problem for the child is not to avoid discriminating certain experiences as self or to delude himself into accepting other experiences as his own. It is simply one of convincing the parent that certain experiences are not his and that certain others are (p. 70).

But eventually the stimuli that arouse or are associated with,

> . . . continued pairings of self-experiences and positive regard satisfactions or frustrations . . . develop reward or punishment value. Gradually the child becomes his own source of positive regard, that is, he develops a need for self regard (p. 70–1).

The conditions of worth that had been required by the parent in order for positive regard to be bestowed become the child's own conditions of worth for self-regard. To avoid loss of self-regard, the child avoids certain experiences or denies certain thoughts or feelings.

> This is not to say, of course, that such experiences will never be clearly discriminated as self. Occasionally they may even be very clearly discriminated, that is, symbolized. But the more clearly any such experience is discriminated as self, the greater will be the experience of loss of self-regard (p. 71).

CHARACTERISTICS OF PSYCHOLOGICAL MALADJUSTMENT

Standal describes psychological maladjustment as having four symptomatic characteristics: 'subverted Needs 1 [basic needs] satisfactions, recurrent losses of self-regard, recurrent anxiety, and subverted positive regard satisfactions' (p. 72),

> The individual will suffer deprivation of certain Needs I satisfactions, either because conditions of worth make it impossible for him to discriminate those needs with sufficient accuracy to institute behavior directed at satisfying them, or because they limit the means of satisfying those needs which he has discriminated with fair accuracy. He will be subjected to recurrent losses of self-regard through the discrimination of experiences which are inconsistent with his conditions of worth. He will be subjected to recurrent anxiety through the anticipation of losses of self-regard. Finally, he will be limited in the range of experiences for which he can receive the positive regard of others (p. 78).

Standal says that four 'complicating factors' help explain why children don't simply adopt their parents' conditions of worth (pp. 78–83). First, there can be problems with 'clarity of discrimination', a phrase which refers to the accuracy of communications between parents and children (pp. 79–81). Parents vary in their abilities to send clear messages, and children vary in their abilities to accurately receive such messages. Second, parents may not share the same conditions of worth, and so their children receive mixed messages (pp. 81–2). Third, the introduction of new social others creates new sources to influence conditions of worth (pp. 82–3). Fourth, the individual may extend conditions of worth to new areas by associating new experiences with previously held conditions of worth (p. 83).

According to Standal, given that nearly everyone probably experiences some personal constriction from at least a single condition of worth, virtually everyone is maladjusted. However, there is variety within this broad schema of psychological maladjustment. Just as children develop conditions of worth in many different ways, the human experience of maladjustment also affects differently situated people differently. Standal distinguishes between 'the adult with congruent conditions of worth' (p. 84) and 'the adult with incongruent conditions of worth' (p. 86). For this distinction, *congruent* means '*internally consistent* and/or *externally consistent*, i.e. consistent with the stimulus characteristics of the environment' (p. 84).

The question is whether or not the individual is living in an environment that is conducive or friendly with respect to her conditions of worth, how culturally well matched she is to her social niche. The closer the match, the more likely it is that a person's basic and secondary needs will be satisfactorily and frequently met, and the less frequently anxiety will occur. Maladjusted persons who are placed in a subculture harmonious with their conditions of worth are fairly comfortable psychologically '. . . but vulnerable to distress in that they cannot withstand certain variations or alterations of milieu beyond rather narrow limits' (p. 86). In contrast, another individual may have no more conditions of worth than the persons described above. However, this last person may have grown up in a social environment where she took on a variety of 'mutually contradictory conditions of worth'. Or, she may have encountered, in her adult life, a social environment that frequently presents self-experiences that challenge conditions of worth formed earlier (pp. 86–7). In either case, such a person is likely to suffer recurrent anxiety in the course of frequently fearing loss of self-regard. She is frequently uncomfortable psychologically and more likely to seek psychotherapy than are individuals culturally better matched and less challenged by their social environments.

This distinction between individuals experiencing more or less internal and external consistency of conditions of worth between self and milieu is very close to Rogers' (1951, pp. 529–30) distinction between individuals who are psychologically more or less vulnerable to threat and more or less likely to enter psychotherapy.

PSYCHOTHERAPEUTIC CHANGE

The result of ideal psychotherapy, according to Standal, is the dissolving of all conditions of worth in the client. Such therapy requires a therapist capable of listening, understanding and discriminating self-experiences of the client in a manner that communicates unconditional positive regard. The therapist needs to be without conditions of worth, so that she is able to:

... react positively to the client and in such a way that the client perceives no self-experience as being more worthy or less worthy of positive regard than any other (p. 90).

Standal describes the psychotherapy process from two viewpoints, the 'molecular' and the 'molar'. He writes:

From the molecular viewpoint, psychotherapy is a matter of countless minute processes, the moment-to-moment interactions that take place within a therapeutic hour. From the molar viewpoint, it is a question of the changed personality structure that emerges from these countless minute processes ... No exact and comprehensive formulation of these relationships has so far been made in client-centered terms beyond that contained in the generally accepted postulate that, through the process of therapy, denied elements are assimilated into the self-structure. I am in agreement with this postulate, but am attempting a somewhat more detailed explanation of what takes place in therapy (p. 91).

Actually, Rogers' 1951 chapter on the 'Process of Therapy' had delineated a couple of possible formulations for further investigation and elaboration. Also, Rogers had described in some detail relevant research to date, which, with varying significance, pointed to trends within therapy of increased positive self-regard and increased acceptance of self. It is this chapter which included Oliver Bown's description of a therapeutic attitude of 'love', and the following statement by Rogers:

As the client experiences the attitude of acceptance which the therapist holds toward him, he is able to take and experience this same attitude toward himself. As he thus begins to accept, respect, like, and love himself, he is capable of experiencing these attitudes toward others (1951, p. 160).

Molecular viewpoint

The molecular viewpoint invites two important questions, according to Standal. First, what motivates a client to express to the therapist her feelings, behavior, and attitudes that she would ordinarily keep to herself? Second, by what mechanism does deeply denied material come to the surface and become available for examination in the course of therapy? (pp. 91–2) Standal finds his answers in the needs for positive regard and self-regard:

The possibility of positive regard satisfaction leads the client to express self-experiences which he has already discriminated but which he normally would not express. The subsequent altering of the conditions of worth governing satisfaction of his need for self-regard makes possible the more accurate discrimination of previously less clearly discriminated experiences (p. 100).

Molar viewpoint

Psychotherapy, viewed from Standal's molar viewpoint, is 'the process by which conditions of worth are removed from the self-structure' (p. 108). The client's unconditional self-regard arises primarily from the therapist's unconditional positive regard for the client throughout the therapy process. In the course of successful therapy the client experiences not only increased self-regard, but also a reduction in anxiety, an increase in the satisfaction of basic needs, and greater satisfaction of the need for positive regard.

PSYCHOLOGICAL MATURITY AND STAYING ADJUSTED

Standal defines 'the psychologically mature person' as 'one whose self-structure not only contains no conditions of worth but can never again have such conditions imposed upon it' (p. 109). Thus, the psychologically mature individual can evaluate experiences, like an infant, through organismic valuing, but, unlike an infant, without taking in introjections from important others. This raises, for Standal, a problem 'of explaining how positive regard transactions can lead to the imposition of conditions of worth before psychological maturity, but do not after it has been reached' (p. 110).

Standal offers a two-part answer to this problem. First, the infant has not developed a self-regard structure whereas the psychologically mature person has. Once a self-regard structure is in place, it is not vulnerable to fundamental change absent 'a sustained relationship characterized by positive regard transactions as extensive as those upon which the present self-regard structure was built' (p. 111). Such a relationship might be found in psychotherapy, where conditions of worth in the self-regard structure could, ideally, be eliminated. However, once that is accomplished, Standal says, it is hard to imagine that self-experiences outside of therapy could overthrow the adjusted self-regard structure and create maladjustment (pp. 111–13).

Secondly, Standal suggests that through completed, ideal psychotherapy, all conditions of worth have been eliminated without any addition of new conditions of worth.

> Henceforth, he [the client] simply *is* whatever self-experience he has. The self-regard he now feels in connection with any given self-experience is communicated to the total self-structure ... [w]ith a self-regard structure based upon his experiencing unconditional positive regard for all aspects of himself ... (pp. 113–14).

The self-structure of the psychologically mature individual is relatively impervious to withdrawals of positive regard from others, parents, close friends, etc. It is not that the psychologically mature individual will not feel a slight, but that she will experience it without denial or distortion. The slight from an important other cannot compete with the mature individual's self-regard while positive regard from others is experienced as reinforcing. ' ... [T]he client's self-regard has become unconditional ... ' (p. 116).

LIMITATIONS TO AN IDEAL PROCESS OF PSYCHOLOGICAL ADJUSTMENT

Standal reiterates what the ideal process would entail:
> (a) the client expresses some self-experience which is discriminated by the therapist in exactly the same fashion that the client is discriminating it; (b) the

therapist communicates to the client that he has accurately discriminated the client's self-experience; c) at the same time, the therapist communicates to the client that his regard for him remains unconditionally positive (p. 118).

Needless to say, this ideal is unobtainable. Standal identifies the personality of the therapist as an important potential limiting factor. The therapist may, for example, not be able to really receive the communications the client is sending, because of the therapist's own conditions of worth, her lack of relevant life experience (called by Standal *range of evocable responses*), or her unfamiliarity with the client's ways of communicating (*range of inferential signs*). Alternatively, the therapist may be unable to communicate back to the client the therapist's empathic understanding and unconditional positive regard (her *range of expressive signs* would then be considered deficient by Standal) (pp. 117–21).

Theoretically and definitionally, in ideal client-centered therapy, the client's limitations cannot be said to work against the psychotherapy process because the process follows the client, is of the client. However, according to Standal, in combination with or in relation to limiting personality qualities of the therapist, qualities of the client can lead to a less ideal process. So, for example, if the client's range of expressive signs is limited at the same time that the therapist's range of inferential signs is limited, the process may be somewhat stymied. A more serious handicap occurs when the conditions of worth of the therapist in combination with the conditions of worth of the client inhibit the process of eliminating the client's conditions of worth. Standal suggests that this might occur if therapist and client had such similar conditions of worth that the therapy was merely reinforcing. But the situation would be far more harmful were it to occur when the therapist's conditions of worth are either imposed upon the client or prevent the therapist from being open to accurate discrimination of and maintaining unconditional positive regard for the client's self-experiences (pp. 132–3).

Barrett-Lennard (1998) has written:

> About the time that Standal was completing his thesis, another major new concept in therapy had begun to germinate, under the name 'congruence'. Used initially in reference to consistency between the perceived actual self, and the ideal or wanted self, the term began to take on another meaning as a core quality of counselor presence in the therapy relationship (p. 65).

Even though Standal does not himself use the term 'congruence' in his dissertation, his discussion of the limitations to psychotherapy might well be seen as having contributed to the deepening redefinition of the concept of a congruent therapist and the position of that concept in the necessary and sufficient conditions.

In 1957, Rogers' statement of the second and third conditions necessary to constructive personality change read:

> *2. That the first [person], whom we shall term the client, is in a state of incongruence, being vulnerable or anxious.*
>
> *3. That the second person, whom we shall term the therapist, is congruent or integrated in the relationship* (p. 96).

Rogers goes on to describe the congruence of the therapist:

> It means that within the relationship he is freely and deeply himself, with his actual experience accurately represented by his awareness of himself . . . His experience may be 'I am afraid of this client' or 'My attention is so focused on my own problems that I can scarcely listen to him'. If the therapist is not denying these feelings to awareness, but is able freely to be them (as well as being his other feelings) then the condition we have stated [that the therapist be congruent in the relationship] is met (1957, p. 97).

In 1959, while discussing the dynamics of family relationships, Rogers explicitly stated that a parent is congruent in relationship with her child to the extent that the parent experiences unconditional self-regard (p. 241).

Similarly, then, a therapist's congruence is present whenever she is experiencing moment-to-moment unconditional self-regard in relationship with the client. Since Standal hypothesized the need for self-regard and argued that the presence of conditions of worth in the therapist was an important potential limitation on the success of the therapeutic process, his contribution to the developing concept of congruence appears to have been significant.

CONCLUSION

Many graduate students, therapists and scholars worked with Rogers in the course of the development of client-centered theory. Discussion, exchanging of ideas, and infusion from various thinkers occurred. Even a detailed bibliographic analysis of every discussion paper, thesis and article authored by students and staff at Ohio State University and at the old Counseling Center would not necessarily tell us who came up with exactly what idea when. The origin of the idea of unconditional positive regard doubtlessly resulted from multiple contributing seminal threads. Certain language constructs and several rationales for client-centered theory written by Stanley Standal contributed to and shaped major portions of the 1957, 1959 and 1961 versions of Rogers' theories. Rogers' 1959 statement incorporates the language of Standal's constructs of *the need for positive regard, the need for self-regard, unconditional positive regard, conditions of worth, regard complex,* and *unconditional self-regard.*

The following statement taken from Rogers' 1959 application of client-centered theory to family life amply illustrates the extent of Standal's influence:

1. The greater the degree of *unconditional positive regard* which the parent experiences toward the child:

a. The fewer the *conditions of worth* in the child.

b. The more the child will be able to live in terms of a continuing *organismic valuing process.*

c. The higher the level of *psychological adjustment* of the child.

2. The parent experiences such *unconditional positive regard* only to the extent that he *experiences unconditional self-regard.*

3. To the extent that he experiences unconditional self-regard, the parent will be congruent in the relationship.

a. This implies genuineness or congruence in the expression of his own *feelings* (positive or negative).

4. To the extent that conditions 1, 2, and 3 exist, the parent will realistically and *empathically* understand the child's *internal frame of reference* and *experience* an *unconditional positive regard* for him.

5. To the extent that conditions 1 through 4 exist, the theory of the process and outcomes of therapy . . . and the theory of the process and outcomes of an improving relationship . . . apply (p. 241).

Standal's hypotheses, language and rationales permeate the central therapeutic constructs of client-centered theory and dominate extensive sections of the 1959 paper, Rogers' most formal theory statement. A therapist's nondiscriminating acceptance of client experience in combination with the client's introjection of the therapist's acceptance had been previously identified as a possible factor for client change (Rogers, 1951, p. 518). Standal postulated an explanation for these phenomena that was adopted in its entirety by Rogers.

REFERENCES

Barrett-Lennard, G. T. (1998). *Carl Rogers' Helping System: Journey and Substance.* London: Sage.

Rogers, C.R. (1947). Some observations on the organization of personality. *American Psychologist, 2,* 358–68.

Rogers, C.R. (1951.) *Client-Centered Therapy: Its Current Practice, Implications, and Theory.* Boston: Houghton Mifflin.

Rogers, C.R. (1956). Client-centered therapy: A current view. In F. Fromm-Reichmann and J.L. Moreno (Eds.), *Progress in Psychotherapy,* Vol. 1, (pp. 199–209). New York: Grune and Stratton.

Rogers, C. R. (1957). The necessary and sufficient conditions of therapeutic personality change. *Journal of Consulting Psychology,* 21, 95–103. Also in H. Kirschenbaum and V. L. Henderson (1989) (Eds.) *The Carl Rogers Reader* (pp. 219–35). Boston: Houghton Mifflin. (Also 1956, Chicago Counseling and Psychotherapy Research Center Discussion Paper, 2 (8).)

Rogers, C. R. (1959). A theory of therapy, personality and interpersonal relationships, as developed in the client-centered framework. In S. Koch (Ed.), *Psychology: A Study of a Science. Vol. 3. Formulations of the Person and the Social context* (pp. 184–256). New York: McGraw-Hill.

Rogers, C. R. (1961). A tentative formulation of a general law of interpersonal relationships. In C.R. Rogers *On Becoming a Person: A Therapist's View of Psychotherapy* (pp. 338–46). Boston: Houghton Mifflin.

Standal, S. W. (1954). The need for positive regard: A contribution to client-centered theory. Unpublished doctoral dissertation, University of Chicago.

van der Veen, F. (1998). Email communication to the cctpca network, Sunday, 29 November 1998.

5   Unconditional Positive Regard Reconsidered

Paul Wilkins

Abstract. *Unconditional positive regard is re-examined in the light of theory and practice in an attempt to understand how it operates. The communication of unconditional positive regard is a major curative factor in any approach to therapy; congruence and empathy merely provide the context in which it is credible. It is possible to demonstrate acceptance in a manner apparently conflicting with the client's frame of reference and for it still to effect positive change. The limiting factor in the effectiveness of counselling and psychotherapy is the extent to which the therapist is able perceptibly to extend unconditional positive regard to the client.*

RE-EXAMINING THE 'CORE' CONDITIONS

There is a plethora of papers addressing empathy from within the person-centred tradition and from other perspectives — perhaps most notably in the work of Kohut (e.g. 1959, 1971, 1980). In an edited collection, Bohart and Greenberg (1997) present a comprehensive 'reconsideration' of empathy, establishing its historical context in the practice of psychotherapy and offering views from client-centred, experiential, psychoanalytic and 'other recent' perspectives. Recently, Warner (1996, pp. 127–43) has shown how empathy cures; Neville (1996, pp. 439–53) describes five kinds of empathy; Wilkins (1997a, pp. 35–45) has indicated its importance in human communication; McMillan (1997, pp. 205–9) has discussed how it occurs; and Binder (1998, pp. 216–30) writes of its significance when working with psychotic clients. Empathy has also been the focus of considerable research effort, some of which is summarised by Rogers (1975, pp. 5–6) and Bozarth (1998, pp. 59–61). Congruence, too, has received attention. For example, Lietaer (1993, pp. 17–46) has shown that 'genuineness' has two aspects (congruence and transparency) and discusses the implications for practice; Tudor and Worrall (1994, pp. 197–206) describe four specific requirements for therapeutic congruence; Wilkins (1997b, pp. 36–41) examines the similarities and differences between congruence and countertransference; and Haugh (1998, pp. 44–50) argues that congruence is misunderstood and sets the record straight.

    Unconditional positive regard has received less attention. Lietaer (1984)

First published in the *British Journal of Guidance and Counselling,* Vol. 28, No. 1. 2000, pp. 23–36, http://www.tandf.co.uk. Reproduced with permission of the publishers, Taylor & Francis/Routledge.

examines the controversy which surrounds it, stating that 'unconditional positive regard is probably one of the most questioned concepts in client-centered therapy' (p. 41).

Kilborn (1996, pp. 14–23) presents the findings from an empirical study of her practice; Purton (1998, pp. 22–37) considers unconditional positive regard and its spiritual implications; and Bozarth (1998, pp. 86–8) offers an overview. It puzzles me that what Bozarth (p. 83) describes as 'the curative factor in client-centred theory' has received more limited attention than the other two core conditions.

For whatever reason, unconditional positive regard, which 'seems effective in bringing about change' (Rogers, 1959, p. 208) and the communication of which (with empathic understanding) is the sixth of Rogers' 'conditions of the therapeutic process' (p. 213), *has* been less examined and is arguably less well understood.

WHAT IS UNCONDITIONAL POSITIVE REGARD?

In 1957, Rogers (reproduced in Kirschenbaum and Henderson, 1990) defined unconditional positive regard thus:

> It involves as much feeling of acceptance for the client's expression of negative, 'bad', painful, fearful, defensive, abnormal feelings as for his expression of 'good', positive, mature, confident, social feelings, as much acceptance of ways in which he is inconsistent as of ways in which he is consistent. It means caring for the client, but not in a possessive way or in such a way as simply to satisfy the therapist's own needs. It means a caring for the client as a *separate* person, with permission to have his own feelings, his own experiences (p. 225).

Rogers associated the terms 'prizing', 'warmth' and 'acceptance' with this quality.

Mearns and Thorne (1988) offer a definition 'in fairly straightforward language':

> Unconditional positive regard is the label given to the fundamental attitude of the person-centred counsellor towards her client. The counsellor who holds this attitude deeply values the humanity of her client and is not deflected in that valuing by any particular client behaviours. The attitude manifests itself in the counsellor's consistent acceptance of and enduring warmth towards her client (p. 59).

These definitions help to get towards an understanding of unconditional positive regard. The first tells what it looks like, what must be done in order to offer it (it is an operational definition), while the latter tells that it is an attitude which must be held towards another. But I have a sense that my understanding of this condition is incomplete, perhaps because I have used the term 'acceptance' as if it were an exact synonym for unconditional positive regard and, although Rogers (1967, p. 283) indicates that he too does this, I wonder if to do so means to miss some essential element.

The sense of this condition is that it has the qualities of being absolute, actual beyond the possibility of doubt, and that it relates to esteem and respect for another. To experience the unconditional positive regard of another, I must be convinced of their deep, unqualified esteem and respect for my total being. This is helpful, but it still leaves me with questions. Just what is being asked of me, and how do I do it?

Also, is unconditional positive regard similar to (or the same as) agape? Setting the counselling relationship in an historical context, Feltham (1999) ponders 'the influence of centuries of religion and religious practice in daily life and ritual' (pp. 6–7), and states:

> secular humanism leaves many without a God to turn to; fragmented and mobile, competitive societies leave many without stable supportive communities and community figures, such as priests, who previously supplied many valued facilities including the confessional; and the breakdown of the concept of selfless duty, altruism or love (agape) also leaves a large hole in the social and interpersonal fabric (p. 7).

Is the unconditional positive regard of a therapist necessary to replace the selfless love which may previously have been offered elsewhere? Arguably, there is a recognition of the value of something like unconditional positive regard to well-being and growth in the tenets of major religions. For example, Purton (1996, p. 459) equates the Buddhist concept of counteracting *lobha* or greed with the development of unconditional positive regard and 'forgiveness' and compassion are at the heart of Christian (and other) belief. If these are to be offered to their fullest extent, perhaps there is a requirement for acceptance of the other on the part of the bestower.

Patterson (1974, pp. 89–90) indicates that love or agape *is* what is offered by a therapist extending the facilitative conditions, and that this reflects the wisdom of thousands of years of human experience and the conclusions of 'great philosophers of various times and cultures' (p. 90). However, unconditional positive regard is only one of these facilitative conditions. When I and my students first heard Brian Thorne describe the quality to which he refers as 'tenderness' (Thorne, 1991, pp. 73–81) which is a sublime culmination of the facilitative conditions in combination, we thought that love (by which we meant agape) would have served equally well as a label. It seems, therefore, that unconditional positive regard is not the same as agape, but is an aspect of it — if undoubtedly an essential aspect and perhaps the most important.

In an attempt to understand unconditional positive regard more completely, I considered what it might mean to reverse each of its elements. *Conditional positive regard* is the offering of warmth, respect, acceptance, etc. only when the other fulfils some particular expectation, desire or requirement; it is offered when one person conveys to another, 'I will only approve of, like, favour you if you do this, give me this, act in this way'. When (for example) a parent does this to a child, in terms of person-centred theory there may be a resulting distortion in the development of conditions of worth (Rogers, 1959, pp. 224–5). Conditional positive regard can also be a facet of therapy when the therapist has an agenda different from that of the client and acts to 'reward' appropriate behaviour; or, as Mearns (1994) warns, when the therapist aligns 'more strongly with one part of the personality against [an]other' and so colludes 'with part of the client to reject another important part of himself' (p. 15). At the very best, supporting 'positive' aspects of the client at the expense of 'negative' aspects, or encouraging and actively approving some patterns of thought or behaviour in preference to others, is — because some element of the client's total being is neglected or ignored — likely to be a block to therapeutic change and may be damaging.

Unconditional negative regard — that is, when one person conveys to another, 'Whatever you say or do, however you are, I will hate, despise, demean or denigrate you' — also has extreme consequences. In its most active and virulent form, it is the root of racism, homophobia, sexism and the like. Unconditional negative regard is also damaging in a more passive form — that is, as the complete neglect by one person of one or more aspects of another. These remain unseen and unresponded to even when warmth and acceptance are extended to other parts. This differs from conditional positive regard (although its effects may be similar) in that the person showing it towards another is unconscious of what they are ignoring, and may even experience themselves as totally warm, accepting and caring towards the other.

Unconditional positive disregard occurs when one person refuses to enter into a relationship of any kind with another. It is paying no attention to and being neglectful of another *whatever* they say or do, or however they act. In an extreme form, it is the complete negation of the existence of one person by another. This can be so powerful that receivers of it come to doubt their right to life. An example of unconditional positive disregard is the psychoanalytic concept of the 'dead mother' (Schutzenberger, 1991), where a child born after the death of a sibling is not seen by the mother, who instead sees only her dead child when she looks at her new baby. Schutzenberger states 'very often, the child of this 'dead mother' will have a difficult life, suicidal tendencies or suffer from schizophrenia or other kinds of problems' (p. 218). A distressed, bored or unengaged therapist is in danger of offering unconditional positive disregard.

In terms of person-centred theory, the consequence of each of these three is the development of conditions of worth because (when experienced by babies from, for example, their mothers) each amounts to the withholding of unqualified love. However it happens, the absence of unconditional positive regard is harmful: as Bozarth (1998) points out, 'conditionality is the bedrock of Rogers' theory of pathology' (p. 83). Although each of these ways of behaving towards another may have the same result, operationally they differ. Understanding this difference leads to a fuller understanding of the benefits of unconditional positive regard.

UNCONDITIONAL POSITIVE REGARD IN OPERATION

The acceptance of the client by the therapist is an essential element of counselling and psychotherapy. How its effectiveness is understood in theoretical terms may differ. For example, Jacobs (1988, p. 13) records that a psychodynamic counsellor would expect 'unconditional regard' to encourage positive transference. From a person-centred perspective, the unconditional positive regard of the counsellor promotes the self-acceptance of the client, and this allows change. Rogers (1951) writes: 'we cannot change, we cannot move away from what we are, until we thoroughly *accept* what we are' (p. 17).

Acknowledging that it is sometimes very difficult to accept another unconditionally, Rogers (in Hobbs, 1987) states: 'If I really care about (another) person in an unconditional way, that's helpful' (p. 20) Barrett-Lennard (1998) outlines person-centred self-theory and states, commenting:

> an effect of conditions of worth is that the individual is no longer freely open to experience ... the resulting *incongruence* between self and experience, involves a state of 'vulnerability' and a degree of dysfunction. However, its effect is also to minimise inner conflict and anxiety (pp. 77–8).

This process results in the development of a psychological defence which 'allows the individual to maintain an acceptable self-concept, while the implicit conditions of worth remain out of view and unaffected' (ibid.). Rogers (1959) states that 'for the process of defense to be reversed', there must be a decrease in the conditions of worth and an increase in unconditional self-regard. He adds that experiencing unconditional positive regard from 'a significant other' is one way of achieving this, and that for unconditional positive regard to be communicated 'it must exist in the context of empathic understanding'. When this happens, conditions of worth 'are weakened or dissolved' (p. 230).

The conclusion drawn from theory is that communicating unconditional positive regard will effect change. However, for a therapist to hold that as an *expectation* and certainly as a *desire* (however well-intentioned) may be counterproductive and may actually limit the effectiveness of therapy. Implicit in the holding of another in unconditional positive regard is an acceptance of their right as a self-determining individual *not* to change, to be 'cured' or to grow. It is natural for a therapist (of whatever complexion) to want the client to change and perhaps even to form a vision of what change might lead to; but, for some clients at least, only when this desire is let go does change become possible. Mearns (1999) has pointed out that one aspect or 'configuration' of many clients is 'not for growth', and gives examples including 'the "me" that just wants to curl up and do absolutely nothing' and 'the part that wants to go back'. He stresses the importance of including these 'not for growth' configurations of self in therapy stating:

> It is not any one configuration within the client's Self which is important but the whole constellation of configurations and the dynamics which define their interrelationship. It is this dynamic integration which will result in an overall picture that reflects the person's Self. If we miss out parts or ban them from therapy because they are too difficult for the therapist, we are offering a conditional relationship and one which is likely to be anti-therapeutic (p. 127).

Offering unconditional positive regard is not always easy, but it is worth the effort. For example:

> A 'difficult' client presented at my place of work. He had previously been seen by one of my colleagues, of whom he had little good to say. In his expressed view, the service for which we worked was useless and counselling was worse. And yet he wanted an appointment. With some foreboding, I agreed to meet with him for counselling. I had a sense of being tested to my limits. This was confirmed when he arrived for his first appointment driving an army surplus armoured car and began telling me of his love of the

military and hatred of women and black people in particular. All this challenged my liberal attitudes, and yet I knew that the efficacy of our relationship depended upon me being accepting, not merely acting the part.

As I listened and responded to him, I began to wonder about what life experiences had led him to his extreme views. The tale he told was of mistreatment as a child and a tempestuous relationship with his wife, who he experienced as 'robbing' him of his house and his business. Between sessions, I read about prejudice and how it might arise. Almost without noticing, I slipped from being challenged by my client's way of being to an appreciation of the person of worth behind the views. As this happened, there was a softening in him, sessions began to include humour and a sense of companionship in the counselling enterprise. It was as if, as he accepted himself more, he became more accepting of the world.

We only met for six sessions and I'm sure that he remained a misogynist and a racist (and I find that I want to say that did not matter to me), but there was an easing of his attitudes. I think we were both changed by the process. Part of my change lay in the realisation that 'acceptance', unconditional positive regard, was exactly that — the issue of my approval or disapproval, my judgement of the views and way of being of another, was impertinent and immaterial. Experiencing an attitude of unconditional positive regard with respect to this client involved a deep acceptance of how he was — he had racist and misogynist views, but these were essential to his way of being in the world. He was doing the best he could, given his antecedents and the way he perceived the world to be. What was required of me was an acceptance of how things were, and this was in some way independent of 'approval' and 'disapproval'.

Unconditional positive regard is the curative factor in therapy. When it is experienced by one person from another, it is growth-promoting regardless of the setting. I am aware of having experienced 'growth' as I have perceived the increasingly unconditional positive regard of clients. The more I perceive myself as being seen and accepted for what I am, the more likely I (as therapist) am to change positively in the therapeutic encounter. I have also noticed that, as my clients approach the end of therapy, they are more likely to offer me unconditional positive regard. For example:

I had been working with Jane for nearly two years. We had been through a great deal together and her perceptions of me had changed a lot. To begin with, I had been the 'expert', owner of some arcane knowledge which would help her through her confusion. As this confusion had cleared, I had become a guide, perhaps even paternal, older, presumed to be wiser, certainly someone in whom she could confide.

As we neared our twenty-fourth month, I was aware of how easy it now was to be with Jane. After the trauma and distress we had been through together, we were at last peaceful in each other's presence. I felt she saw me as I was and that she was happy for me to be however I was. It was then that she told me she didn't need to come any more — I had no doubt that she was right. We ended well, with some sadness at our parting, but no regret.

Six months later I had a postcard from the South Seas to tell me of the adventure she had embarked on as a consequence of our time together.

Jane's journey could be understood as one from incongruence and anxiety, through self-acceptance and 'mutuality' (see Mearns and Thorne, 1988, pp. 126–9) to an ability to accept others. An alternative but related view would be that of Brazier (1993, pp. 72–90): that Jane rediscovered her ability to *give* unconditional positive regard rather than to receive it, and that it was this that was transformative.

Bozarth (1998) qualifies the view that unconditional positive regard is 'the curative factor of [person-centred] theory' stating:

> It is [the actualising] tendency that is the fundamental curative factor lying within the person. The reference to unconditional positive regard as the curative factor assumes the thwarting of the natural tendency; hence, making it necessary that the client become more directly connected with the actualising tendency through unconditional positive self-regard (p. 82).

This does not conflict with Rogers' (1957, p. 96) integrative statement which asserts that *any* therapist who demonstrates an accepting understanding of the client while being fully present in the relationship will facilitate change. To restate this: any person regardless of the setting or their belief in the nature of humans is likely to promote positive change in another if they communicate their undoubtable unconditional positive regard for this second person.

Mearns (1994, pp. 3–5) points out that accepting somebody is very different from liking them: 'liking' is based in shared values or complementary needs — in other words, 'liking' is conditional. He also points out that person-centred counsellors seek to be 'beside' their clients, not 'on their side' (p. 54): that is, to be as close to the client's experiencing as possible, not allying with their thoughts and feelings. The first is an accepting position; the second is, or may become, conditional.

Lietaer (1984) considers that unconditionality has its problems:

> (1) There is a potential conflict between genuineness or congruence on the one hand, and unconditionality on the other; (2) It is a rare person and a rare time in which the constancy of acceptance can be provided by any therapist for any client. Thus, while unconditionality is not impossible, it is improbable; (3) Unconditionality calls upon the therapist for a devoted self-effacing that often leads to a compensatory reaction in which confrontation becomes a form of self-assertion (p. 41).

Lietaer sees that these questions and difficulties arise as client-centred therapy becomes more relationship-centred, with a resulting increased prominence given to the therapist's congruence ('which implies, among other things, feedback and confrontation'). Bozarth (1998) believes Lietaer to be in error, expressing the view that 'client-centred' and 'relationship-centred' are not differently defined and that Lietaer's 'behavioral definition of genuineness as involving feedback and confrontation' leads to a shift in emphasis from trusting the client's experience towards trusting the 'expertise' of the therapist (p. 85). I am inclined to accept

Bozarth's view.

In the eighteenth proposition of his personality theory, Rogers (1951) explains the link between self-acceptance and the acceptance of others:

> When the individual perceives and accepts into one consistent and integrated system all his sensory and visceral experiences, then he is necessarily more understanding of others and is more accepting of others as separate individuals (p. 520).

Lietaer (1984) links congruence and 'acceptance', seeing them as 'parts of a more basic attitude of "openness"'. Congruence is openness towards one's self, while unconditional positive regard is openness towards another. He states:

> The more I accept myself and am able to be present in a comfortable way with everything that bubbles up in me, without fear or defense, the more I can be receptive to everything that lives in my client. Without this openness, without this acceptance, it is not possible to let the experience of my client unfold, to let it come to life fully; for with a conditional attitude the chances are great that I dare not see certain parts of the client's experience, and that I will minimise or reject some of them (p. 44).

Because it depends on the attitude individuals hold towards themselves, unconditional positive regard is the hardest therapeutic attitude to develop. It cannot be effectively faked, and tolerance (the ability to patiently endure or 'allow') is quite different. I have doubts, too, about the much-repeated notion of accepting the person but not the behaviour. While it is neither ethical nor appropriate for a therapist to condone antisocial or harmful behaviour or to collude in its perpetuation, there is a real risk that in attempting to hold the attitude 'I disapprove of what you do but I accept you', the therapist will fail to offer unconditional positive regard, and the client experience is then one of censure and perhaps rejection. What is required is an ability to see and connect with the person behind the 'repulsive' or 'repugnant' behaviour or attitude (perhaps as in the case history above). In some way this reduces the need to tolerate or judge the reprehensible thought, act or deed. This necessary paradox is essential to effective therapy. The attitude of unconditional positive regard requires that, while the therapist does not collude with harmful or antisocial behaviour, it is neither condoned nor opposed.

This may not mean that 'confrontation' is impossible in person-centred therapy. Lietaer (1984) discusses 'confrontation and unconditionality', and points out that 'confrontation does not in any way mean that I reject my client as a person or that I stop trying to understand his experience' (pp. 54–7). If the unconditional positive regard of the therapist is experienced by the client, then challenge and confrontation may play a useful part in therapy. Certainly, being person-centred is not about being passive or 'nice', but a necessary component of unconditional positive regard is an acceptance of the client's authority and self-expertise. It is not for the therapist to decide on or direct the course of change, or even to assume it must happen.

If the proposition is accepted that 'psychopathological' and/or antisocial ways of being are induced by conditions of worth, and that communicating unconditional positive regard is a way of redressing these, then it is implicit that effective therapy is limited only by the therapist's ability to experience and convey this attitude to the client. If the first of Rogers' (1957, p. 96) six conditions — that is, the requirement for psychological contact — can be met [and Prouty (1976, pp. 290–5) shows that even this requirement is not absolute], then there are no clients who are by definition unsuitable for psychotherapy. Although the terms used may be different, this is not necessarily a problem from other theoretical perspectives. Any apparent difference seems to reside in the issue of 'contact'. For example, Jacobs (1988, p. 53) lists distinguishing features which suggest that a potential client is unsuitable for psychodynamic therapy. These can be understood as restricting psychological contact.

The experience of person-centred therapists challenges some of these 'disqualifications'. There are published accounts of the usefulness of person-centred therapy when working with people described as schizophrenic (e.g. Teusch, 1990, pp. 637–44; Berghofer, 1996, pp. 481–94) and people seen as having a learning difficulty (e.g. Pörtner, 1990, pp. 659–70), and Lambers (in Mearns, 1994, pp. 110–20) has written of person-centred therapy with people with a variety of 'psychopathologies'. Although empathy and congruence are seen as playing an important part in working with these clients, it is the ability of the therapist to accept unconditionally the (sometimes bizarre) nature of the client's inner world and its subjective reality, as well as some notional 'healthy' core or rational facet, that increases the likelihood of psychological contact and therefore therapeutic change. For example:

> *One of my students came to me one day to tell me that her supervisor thought she should stop seeing one of her clients because he was 'psychotic'. My student felt very strongly that she had a relationship with this client and that the point of counselling was not to 'cure' the psychosis (which in any case seemed of marginal relevance to her) but to stay alongside her client as he travelled what was a traumatic and difficult path. She did not know that psychotic people were not susceptible to counselling interventions and that they were thought by some people to be incapable of forming a therapeutic relationship.*
>
> *So, with the agreement that she ensure her personal safety in a variety of ways, she continued to see this client and carried on responding to him in a person-centred way. While firmly rooted in her reality, she entered into his delusional world to some extent 'as if' it were her own, and noticed that as she did so his periods of rationality began to increase. He would still behave bizarrely in her presence but, every so often, his voice and demeanour would return to normal and he would thank her for staying with him through what he knew was a difficult episode for them both.*
>
> *This continued for some weeks until the client was once again able to encounter the world with confidence and to connect with people. He said to my student that it was the first time anybody had attempted to stay with him throughout a florid episode. He reported that even at his most delusional he had been aware of her presence and that her steadfast and accepting nature and her obviously genuine desire to understand what it was like to be him had been very comforting, reassuring and helpful. His*

> *psychotic episode had been relatively short in comparison to his previous experience.*

In our conversations during and after this therapeutic relationship, I was aware of my student's insistence that her client was worthy of deep respect and of his right to his fantasy world and odd behaviour — that is, his right to be himself as he was at any time.

The reason that psychotherapeutic interventions are seen not to 'work' with, for example, people in a psychotic state, and paedophiles, may have much more to do with the belief, fear, disapproval and revulsion of the therapists than with the supposed intractable nature of the clients. However open-minded therapists believe themselves to be, however tolerant they are, if the client does not experience unconditional positive regard, then the likelihood is that therapy will fail. There is limited support for this view from research (perhaps because research into the effectiveness of person-centred therapy centres on *all* the conditions or on the relationship *per se*), but examples include Eckert and Wuchner (1996), which is a study of work with people diagnosed as having a borderline disorder. They emphasise the need for client-centred psychotherapists to 'hang on tightly' to their unconditional positive regard when working with this client group:

> As a result of what they have already been through, these patients are profoundly frightened of being manipulated and misused. One form of misuse they are particularly wary about is that the therapist hopes their symptoms will vanish soon, confirming that he is a 'good' therapist. So the client-centred therapist is well-advised to aim genuinely at nothing other than really understanding his borderline client. Faced by this kind of fear once, I remarked to the patient: 'I am not interested in making you better but in helping you to understand yourself better', and the patient was quite obviously very relieved (pp. 213–33).

That the ability to offer effective therapy is limited by the therapist's qualities, and not those of the client, lays a great responsibility on the therapist, for we will each only become more effective by addressing our own issues. Our ability to offer unconditional positive regard to others depends on our capacity for unconditional self-regard. Rogers (in Kirschenbaum and Henderson, 1990) wrote about the challenge of self-acceptance and its value to the counsellor:

> If I can form a helping relationship to myself — if I can be sensitively aware of and acceptant toward my own feelings — then the likelihood is great that I can form a helping relationship with another (p. 120).

THE RELATIVE IMPORTANCE OF UNCONDITIONAL POSITIVE REGARD

In a way, it is nonsense to attempt to rank Rogers' six conditions. He states (1957) that all six, if they exist over a period of time, are necessary and sufficient to ensure 'constructive personality change' (p. 96). Bozarth (1998) argues persuasively that empathy, unconditional positive regard and congruence 'are really, ultimately and functionally, one condition' (p. 80). However, Lietaer (1993, p. 17) asserts that from 1962 Rogers called congruence the most fundamental of the core conditions. Thorne (1991) writes:

Acceptance, empathy and congruence — these three, as always, but the greatest and the most difficult and the most exciting and the most challenging is congruence (p. 189).

Person-centred therapists often believe that congruence takes precedence over the other core conditions. However, in both terms of theory and my personal experience, I find it hard to accept that congruence is the most important condition. It is challenging, it is exciting, but if any condition is more important than the others it is surely the sixth — that empathic understanding and unconditional positive regard are communicated. Also, though perhaps only in unusual circumstances, constructive personality change can occur when unconditional positive regard is communicated in the apparent absence of empathic responses.

I agree with Bozarth (1998) that 'the interrelationship of the conditions of congruence, empathy and unconditional positive regard is so high that they are inseparable in the theory' (p. 83), and I extend this to practice. This is because empathy and congruence provide a framework in which unconditional positive regard is believable, but it is also because it is impossible to be truly accepting of another without being open to one's own inner experience and being in a personal state of harmony. Also, in operation, there is sometimes little to distinguish deep empathy from unconditional positive regard. For example:

Jim held a position of considerable responsibility and authority in a large corporation. The efficacy of his work was dependent upon a close collaborative relationship with his colleagues. Jim was experiencing one of his colleagues as not pulling his weight and a formerly cordial relationship between them had broken down. Jim was currently feeling very hurt and damaged by his colleague's behaviour.

As he described all this to me, without really thinking, I said, 'You wish he would fuck off and die.' There was instantly a look of profound relief on Jim's face and, at first softly and then with increasing vehemence, he repeated my phrase several times.

Somehow the phrase I used seemed to have the right force. Perhaps I had empathically sensed Jim's desire that his colleague cease to exist but, as I spoke, I sensed that what was important was that I knew Jim felt as he did and that I accepted him. Jim later confirmed that the way I had acknowledged and accepted an extreme negative feeling he had not previously admitted to himself was crucial to our relationship and to his resolving his workplace issues. In some way he was changed by hearing me acceptingly voice his hidden wish.

In therapy and other relationships, there have been times when I have been similarly affected. It has been like the flicking of a switch; whether something has been turned on or off I am unsure, but I do know that the transformation is abrupt and apparently complete and everlasting. I have not necessarily been aware of the empathic understanding of the other person, but I have been sure that they have accepted in me what has hitherto been so unacceptable to me that I have not even recognised its existence. I cannot begin to do justice to the power of this experience as I have felt it for myself and witnessed it happen to others. When this occurs, there is an equivalent in terms of unconditional positive regard of what Mearns and Thorne (1988) define as 'depth reflection' (p. 42) — that is, the communication of an empathic sensing of something just below the level of the client's awareness.

This leads to the conclusion that, if any condition is more important than another, it is the communication of unconditional positive regard. This can itself effect constructive change. In this respect, unconditional positive regard is unique. Rogers (1954, p. 33; 1956, pp. 199–200) may be interpreted as suggesting that congruence is itself transforming (because it provides a context of 'reality'), but this is only because the realness of therapists gives credence to their unconditional positive regard and their empathic understanding.

IMPLICATIONS FOR PRACTICE

If unconditional positive regard is the most crucial therapist attitude (regardless of the nature of therapy), there are profound implications for practice. Even given that to hold someone in unconditional positive regard is 'sometimes very difficult' (Rogers quoted in Hobbs, 1987, p. 20) and that for the therapist to accept the client *in the moment* is desirable, not mandatory, if when therapy breaks down a likely cause is the limited acceptance of the therapist, and if 'untreatable' clients are unacceptable clients, then there is an implicit duty on therapists to maximise their ability to accept others. Because of this, it is not congruence which presents the greatest challenge to therapists, but unconditional positive regard. This requires that therapists approach their clients without prejudice, with respect for who and what they are, and with a recognition that they are self-determining persons. Because we have values and opinions, because few of us are without our own pain and shame, this is very difficult. Perhaps the first thing each of us needs to accept is that our ability to offer unconditional positive regard is limited; the second is to discover those limits and to seek to expand them (while working within them in the interim). How to do this is a matter of choice and opportunity. Personal therapy is a well-known route, joining a self-development group may be helpful, but it might be that meditation or some other contemplative practice serves as well.

On a practical level, it may help to re-evaluate attitudes to practice and to clients. Dogma is the enemy of unconditional positive regard. Certainly it is worth critically appraising existing conventions of practice and developing a credulous attitude to clients and the ways in which we behave towards them.

Any notion of the client as attention-seeking or manipulative seems to have little to do with unconditional positive regard. If someone is attention-seeking, does this not bespeak a deep need to be attended to? Similarly, when a client is late for an appointment or misses it altogether, does this merit a punitive response, or should I be attending to and accepting of the implied message or obscurely expressed need? Is it accepting to insist that clients meet with me for one hour a week at a place of my choosing? I am not suggesting that the communication of unconditional positive regard necessitates a permissive attitude towards clients, but I do suggest that sometimes the structures of therapy are relied upon uncritically and that this may lead to less effective practice. The ability to develop and convey an attitude of unconditional positive regard depends on a willingness to approach each person as an individual with unique needs. This is not without tensions. These can only be resolved on a case-by-case basis.

REFERENCES

Barrett-Lennard, G.T. (1998). *Carl Rogers' Helping System: Journey and Substance.* London: Sage.

Berghofer, G. (1996). Dealing with schizophrenia — a person-centered approach providing care to long-term patients in a supporting residential service in Vienna. In R. Hutterer, G. Pawlowsky, P.F. Schmid and R. Stipsits (Eds.), *Client-Centered and Experiential Psychotherapy: a Paradigm in Motion.* Frankfurt-am-Main: Peter Lang.

Binder, U. (1998). Empathy and empathy development with psychotic clients. In B. Thorne and E. Lambers (Eds.), *Person-Centred Therapy: a European Perspective.* London: Sage.

Bohart, A. C. and Greenberg, L.S. (Eds) (1997). *Empathy Reconsidered: New Directions in Psychotherapy.* Washington, DC: American Psychological Association.

Bozarth, J.D. (1998). *Person-Centered Therapy: a Revolutionary Paradigm.* Ross-on-Wye: PCCS Books.

Brazier, D. (1993). The necessary condition is love: going beyond self in the person-centred approach. In D. Brazier (Ed.), *Beyond Carl Rogers.* London: Constable.

Eckert, J. and Wuchner, M. (1996). Long-term development of borderline personality disorder. In R. Hutterer, G. Pawlowsky, P.F. Schmid and R. Stipsits (Eds.), *Client-Centered and Experiential Psychotherapy: a Paradigm in Motion.* Frankfurt-am-Main: Peter Lang.

Feltham, C. (1999). Contextualising the therapeutic relationship. In C. Feltham (Ed.), *Understanding the Counselling Relationship.* London: Sage.

Haugh, S. (1998). Congruence: a confusion of language. *Person-Centred Practice, 6(1),* pp. 44–50.

Hobbs, T. (1987). The Rogers' interview. *Counselling Psychology Review, 4(4),* pp. 19–27.

Jacobs, M. (1988). *Psychodynamic Counselling in Action.* London: Sage.

Kilborn, M. (1996). The quality of acceptance. *Person-Centred Practice, 4(1),* pp. 14–23.

Kirschenbaum, H. and Henderson, V.L. (Eds.) (1990). *The Carl Rogers Reader.* London: Constable.

Kohut, H. (1959). Introspection, empathy and psychoanalysis. *Journal of the American Psychoanalytic Association, 7,* pp. 459–83.

Kohut, H. (1971). *The Analysis of Self* New York: International Universities Press.

Kohut, H. (1980). Reflections. In A. Goldberg (Ed.), *Advances in Self Psychology.* New York: International Universities Press.

Lietaer, G. (1984). Unconditional positive regard: a controversial basic attitude in client-centered therapy. In R.E. Levant and J.M. Shlien (Eds.), *Client-Centered Therapy and the Person-Centered Approach: New Directions in Theory, Research and Practice.* New York: Praeger.

Lietaer, G. (1993). Authenticity, congruence and transparency. In D. Brazier (Ed.), *Beyond Carl Rogers.* London: Constable.

McMillan, M. (1997). The experiencing of empathy: what is involved in achieving the 'as if' condition? *Counselling, 8(3),* pp. 205–9.

Mearns D. (1994). *Developing Person-Centred Counselling.* London: Sage.

Mearns, D. (1999). Person-centred therapy with configurations of self. *Counselling, 10(2),* pp. 125–30.

Mearns, D. and Thorne, B. (1988). *Person-Centred Counselling in Action.* London: Sage.

Neville B. (1996). Five kinds of empathy. In R. Hutterer, G. Pawlowsky, P.F. Schmid and R. Stipsits (Eds.), *Client-Centered and Experiential Psychotherapy: a Paradigm in Motion.* Frankfurt-am-Main: Peter Lang.

Patterson, C.H. (1974). *Relationship Counseling and Psychotherapy.* New York: Harper and Row.

Pörtner, M. (1990). Client-centered therapy with mentally retarded persons: Catherine and Ruth. In G. Lietaer, J. Rombauts and R. Van Balen (Eds.), *Client-Centered and Experiential*

Psychotherapy in the Nineties. Leuven: Leuven University Press.

Prouty, G.F. (1976). Pre-therapy, a method of treating pre-expressive psychotic and retarded patients. *Psychotherapy: Theory, Research and Practice, 13(3),* pp. 290–5.

Purton, C. (1996). The deep structure of the core conditions: a Buddhist perspective. In R. Hutterer, G. Pawlowsky, P.F. Schmid and R. Stipsits (Eds.), *Client-Centered and Experiential Psychotherapy: a Paradigm in Motion.* Frankfurt-am-Main: Peter Lang.

Purton, C. (1998). Unconditional positive regard and its spiritual implications. In B. Thorne and E. Lambers (Eds.), *Person-Centred Therapy: a European Perspective.* London: Sage.

Rogers, C.R. (1951). *Client-Centered Therapy.* Boston: Houghton Mifflin.

Rogers, CR. (1954). The case of Mrs Oak. In C.R. Rogers and R.F. Dymond (Eds.), *Psychotherapy and Personality Change.* Chicago: University of Chicago Press.

Rogers, C.R. (1956). *Client-Centered Therapy* (3rd edn). Boston: Houghton-Mifflin.

Rogers, C.R. (1957). The necessary and sufficient conditions for therapeutic personality change. *Journal of Consulting Psychology, 21,* pp. 95–103.

Rogers, C.R. (1959). Therapy, personality and interpersonal relationships. In S. Koch (Ed.), *Psychology: A Study of a Science, Vol 3: Formulations of the Person and the Social Context.* New York: McGraw-Hill.

Rogers, C.R. (1967). *On Becoming a Person.* London: Constable.

Rogers, C.R. (1975). Empathic: an unappreciated way of being. *Counseling Psychologist, 5(2),* pp. 2–10.

Schutzenberger, A.A. (1991). The drama of the seriously ill patient: fifteen years' experience of psychodrama and cancer. In P. Holmes and M. Karp (Eds.), *Psychodrama: Inspiration and Technique.* London: Routledge.

Teusch, L. (1990). Positive effects and limitations of client-centered therapy with schizophrenic patients. In G. Lietaer, J. Rombauts and R. Van Balen (Eds.), *Client-Centered and Experiential Psychotherapy in the Nineties.* Leuven: Leuven University Press.

Thorne, B. (1991). *Person-Centred Counselling: Therapeutic and Spiritual Dimensions.* London: Whurr.

Tudor, K. and Worrall M. (1994). Congruence reconsidered. *British Journal of Guidance and Counselling, 22(2),* pp. 197–206.

Warner, M.S. (1996). How does empathy cure? A theoretical consideration of empathy, processing and personal narrative. In R. Hutterer, G. Pawlowsky, P.F. Schmid and R. Stipsits (Eds.), *Client-Centered and Experiential Psychotherapy: a Paradigm in Motion.* Frankfurt-am-Main: Peter Lang.

Wilkins, P. (1997a). Empathy: a desirable quality for effective interpersonal communication? *Applied Community Studies, 3(2),* pp. 35–45.

Wilkins, P. (1997b). Congruence and countertransference: similarities and differences. *Counselling, 8(1),* pp. 36–41.

6   Acknowledgement: The art of responding. Dialogical and ethical perspectives on the challenge of unconditional relationships in therapy and beyond

Peter F. Schmid

Abstract. *The practice of person-centred psychotherapy works with an image of the human being, which understands the human being as a person and thus respects his or her being different. To accept one another as being truly an Other and therefore always also 'being counter', is described as the foundation for the possibility of encounter within and beyond therapy. The well-known attitude of unconditional positive regard in psychotherapy is discussed more fundamentally from a dialogical or encounter philosophical perspective, as the human possibility of, and the need for, acknowledgement without conditions — a basic quality in the relationship among persons. It means both to praise somebody's uniqueness as a person full of worth — to be loved, and to respond to the Other's need for understanding and solidarity. (The latter denotes its ethical aspect.) To encounter another person with acknowledgement instead of objectifying him or her by trying to get knowledge about the Other, is an essential paradigm shift in psychotherapy and helping relations of various kinds. It implies a person-centred understanding of aggression as a movement towards the Other out of the need for identity as well as contact. It is shown that acknowledgement as an ethically founded 'way of being with' — in therapy and beyond — rests on the well-known, though often misunderstood, quality of personal love.*

> *Toleranz sollte eigentlich nur eine vorübergehende Gesinnung sein:*
> *Sie muss zur Anerkennung führen. Dulden heißt beleidigen.*[1]
> (Johann Wolfgang Goethe, Maximen und Reflexionen)

Unconditional acceptance will be examined in this chapter from the perspective of personal or dialogical anthropology[2] and a socio-ethical point of view as a fundamental quality of being and becoming a person. Thus it is seen as more than a therapeutic condition or an attitude of the therapist or counsellor. It has been referred to in many ways, including 'unconditional positive regard', 'acceptance', 'non-possessive warmth', 'emotional warmth', 'liking', 'prizing', as a way 'to love, to like, to regard, to respect'. It has been described many times (in its

---

Acknowledgement: I am very grateful to Pete Sanders for his help in making the text understandable to the English reader.
1. 'Tolerance should only be a temporary cast of mind: it has to lead to acknowledgement. To tolerate means to offend.'
2. See Schmid, 2001a, footnote 2.

49

facilitative impact in relationships) mainly from a therapeutic perspective by Carl Rogers and other theoreticians.[3] Together with authenticity and empathy, it makes up the basic 'way of being with' which is called 'presence' (see Schmid, 2001c) and thus — beyond therapy and helping relationships — is an elementary constituent of human communication and the conditio humana in general.

Based on dialogical or encounter philosophy, here it is referred to as *acknowledgement.*

TO SAY 'YES' TO THE OTHER: THE MEANING OF ACKNOWLEDGEMENT

Acknowledgement without conditions denotes an attitude of life which says 'yes' to the Other[4] as a person, in his or her essence. It accepts the Other as he or she is — the Other is not evaluated nor assessed nor judged. But acknowledgement is more than the absence of judgements. It is an active and pro-active way of *deliberately* saying yes to the Other as a person.

The crucial point here is the unconditionality. There is no 'but', i.e. 'I accept you, *but* I expect you to do this or that'. There is no 'if', i.e. 'I like you, *if* you do this and avoid that'. On the contrary, it is a cordial attention which is not tied to conditions (such as that the Other is required to behave or develop in a way one likes to see — a trap frequently observed in the process of therapy), which 'guarantee' the constancy of acknowledgement.

Acknowledgement[5] starts with *interest* (the Latin word 'inter-esse' means 'being in between'), and with curiosity and is followed by *facing* the Other. As a process quality it is deeply connected with *empathy* in an open dialectical process: you can only accept what you understand to a certain degree, and only understand what you accept. Acknowledgement is only possible if one tries to view the Other as he or she views himself (see Schmid, 2001b), which itself again promotes acceptance. Hence it is also obvious that there cannot be acknowledgement without self-acknowledgement and vice versa.

To acknowledge means not only to become aware. Acknowledgement rather means being open for the Other in his or her concrete, typical, unique way of being. In encounter philosophy this is called the 'realization of the Other' — an attitude which sharply contrasts with observing them as an object. This is in itself an existential confirmation of the person of the Other (see below).

To acknowledge somebody is an affection for the person based on respect, a way

---

3. E.g. Rogers, 1957, 1959, 1961, 1962, 1969, 1970, 1980b, 1986; Wood, 1988; Tausch and Tausch, 1990; Thorne, 1991; Lietaer, 1984; Finke, 1994; Biermann-Ratjen, Eckert and Schwartz, 1997.
4. To emphasize the encounter philosophical meaning of the Other (see below), the word is written with a capital letter.
5. A lot of terms can be used to catch the specific notion of this attitude: to accept somebody (etymological from the Latin word 'ac–cipere', which means 'take', 'receive', 'take upon', 'accept', 'perceive', 'approve') stands for 'to receive and acknowledge somebody, to say yes to somebody, to give a positive response'. In German, besides 'annehmen' ('accept'), the verb 'anteilnehmen' exists, which literally means 'to become a part' of the other's life, to share his or her fate. The German word 'wertschätzen' expresses 'to esteem or appreciate somebody's worth', 'to value somebody as a treasure'. 'Sich zuwenden' means 'to turn to somebody', in this context, i.e. in a loving and caring way. 'To care' has the meaning of 'to pay serious attention to somebody' (see Hoad, 1986).

of approaching the Other with emotional warmth, 'a warm interest without any emotional over-involvement' (Rogers, 1961, p. 44), a way of caring without taking possession. It means to be with the Other whatever might happen to, or in, him or her. It is an expression of trust in the person and his or her actualizing tendency.

This does not mean one has to approve of everything the Other does or says, to agree with him or her, to applaud, not to contradict him or her, or to support their attitudes, ideas or intentions. It goes deeper: it means the person as such is 'ap-preciat-ed' in his or her worth and dignity — esteemed as a 'precious' being. This means not to *imagine* what the Other actually might want to say (see Rogers, 1970, p. 50), but bona fide, in good faith and without hidden suspicion or evaluation, to *take* ('ac-cept') the Other as he or she describes, exposes, discloses him- or herself, namely, 'at the face value'.

The otherness of the Other is not seen as a danger (hence to be feared and repulsed), but welcomed as an enrichment. Even socially undesirable behaviour or 'negative feelings' of the Other are not able to persuade the accepting person out of true acknowledgement.

This attitude can be compared with a parental way of being and behaving towards a child, especially an infant, in-as-much as it is loved without the parents approving or welcoming everything it does (see Rogers, 1992, p. 25). It is particularly evident in upbringing and education how much a person can be harmed by conditional appreciation which happens when parents make their attention and love conditional on the good behaviour and achievements of their children. Unconditional prizing and caring is one of the most powerful positive attitudes in the upbringing of children for their emotional and personal growth. This has tremendous implications for pedagogy and learning. The developmental-psychological importance must not be underestimated. Rogers (e.g. 1959) is convinced that the need for positive regard is essential and omnipresent for humans.[6]

Acknowledgement without restrictions fosters self-acknowledgement, self-acceptance and self-esteem. As a consequence, it provides protection and care for the person: irrespective of what he or she thinks and does, the person can rely on acknowledgement. To be loved by others is a precondition for loving oneself — the source of trust and the ability to be critical towards oneself. To accept each other leads from discussion and talking something over, to dialogue. It aims towards a *mutual acknowledgement* as persons instead of *knowledge about* another.

TO MEET FACE TO FACE: THE IMPORTANCE OF 'BEING COUNTER'

Person-centred psychotherapy appreciates the human being as a person (taking

---

6. Eva-Maria Biermann-Ratjen (1989, 1996) based a person-centred model of developmental psychology on these foundations and on the importance of empathic understanding, i.e. a child integrates only those experiences and the values connected with them into the self-concept which are understood and unconditionally accepted by a congruently interacting person. It is a process lasting the whole life long: Experiences want to be unconditionally accepted and understood in order to be symbolized correctly. This, by the way, implies that the experiences making up the self-concept of a person are always also *relational* experiences. They are intrapersonal as well as interpersonal from the very beginning.

the meaning of the term 'person' in the western tradition deriving from Jewish-Christian roots).[7] Although this represents a major paradigm shift from an expert-centred to a client-centred position, the full consequences of what it means in many respects are not yet fully appreciated. Among these is the realisation that accepting another person means to truly acknowledge him or her as an Other.

He or she is no alter *ego*, no close friend a priori, no identifiable person. He or she is an entirely different person. Only when fully appreciating this fact of fundamental difference do encounter and community become possible. To encounter another person first of all means to take into consideration that the Other really 'stands counter' because he or she is essentially different from me.

The German philosopher and Catholic theologian Romano Guardini (1885–1968) defined encounter as an amazing meeting with the reality of the Other. According to him, encounter means that one is touched by the essence of the opposite (Guardini, 1955). To let this happen, a non-purpose-oriented openness, a distance which leads to amazement and the initiative of man in freedom, are indispensable conditions: encounter cannot be created, it is, at one and the same time, both being touched and touching. The relationship 'centres in the Other': in encounter with nature or art, just as in personal encounter.

According to the great Protestant theologian Paul Tillich (1886–1965), with whom Rogers entered into an open dialogue (Rogers/Tillich, 1966), the person emerges from the resistance in the encounter of the Other, if the person:

> were not to encounter the resistance of other selves, then every self would try to take itself as absolute. . . An individual can conquer the entire world of objects, but he cannot conquer another person without destroying him as a person. The individual discovers himself through this resistance. If he does not want to destroy the other person, then he has to enter into a community with him. It is through the resistance of the other person that the person is born (Tillich, 1956, p. 208).

Martin Buber (1878–1965), Jewish philosopher and theologian, and another partner of Rogers in dialogue, points out that being human means to be '*the* being counter' (Buber, 1986, p. 83). The specific human relationship, according to Buber (1953), is the relationship opposite to each other. What makes up a human is the possibility to gain distance — as a precondition for encounter. 'Being counter' is the foundation for meeting face to face. To be opposite to the Other offers the possibility to face and to acknowledge him or her.

This can be easily understood by thinking of standing aside and making a step towards each other: it starts with a step to bring oneself opposite to the other. However, such a seemingly simple step is fundamental: to make a step away and face the other person, thus standing opposite or 'counter' to him or her. This 'position' appreciates the Other as somebody independent, as an autonomous individual, different and separated from me, worthy of being dealt with. In being counter, the otherness of the Other is protected and appreciated. Standing face to face avoids both, identification and objectification. It enables encounter. Before the step to stand opposite and face the Other is taken, there is no possibility to encounter him or her. It is — literally — the turning point: I turn

---

7. This is explained in detail in Schmid, 1991 and 1998c.

towards the Other.

To stand counter also means to give room to each other and to share a common room. It expresses respect. In facing the Other I can see him and acknowledge his uniqueness and qualities. In facing him I do not think what I could *know* about him, but I am ready to *accept* what he is going to disclose.

To take such a step is not an insignificant action, no harmless, risk-free or 'soft' action. To stand counter always implies 'confrontation' (the Latin word 'frons' means 'forehead'), it might even imply conflict. Thus it is essential for the understanding of encounter and acknowledgement to deal with aggression (see below).

TO BE KEPT AWAKE BY AN ENIGMA: THE CHALLENGE OF ENCOUNTER

The French existential philosopher Gabriel Marcel (1889–1973) emphasizes that the Other has always been there in advance (1928; 1935). Similarly Emmanuel Levinas (1905–95)[8] lays emphasis on the truth, which can be observed phenomenologically and developmental psychologically, that the Other always comes first, and shows that this is a fundamental ethical issue (Levinas, 1961, 1974, 1983).

Levinas points out that all of the occidental philosophy has remained 'egology' (and this also applies to psychology as its 'daughter' and to psychotherapy as its 'grand-daughter', including its so-called humanistic orientation in the twentieth century). This fixation on the I is clearly predominant in the terminology of those forms of humanistic psychology who are only concentrated on self-development (note the numerous 'self-terms' employed). Despite all positioning against an objectivation and instrumentalization, it finally indicates a reduction of the Other, of what the Other means to *me*. In this connection, even a well-known sentence by Martin Buber (1923, p. 18) like 'I become through the Thou' suddenly sounds quite different: even here, as is to be suspected, everything is still focused on *me*. This, however, presents the ideals of the humanistic movement in a new light. According to Levinas: what once seemed to be a distinctive human quality, the absolute desire to determine and realize oneself, 'self-determination' and 'self-realization', has proved the reason for violence against the other human being in the history of the twentieth century. Thus 'the enforcement of the ego's objectives must [not] become the basis . . . [of the thinking and acting of humans] . . . but [rather] the perception of the other. This is an ethical relation' (Waldschütz, 1993).

In his main work *Totalité et infini* Levinas (1961) points out that to exist means to be entangled in oneself, caught in the totality of one's own world. According to Levinas the first alienation of the human being is not being able to get rid of oneself. Wrongly, the intention of a simplistic moral goes toward being one's own master. But the awakening from the totality of the being-caught-in-oneself does not happen through 'being independent'. Rather, the Other is the power which liberates the I from oneself. The foundation of self-confidence is not the reflection

8. I consider the Lithuanian Jewish encounter philosopher and professor at the Sorbonne in Paris, who lost his whole family in the holocaust, to be a thinker of tremendous importance for a person–centred approach.

on oneself, but the relationship to the Other. This overcomes the limits of the self and opens up in-finity. The self is born in the relationship to another person.

The Other — who is absolutely different, not an alter ego, thus not to be seen from my perspective — is the one coming towards me, approaching me. The Other 'enters' the relationship — what Levinas calls a 'visitation'.[9] He uses the metaphor of 'visage [face]': my look is touched by the look of the visage. Hence the Other is not in my view, but I am in the view of the Other. The movement goes from the Thou to the I. Also from a developmental perspective the movement always originates from the Thou: it is the call, the addressing of another human being, which evokes a response, confronts with freedom and risk. Encounter happens to a man long before he can aim at obtaining such an experience.

Thus, encounter in dialogue turns out to be a condition for self-consciousness, to be an in-finity, to be a common transcendence of the (totalitarian) status quo, to be a start without return: Abraham, who starts his journey to an unknown country without return, and not Ulysses, who at the end returns to his starting-point, is to be seen as the symbolic character.[10]

In other words, encounter is always a challenge: 'Encountering a human being means being kept awake by an enigma', states Levinas (1983, p. 120).

TO BE ADDRESSED TO RESPOND: FROM KNOWLEDGE TO ACKNOWLEDGEMENT

The Other, however, does not come up to me as an anonymous stranger, but as a *Thou*. In reflection, the Other can be generalized, as if he or she were a thing. For 'the Thou' — now it is more correct to say 'for you' — this is entirely impossible. You have essentially nothing in common with a thing anymore.

He or *she* (the object which I talk to you about) is not capable of responding, but *you* respond — to you I am responsible. What we talk about is the object. You are never an object, but invocation and presence. I can judge objects, in you I have to believe. You are only accessible through love.

Thus it is not knowledge which is required but ac-knowledge-ment, the personal way of realizing.

Justice to the Other can only be done by carrying out the shift from per-cept-ion to ac-cept-ance, from knowledge to acknowledgement — an epistemological paradigm change of tremendous importance for the understanding of dialogical or encounter philosophy in general, the person-centred approach in particular.

As a person, the Other breaks the limits of our knowledge, of what we can perceive. Instead of (factual) knowledge, acknowledgement is required. We cannot comprehend him or her (which originally means 'surround' or 'encircle' somebody). It is the Other who is opening up, revealing him- or herself. Being truly an Other, he or she can never be *known* or *recognised* by somebody else but has to be *respected* in his or her uniqueness. To become acquainted with the Other requires that we are open to what the Other is going to make known, what

---

9. This reminds of the Greek origin of the Latin word 'person': 'πρόσωπον [prósopon]' which means 'face'.

10. More on encounter as a basic category for the person-centred approach: Schmid, 1991, 1994, 1998b, 2002.

he or she is showing, disclosing, revealing.

With knowledge comes judgement, whereas with acknowledgement comes belief. Encounter does not aim at the certainty of knowledge, but it is a belief: acknowledgement equals love. (As in the old meaning of the word 'to know' in the sense of sexual contact, this meaning of 'acknowledging' implies an intimate and intensive form of human communication.)[11]

The Other is the one who cannot be comprehended but empathised with (see Schmid, 2001b). Being aware of the fundamental otherness of the Other, we can facilitate their process of opening-up but in no way direct or guide it.

Epistemologically speaking this reverses the order of usual communication: the direction goes from the Other to me, not from me to the Other. It denotes a Thou-I-relationship. We do not try to understand the Other by making analogies from us to them, by estimating how and who they are. Rather we try to understand the Other by opening up to whatever they show, experience, communicate or reveal.

And, as stated above, acknowledging them we are able (and urged) to respond, and from this our respons-ability is derived. That is why, to authentically respond to another person, whether it be in therapy, or in any personal relationship, is *the* ethical challenge (see Schmid, 2001a).

TO PRAISE AND RESPOND: THE SUBSTANTIAL AND RELATIONAL DIMENSIONS OF ACKNOWLEDGEMENT

The meaning of 'person' developed in the occidental tradition equally values both his or her individuality and autonomy, *and* his or her interconnectedness and capability or need for reciprocal solidarity — dimensions which can be seen very clearly in Rogers' image of the human being (see Schmid, 2001a, pp. 202–3).

As his writings progressed, Rogers gave more equal stress to both of these aspects. In the dialogue with Buber, e.g. he states:

Acceptance of the most complete sort, acceptance of this person, as he is, is the strongest factor making for change that I know. In other words, I think that does release change or release potentiality to find that as I am, exactly as I am, I am fully accepted — then I can't help but change. Because then I feel there is no longer any need for defensive barriers, so that what takes over are the forward moving processes of life itself, I think (Rogers and Buber, 1960, p. 219).

From the *substantial point of view* to acknowledge somebody means to praise his or her uniqueness as a person full of worth to be loved, it is the answer to his or her worth in him- or herself.

Whereas, from the *relational dimension,* acceptance is the answer to the Other's need for understanding and solidarity.

To acknowledge the possibilities: the challenge to become what we might be

In regard to the substantial meaning of the person, acknowledgement denotes

---

11. Gabriel Marcel (1978) shows the parallels of 'acknowledgement' and 'awareness' in the sense of an 'inner becoming aware of' which cannot take place without the body — itself seen not as an instrument but as the gestalt for the relationship with others.

the importance of valuing a person's capability to transcend their status quo.

In their dialogue (Rogers and Buber, 1960) it became clear that — at this stage of development of their ideas — Buber focuses more on the relationship, while Rogers focuses more on the inner growth aspect, the actualizing tendency.[12] Buber (1962/3) makes a distinction between 'acceptance, affirmation' and 'confirmation'. In his terminology, acceptance is the beginning of a relationship in which the other person is recognised as truly being an Other and as what he or she *is* in the moment. 'Confirming', though, denotes more: the Other is also seen as what he or she can *become*, as 'the person he has been created to become' (Rogers and Buber, 1960, p. 219). The emphasis is not only on what is, but also on what is possible. The unlived possibilities of the Other come into play. According to Buber this implies — out of love — an existential challenge for the Other: to become what he might be. Buber thinks of a dialogue of this kind as a joint fight, a fight of partners. Mutuality becomes essential. This understanding reminds of Pindar's 'Become what you are' and Kierkegaard's 'To be that self which one truly is', often quoted by Rogers (e.g. 1961, p. 163).

Buber tends to think that the person encountering another discovers the real potential of the Other through confirming him or her, including even 'the best that the Other might be able to become'. This seems to imply a directive moment. Rogers, on the contrary, thinks that this process of discovering what one might become is made possible by and is achieved by the person themselves.

Buber emphazises that every real relationship begins with acceptance, but that confirmation goes beyond this. To illustrate his point, he uses an example of a husband and wife:

> He says, not expressly, but just by his whole relation to her, that 'I accept you as you are'. But this does *not* mean 'I don't want you to change'. But it says 'I discover in you just by my accepting love, I discover in you what you are meant to become' (Rogers and Buber, 1960, p. 219).

Rogers agrees: 'I think that we do accept the individual *and* his potentiality.'[13]

In 1958 (p. 14) Rogers explicitly refers to Buber's 'confirmation' and stresses — one year after their dialogue — the process quality:

> If I accept the other person as something fixed, already diagnosed and classified, already shaped by his past, then I am doing my part to confirm this limited hypothesis. If I accept him as a process of becoming, then I am doing what I can to confirm or make real his potentialities . . . I have then — to use Buber's term — confirmed him as a living person, capable of creative inner development (ibid., pp. 14–15).

Here Rogers sees the actualizing tendency intrinsically linked to creativity.[14]

---

12. It is obvious that the confrontation with Buber had tremendous impact on Rogers' development of the relational aspect of the therapeutic relationship and the understanding of the image of the human being out of interconnectedness.

13. A more detailed discussion of the differences between Buber and Rogers and their dialogue can be found in Schmid, 1994, especially pp. 178–1801, 183–200.

14. More on the understanding of the specific human actualizing tendency ('personalisation') as creativity: Schmid, 1994, pp. 413–23.

Thus acknowledgement means both: acceptance and confirmation, challenge and pro-vocation. Both are mutually and dialectically connected with each other.

Buber's view also shows the close relationship of empathy and acknowledgement. And Rogers (1975) stresses that empathy provides the confirmation that somebody exists as a special and respected person in his or her own identity. Here acknowledgement and empathy unite (see Schmid, 2001b).

To acknowledge the pro-vocation: the art of responding to the call of the Other

Taking the relational notion of the person into consideration, acknowledgement points to the challenge of responding.

As already stated, from a developmental perspective we enter the world by con-ception, by being conceived. In this very moment we enter into a relationship and are ac-cepted. Under normal circumstances being born means being awaited and received. Thus from the first moment of our existence there are Others and we are born into the relationships to them.

The Other or the Others are here 'before' me. They both expect and welcome us and they are strange and surprising to us. In this view, the Other always is seen as a call and a provocation. As stated above, the fellow being is the one strange to me, who surprises me, and who I find myself opposed to, who I have to face — neither monopolizing nor rejecting him or her — face to face. The presence of the Other which always 'comes first' is a call for a response (see Schmid, 2001a) from which I cannot escape, because nobody can respond in my place. We are *obliged and responsible* to the Other and owe him an answer — making a 'priority' of the Other.

Therefore, in every encounter there lies the response to a call. And from the response follows respons-ability which is grounded in the above-mentioned fact that nobody else can respond instead of me. Thus, the ethical dimension of encounter is denoted: the Other is an appeal and a provocation and the relationship to him in principle is asymmetrical. He represents a demand. Out of the being addressed by the Other grows a fundamental responsibility, called 'diakonia [service]'. By responding to the Other, I only fulfill my duty.

Both dimensions are dialectically related: with oneness, otherness also grows: just as independence grows with being Thou-related. The person opposite initiates the individual into becoming a person and initiates community. The most adequate form of communication is dialogue in the sense of having an (at least a kind of) exchange which aims at reciprocity, as an 'understanding confrontation'.

TO BE AGGRESSIVE: TAKING STEPS TOWARDS EACH OTHER

In connection with unconditional positive regard, the issue of confrontation is often discussed. Particularly where confrontational statements made by the therapist towards the client, conflict with positive regard. This leads to the fundamental issue of aggression and its meaning for, and in, both personal and person-centred relationships. It is a subject which is often seen as taboo theoretically and practically in the person-centred context, yet it is a vital part of human life and crucial for the understanding of the person and their relationships.

Real encounter means to 'ag-gredi', to make steps towards each other, approach each other. 'Aggredi' — hence the term 'aggression' — means 'to turn to somebody, to approach, to attack, to commence'. From a person-centred perspective, in principle, aggression (singular) must be seen as a constructive force of the human being, realized in several form of aggressions (plural), e.g. anger, rage, hatred, ignorance, refusal, cynicism, sarcasm, forceful activity, etc. From the substantial view, aggression is an expression of the actualizing tendency and the experiencing of a person. From the relational view, it means turning towards the other in order to handle a conflict. On the one hand, in aggression, the individual's striving for independence becomes obvious as the person aims at identity by differentiation (saying no, i.e. in puberty, etc.). In this movement of separation the basis for acknowledgement of the self and of the Other is set. On the other hand the interconnectedness becomes obvious as aggression approaches the Other ('ag-gredi') and through confrontation accepts the Other as partner in the relationship. In this 'against one another' situation, facing the Other makes aggression indispensable for the 'counter' of the en-counter. Aggression regulates, and assures, both closeness and distance and protects from loosing one's identity by either merging or alienating. Being able to bear conflicts is not only a sign of maturity, but also of tremendous importance for the prevention of violence.

Aggressions may become destructive, if they are denied or symbolised incompletely, incorrectly or distortedly. Such destructive forms can be shown in the aggressive and auto-aggressive elements of having pity on someone or of depression or of suicide. Other examples might include psychosomatically suffering persons, when the body tries to symbolise those parts of the self which are not understood and not accepted well enough, or addictions, which can also be understood as aggression against oneself. If aggression is accepted or transparent, it is not destructive (Rogers 1961, p. 177).

Thus, particularly for person-centred therapy, to deal openly with aggression is vital. Therapists must be open to conflicts, if the constructive and vital aspects of aggression are not to be ignored or covered up. For effective therapy, it is necessary that acceptance, understanding, symbolisation and integration of aggressive feelings and impulses are achieved as fully as possible.[15]

TO LOVE IN A PERSONAL WAY: 'A KIND OF LIKING WHICH HAS STRENGTH'

Acknowledgement is the personal response to another person's presence and call, which we owe each other. But what people do owe each other is love. Although it may sound unusual to some (and others might find it not scientific, and therefore disapprove of it), the way of being described here converges into this simple, often used and often misused word (and used by several authors): love.

Of course it is necessary to clearly state what is meant exactly by this word. It is not the sexual or erotic love, nor the paternal love or the love in a friendship or

15. A more detailed discussion of aggression from a person-centred view can be found in Schmid 1995.

in a religious sense. It is the notion of love as developed in the Jewish-Christian tradition which denotes a fundamental way of being in the relationship of humans as fellow human beings — which aptly can be called 'personal love'. It is love towards oneself as well as love towards the other. Personal love means: somebody is loved as a person.

Carl Rogers himself understood unconditional positive regard as love, 'easily misunderstood though it may be' (Rogers, 1951, p. 159), and stressed its importance as a therapeutic agent, when he writes that:

> the client moves from the experiencing of him- or herself as an unworthy, unacceptable, and unlovable person to the realization that he is accepted, respected, and loved, in this limited relationship with the therapist. 'Loved' has here perhaps its deepest and most general meaning — that of being deeply understood and deeply accepted (ibid., 160).

Positive regard:

> means a kind of love for the client as he is, providing we understand the word 'love' as equivalent to the theologian's term *agape*, and not in its usual romantic and possessive meanings. What I am describing is a feeling which is not paternalistic, nor sentimental, nor superficially social and agreeable. It respects the other person as a separate individual, and does not possess him. It is a kind of liking which has strength, and which is not demanding. We have termed it 'positive regard' (Rogers, 1962, p. 94).[16]

It can be shown that the understanding of love as agape, as St Paul uses it for the first Christian communities (Gal. 5:13), parallels the understanding of solidarity (Comblin ,1987, p. 20f), thus denoting the social and political implications of love and acknowledgement.[17]

Seen from an dialogical philosophical perspective, in encounter, only *love* is the adequate communication. But it is especially in love that encounter transcends the duality, the couple, and opens up for the Third One (as a chiffre for the many Others and for the Others of the Other). Levinas points out that we do not live in the world of *the* human being, but in the world of human beings. Encounter transcends the synchronicity of the I-Thou, the onesidedness of orientation, the unquestionability of this closeness, and goes towards the diachronism in the relationship. To love always implies a transcendence of the dual-unity. Hence, plural is essential for encounter: it transcends the duality and is open for a Third One, for the *group*, for the community which itself offers space for encounter. This 'complete-together' lies beyond the relative closedness of the I-Thou, it lies in the We, in being-together. That is where the source of freedom

---

16. See also Rogers, 1951, pp. 160–72; 1956, p. 14; 1971; 1980a, pp. 23, 204; Rogers and Buber, 1960, p. 219; Rogers and Tillich, 1966, pp. 21-2 ('listening love') and his understanding of 'presence' (e.g. Rogers, 1986). Similar connections between the basic attitude of unconditional positive regard and love can be found, e.g. at Bowen (1984), Bozarth (1992) or Thorne (1991); see also Binswanger (1942); Thomas (1969) (authentic 'game of love' without rules); May (1969), Maslow (1962), Yalom (1980) ('psychotherapeutic eros'). The German empirical researcher Dieter Tscheulin (1995) sees in 'healing through love' the common denominator of all the technical, relational and personal variables of the structure of therapeutic interaction and the process of change.
17. See Schmid, 1994, pp. 154–5; 1996, pp. 533–40; 1998a, p. 142.

lies; that is what leads to the necessity for decision, for justice; that is what makes love become '*love-with* (condilectio)'[18] in which nobody is an instrument, a means, but everybody is a setting-out and a goal: vivid plurality, which conquers the dialectic of difference and identity, of alienation and loneliness.

TO PRACTICE THERAPY AS ACKNOWLEDGEMENT: ASPECTS OF ACKNOWLEDGEMENT IN SINGLE AND GROUP THERAPY

So far I have looked at acknowledgement related to the human condition in general. In therapy it takes on a special meaning. The practice of person-centred psychotherapy works with an image of the human being in which the human being is understood as a person. The therapist, then, encounters him or her *personally*, acknowledging him or her as the Other instead of objectifying him or her by trying to know him or her, or to get knowledge over him or her.

To encounter a human being in therapy means to provide space and freedom for the client to develop out of themselves. It is the presence of the therapist as a person which facilitates this process of development. This is opposed to any intention or aim, and to any acting out of a role or function. According to Martin Buber (1962/63) encounter is characterized by '*authenticity*' (see Schmid 2001a). This is achieved by *being* instead of the 'breaking-in of seeming'. It is also achieved by '*acceptation* (akzeptation)', i.e. to say yes to the Other as a person (not simply being aware of him or her). And it is achieved through '*comprehension* (Umfassung)' and '*inclusion* (Innewerden)' (see Schmid, 2001b), i.e. accepting and confirming and being open for the uniqueness of the Other. These dimensions of presence developed and described in dialogical philosophy correspond very closely to the three so-called 'core conditions' described by Carl Rogers.[19]

To do therapy along these lines turns the conventional and established understanding of psychotherapy completely on its head (since it rests on the idea that it is the therapist who has to gain knowledge about the client in order to treat them), paralleling the traditional medical model Carl Rogers so strongly opposed.

Now it is the client who is the expert; he or she is the one opening up and directing the way of the process. And it is the therapist's task to respond as a person by acknowledging whatever the client reveals — without any conditions. Thus, first of all, the task is to let go of one's good ideas about the client. Sidney Jourard (1968) points out that disregarding one's prejudices is an invitation to the Other to also let go — let go of yesterday's ideas, interests and goals and explore new ones. Thus both therapist and client transcend their ideas about the client and provide the chance for new, creative possibilities. It is obvious that a fundamental and principled non-directivity is the logical consequence of an image of the human being which prefers the uniqueness of the Other to standardising diagnosis and prioritizes acknowledgement rather than knowledge

---

18. In the sense of Richard of St Viktor, Levinas, Splett, Windisch, etc. (see Schmid. 1994, pp. 154–5).
19. Whose aim was different, namely to describe the sufficient necessities for therapeutic personality development.

(see Schmid, 2001a).

It seems clear that this attitude must not be mixed up with 'tolerance' neither in its superficial sense as 'anything is okay; I don't bother you, if you don't bother me' and more or less ignoring the other nor in its deeper sense as an attitude of allowing everybody to have his or her own convictions and fostering a climate of patience, openness and open-mindedness (see footnote 1). Acknowledgement in therapy means more: it is to actively encourage the client to trust in their own potentialities and to acknowledge themselves. Jerold Bozarth (1992) is convinced that acknowledgement is the primary condition of all, not only because the actualizing tendency is fostered — thus the need for positive regard and self-respect is met, but because it expresses person-centred *being* and not only person-centred *behaving* (or *doing*).

For many therapists the most difficult task is to continuously give up control over the person(s) and the process. This can only be achieved by having respect for the person of the Other, by realizing that control *opposes* interest, and that ultimately it turns out that it is impossible to control a person, if one is aware that he or she really is an Other.

An aspect of acknowledgement is to take and accept whatever comes from the client, be it feelings, ideas, memories or whatever. The therapist does not openly (or secretly) promote specific ways of expression or particular subjects or certain ways of symbolizing, or the like. The therapist also does not set up rules such as 'we only talk about the here and now' or 'you must concentrate on feelings', etc.[20] In person-centred therapy the client is regarded to be not only the expert for the *contents*, he or she is also regarded to be the expert of the ways to deal with their issues (the *process*).

In group therapy it is necessary to accept the individual members, as well as the group as such, and contribute to a climate of acknowledgement in trusting its constructive potential. On the one hand this is a more difficult task than in a one-on-one relationship, on the other hand the group can be a relief because the facilitator is not the only person on whom the acceptance depends. To accept the group means not to be preoccupied with thinking about whether the group does the right thing, is going at the right speed, observes the correct rules, moves in the right direction, etc. It is necessary to be aware that under certain, for example institutional conditions with preset goals it is not possible to accept unconditionally without producing conflicts with the authorities. Unfortunately this is often the case in clinical settings, for example, psychiatric hospitals.

How can acknowledgement be learned? By being acknowledged and thus acknowledging oneself. Maybe the most difficult task is to learn to let oneself be liked and loved. There is no acknowledgement towards the other without acknowledgement towards oneself. This is an old wisdom: 'You shall love your neighbour as yourself'. (Matt. 22:39) which often is distorted into 'Love your neighbour instead of yourself or more than yourself'.

---

20. The interest — less on the contents and more on the meaning — it has for the client will be discussed in Schmid, 2001c.

TO RESPOND AS A PERSON: A MATTER OF COURAGE

In the perspective of Levinas' view of the Other, psychotherapy — and indeed all psychosocial, pedagogic, political, pastoral 'acting' — takes on a socio-ethical dimension. This leads us from the categories 'response' and 'responsibility' to a new understanding of self-realization which can only become reality in what Levinas called 'diakonia (diakony)' — a term with the same meaning as 'therapy', i.e. 'service'. In the interpersonal encounter which we call therapy, when addressed and asked to respond, we assume a deep responsibility, an obligation in which our fellow man expects us to render the service we owe to each other: nothing else but love.

Acknowledgement, understood as personal love, can be seen as the 'art of answering' (Pagès, 1974, p. 307): a way of responding to the other persons and the world, out of inner freedom, out of detachment (see Coulson, 1983, p. 24) — not by *giving simple answers* but by *being an answer* as a person oneself.

It is a matter of courage, I suppose. It needs bravery to see oneself as a therapist, as an 'artist of responding' and as somebody who is capable of 'a kind of liking which has strength'. Put in simple words, it is the question of whether we dare to love our clients.

It needs courage to trust in the client's and one's own abilities instead of falling back on behaviours, methods and techniques which provide security because we *know* what will come next (but paradoxically in these cases we also more or less *determine* what comes next). The risk is to *acknowledge* what is opening up and disclosing itself, to be surprised by the mystery of the Other and to dare to *receive, to ac-cept.*

REFERENCES

Biermann-Ratjen, E.-M. (1989). Zur Notwendigkeit einer Entwicklungspsychologie für Gesprächspsychotherapeuten aus dem personenzentrierten Konzept für die Zukunft der klientenzentrierten Psychotherapie. In Sachse, R. and Howe, J. (Eds.), *Zur Zukunft der Klientenzentrierten Psychotherapie*, Heidelberg: Asanger, pp. 102–25.

Biermann-Ratjen, E.-M. (1996). Entwicklungspsychologie und Störungslehre. In Böck-Singelmann, C., Ehlers, B., Hensel, T., Kemper, F. and Monden-Engelhardt, C. (Eds.), *Personzentrierte Psychotherapie mit Kindern und Jugendlichen*. Vol. 1: Grundlagen und Konzepte, Göttingen: Hogrefe.

Biermann-Ratjen, E.-M., Eckert, J. and Schwartz, H.-J. (1997). *Gesprächspsychotherapie. Verändern durch Verstehen*. Stuttgart: Kohlhammer, 8th ed.

Binswanger, L. (1942). *Grundformen und Erkenntnis menschlichen Daseins*. München: Reinhardt.

Bowen, M. C. (1984). Spirituality and person-centered approach: Interconnectedness in the universe and in psychotherapy. In Segrera, A. S. (Ed.) *Proceedings of the First International Forum on the Person-Centered Approach*. Oaxtepec: Universidad Iberoamericana, pp. 197–222.

Bozarth, J. (1992). A theoretical reconceptualization of the necessary and sufficient conditions for therapeutic personality change. Paper given at the Fifth Forum on the Person-Centered Approach, Terschelling.

Buber, M. (1923). *Ich und Du*. Heidelberg: Lambert Schneider, 8th ed. 1974; orig. 1923.

Buber, M. (1953). Elemente des Zwischenmenschlichen. In Buber, M. *Das dialogische Prinzip*. Heidelberg: Lambert Schneider, 5th ed.1984, pp. 271–98; orig. 1953.

Buber, M. (1962/63). *Werke*, 3 vol. München: Kösel.

Buber, M. (1986). *Begegnung: Autobiographische Fragmente.* Heidelberg: Lambert Schneider, 4th ed. 1986.

Comblin, J. (1987). *Das Bild vom Menschen.* Düsseldorf: Patmos.

Coulson, W. R. (1983). Über therapeutische Disziplin in der klient-zentrierten Therapie. Was lehren uns kritische Ereignisse in Einzel- und Gruppentherapie? In: Tscheulin, D. (Ed.) *Beziehung und Technik in der klientenzentrierten Therapie.* Weinheim: Beltz, pp. 15–29.

Finke, J. (1994). *Empathie und Interaktion. Methode und Praxis der Gesprächspsychotherapie.* Stuttgart: Thieme.

Hoad, T. F. (1986). (Ed.) *The Concise Oxford Dictionary of English Etymology.* Oxford: Clarendon.

Guardini, R. (1955). Die Begegnung: Ein Beitrag zur Struktur des Daseins. *Hochland,* 47,3, 224–34.

Jourard, S. M. (1968). *Disclosing Man to Himself.* New York: van Nostrand.

Levinas, E. (1961). *Totalité et Infini : Essai sur l'extériorité.* Den Haag: Nijhoff.

Levinas, E. (1974). *Autrement Au'être ou au Delà de l'Essence.* Den Haag : Nijhoff.

Levinas, E. (1983). *Die Spur des Anderen: Untersuchungen zur Phänomenologie und Sozialphilosophie.* Freiburg: Alber.

Lietaer, G. (1984). Unconditional positive regard: A controversial basic attitude in client-centered therapy. In Levant, R. F. and Shlien, J. M. (Eds.), *Client-centered therapy and the person centered approach.* New York: Praeger, pp. 41–58.

Marcel, G. (1928). *Journal Métaphysique.* Paris: Gallimard.

Marcel, G. (1935). *Être et Avoir.* Paris: Aubier.

Marcel, G. (1978). Leibliche Begegnung. In Kraus, A. (Ed.) Leib, Geist, Geschichte. Heidelberg: Hütig, pp. 47–73.

Maslow, A. H. (1962). *Toward a Psychology of Being.* Princeton: van Nostrand.

May, R. (1969). *Love and Will.* New York: Norton.

Pagès, M. (1974). *Das Affektive Leben der Gruppen: Eine theorie der menschlichen Beziehung.* Stuttgart: Klett; orig.: *La vie affective des groupes.* Paris: Dunod, 1968.

Rogers, C. R. (1951). *Client-Centered Therapy. Its Current Practice, Implications, and Theory.* Boston: Houghton Mifflin.

Rogers, C. R. (1956). Review of Reinhold Niebuhr's 'The self and the dramas of history'. In *Chicago Theological Seminary Register* XLVI,1, pp. 13–14.

Rogers, C. R. (1957). The necessary and sufficient conditions of therapeutic personality change. In *Journal of Consulting Psychology,* 21,2, pp. 95–103.

Rogers, C. R. (1958). The characteristics of a helping relationship. In *Personnel and Guidance Journal,* 37,1, pp. 6–16.

Rogers, C. R. (1959). A theory of therapy, personality, and interpersonal relationships, as developed in the client-centered framework. In Koch, S. (Ed.), *Psychology. A study of science. Vol. III: Formulations of the person and the social context.* New York: McGraw Hill, pp. 184–256.

Rogers, C. R. (1961). *On Becoming a Person: A therapist's view of psychotherapy.* Boston: Houghton Mifflin.

Rogers, C. R. (1962). The interpersonal relationship: The core of guidance. In Rogers, C. R. and Stevens, B. *Person to Person. The Problem of Being Human.* Moab: Real People Press, pp. 89–104.

Rogers, C. R. (1969). *Freedom to Learn. A view of what education might become.* Columbus: Charles Merrill.

Rogers, C. R. (1970). *On Encounter Groups.* New York: Harper and Row.

Rogers, C. R. (1971). Interview with Dr. Carl Rogers. In Frick, W. B. (Ed.), *Humanistic Psychology: Conversations with Abraham Maslow, Gardner Murphy and Carl Rogers.* Columbus: Charles E. Merrill, pp. 86–115.

Rogers, C. R. (1975). Empathic — an unappreciated way of being. In: *The Counseling Psychologist,* 5,2, pp. 2–10.

Rogers, C. R. (1980a). *A Way of Being.* Boston: Houghton Mifflin.

Rogers, C. R. (1980b). Client-centered psychotherapy. In Kaplan, H. I., Freedman, A. M. and Sadock, B. J. (Eds.), *Comprehensive Textbook of Psychiatry, III,* Vol. 2, Baltimore, MD: Williams and Wilkins, 3rd ed. 1980, pp. 2153–68.

Rogers, C. R. (1986). A client-centered/person-centered approach to therapy. In Kutash, I. L.

and Wolf, A. (eds.), *Psychotherapist's Casebook: Theory and technique in the practice of modern times*. San Francisco: Jossey-Bass, pp. 197–208.

Rogers, C. R. (1992). The best school of therapy is the one you develop for yourself. Lecture and discussion with psychotherapists in Vienna. Manuscript.

Rogers, C. R. and Buber, M. (1960). Martin Buber and Carl Rogers. In *Psychologia. An International Journal of Psychology in the Orient* (Kyoto University), 3,4, 208–21.

Rogers, C. R. and Tillich, P. (1966). *Dialogue between Paul Tillich and Carl Rogers, Parts I and II*. San Diego: San Diego State College.

Schmid, P. F. (1991). Souveränität und Engagement: Zu einem personzentrierten Verständnis von 'Person'. In Rogers, C. R. and Schmid, P. F., *Person-zentriert: Grundlagen von Theorie und Praxis*. Mainz: Grünewald 1991, pp.15–164; 4th ed. 2000.

Schmid, P. F. (1994). *Personzentrierte Gruppenpsychotherapie: Ein Handbuch. Vol. I: Solidarität und Autonomie*. Köln: Edition Humanistische Psychologie.

Schmid, P. F. (1995). Auseinandersetzen und Herangehen. Thesen zur Aggression aus personzentrierter Sicht. In *Personzentriert*, 2, 62-94

Schmid, P. F. (1996). *Personzentrierte Gruppenpsychotherapie in der Praxis: Ein Handbuch. Vol. II: Die Kunst der Begegnung*. Paderborn: Junfermann.

Schmid, P. F. (1998a). *Im Anfang ist Gemeinschaft: Personzentrierte Gruppenarbeit in Seelsorge und Praktischer Theologie. Vol. III: Beitrag zu einer Theologie der Gruppe*. Stuttgart: Kohlhammer.

Schmid, P. F. (1998b). Face to face: The art of encounter. In Thorne, B. and Lambers, E. (Eds.) *Person-Centred Therapy: A European Perspective*. London: Sage, pp. 74–90.

Schmid, P. F. (1998c). On becoming a person-centered approach: A person-centred understanding of the person. In Thorne and Lambers (eds.) *Person-Centred Therapy: A European Perspective*. London: Sage, pp. 38–52.

Schmid, P. F. (2001a). Authenticity: the person as his or her own author. Dialogical and ethical perspectives on therapy as an encounter relationship. And beyond. In Wyatt, G. (Ed.), *Rogers' Therapeutic Conditions. Evolution, theory and practice. Volume 1: Congruence*. Ross-on-Wye: PCCS Books.

Schmid, P. F. (2001b). Comprehension: The art of not knowing. Dialogical and ethical perspectives on empathy as dialogue in personal and person-centered relationships. In Haugh, S. and Merry, T. (Eds.), *Rogers' Therapeutic Conditions. Evolution, Theory and Practice. Volume 2: Empathy*. Ross-on-Wye: PCCS Books.

Schmid, P. F. (2001c). The therapeutic relationship — a dialogical perspective (working title). In Wyatt, G. and Sanders, P. (Eds.), *Rogers' Therapeutic Conditions. Evolution, Theory and Practice. Volume 4: Contact and Perception*. Ross-on-Wye: PCCS Books.

Schmid, P. F. (2002). The necessary and sufficient conditions of being person-centered: On identity, integrity, integration and differentiation of the paradigm. In Watson, J. (Ed.), *Client-centered and experiential psychotherapy in the 21st century: Advances in theory, research and practice*. Ross-on-Wye: PCCS Books.

Tausch, R. and Tausch, A. (1990). *Gesprächspsychotherapie: Hilfreiche Gruppen- und Einzelgespräche in Psychotherapie und alltäglichem Leben*. Göttingen: Hogrefe, 9th ed.

Thomas, H. F. (1969). Encounter: The game of no game. In Burton, A. (Ed.) *Encounter: The theory and practice of encounter groups*. San Francisco: Jossey-Bass.

Thorne, B. (1991). *Person-Centred Counselling: Therapeutic and spiritual dimensions*. London: Whurr.

Tillich, P. (1956). *Systematische Theologie*. Vol. 1. Berlin: de Gruyter, 3rd ed.

Tscheulin, D. (1995). *Heilung durch Liebe? Die Struktur der psychotherapeutischen Situation*. In Eckert, J. (Ed.) *Forschung zur Klientenzentrierten Psychotherapie: Prozesse — Effekte — Vergleiche*. Berlin: Springer, pp. 51–69.

Waldschütz, E. (1993). Was ist „Personalismus"? In *Die Presse, Spectrum*, 24 December 1993, p. XII.

Wood, J. K (1988). *Menschliches Dasein als Miteinandersein: Gruppenarbeit nach personenzentrierten Ansätzen*. Köln: Edition Humanistische Psychologie; American orig.: manuscript.

Yalom, I. D. (1980). *Existential psychotherapy*. New York: Basic Books.

Unconditional Positive Regard:
A misunderstood way of being
Ruth Sanford

Because the focus of this paper has meaning only within the context of the client-centered, person-centered approach to psychotherapy and other interpersonal relationships as it has evolved through the works of Carl Rogers over the period of his professional life, it seems appropriate, at the outset, to review for or to acquaint the reader with the essential theoretical formulations of the approach, as summarized in brief form by Rogers in his most recent publication on the subject (Rogers, 1986):

> What do I mean by a client-centered, person-centered approach? For me it expresses the primary theme of my whole professional life, as that theme has been clarified through experience, interaction with others, and research. This theme has been utilized and found effective in many different areas, until the broad label 'a person-centered approach' seems the most descriptive. The central hypothesis of this approach can be briefly stated. It is that the individual has within him- or herself vast resources for self-understanding, for altering her or his self-concept, attitudes, and self-directed behavior — and that these resources can be tapped if only a definable climate of facilitative psychological attitudes can be provided. There are three conditions which constitute this growth-promoting climate, whether we are speaking of the relationship between therapist and client, parent and child, leader and group, teacher and student, or administrator and staff. The conditions apply, in fact, in any situation in which the development of the person is a goal. I have described these conditions at length in previous writings (Rogers, 1959, 1961). I present here a brief summary from the point of view of psychotherapy, but the description applies to all of the foregoing relationships. The first element has to do with genuineness, realness, or congruence. The more the therapist is him- or herself in the relationship, putting up no professional front or personal facade, the greater is the likelihood that the client will change and grow in a constructive manner . . . The second attitude of importance in creating a climate for change is acceptance, or caring or prizing — unconditional positive regard. It means that when the therapist is experiencing a positive, nonjudgmental, accepting attitude toward whatever the client is at that moment, therapeutic movement or change is more likely . . . The third facilitative aspect of the relationship is empathic understanding. This means that the therapist senses accurately the feelings and personal meanings that are being experienced by the client and

communicates this acceptant understanding to the client (Rogers, 1986, pp. l, 2, 3).

The present inquiry into the meaning and use of the term, 'unconditional positive regard', has grown from a personal need to respond in a thoughtful way to comments of professional people made frequently in discussions of the three 'necessary and sufficient conditions' conducive to therapeutic growth. Many of these comments are typified by, 'Yes, I believe that realness and deep empathic listening are essential elements in creating a growthful climate, but I have many questions about unconditional positive regard. What does it mean?' Or 'Does it mean that I put aside my own values and assume the attitude that anything goes?' or 'I can't feel unconditional positive regard for everyone!' or 'Positive regard for most people I can see, but unconditional?'

I carefully considered using the traditionally impersonal third person in the writing of this paper, but an impersonal style seems inappropriate to me as I invite others to join me in my own personal search into the meaning and application to significant relationships, including the relationship between client and therapist, of this term which has become so central to the way of being known as the person-centered approach. My inquiry led me first to *Client-Centered Therapy: Its Current Practice, Implications and Theory* (Rogers, 1951). In this work I found the first reference to the condition or attitude which later evolved into 'unconditional positive regard'. It is here that the present inquiry begins with an illustration of the therapeutic process between a client and a therapist who approaches the relationship in a client-centered way (p. 144):

> Characteristically the client changes from high level abstractions to more differentiated perceptions, from wide generalizations to limited generalizations closely rooted in primary experiences. The client who commences therapy with the stated feeling that he is a hopeless and useless person comes, during therapy, to experience himself as indeed useless at times, but at other times showing positive qualities, at still other times exhibiting negative aggression. He experiences himself as being quite variable in functioning — in short, as a person who is neither all black nor all white, but an interesting collection of varying shades of gray. He finds it much easier, as has been indicated, to accept this more differentiated person. Or take the client whose expressed attitude in therapy, is that 'My mother is a bitch!' During therapy she begins to perceive in differentiated fashion her varied experiences of her mother. Her mother rejected her in childhood, but occasionally indulged her; her mother means well; she has a sense of humor; she is not well educated; she has a violent and unreasonable temper; she wants very much to be proud of her daughter. The relationship with mother in childhood is examined and differentiated from the relationship with mother today. As this process goes on, the overall generalization, 'Mother is a bitch and I can't possibly get on with her', is seen to be quite inadequate to fit the complex facts of primary experience. With almost every client this process can be observed. He moves from generalizations which have been found unsatisfactory for guiding his life, to an examination of the rich primary experiences upon which they are based, a movement which exposes the falsity of many of his generalizations, and provides a basis for new

and more adequate abstractions. He is customarily in the process of formulating these new guides for himself as therapy concludes. It is obvious that this process does not just happen. It is facilitated by the special conditions of the therapeutic relationship — *the complete freedom to explore every portion of the perceptual field, and the complete freedom from threat to the self which the client-centered therapist in particular provides* (emphasis added).

Drawing from my own experience with a client whose perception of his mother at the beginning of therapy was similar to that of the woman client in the hypothetical case just quoted, I found that he moved, over the period of a year, to acceptance of his mother as a person, with fewer conditions. He could say in essence, 'I still hate it when she whines, and I still feel like walking away from her when she tries to tell me what to do, but I know that she loves me in her own way and that she will never abandon me. I can live with that. Not that I want to live in the same house with her. But I can see that she's had a hard time herself, that she has her own problems and reasons for what she does — just the way I have mine. When I visit her now, we sometimes even enjoy each other!'

From saying, 'She's a bitch, I hate her and I can't stand to be around her ever again!' he moved a long way toward acceptance of her as a person, and of his own positive as well as negative feelings toward her. After a year in therapy he was saying that he could hear her disparaging remarks as her own opinion spoken in hurt or anger without feeling worthless himself or taking them as evidence that she did not love him, or wished him harm. When he was able to accept his own feelings, negative as well as positive, as the therapist had accepted them, he could also accept his mother as a person — imperfect as they both were — and experience warm feelings toward her.

THE QUALITY OF THE CLIENT-THERAPIST RELATIONSHIP

It is important here to return to the hypothetical case cited earlier and to Rogers' comment following it:

> It is obvious that this process does not just happen. It is facilitated by the special conditions of the therapeutic relationship — the complete freedom to explore every portion of the perceptual field, and the complete freedom from threat to the self which the client-centered therapist in particular provides (ibid, p. 144).

Both of these clients were interacting with the therapist in verbal as well as in nonverbal ways, as the therapist communicated to the client complete acceptance of the client as he or she was at the moment. Sometimes in the experience of every therapist, verbal communication is very slight or nonexistent, and the question arises: is it possible then to convey to the client the sense of unqualified acceptance? Rogers, in Chapter 4, 'Process of Therapy' (ibid, p. 158), poses the question in this way:

> What are we to regard as essential to psychotherapy if success occurs in dealing with a child when there have been no verbalized insights, little expression of attitudes towards the self, no certain expression of denied experience of self?

He answers his own question in part by referring to the experience of a counselor with Joan, a nonverbal, isolated high-school girl, in which the counselor concludes her report with, 'What happened in those hours of silence? My faith in the capacity of the client was sorely tested. I am glad it did not waver.'

At this point it seems important to accompany Rogers in his further inquiry:

> Whatever happened here seems not to have happened as the result of verbal interchange . . . How, then, can we formulate therapeutic process in terms of a relationship? One hypothesis is that the client moves from the experiencing of himself as an unworthy, unacceptable, and unlovable person to the realization that he is accepted, respected, and loved in this limited relationship with the therapist. 'Loved' has here perhaps its deepest and most general meaning — that of being deeply understood and deeply accepted. In terms of this hypothesis we might speculate on the case of Joan. Feeling that she is a person who is unworthy of having friends, partly because she is so shy and uncommunicative, she enters a relationship with the counselor. Here she finds acceptance — or love, if you will — as much evident in her periods of silence and shyness as in the times when she can talk. She discovers that she can be a silent person and still be liked, that she can be her shy self and still be accepted. Perhaps it is this which gives her more feeling of worth and changes her relationship to others. By believing herself lovable as a shy and withdrawn person, she finds that she is accepted by others and that those characteristics tend to drop away (ibid, pp. 159-60).

One thread running through these references is complete acceptance of the client without the threat of judgment and rejection. In the words of Joan's counselor, although her faith in the capacity of the client for self-understanding and change was severely tested by hours of silence, she did not waver in her trust in Joan — and in the verbal and nonverbal ways in which she communicated her trust. The other thread is love, respect and deep understanding, also communicated to the client so as to be perceived by the client. Oliver Bown in this same chapter (p. 160) states very clearly his conviction that love is the most expressive term for this element in the relationship, although he is aware that it is easily misunderstood in this society. In his words, 'If a client is hostile toward me and I can see nothing in the moment except hostility I am quite sure that I will react in a defensive way to the hostility. If, on the other hand, I can see this hostility as an understandable component of the person's defense against feeling the need for closeness to people, I can then react with love toward this person, who also wants love, but who at the moment must pretend not to.'

On the one hand the therapist would be responding to hostility, perceived hostility or an act of hostility, on the other hand to a person who needs and wants to love and be loved, in spite of present, apparent denial. The therapist, then, is responding to a person rather than to an act that repels or threatens him. His response stems from his belief that the client is a trustworthy person capable of and desiring positive growth. There is trust that, as the therapeutic relationship continues, the therapist can expose more tender and caring parts of himself without fearing 'that they would be trampled on, misused or perhaps ridiculed', and that, in experiencing the trust and love or caring, the client becomes more able to establish similar, less limited, relationships with others in her life.

Acceptance, or love as it is used here, is not dependent on the other's conformity to preconceived conditions existing in the therapist. It is not placing critical interpretations upon the client's behavior or saying, in effect, 'I am accepting you if you behave in a friendly way to me or conform to my values', Again I return to the text of the chapter, 'The Process of Therapy':

> It is our experience in therapy which has brought us to giving this proposition central place. The therapist becomes very much aware that the forward-moving tendency of the human organism is the basis upon which he relies most deeply and fundamentally. It is evident not only in the general tendency of clients to move in the direction of growth when factors in the situation are clear, but is most dramatically shown in very serious cases where the individual is on the brink of psychosis or suicide. Here the therapist is very keenly aware that the only force upon which he can basically rely is the organic tendency toward growth and enhancement (Rogers, 1951).

THE COINING OF A NEW TERM

I have chosen to explore the term which is the subject of this paper by beginning with the concept as expressed in the originator's early work (1951), as acceptance, respect, understanding, love.

Qualifying modifiers included deeply, completely or deep, complete. In the five other references cited in this paper published in 1957, 1959, 1961, 1980 and 1986, these elements have been put together in the term 'unconditional positive regard', and included in the 1957 paper as one of the six 'necessary and sufficient conditions' for creating a psychological climate conducive to positive therapeutic growth. What appeared earlier as love or respect or complete acceptance evolved into unconditional positive regard. It is possible that Oliver Bown's awareness of risk of misunderstanding played a large part in replacing the word 'love'. The creation, then, of the new term, fresh and unclouded by a variety of meanings attached to it by the society in general, was undoubtedly a wise choice in keeping with Rogers' lifetime search for the simplest and most accurate terms to express his meaning.

Eight years later (Rogers, 1959), unconditional positive regard is included in 'A. Conditions of the therapeutic process' (p. 213):

> For therapy to occur it is necessary that these conditions exist:
>
> 1. That two persons are in contact.
>
> 2. That the first person, whom we shall term the client, is in a state of *incongruence, vulnerable, or anxious.*
>
> 3. That the second person, whom we shall term the therapist, is *congruent*, in the relationship.
>
> 4. That the therapist is *experiencing unconditional positive regard* toward the client.
>
> 5. That the therapist is *experiencing* an *empathic* understanding of the client's *internal frame of reference.*
>
> 6. That the client *perceives*, at least to a minimal degree, the *positive regard* of the therapist for him, and the understanding of the therapist. The process

often commences with only these minimal conditions, and it is hypothesized that it never commences without these conditions being met (original emphasis).

For the purpose of stressing the importance of communicative aspects in the process, a qualifying statement is added as an alternative to item 6, 'That the communication to the client of the therapist's empathic understanding and unconditional positive regard is, at least to a minimal degree, achieved'.

EACH 'OTHER', A UNIQUE PERSON

As I experience more and more the one-to-one relationship in therapy and in group situations in which participants are seeking personal growth and a deeper understanding of the person-centered approach in their personal lives and in their professional work, I am affirmed in my conviction that this way of being cannot be viewed as a technique or a strategy to be applied in different ways with persons who come with different needs or anxieties. I find, if I am to be real and to have within myself an unconditional positive regard for whoever that person is and how he/she is feeling at the moment, if I am to be able to hear the experiencing of the other at the moment, I cannot be aware of categories of behavior or 'presenting problems'. For this reason, I find diagnoses of this nature at least irrelevant and at worst destructive of the therapeutic or growth process. For this reason I experience an increasing impatience with prescriptions in professional journals for how to 'treat' the divorced or bereaved or alcoholic or deviant or other specialized client. Not only do I find this specialized approach unhelpful, but to work against the realness of the relationship, and to be manipulative in its very nature.

The client, in the process of client-centered therapy, moves to a more open expression of his/her feelings and awareness of incongruity between experiencing of self in that situation and his concept of self. He/she also becomes increasingly aware of the threat of such incongruence. Being able to let in the experience of threat to his concept of self can take place only because unconditional positive regard of the therapist has been communicated to him/her. Only as the need for defensiveness or the felt need for defensiveness decreases in this safe relationship can the client begin to feel self-regard without conditions — or unconditional positive self-regard. Perhaps more accurately, to the degree that the felt need for defensiveness or self-protectiveness decreases, the fewer conditions the client places on his own sense of self-worth. And to the degree that the client perceives from the therapist unconditional positive regard is it possible for this shift or movement to take place. Evidence in support of this process is cited in studies by Snyder, Seeman, Lipkin, Raskin, Kessler and others. For more complete findings the reader is referred to Rogers, 1959, pp. 217–19. The importance of positive regard in self-concept is clearly stated in C and D, pp. 223 and 224:

> As the awareness of self emerges, the individual develops a 'need for positive regard'. This need is universal in human beings, and, in the individual, is pervasive and persistent. Whether it is an inherent or learned need is irrelevant to the theory.

The need and satisfaction of the need is seen as reciprocal in a relationship with significant other or others. Development of the need for self-regard and development of conditions of worth or of unconditionality are basically important to the development of personality. Rogers continues:

> Hypothetically, if an individual should experience only unconditional positive regard, then no conditions of worth would develop, self-regard would be unconditional, the needs for positive regard and positive self-regard would never be at variance with the organismic evaluation, and the individual would continue to be fully functioning. This chain of events is hypothetically possible, and hence important theoretically, though it does not appear to occur in actuality.

RECIPROCITY: A BASIC HUMAN NEED AND ITS FULFILLMENT

Reciprocity in the experiencing of unconditional positive regard has been briefly mentioned and frequently implied in this paper — reciprocity in the experiencing of it in the therapeutic relationship as well as in other significant relationships. In the therapeutic relationship the communication of it is not so clearly defined as reciprocal, nor found to be expressed reciprocally. Because of the nature of the process itself, the therapist, in helping to create a climate for growth, is active in communicating to the client her own experiencing of unconditional positive regard.

Nowhere, in my search, has the intricate, delicate and durable organismic fabric become more clear to my vision than in Rogers, 1961, pp. 51–5, as Rogers poses and answers from his own experience the question, 'How Can I Create a Helping Relationship?'

> 1. Can I be in some way which will be perceived by the other person as trustworthy, as dependable or consistent in some deep sense? Both research and experience indicate that this is very important.
>
> 2. Can I be expressive enough as a person that what I am will be communicated unambiguously? I believe that my failures to achieve a helping relationship can be traced to unsatisfactory answers to these two questions. When I am experiencing an attitude of annoyance toward another person but am unaware of it, then my communication contains contradictory messages. When as a parent or therapist or a teacher or an administrator I fail to listen to what is going on in me, fail because of my own defensiveness to sense my own feelings, then this kind of failure seems to result . . . if I can be sensitively aware of and acceptant toward my own feelings then the likelihood is great that the relationship will be a helpful one.
>
> 3. Can I let myself experience positive attitudes toward this other person? It is not easy. I find in myself, and feel I often see in others, a certain amount of fear of these feelings. We are afraid that if we let ourselves freely experience these positive feelings toward another we may be trapped by them.
>
> 4. Can I be strong enough as a person to be separate from the other? Can I be a sturdy respecter of my own feelings, my own needs, as well as his? . . . Is my inner self hardy enough to realize that I am not destroyed by his anger, taken

over by his need for dependence nor enslaved by his love, but that I exist separate from him with feelings and rights of my own? When I can freely feel this strength of being a separate person, then I find that I can go much more deeply in understanding and accepting him because I am not fearful of losing myself.

5. Can I permit him to be what he is — honest or deceitful, infantile or adult, despairing or over-confident? Can I give him the freedom to be? . . . In this connection I think of the interesting small study by Farson which found that the less well-adjusted and less competent counselor tends to induce conformity to himself, to have clients who model themselves after him.

6. Can I step into his private world so completely that I lose all desire to evaluate or judge it?

. . . For myself I find it easier to feel this kind of understanding and communicate it to individual clients than to students or staff members in a group in which I am involved. There is a strong temptation to set students 'straight' or to point out to a staff member the errors in his thinking.

[In the service of brevity I have become highly selective as I pass on to question 9 (p. 54):]

9. Can I free him from the threat of external evaluation? 'That's good; that's naughty. That's worth an A; that's failure. That's good counseling; that's poor counseling.'

10. Can I meet this other individual as a person who is in the process of becoming or will I be bound by his past and by my past?

In quoting Buber, Rogers here uses the phrase, 'confirming the other'. 'Confirming means accepting the whole potentiality of the other' (p. 55).

This has been an extensive, though incomplete, quotation which seems for me a tying together and rounding out of the various aspects of unconditional positive regard and the way of being in any significant relationship which enhances the persons involved — both or all. It relates unconditional positive regard to empathic understanding and to realness. It again places it close to the heart of a person-centered way of being in relationship to oneself and to others — including but not exclusive to the therapeutic relationship (Rogers, 1980).

RETURN TO A PERSISTENT QUESTION: SIGNIFICANT RELATIONSHIPS

For me there remains the question, 'Can one have unconditional positive regard for everyone?' I can speak only for myself, limited as I am in my thoughtful exploration of this aspect of the subject. 'In one's significant relationships' is helpful to me as I try to define the place in my 'larger' relationships which this condition or characteristic implies.

Some relationships are of great significance to me; some relationships with persons remote from me or having slight or no definable impact on my life and awareness are much less significant for me. At one end of the continuum are my family, friends, clients, colleagues, and those with whom I have more brief though fairly close contact. At the other end are persons I meet casually or more remotely, like the salespersons, servicepersons, journalists, politicians, and the like.

It is clear to me that close to the very core of my intimate and significant relationships dwells unconditional positive regard as an integral part of my way of being. But all of these less significant, more peripheral and even distant relationships? The further I go in my search the more I am aware that the attitude seeps in to touch in some way my feeling about persons in my city, my town, or the broader arena of community life. I wonder how a commissioner, mayor or delegate to the UN has come to a decision, how she/he feels, what the pressures are.

Or, as I read of the events in South Africa as reported in the papers, I am re-experiencing how the black members of a group with which I met in Johannesburg felt as they faced white participants in the apartheid government. I hear again the feelings of the white members, their fear, their anger, their confusion. I feel fear and anger and I hate the injustices, I feel the pain of their hopelessness and striving. Having experienced meeting with them I am better able to differentiate between the person and the act, to feeling caring for a person even as, on this level and national levels, I must speak my convictions. I can do no less and be the person I am.

Even as I speak out on an issue that has become very important to me, I am thinking of women and men with various shades of skin color, of life experience, convictions of their own growing from their unique life experiences and each one feeling as I feel, 'I must speak my own convictions if I am willing to take the risk'. I am, then, looking at persons, not acts or words alone, not at labels or classes or classifications. When I can say, 'I want to hear what they are thinking and feeling, the reasons for their choices' — even when I am feeling anger or am diametrically opposed to their beliefs as they have expressed them in words or action — I am, in essence, saying that these individual human beings are worth listening to, that their reality is as real for each of them as mine is for me, I am experiencing positive regard. If I have the experience of genuinely caring for them as persons my regard becomes unconditional. The channel for communication and understanding is then open.

The men and women to whom I refer are real. I met with them in a group in Johannesburg, South Africa; with them and from them I learned again the meaning of positive regard and the power of unconditionality in the resolution of conflict and misunderstanding. The encounter was brief and open within a climate created by experienced facilitators.

More than other group experiences, that afternoon in Johannesburg gave me the opportunity to venture beyond familiar territory in my search for an answer to my question, 'Is it possible for me to have positive regard for everyone and if not, what limitations do I impose?' That day in 1982 has made it possible for me to venture further, to move toward the far end of the continuum.

Alice Miller, the Swiss analyst-teacher, in her book, *For Your Own Good* (Farrar, Straus, Giroux: New York, 1983) took a step far out into my unknown as she examined the most extreme point on the continuum which I have envisioned. Briefly, her thesis as stated in the chapter, 'Adolph Hitler's Childhood: From Hidden to Manifest Horror', is that even the worst criminal of all time was not born a criminal; that empathizing with a child's unhappy beginnings does not imply exoneration of the cruel acts he later commits, and, finally, the fact that a situation is ubiquitous does not absolve us from examining it. 'On the contrary,' she continues, 'we must examine it for the very reason that it is or can be the fate of each and every one of us.' Miller, after an extensive and scholarly study of the life of Adolph Hitler beginning with his parents and continuing through his birth, infancy, early childhood and adulthood, raises a thought-provoking question. If one person, parent, servant, friend or teacher had listened to his pain, anger, frustration and accepted him and his anger before it was turned in upon himself, where in time it burned out of control, would it have become the fiery cauldron of rage and hate that destroyed millions and himself? It may be my heightened awareness on the subject that I hear so clearly, but I believe I hear in that question a plea for what Carl Rogers has described as unconditional positive regard, particularly as it relates to the rearing and nurturing of children. I hear in it a strong statement of the effectiveness, socially and even politically, of meeting the pervasive and persistent need of human beings for unconditional positive regard, somewhere, sometime, from someone, and the terrible consequences of what appears to be complete lack of response to that need. Alice Miller has forced me to look with clear eyes at what I have learned from Carl Rogers about regard for the person by right of our being human, and to listen to that person deeply before I build a wall of the stuff of my own arrogance against another's reality.

SUMMARY

This paper is a personal inquiry into: (1) the evolution, meaning and application of unconditional positive regard as found in the work of Carl Rogers and (2) an exploration of its meaning for me as I accept it as a central and integral part of my way of being with myself and others. Unconditional positive regard, as it is described and discussed, is a term which evolves in the work of Rogers over a period of many years from the earlier concept described as deep or complete acceptance, understanding, respect or love felt by a therapist for a client within the limits of the therapeutic relationship. The concept has broadened in recent years to include a wide range of relationships and is referred to as the person-centered approach to interpersonal relationships.

1. Unconditional positive regard is a basic human need — pervasive and persistent.
2. An individual, in order to experience and express unconditional positive regard, must first have experienced it from another significant person.
3. It exists as unconditional positive regard for self and for others.
4. Rogers hypothesizes that it is one of three essential elements in the creation of a psychological climate, by a therapist, in which a client can experience positive growth toward becoming a fully functioning person.
5. It is effective, as well, in any interpersonal relationship in which growth and the fostering of an intimate or significant relationship is the intent.
6. It is my present opinion that unconditional positive regard is an attitude varying along a continuum from intimate and long-term relationships to remote and brief contacts.
7. There is strong support for the belief that its presence or absence can have

far-reaching social and political impact in diplomacy and negotiations as well as a marked positive, or negative and destructive, influence on personal relationships.

8. As a result of this inquiry I have become firm in the opinion that unconditional positive regard, once it has reached into intimate and significant relationships in one's personal life, also impinges upon and finally pervades the attitude one holds in response to others along the continuum. Absence or presence of this way of relating to others determines the tone or tenor of that person's life and its impact.

A PERSONAL NOTE

If I am to enter into the full meaning of this, my strong opinion, I need to bring it back to my own living experience. When I can look beyond the act which I deplore to the creator of the act *as a unique person*, human and flawed as I am, and still trust my own deep experience; when I can be firm in my convictions and leave room for the other's, I am learning to live unconditional positive regard in a wide range of relationships. Hypotheses and opinions are tentative, but it is at the times when I am thus open to my real self, to others and to new experience that I feel best about myself and others, feel most effective as a person and as a responsible resident of this planet.

REFERENCES

Rogers, C. R. (1951). *Client-Centered Therapy: Its Current Practice, Implications and Theory.* Boston: Houghton Mifflin. (paperback edition 1965).

Rogers, C. R. (1957). The Necessary and Sufficient Conditions of Therapeutic Personality Change. *Journal of Consulting Psychology,* 21, pp. 95–103.

Rogers, C. R. (1959). A Theory of Therapy, Personality, and Interpersonal Relationships, as Developed in the Client-Centered Framework. In S. Koch (Ed.), *Psychology: A Study of Science, Vol. III, Formulations of the Person and the Social Context.* New York: McGraw-Hill, pp. 184–256.

Rogers, C. R. (1961). *On Becoming a Person: A Therapist's View of Psychotherapy.* Boston: Houghton Mifflin.

Rogers, C. R. (1980). *A Way of Being.* Boston: Houghton Mifflin.

Rogers, C. R. (1986). Client-centered Approach to Therapy. In I. L. Kutash and A. Wolf (Eds.), *Psychotherapist's Casebook: Theory and Technique in Practice.* San Francisco: Jossey-Bass.

8 Unconditional Positive Regard and Pre-Therapy: An exploration

Garry Prouty

INTRODUCTION

Although Pre-Therapy (Prouty, 2000) is a new theoretical statement which expands Rogers' (1959) notion of psychological contact, little has been written about the interface between Pre-Therapy and the 'core attitudes'. The exception is a chapter which appears in a book on empathy edited by Haugh and Merry (Prouty, 2001b).

The present chapter will explore the relation between unconditional positive regard and Pre-Therapy.

UNCONDITIONAL POSITIVE REGARD

Unconditional Positive Regard, as a part of the client-centered tradition was first presented by Standal (1954). Rogers (1957) defined Unconditional Positive Regard(UPR) attitudinally in the following manner:

> To the extent that the therapist finds himself experiencing a warm acceptance of each aspect of the client's experience as being a part of that client, he is experiencing unconditional positive regard . . . It means there are no conditions of acceptance . . . It means a prizing of the person (p. 98).

Bozarth (1998) describes Rogers' theoretical view that UPR is the core condition for fostering psychological growth and the self-actualizing process. He describes parent-unconditional positive self-regard as the preliminary condition enunciated by Rogers for psychological growth and the self-actualizing process for children.

Mearns and Thorne (1988) describe UPR in more communicative terms. They say, 'Each individual counselor will have her own repertoire of ways of communicating warmth. It is interesting to reflect on how easy or how hard it might be to use each of the following' (p. 69). Simple communicative examples of UPR are: going to the door to meet the client, shaking hands with the client, using the client's first name, smiling, using a 'warm' tone of voice, holding eye contact, genuinely laughing as the client recounts a funny incident, agreeing to extend the session where that is possible and appropriate, using words to show warmth, showing genuine interest in the client, physically moving towards the client, touching the client's arm, touching the client's shoulder, holding hands, hugging the client. This author would like to recount that offering coffee to a psychotic client, helped her feel worthwhile and accepted. She also, later, was able to verbalize that my ability to value her, despite her homicidal feelings, was deeply therapeutic.

Schizophrenia and unconditional positive regard

Rogers (1967) describes the critical significance of unconditional positive regard in the treatment of schizophrenic clients. He states:

> Finally, contrasting our Relationship Inventory findings with those of Barrett-Lennard (1962) on his group of psychoneurotic subjects, we found that the therapist relationship factors were relatively more crucial for schizophrenic patients. While therapist congruence seemed to be equally crucial for both groups, the schizophrenics focused additionally on therapist's positive regard, while the psychoneurotics tended to emphasize the therapist's empathic understanding. In other words the actual relationship with their therapist seems more pivotal for schizophrenics, while psychoneurotics tend to focus more on the therapist's empathic capabilities (p. 296).

In the Wisconsin research (Rogers, 1967), Truax developed a separate scale for measuring UPR in which the variable moves from negative to positive scoring. The following is a general outline of levels of regard:

Stage 1 describes the therapist as actively giving advice or clear negative regard. The therapist may be approving or disapproving in a manner that makes him the locus of evaluation.

Stage 2 The therapist responds mechanically to the client and indicates little positive regard. The therapist may ignore the patient or his feelings or display a lack of concern. The therapist shows complete passivity that communicates almost unconditional lack of regard.

Stage 3 The therapist indicates a positive caring for the client, but it is a semi-possessive caring in that he communicates that what the client does or does not do matters to him. The therapist sees himself as responsible for the client.

Stage 4 The therapist clearly communicates a very deep interest and concern for the welfare of the client. The therapist communicates a non-evaluative and unconditional positive regard in almost all areas of his functioning. Thus although there remains conditionality in the more private areas, the patient is given the freedom to be himself.

Stage 5 At this stage, the therapist communicates UPR without restriction. There is a deep respect for the patient's worth as a person and his right to be free. At this level, the patient is free to be himself even if this means regressing, being defensive, or even disliking or rejecting the therapist.

However, the utility of this scale was not satisfactory. As Rogers stated, 'a reliable rating scale for measuring unconditional positive regard was not fully achieved. The ratings on this quality tended to be unreliable, and so had limited use in this study' (Rogers, 1967 p. 73–4).

Further explorations of unconditional positive regard

It should be noted that Wilkins' (2000) description of *Conditional Positive Regard, Unconditional Negative Regard* and *Unconditional Positive Disregard* are similar to Truax's attempt at describing negative dimensions. Perhaps Wilkins' clinical descriptions are a better way to approach the issues than quantitative scales that often do not capture full reality. Further, Kilborn (1996) provides a qualitative description of UPR through exploring the perceptions of therapists, clients and supervised students. Some of the more unusual *therapist* findings are:

One therapist 'felt that her unconditional positive regard could be so strong, flow so naturally, that some of her clients have felt unable to bring up the negative side of themselves' (p.16).

Another therapist states the view 'that British counseling culture often substitutes a kind of "polite withholding" for unconditional positive regard' (p.16).

A further therapist expressed UPR by 'the non-disclosure of illegal actions and also acceptance of the failure to attend' (p. 16).

In approaching *clients'* experience of UPR, Kilborn expresses the hope that 'the very taking part in the project would become part of and enhance the therapeutic process' (p. 19).

One client welcomes her attempt at UPR 'but wishes I would make more use of the dynamic that I don't succeed !' (exclamation from client). Still yet another client: 'I often have the experience that you practice total acceptance to the point of denying me as an individual . . . At times, I experience your total acceptance as a mask behind which you hide' (p. 19).

Another interesting point described by Kilborn: 'They are looking for more active acceptance, otherwise they make assumptions about what I am thinking, and that I am judging them' (p. 20).

In conclusion, Kilborn reports that several clients report lack of self-acceptance as blocking the reception of UPR.

Moving to *supervisees,* one student, who was a pastoral counselor, said she felt 'my wariness and lack of acceptance of her faith and spiritual issues'. This correlates with an earlier description that Kilborn was not accepting of a client's spirituality. Obviously values were possibly affecting the interaction. This variety of responses illustrates problems and complexities associated with the expression and reception of UPR. This is an area currently not examined in client-centered qualitative or quantitative study.

Facets of unconditional positive regard

Following the earlier work on schizophrenia, this writer would like to add that mentally retarded/psychotic persons, suffer *many conditions of worth.* Also, it is possible that '*conditions are not present for worth to develop*' (Haugh, p. 127). These clients need a deep experience of unconditional positive regard (Peters, 1999; Pörtner, 2000; Prouty, 2001a). As a function of working with these populations, this writer would like to present an expansion or 'widening' of the concept of UPR.

In working with these more regressed populations, it has been helpful to understand UPR as a multifaceted capacity that can be expressed in many forms. Students are taught to identify those aspects of their personality that *naturally* express UPR for themselves. They are taught to use these so as not to develop a *role* that a client will sense as artificial and further collapse into psychosis. This is where the congruence plays a necessary role and intertwines with UPR rather than being 'polarized' as suggested by Lietaer (1984). Prouty (1994) describes these possible components in the following way. These are reported from therapy sessions.

Love

UPR can be expressed as love. There are times in therapy when the counselor can have a feeling of love toward the client — not sexual love nor family love, but human loving of the client for their true self. One client expressed this as looking into the therapist's eyes and seeing her self expressed.

Care

Rogers indicated that UPR can be expressed as care. This can mean that what happens to the client really matters to the therapist on a personal level. I remember a client who was schizo-affective, with secondary symptoms of drug abuse. She was also suicidal.

One night a physician at the local hospital called to say they were not sure they could save the client's life after a drug overdose. I remember crying for the client and the possible ending of her life. It really mattered. Her possible death was not an objective affair. I was quite relieved when word reached me that she had survived.

Compassion

Compassion is another dimension of UPR. This is the therapist's reaction to the client's suffering. Suffering receives little attention in professional writing about mental health yet it is, however, a major experience in the seriously disturbed client. I recall a dual-diagnosed mentally retarded/schizophrenic client who was agonized, terrorized and deeply pained over a hallucination involving an indistinct, purple, devilish apparition that laughed menacingly and mockingly at him. This would occur, very frequently, during each day while the client was trying to work in a rehabilitation center. One could not but experience compassion for this person who was going mad while trying to cope with expectations of a work situation.

Non-judgment

Also, as Rogers indicated, a non-judgmental attitude is an aspect of UPR. It can be illustrated as follows. The client, a paranoid-schizophrenic with suicidal and homicidal symptoms was successfully treated without medications. After treatment, she expressed the conviction that treatment would have been impossible without my capacity to 'separate the person from the disease'. In this conviction, she is describing her experience of my non-judgmental attitude.

Acceptance

In addition, according to Rogers, acceptance is a necessary component. Perhaps acceptance can be modeled in this fashion: in teaching acceptance it is described as allowing the therapist to become 'pregnant' with the meanings of the client. The client's meanings are welcomed deeply into your experience. You can accept the client's feelings inside yourself. You can open yourself and experientially receive the client's meanings. The client is alive inside you and the client experiences being taken in. This is difficult when exploring suicidal, homicidal and bizarre sexual feelings.

Nurturance

Nurturance is also considered part of UPR. Nurturance is often expressed in therapy by a deeply sustaining and supportive attitude. For example being available during a client's crisis is often significant. One client, who was suicidal, often called me when I was asleep. On these occasions she would hold a gun in her mouth, clicking it against her teeth in a way that I could hear it. The client experienced my response of 'I'm here, I'm here' as supporting her efforts not to impulsively shoot herself. A female therapist reported a male schizophrenic regressing into a fetal position. Her subsequent holding of him expressed a deep accepting and nurturant attitude.

Valuing

Valuing is communicating to clients aspects of their being that, *in fact,* you do value. Very often, in therapy, I will value a client's courage. A client was very hallucinatory, psychotic and alcoholic. She came to therapy for many years and struggled with these problems. Even though she was psychotic and dangerous, she courageously struggled through to health. Very often, I expressed my admiration for her strength and personal responsibility.

Prizing

Prizing, according to Rogers, is still another part of UPR. It refers to an attitude of the therapist toward the life growth of the client. Many clients take small steps toward enhancing their existence: for example, a client who had been very psychotic improved sufficiently to enter a college computer-training program. I was clearly happy for the expansion of the client's life.

Respect

Last, but not least, is the attitude of respect. Respect conveys the feeling that clients have positive resources in themselves. You have the capacity to make this decision. A client who had been sexually abused, sodomized by his father and fixated with animal sexuality eventually, through therapy, humanized himself into a homosexual lifestyle. He then decided to leave treatment and enter the U.S. Marine Corps. The therapist was concerned that this would lead to a sexual episode with a psychotic relapse. However, the therapist respected the capacity of the client to make his own life decisions. The client did successfully complete service in the Marines. He came back stronger and more self-respecting.

PRE-THERAPY

Pre-Therapy is first and foremost a theory of psychological contact. Rogers (1957) approaches the issue of psychological contact in the following manner:

> All that is intended by this first condition is to specify that the two people are to some degree in contact, that each makes some perceived difference in the experiential field of the other. Probably it is sufficient if each makes some 'subceived' difference even though the individual may not be consciously aware of this impact. Thus it would be difficult to know whether a catatonic patient perceives a therapist's presence as making a difference to him — a difference of any kind — but it is almost certain that at some organic level he does sense it (p. 96).

Prouty (2002) offers a different description of Psychological Contact. It is defined in existential phenomenological terms as the *lived, pre-reflective consciousness of the world, self or other.* Theoretically it further defines psychological contact on three levels: (a) Contact Reflections, (b) Contact Functions and (c) Contact Behaviors. In essence, the therapist's work, the psychological functions of the client and behaviors for measurement, the development of case histories and empirical explorations inductively lead to the concept of the 'Pre-Expressive Self' (Prouty, In Press)

Contact Reflections

This portion of the paper will address the Contact Reflections. In brief terms, there are five contact reflections: Situational, Facial, Word-for-word, Bodily and Reiterative. These are very concrete reflections of the client's *pre-expressive* communications. It is important to realize that the therapist is responding in a non-directive manner, i.e. following the process of the client's expressive behavior.

Situational Reflections (SR)

Existential thinkers often describe humans as 'in situations' meaning they are relationally imbedded in their *world* (Brockelman, 1980). In concrete terms this means the client participates in his environment or milieu. It may be as simple as looking out the window. In this case the therapist would reflect, 'You are looking out the window'. Such reflections facilitate the client's reality contact.

Facial Reflections (FR)

Arthur Burton (1973) views the human face as the expressive 'organ' of the uniquely human. I would reformulate this sense of the face to suggest it is expressive of the self. Many regressed and chronic patients embody their feelings in their face due to psychosocial isolation, institutionalization and over-medication (Reiss, 1994). An example of a facial reflection would be: 'You look scared'. An even more concrete example would be: 'Your eyes are wide'. Such reflections assist the client in their contact with *self.*

Word-for-Word Reflections (WWR)

Word-for-word reflections are attempts to develop contact with clients who are communicatively impaired. Psychotic or brain-damaged clients display symptoms such as sentence/word fragments, echolalia, neologisms or word salads. Consequently, a client may express themselves through a mixture of intelligible and unintelligible words. The therapist is taught to reflect the intelligible language. The client experiences being 'received' and validated. It is not important for the therapist to understand the meaning being communicated. What is important is that the therapist have empathy for the client's effort at communication. Such reflections help the client make contact with the *other*.

Body Reflections (BR)

In the existential language of Meddard Boss (1994), the organism can be described as 'bodying forth'. This means the human body is expressive concerning *existence* as the person experiences it. Body Reflections are empathic reflections to the clients 'bodying forth'. They often result in shifts to verbal expression. This can be seen in explorations of catatonic symptoms (Prouty and Kubiak, 1988). There are two types of reflection — verbal and literal body responses by the therapist. An example would be: 'You are holding your arm in the air' or the therapist holds his/her arm in the air.

Reiterative Principle (RP)

Reiterative reflections are not a specific technique. If any of the particular reflective techniques succeed in a client response, *repeat it*. This embodies the principal of *re-contact*. There are 'short-term' and 'long-term'. Short-term responses are reiterating a expression that the client initiated which seemed particularly congruent, and temporally close. The long-term reiteration is more remote, e.g. 'Last week you said' or 'Last session you said'. Very often the reiteration will start a process in the client from their own 'place'. Another way to reiterate reflect has to do with 'stuck places'. It has been discovered (Prouty, 1977) in treating hallucinations that frozen or 'structure-bound experiencing' (Gendlin, 1964) is resolved by the repeated reflections of the structure and/or slow processing of the hallucinatory image.

These reflections provide the client with a 'web of contact' enabling him to respond to the world, self and other. The theoretical aspects of Pre-Therapy (Contact Functions) and the operational aspects (Contact Behaviors) can be found in Prouty (1998). It has been expanded for use with geriatric clients, trauma clients and aspects of the multiple personality

PRE-THERAPY AND UNCONDITIONAL POSITIVE REGARD

Pre-Therapy cannot be undertaken without the attitude of unconditional positiveregard. One is presented with clients who have been exposed to conditions of worth from many sources: parents, peers, and professionals. Also 'normal' lower-class persons have chronic feelings of inferiority, as revealed by years of testing by school psychologists.

Schizophrenic clients, in addition, have intense feelings of worthlessness. I recall a woman who felt she was a dirty garbage can because of her menstruation. I remember a retarded boy who would flash a knife at the slightest perceived hint of inadequacy, i.e. the reactive dynamic to inferiority and worthlessness. In addition these clients have powerful feelings of rejection from friends and society. All of this points to more of a need for an emphasis on UPR, as indicated by Rogers' earlier (1967) research.

Tom Greening (1999) describes Pre-Therapy as a form of 'being there'. I would add to this existential metaphor that it is not only a description of therapist presence, but also a facilitation of the client's 'being there'. These remarks are very close to Marcel's idea of consciousness: 'Consciousness is first and foremost *"being with"* a lived experience of presence' (Marcel, p. 71).

Vignette

There is perhaps no better conclusion to this paper than a final episodic example of UPR within contact.

Van Werde and Morton (1999) present a process involving a mother dying of a brain tumor. The essential point of the vignette is that *contact techniques enable the communication of unconditional positive regard* between son and mother and even, ultimately, between mother and son. The demonstration of the son's *'being there'* and the mother's last and final *'being there'* is also expressed.

SON	(SR)	*Now I'm sitting on this side of the bed*
	(SR)	*There is more light here*
	(SR)	*I can read better here*
		...
	(SR)	*I'm writing a bit*
		...
	(BR)	*You hold your hands to your head*
MOTHER		*I was going to read*
SON	(WWR)	*You were going to read*
MOTHER		*Another paper*
SON	(WWR)	*Another paper*
MOTHER		*Kellogs? Or what is the name*
SON (Congruently)		*Maalox?*
MOTHER		*Yes. What?*
SON	(WWR)	*What*
MOTHER		*What?*
SON	(WWR)	*What*
MOTHER		*And which do you have to take then?*
SON	(WWR)	*And which to take?*
	(BR)	*You keep your hands to your head*
MOTHER		*Yes*
		...
SON	(FR)	*... and you yawn*
MOTHER		*Yes. But I have to yawn*
SON	(WWR)	*Yes, I have to yawn*

MOTHER		*Yawn, yawn*
SON	*(WWR)*	*Yawn*
MOTHER		*Yes, Kellogs*
SON	*(WWR)*	*Kellogs*
MOTHER		*Yes. The Kellogs Book. Yes*
SON	*(WWR)*	*Yes*
	(RP)	*I came to sit on this side of the bed . . . You were talking and your hand was on your head*
MOTHER		*And that was it*
SON	*(WWR)*	*That was it*
MOTHER		*That was it, the deliberation*
SON	*(WWR)*	*The deliberation*
		. . .
SON	*(FR)*	*. . . and you cough . . .*
MOTHER		*Yes, a bad cough . . . I don't like it a bit*
SON	*(WWR)*	*You don't like it a bit*
	(RP)	*You cough and say: I don't like it*
MOTHER		*I like it, I don't like it*
		Praying
SON	*(WWR)*	*Praying*
		I like it, I don't like it
	(RP)	*and you say: 'praying'*
MOTHER		*Now I am happy*
SON	*(WWR)*	*You're happy*
MOTHER		*Now I'm happy*
		Where I'm not happy, I am not happy . . .
		And now I'm happy
SON	*(WWR)*	*Now you are happy*
MOTHER		*Yes, that is fine, isn't it*
SON	*(WWR)*	*That's fine*
MOTHER		*Voila, that is the way it is. Am I happy, am I happy, am I not happy, am I not happy? That's it*
SON	*(WWR)*	*That's it*
		. . .
	(RP)	*You cough and you said: that's it*
MOTHER		*And I cough and cough and cough*
SON	*(WWR)*	*And you say: I cough*
SON	*(FR, RP)*	*A big yawn and you say: I cough*
		. . .
		. . .
		. . .
	(SR)	*. . . and you are silent now*
MOTHER		*Yes*
		. . .
		. . .
		Three times, I do good
SON	*(WWR)*	*Three times, I do good*

Mother		*Mhm, mhm . . .*
		. . .
		. . .

(Mother wipes her hand over the sheets.)

Son	(BR)	*You wipe your hand*
Mother		*My hand wipes the little chair*
Son	(WWR)	*Your hand wipes the little chair*
Mother		*I wiped the chair*
		Than I wipe loose
		Than I don't wipe loose
Son	(RP)	*You wiped the chair*
Mother		*Than I wipe it loose*
Son	(SR)	*Your hand is on the pillow*
Mother		*It looks like it, doesn't it . . .*
Son	(WWR)	*It looks like it, doesn't it . . .*
Mother		*Does somebody finally helps me?*
Son	(WWR)	*Does somebody finally helps me?*
Mother		*Do I get help? Yes, don't I?*
Son	(WWR)	*You ask if you are getting help*
Mother		*Yes . . .*
		It is good, isn't it?
Son	(WWR)	*You say it is good*
Mother		*It is [unclear . . .]*
Son	(WWR)	*It is of the boys?*
Mother		*Grandiose*
Son	(RP, WWR)	*I heard of the boys and you say grandiose*
Mother		*That's what I also heard in the beginning, and it isn't true*
Son	(RP)	*Grandiose*
Mother		*Why isn't that OK?*
Son	(WWR)	*Why isn't that OK?*
Mother		*It is goo.*
		. . .
		Yes
		What is there left to do? What is there left to do?
Son	(WWR, BR)	*What is there left to do? And you hold your hand to your head*
Mother		*What is there still left over than? I want to do something about it though . . .*
Son	(WWR)	*I do want to do something about it though*
Mother		*But what?*
		Muscles. If all that is food for us . . .
		Goody, goody, good . . .
Son	(WWR, RP)	*Goody, goody, good . . . What there is still left over*
Mother		*If there still is something left over . . . You know what I mean, 'S'*
Son	(WWR)	(surprised and very touched) *'You say my Christian*

		name, 'S'
MOTHER		*'S' I say, 'SQ'.*(Forename and family name!*)*
SON	*(WWR)*	*'SQ', that's my name!*
MOTHER		*That's your name. That's a beautiful name*
SON		(S sits closer and caresses the hand of his mother.*)*
		. . .
		. . .
	(SR)	*And it turned a little bit darker outside . . .*
MOTHER		*. . . and more quiet . . .*
SON	*(WWR)*	(agreeing and confirming*) . . . more quiet . . .*
MOTHER		*. . . and more quiet, that pleases me*
SON	*(WWR)*	*and more quiet, that pleases you*

Quiet

REFERENCES

Barrett-Lennard, G.T. (1962). Dimensions of therapist responses as causal factors in therapeutic change. *Psychological Monographs, 76.* No. 43, (Whole No. 562).

Boss, M. (1994). *Existential Foundations of Medicine and Psychology.* London: Jason Aronson, pp. 100–6.

Bozarth, J. (1998). Unconditional Positive Regard. In *Person Centered Therapy: A Revolutionary Paradigm.* Ross-on-Wye: PCCS Books, pp. 83–8.

Brockleman, P. (1980). *Existential Phenomenology and the World of Ordinary Experience.* New York: University Press.

Burton, A. (1973). The presentation of the face in psychotherapy. *Psychotherapy, Theory, Research and Practice.* 10, 4, p. 301.

Gendlin, E.T. (1964). A theory of personality change. In Worchel, P. and Byrne (Ed.) *Personality Change.* New York: J. Wiley and Sons, pp. 102–48.

Greening, T. (1999). Commentary. *Journal of Humanistic Psychology.* 39, 4, 4.

Haugh, S. (2001). A historical review of the development of the concept of congruence in person-entred theory. In G. Wyatt (Ed.), *Rogers' Therapeutic Conditions: Evolution, Theory and Practice, Vol. 1 Congruence.* Ross-on-Wye: PCCS Books, pp. 1–17.

Haugh, S. and Merry, T. (2001). A New Mode of Empathy. In *Rogers' Therapeutic Conditions: Evolution, Theory and Practice. Vol. 2: Empathy.* Ross-on-Wye: PCCS Books, pp. 155–62.

Kilborn, M. (1996). The Quality of Acceptance. *Person Centered Practice.* 4, 1, pp. 14 –23.

Lietaer, G. (1984). Unconditional Positive Regard: A Controversial Basic Attitude in Client-Centered Therapy. *In Client-Centered Therapy and the Person-Centered Approach: New Directions in Theory, Research and Practice.* Levant R., Shlien J. (Eds.), New York: Praeger, pp. 41–58.

Marcel, G. (1994). The Philosophy of Gabriel Marcel. In *Existentialism and Human Existence.* Malabar Florida: Kreiger Publishing Company, p. 71.

Mearns, D. and Thorne, B. (1988). Unconditional Positive Regard. In *Person-Centered Counselling in Action.* London: Sage, pp. 59–74.

Morton, I. and Van Werde, D. (1999). The Relevance of Prouty's Pre-Therapy to Dementia Care, In *Person-Centered Approaches to Dementia Care.* Bicester, UK: Winslow Press, pp. 139–66.

Peters, H. (1999). Pre-Therapy: An Approach to Mentally Handicapped People. *Journal of Humanistic Psychology.* 39(4), pp. 8–29.

Pörtner, M. (2000). *Trust and Understanding — The Person-Centered Approach to Everyday Care for People with Special Needs.* Ross-On-Wye: PCCS Books.

Prouty, G. (1977). Protosymbolic method: A Phenomenological treatment of schizophrenics.

International Journal of Mental Imagery. 1 (2), pp. 339–44.

Prouty, G. (1994). *Theoretical Evolutions in Person-Centered/Experiential Therapy: Applications to Schizophrenic and Retarded Psychoses.* Westport, Conn: Praeger.

Prouty, G. (1998). Pre-Therapy and Pre-Symbolic Experiencing: Evolutions in Person-Centered/ Experiential Approaches to Psychotic Experiencing. In *Handbook of Experiential Psychotherapy.* Greenberg, L., Watson, J. and Lietaer, G. (Eds.), New York: Guilford Press, pp. 388–409.

Prouty, G. (2000). Pre-Therapy and the Pre-Expressive Self. In *Person Centred Practice: The BAPCA Reader.* Tony Merry (Ed.), Ross-on-Wye: PCCS Books, pp. 68–76.

Prouty, G. (2001a). Pre-Therapy: A Treatment Method for People with Mental Retardation who are also Psychotic. In *Children and Adults with Mental Retardation.* Dosen, A. and Day, K. (Eds.), Washington, D.C.: American Psychiatric Press, pp. 155–66.

Prouty, G. (2001b). A New Mode of Empathy: Empathic Contact. In *Rogers' Therapeutic Conditions: Evolution, Theory and Practice. Volume 2: Empathy.* Haugh, S. and Merry. T. (Eds.), Ross-on-Wye: PCCS Books.

Prouty, G. (2002). Humanistic Research and Practice with Schizophrenic Persons. In *Handbook of Research and Practice in Humanisitic Psychotherapies*, Washington, D.C.: American Psychological Association.

Prouty, G. (In Press). Pre-Therapy: An Introduction to Philosophy and Theory In: Kiel, W., and Stumm, G., *The Many Faces of Client-Centered Therapy*, Vienna, Axel, Springer, Verlag.

Prouty, G. and Kubiak, M. (1988). The development of communicative contact with a catatonic schizophrenic. *Journal of Communication Therapy.* (2) 1, pp. 13–20.

Reiss, S. (1994). Overmedication. *Handbook of Challenging Behaviors: Mental Health Aspects of Mental Retardation.* Worthington: IDS Corporation, p. 171.

Rogers, C.R. (1957). The Necessary and Sufficient Conditions of Therapeutic Personality Change. *Journal of Counseling Psychology.* (21),2, pp. 95–103.

Rogers, C. R. (1959). A theory of therapy, personality, and interpersonal relations as developed in the client-centered framework. In S. Koch (Ed.) *Psychology: A study of a Science, Vol. 3: Formulations of the Person and the Social Context.* New York: McGraw Hill, pp. 184–256.

Rogers, C.R., Gendlin, E.T., Kiesler, D.J. and Truax, C.B. (1967). Appendix B: A Tentative Scale for the Rating of Unconditional Positive Regard. In, *The Therapeutic Relationship and Its Impact: A Study of Psychotherapy with Schizophrenics.* Madison: University of Wisconsin Press .

Standal, S. (1954). The need for positive regard: a contribution to client-centered theory Unpublished doctoral dissertation, University of Chicago.

Wilkins, P. (2000). Unconditional positive regard reconsidered. *British Journal of Guidance and Counseling.* (28), 1, pp. 25–6.

9   Unconditional Acceptance and Positive Regard

Germain Lietaer

PRELIMINARY DEFINITION OF UNCONDITIONAL POSITIVE REGARD

The therapist condition 'unconditional positive regard' is in fact a multidimensional concept. In the clinical descriptions of this basic attitude one can distinguish different components, which are interrelated to a certain degree, but which are specific enough on their own to be dealt with separately (see, among others, Barrett-Lennard, 1962; Rogers, 1957, 1961, 1962, 1966; Rogers and Truax, 1967; Rogers and Wood, 1974; Truax and Kiesler, 1967; Truax and Mitchell, 1971, pp. 315–17; Vandevelde, 1977). Also, in the empirical, factor analytic research, this basic attitude seems to be composed of a number of relatively independent dimensions (Barrett-Lennard, 1978; Gurman, 1977, pp. 508–14; Lietaer, 1976), namely: positive regard, non-directivity, and unconditionality.

Positive regard refers to the affective attitude of the therapist toward his client: the extent to which he values his client and welcomes his coming, believes in his potentialities and engages him in a non-possessive way. This attitude is also called 'caring' or 'non-possessive warmth'.

Non-directivity — a dimension more accurately termed 'client-centeredness' — refers mainly to an attitude of non-manipulation: to approach the client as a unique and independent person, with the right to live according to his own viewpoint. In contrast to this stands a more paternalistic attitude in which one treats the client from one's own frame of reference. Some aspects of the contrasting paternalistic attitude are: lack of respect for the privacy and the pace of the client, and the intention to mold the client toward one's own patterns of feeling, thinking and behaving.

Finally, *unconditionality* refers to the *constancy* in accepting the client, the extent to which the therapist accepts his client without 'ifs'. Unconditional acceptance means that the attitude of the therapist toward his client does not fluctuate as a function of either the emotional state or the behavior of his client, or of the client's attitude toward the therapist, or of what other people think of the client (Barrett-Lennard, 1962, p. 4). Rogers (1961, p. 54) expresses the importance he attaches to this aspect of the helping relationship as follows:

> Still another issue is whether I can be acceptant of each facet of this other person which he presents to me. Can I receive him as he is? Can I communicate

this attitude? Or can I only receive him conditionally, acceptant of some aspects of his feelings and silently or openly disapproving of other aspects? It has been my experience that when my attitude is conditional, then he cannot change or grow in those respects in which I cannot fully receive him.

Thus unconditional acceptance implies, among other things, an evaluative moratorium: no judgment from the outside and no approval or disapproval stemming from the frame of reference of the therapist. As Truax and Mitchell (1971, p. 316) tersely put it: '. . . it does involve an acceptance of what is, rather than a demand of what ought to be'. A client of a colleague of mine, who used to write down his therapy experiences, phrased the 'unusual side' of this attitude of the therapist as follows: 'On the faces of the people who are nevertheless favorably disposed towards me, I always read a norm, or set of expectations, and I feared not to live up to it. On your face, however, from the first conversation on I did not read a norm' (Jennen, 1974, p. 25). This attitude of unconditionality has much in common with the psychoanalytic rule of 'neutral benevolence'; it also belongs to the core of the focusing attitude (Leijssen, 1990): a friendly welcoming of whatever emerges at the felt sense level of the client's experiencing.

It is mainly the dimension of unconditionality that will be discussed at full length. First I will point out the importance of it in the therapeutic process. Second, I will briefly consider some criticisms of this concept. Third, I will provide a more precise definition of the essence of this basic attitude. Fourth, using this more elaborate definition as a frame of reference, I will deal in more detail with some of the limitations and difficulties in experiencing and communicating this basic attitude (including a discussion of the issue of 'verbal conditioning') and with the way in which confrontational interventions may be integrated into a climate of acceptance. The final part of the chapter will be devoted to a description of the dimension 'positive regard'.

THE FUNCTION OF UNCONDITIONAL ACCEPTANCE IN THE THERAPEUTIC PROCESS

Why did Rogers attach so much weight to this attitude? What is the importance of this attitude in the therapy process? The answer to this question obviously cannot be viewed apart from the objectives of client-centered/experiential therapy and from the way in which we believe we are able to achieve these objectives.

The major aim of client-centered/experiential therapy can be very generally described as an attempt to get the experiencing process of the client going again, or to help it function in a richer and more flexible way (Rogers, 1961; Gendlin, 1964). We want to help the client to live through fully, and to integrate, elements of her experience she was not able to face until then. We help the client come to a larger unity with herself, to become 'congruent'. This means that a continuous zigzag between the more conscious symbolization and the underlying stream of experience becomes possible. Thus the person becomes less rigid in her manner of experiencing, becomes more open to *all* aspects of her experience, and begins to trust more fully her own experience — in all its complexity, layers, and change — as a valuable guide for a process-like way of living.

In this 'journey into self' we try to assist the client by continuously being personally centered on, and responsive to, her experiential world (Gendlin, 1968; Rogers, 1975b). The actual 'work' of a client-centered therapist consists mainly in being in touch with, and communicating, the explicit, and, above all, the implicit felt meanings in the message of the client about herself, in what is welling up in myself, and in what is going on between the two of us. Empathy and (more sporadically) self-expression form the most tangible aspects of our contributions as therapists.

What, then, is the importance of an attitude of unconditionality? Together with the congruence of the therapist, I consider these two attitudes to be the foundation, the deeper-lying fertile soil, necessary to enable the therapist to respond sensitively to the experiential world of the client. They are basic attitudes that are not readily visible in the therapist's responses, but nonetheless constitute indispensable basic conditions. As a matter of fact, congruence and acceptance are thought to be closely related to one another; they are parts of a more basic attitude of 'openness' (Truax and Carkhuff, 1967, p. 504): openness toward myself (congruence) and openness toward the other (unconditional acceptance). The more I accept myself and am able to be present in a comfortable way with everything that bubbles up in me, without fear or defense, the more I can be receptive to everything that lives in my client. Without this openness, without this acceptance, it is not possible to let the experience of my client unfold, to let it come to life fully; for with a conditional attitude the chances are great that I dare not see certain parts of the client's experience, and that I will minimize or reject some of them.

The importance that Rogers attaches to an attitude of unconditional acceptance must be viewed in the context of his view of the origin of psychological dysfunctions (Rogers, 1959, 1963a, 1964; Standal, 1954; Wilkins, 2000). Indeed, he considers the conditional love of parents and significant others to be the basic source of alienation. In order to retain the love of the people who are important to him, a person internalizes norms that may be contrary to his desires and experience. A dissociation thus arises between what we strive after consciously and our true self; we become alienated from our deeper core. In therapy, then, the attitude of unconditionality of the therapist serves as a 'counterbalancing force', as a kind of 'counterconditioning' in the corrective experience which the client hopefully has during therapy! As a result of the unconditional acceptance of the therapist, the client gradually feels safe enough to explore himself more deeply, to face aspects that up to that moment had been too threatening or too shameful. So the acceptance by the therapist facilitates self-acceptance and subsequent change. That this corrective influence may be very powerful, should not be at all surprising. Indeed, as Yalom writes (1980, p. 406): not only is the therapist usually somebody whom the client values highly; at the same time he often is the only person who knows the 'shadow side' of the client so thoroughly.

When experiencing a sufficient degree of interpersonal safety, the client dares to let go of his defensive attitude and succeeds in having closer contact with himself. Therefore, an attitude of acceptance does not lead to stagnation, but rather enables evolution of 'frozen' aspects of ourselves. Growth and change become possible precisely when we are able to accept ourselves as we are. In this respect, the above-mentioned client wrote: 'From the beginning I experienced this as if light was shining for the first time on dark chilly spots where nobody had ever come before. It was not cold neon-light but a warm benevolence by which something could start living. It is as if you pass a lamp over all kinds of sore places which then heal and begin to live' (Jennen, 1974, p. 25). At the same time, this absence of external judgment stimulates the client toward more independence and self-responsibility: not what others think or expect, but the individual's own experience becomes the major basis of choices and decisions.

SOME CRITICISMS

Unconditionality is probably one of the most questioned concepts in client-centered/experiential therapy (e.g. Schmitt, 1980). Both within and without client-centered therapy this basic attitude has not always been welcomed in an unconditionally positive way. In my view, part of this ambivalence is related to the fact that Rogers did not elaborate on this basic attitude or at least did not go into detail regarding its problems. The questions and the difficulties with regard to this basic attitude came more distinctly to the foreground as client-centered therapy became more relationship-centered, and as the genuineness of the therapist — which implies among other things feedback and confrontation — became more prominent (Van Balen, 1990). Here is a brief formulation of the most pertinent of those criticisms. (Because some criticisms arise from a misunderstanding of the concept, they are consequently not to the point.)

The learning theorists and behavior therapists tell us that it is naive to believe that unconditionality is possible at all. According to them, selective reinforcement is inevitable. They do not believe, for that matter, that this is bad, at least when the therapist reinforces in a good way, that is, in the direction of more adaptive behavior. In their criticism they refer to the effects of modeling, which they believe occurs in every therapeutic encounter. In particular, they point to research (Murray, 1956; Truax, 1966) that claims to demonstrate that Rogers does reinforce selectively.

Systems theory stresses that we cannot 'not influence'; consequently, 'non-directive' therapy is inherently an illusion. There is directive influencing in every therapy session, although one therapist may be more subtle than another.

Within client-centered therapy this attitude of unconditionality has been questioned as well. On the occasion of his work with more seriously disturbed clients (Rogers, Gendlin, Kiesler and Truax, 1967a), Rogers himself wrote that the client often experiences an attitude of unconditionality on the part of the therapist as indifference and that — at least in the first phase of therapy — a more conditional, demanding attitude would probably be more effective in building up a relationship (Rogers, 1966, p. 186). Through this work with schizophrenics, but also through their experience with encounter groups and under the influence of their contacts with the existential orientation in American psychotherapy, client-centered therapists started to put more emphasis on genuineness and on bringing in one's own experience. In this context, an attitude of unconditionality was sometimes seen as unnecessary self-effacement in the therapeutic relationship, since the client can be helped forward through the feedback with which the therapist confronts him (Rogers et al., 1967b; Gendlin, 1967; Lietaer, 2001).

These then are some of the criticisms of the concept of unconditional acceptance. They provide reason enough to make an attempt to describe this attitude more precisely.

A MORE PRECISE DEFINITION OF UNCONDITIONAL ACCEPTANCE

It is important to make a distinction between experience and external behavior — between, on the one hand, all my client's feelings, thoughts, fantasies, desires, and, on the other hand, his actual behavior. Unconditionality refers to my acceptance of his experience. My client ought to experience the freedom to feel *anything* with me; he should sense that I am open to his experience and will not judge it. In behavioristic terms this is a client-centered form of desensitizing. My client will only be able to explore further, and live through more deeply, those experiences which are anxiety-provoking when he feels that I am able to be present in a comfortable way. When someone tells me that he is looking forward to the moment that his father is dead, or when a client tells me that she secretly wishes her friend to have a miscarriage, or when someone lets his deep feelings of despair emerge . . . then it is important that I be able to go along with this experience without indignation or anxiety. Only then is the client able to explore the deeper needs underlying this experience.

This attitude of receptivity toward the inner experiential world of my client does not mean that I welcome all behavior equally. Both within and without the therapeutic relationship there can be specific behaviors of which I disapprove, would like to change, or simply do not accept. Often the person himself does not advocate this behavior; that may be why he came into therapy in the first place. When someone tells me that he never dares to refuse anyone, that he steals, that he withdraws more and more from all relationships, that he has thrashed his child, and so on . . . then these are behaviors that I — as much as my client — would like to see change. It remains, however, important that I do not merely look at this behavior from the outside, but try to understand it from the perspective of everything that the client experienced in his life (Rogers and Truax, 1967, p. 103). Without approving of it, I accept his behavior as something that is there 'for the time being' and go with him into the personal problems that lie behind it. Sometimes, however, it happens that I feel disapproval or irritation toward behavior that my client hardly questions or does not question at all, or that I cannot comply with what the client requests of me. The former situation can lead to confrontations in which I give my client clear feedback about the consequences of his behavior for himself or for others. In the case of difficulties within the therapeutic relationship itself, I can express to her what kind of feelings she stirs in me and what my limits are. For instance, my client might take a very dependent position, be mad at me, want to dominate me, or wish to have a more informal friendship relationship or even a sexual relationship with me. It remains important that she can express and discuss everything that she experiences with respect to me, without my becoming reluctant or rejecting her as a person; but with regard to her behavior, I do confront her with my limits.

Unconditionality, then, means that I keep on *valuing the deeper core of the person, what she potentially is and can become* (for a similar point of view: see Purton, 1998). My client must sense that I continue to stand beside her, that I will not let her down in spite of her disquieting fantasies, in spite of her antisocial or self-destructive behavior, or in spite of the difficulties we are having in our relationship. Unconditionality in its optimal form has consequently nothing to do with indifference but rather points to a deep involvement with and belief in the other. It is accepting the other as a person in the process of becoming, through which I confirm her in her potentialities and help her to realize them (Rogers, 1961, p. 55). In a revised definition of unconditionality, Barrett-Lennard (1978, p. 5) also stresses that this attitude is directed at the person of the other and not at concrete behaviors.

> . . . variation in regard toward another is conditional to the extent that (a) it is contingent on varying or alternative behaviors, attitudes, feelings or ways of being of the other and (b) is experienced in the form of a response to the person or self of the other . . . In the event that differentially positive or negative reactions to particular behaviors carried no message of approval/disapproval, liking/disliking, etc., for the self or personhood of the receiving individual then they would not imply conditionality.

My acceptance of my client is something that grows. I cannot force it, but my attitude of understanding him from the inside helps me in it. Truax and Mitchell (1971, p. 315) compare it to reading a good novel: as I continue reading a book I become more and more familiar with the inner world of the main characters and my external judgment fades away. In the same way, in therapy I try to keep in touch with what lies behind the behavior of my client. This is not always easy. Sometimes we cannot 'find' each other; sometimes I do not succeed in getting in touch with the inner side of my client but remain stuck on particular behaviors that disturb me. A few moments of personal encounter may weaken my irritation; then I know: 'Basically he is different'. When, however, this does not occur, I believe that therapy with this client will not be a very successful endeavor. With this I arrive at the topic of the limitations and difficulties in realizing this attitude.

LIMITATIONS AND DIFFICULTIES: SOURCES OF CONDITIONALITY

Like the other basic attitudes that Rogers described, unconditional acceptance is described in ideal terms. We can never attain a total openness to the experiential world of the other, but we can nevertheless try to raise our personal limits. In connection with our own limitations, I see three sources of conditionality: our own vulnerabilities; the repercussions of the other's life on our own life; and, finally, problems that relate to the fundamental objective of therapy, which is to facilitate change in our client.

Therapist vulnerabilities or incongruencies

I have already indicated the close tie between congruence and acceptance. Sometimes we cannot let the experience of our clients be fully what it is because of our own personal difficulties. Themes of life with which we have not come to terms, personal needs that interfere with therapy, and our own vulnerabilities and blind spots sometimes cause us to feel threatened and to be unable to respond to certain feelings of our clients in a serene way. This seems to me to be an important source of conditionality to which much attention ought to be paid in training programs. Indeed, our own person is the most important tool with which we work. Entering into the experiential world of someone with values totally different from our own, allowing feelings of helplessness and despair, empathizing with peak experiences of happiness, responding in non-defensive ways to strong negative or positive feelings of a client toward us: these are not easy things to do. That is why I feel rather skeptical about 'crash courses' in which the basic client-centered attitudes are trained at a rushed pace. Personal growth and the development of an understanding of the impact our own difficulties have on our therapeutic work are processes that can probably only take place thoroughly during a training of longer duration, in which the person of the therapist has a more central position (Lietaer, 1980).

Conflicts of interests

Often we cannot fully hear the experience of the other because of what it entails for our own life. This is especially true for real life relationships in which we are interdependent as partners and in which conflicts of interests occur. What my partner experiences can be an obstacle to how I want to live. If my wife is scared to be alone at night, or is jealous, or is afraid of people, or is compulsively orderly, it may be difficult for me to accept and understand her experience. This is because she probably would not expect me 'merely' to understand, but also would want me to take it into account in the way we live together. In the therapeutic relationship this problem plays a much smaller role because therapist and client are less interdependent in their daily living. How my client feels or what he does usually has no direct repercussions for my own life. The structure of the therapeutic relationship protects me on this point. There is the outer structure: he comes only once or twice a week, at fixed hours. There is also the inner structure, my inner attitude: for in the therapy I have fewer expectations for myself; I mainly want to be occupied with him, to carry *his* process further. This distance, the fact that I am more protected and less self-interested, enables me to be closer and helps me attune myself better to his experience (Lehmann, 1975). That is why parents are at times bad counselors for their growing children. Because of their own needs and expectations, they might not be capable of accepting and understanding their children's evolution toward more independence.

The fact that acceptance is less difficult to experience in a therapeutic relationship than in daily life poses some problems, particularly in the client-centered orientation, where the distinction between professional-therapeutic relationships and real life relationships is less sharply drawn than in other orientations. First and foremost there is the problem of 'unfair competition', Sometimes my client finds I understand him much better than his partner does. This can create secondary problems in his or her relationship at home. In this respect, I sometimes wonder if I am not providing my client with an illusory model, something that is many times more difficult to reach in real life relationships. Usually, however, the client himself recognizes that the comparison is invalid, and I do not neglect to underscore this when my client mentions the subject. An experience that is rather contrary to the problem of unfair competition is the feeling of 'acceptance at a distance', in which the client wonders: 'Is your acceptance authentic? What can I do with your acceptance, when you could not live with me after all?' As mentioned above, the structure of the therapeutic relationship makes it less difficult indeed to accept our client. And precisely as a consequence of this special structure we are able to offer him something which he most often doesn't find in ordinary life: to explore 'without being disturbed' everything that lives in him, to go to the depth of his feelings and draw understanding and strength from them in order to grow. At its best, however, our acceptance is not aloof but implies a warm involvement with the other. It is usually the fruit of a persistent and disciplined focus on the client's frame of reference and — when needed — a working through of the problems we are having in our here-and-now relation. It remains of course that with most of our clients we would not want to 'live'. But this does not belong to the essence of our therapeutic task, which is: to help our clients relate in a better way with themselves and with the important persons in their *own* life circle.

Selective reinforcement and the objective of therapy

Is acceptance necessarily selective and consequently 'conditional' simply because of the objective of therapy, which is to bring about change in the client? Is it true that we are not able and even do not want to be 'non-directive', since we hope to have an impact on the life of our client in our role as 'change agents'?

One form of directivity and selectivity is abundantly plain and has been readily admitted by Rogers and other client-centered therapists — and that is that we are experience-oriented. Not every statement of the client receives equal attention. We always try to shift from the narrative to the felt meanings, from the theoretical-abstract level to what is concretely lived through. Rogers writes in this sense about his interventions in an encounter group (1970, pp. 50–1):

> There is no doubt that I am selective in my listening, hence 'directive' if people wish to accuse me of this. I am centered in the group member who is speaking, and am unquestionably much less interested in the details of his quarrel with his wife, or of his difficulties on the job, or his disagreement with what has just been said, than in the *meaning* these experiences have for him now and the *feelings* they arouse in him. It is to these meanings and feelings that I try to respond.

Consequently there is a formal kind of directivity, which amounts to a reinforcement of the client's experience. In addition, we support our client as she evolves toward a more experience-oriented way of living, holds on less tightly to external norms, undertakes actions toward more autonomy, dares to risk herself more personally in relationships — in short, when she changes in the direction of our concept of the 'fully functioning person' (Rogers, 1963b).

The question remains, however, whether we also reinforce selectively *within* experience itself, whether our directivity is also content-oriented. Rogers hopes it is not. He believes that he does therapy at its best when every feeling of the client is welcome, when the client is 'rewarded' through therapy for *each* expression of herself, whatever the content of the feeling (Rogers et al., 1967, p. 519). Also, when a client secludes herself, for instance, or decides to quit the therapy because she shrinks before everything it might entail, or falls back on former ways of behavior, and so on . . . in such moments we can help our client best of all by accepting where she finds herself now, by focusing on and exploring more in depth what she experiences *now*. Another aspect of this non-directivity with regard to experiential content lies in the fact that in client-centered therapy there is no preliminary strategy nor planning for therapy. Rather, therapy is considered to be an adventure from moment to moment, in which it is not necessary that the therapist understand in advance the heart of the client's problem (Rogers et al., 1967, p. 509). As a matter of fact, we rely on the assumption that what is really important to the client will come up in therapy. The only instruction we give ourselves is to follow as receptively as possible the experiential flow of our client. Neither the therapist nor the client knows in advance where this will lead. Thus we have not 'mapped out' anything, nor have we decided in advance that certain contents *must* be explored.

With this difference between content and form in mind, it seems sensible to have a closer look at the research of Truax (1966) and Murray (1956). Their findings are sometimes quoted in support of the thesis — which in my opinion is not qualified sufficiently — that Rogers 'conditions verbally' and thus that he 'controls' the content of what a client tells (see also Lieberman, 1969a, 1969b; Truax, 1969; Wachtel, 1979). Both authors examine whether certain modes of behavior of the client are reinforced more than others, and whether the more frequently reinforced behaviors increase as therapy progresses. Truax (1966), in a case study of 85 sessions, viewed empathy, acceptance, and non-directivity as social reinforcers[1] and examined whether the level at which Rogers offers these attitudes correlates with the level of nine dimensions of client behavior. Positive correlations were obtained between the therapeutic attitudes and five dimensions, and four of the dimensions showed higher levels in the later therapy sessions. These four dimensions include differentiation of feelings, the development of understanding, problem-orientedness, and the degree of similarity in style of expression between the client and the therapist. These results clearly indicate that Rogers reinforces experiential depth, but they do not support any conclusions with regard to content selectivity, because the dimensions refer to formal qualities of the process of exploration. This is less clear with regard to the dimension 'similarity in style of expression'. Truax did not define what he really meant by this dimension. Elsewhere in his article he described the 'stylistic characteristics of the therapist' as the therapist expressing himself in a personal, concretely simple, and tentative way (Truax, 1966, p. 4). These are characteristics

---

1. Together with Gurman (1977, p. 536), I believe that it is simplistic to understand the Rogerian basic attitudes as mere reinforcers. Certain clients can experience these attitudes as 'aversive stimuli' because of their personal learning history. This can, for instance, be the case for non-directivity with dependent clients and for warm acceptance with suspicious clients.

that can, through modeling if you will, direct the client in a vivid and receptive manner toward his own experience. Furthermore, it was also found that the two most content-oriented dimensions of client behavior are not differentially responded to by the therapist. These dimensions are the degree of anxiety of the client and the extent to which she expresses negative as opposed to positive feelings.

In contrast, the research of Murray (1956) indicates that Rogers reinforces some experiential contents more than others. In a case study of eight sessions, Murray examined the effect of subtle approvals and disapprovals on the verbal behavior of the client and found that Rogers approves of desires, plans, and ways of behavior in the direction of independence and self-assurance (for instance: 'And that makes you feel pretty good, I presume'; 'That sounds like quite a step'), whereas he responds slightly disapprovingly to intellectual defense (for instance: 'Can you really consider your own reactions, not an intellectualized abstracted picture of them?') and to a number of aspects of the client's sexual problems. Murray also found that the approved categories increased and the disapproved categories decreased as therapy progressed. Do these data confirm more than a formal experience-orientedness: that is, that Rogers accepts some experiences — in casu the clearly content-laden category 'sexuality' — less than others? I would tentatively answer that it is not always possible to separate form and content in the concrete therapeutic process: trying to deepen the process of experiential exploration of the client sometimes means that the therapist looks for openings to shift the conversation to other layers of experience, which at the same time may mean: to other contents. This is the case with sexuality in Murray's case study. Whereas in the beginning phase of the therapy the client believed that his problems were mainly of a sexual nature, Rogers sensed that his sexual problems were in fact an expression of a more fundamental problem of self-respect and maturity. That is why he tried to push through to what he believed to be a deeper level. Moreover, supporting and encouraging the growth to more independence is probably co-determined by Rogers's view of optimal functioning: he sees self-determination and self-responsibility as the offshoots of an experiential way of living. The slight disapprovals with regard to certain experiential contents (for instance, fear of independence) do not signify that Rogers fails to accept and understand these feelings, and certainly not that he rejects his client as a person. The fact is that he does not support these experiences or assent to them as a positive end point, but on the contrary seeks to differentiate them further in the hope that they will evolve in a constructive way. Rogers has never been explicit about it, but careful analysis of the many session transcripts he left shows that in his responses he selectively chooses the side of 'the experiencing self' in contrast to the inner critic or societal voices which tend to interfere (Lietaer, 1995; Gundrum, Lietaer and Van Hees-Matthyssen, 1999). Authors like Greenberg, Rice and Elliott (1993) are more explicit about it. They formulate as one of the task principles of process-experiential psychotherapy:

> to encourage client's growth and self-determination . . . The major method for doing this is 'empathic selection.' That is, the therapist reflects aspects of client experience that involve emerging experience, or ownership; strengths, progress or active coping; desire for change, mastery, or contact with others; personal

rights, mature interdependence and mutuality; positive aspects of self; and plans or projects for the future (p. 114).

From all this it may appear that even client-centered/experiential therapy cannot be anything else than a directive process. We are formally directed toward keeping in touch with and expanding the experiential field of the client, and we also have an ideal of optimal functioning that may direct our interventions as well; here formal and content selectivity almost coincide. Throughout the therapeutic process, however, it remains important that we remain open to what the client experiences at every moment, whatever the content may be. This is of course an ideal that is never fully realized. Our own personalities and blind spots prevent us from noticing certain experiential contents of our clients or require that we leave them untouched and dare not really deal with them. Also our training within a certain therapeutic orientation can sharpen or blunt the sensitivity for certain experiential contents. This shows, for example, in the reactions of some psychoanalytically oriented and existential therapists to fragments of three client-centered therapies with schizophrenics. Truax and Carkhuff (1967, p. 503) summarize their comments as follows:

> Particularly striking were the observations by almost all the theorists that the client-centered process of therapy somehow avoids the expected and usual patient expressions of negative, hostile, or aggressive feelings. The clear implication is that the client-centered therapist for some reason seems less open to receiving negative, hostile, or aggressive feelings. Is it that the therapists have little respect for, or understanding of, their own negative, hostile, or aggressive feelings, and are thus unable to receive those feelings from the patient? Do they simply 'not believe' in the importance of the negative feelings?

We can only hope that training and experience help to restrict such non-task-oriented forms of selectivity to a minimum, in order to keep our influence on the process of change of the client as clean as possible. Rogers evidently does not object to influencing; in his later years he has revealed himself as a 'quiet revolutionary' (Rogers, 1977). What he does object to is control and manipulation, external pressure, and the use of power (Rogers and Skinner, 1956). A central idea of client-centered therapy is that in the end the client himself leads the show. As 'process experts' we contribute to it; but the client decides whether he responds to it or not, how fast and how far he goes, to what extent our interventions bring new life to his experience, and so on. Such a process is consequently not a blind conditioning in the orthodox sense, but a personally desired process of influencing that takes place as consciously as possible, and in which the client gets the last word. (For a broader discussion of the concept of non-directivity in client-centered/experiential psychotherapy: see Lietaer, 1998.)

CONFRONTATION AND UNCONDITIONALITY

Against the background of the above statements I want to formulate some reflections with regard to confrontation in client-centered/experiential therapy. Client-centered therapy is known as a 'soft' therapy. It can be asked to what extent a client-centered therapist confronts his client and whether such confrontation is compatible with an attitude of unconditional acceptance.

1. First and foremost I believe that client-centered therapists aim toward a high degree of *self*-confrontation within the client. Rogers' basic idea has always been that the main task of the therapist consists of creating a safe climate in which the client can focus on his or her inner experience. This reduced interpersonal fear and increased inner concentration (Rice, 1974, p. 302) allows the client to go deeper into his own experience. A 'self-propelling process' is started through which the client integrates the parts of his experience that he had previously denied to awareness and evolves further from it. The acceptance of the therapist becomes an important support for the client in this often painful process of self-confrontation. At the same time, an attitude of acceptance assures that the therapist will not stand in the way of this unfolding experiential process or sidetrack it.

2. Although this central idea retains its importance, the contribution of the therapist has been gradually reformulated in more active terms. Whereas, in the initial period, theory postulated what the therapist should not do (the so-called 'don't rules'), later on his contribution has been described in a more positive way — namely to maximize the experiential process of the client (Gendlin, 1970). In this perspective, the therapist's receptive attitude remains important, but this does not exclude the therapist from taking initiative at certain moments in order to stimulate the client's experiential process. It is in the framework of this evolution that confrontational interventions have increasingly obtained a place within client-centered therapy. Without going into great detail I would like to illustrate this more concretely. First, with regard to empathy, it is clearly indicated in the more recent formulations that the therapist reflects deeper-lying meanings. [2] Rogers speaks of feelings the client is hardly aware of. Gendlin talks about implicitly felt meanings. Rice contrasts maintenance reflection to *evocative reflection,* by which she means that the therapist tries to open up the experience of the client through evoking experiential elements that are not yet integrated into his cognitive construct of self. Thus a confrontational aspect of empathy is now explicitly acknowledged. On a more concrete level this has been illustrated in an article written by Troemel-Ploetz (1980), in which the author reveals the restructuring, interpretive, and even paradoxical aspects of three empathic interventions.

Furthermore, client-centered therapists have come to attach more importance to bringing in their own here-and-now experiences. The impressions I form about my client and the feelings he stirs in me can be

---

2. Some quotations will serve as illustrations. Rogers (1975a, p. 1833): 'At its best, such understanding is expressed by comments that reflect not only what the client is fully aware of but the hazy areas at the edge of awareness'. Gendlin (1967, p. 399): '[My response] lets the patient experience not only what he already knows he feels, but also what he almost but not quite feels (so that he feels it clearly, after it is spoken of)'. Rice (1974, p. 298): '[The therapist] tries to sense as accurately as possible "this is what it was like to *be* the client at that moment". It is his flavor of the total experience that he tries to give back to the client as concretely and vividly as possible. Hopefully, the client can then use this reflection to deepen and enrich his own awareness of the total experience and thus to broaden his construction of it.'

important material for the client; it can be useful as a stimulus to explore further himself and his relational patterns (van Kessel and Lietaer, 1998). This does, however, involve a loosening of the client-centered principle of *continuously* staying in the experiential field of my client (Rogers, 1966, p. 190): when giving feedback, I indeed confront the client from my own frame of reference with something that does not explicitly, and sometimes not even implicitly, occupy him or her.

As a matter of fact, client-centered therapy is in the process of evolving toward a more broadly conceived experiential psychotherapy (Gendlin, 1974), in which there is room for a variety of interventions. Thus the former non-directive rules can be transcended in an experiential way: using clinical concepts, giving 'homework', bringing in auxiliary techniques — all of these can be done in a client-centered manner, as long as the experience of the client remains the continuous touchstone with regard to anything brought in by the therapist.

3. Are such confrontational interventions at odds with an attitude of unconditional acceptance? According to the meaning I have given to unconditional acceptance, I believe they are not. For confrontation does not in any way mean that I reject my client as a person or that I stop trying to understand his experience. First of all, not every confrontation stems from feelings of irritation. For instance, I might confront my client with his strengths and possibilities, or with facets of his experience that are hardly conscious, or even with positive feelings on my part. In addition, there are of course confrontations that have to do with difficulties in our relationship. Such moments of confrontation stand the best chance of having a constructive effect when at the same time I can experience and communicate a deep feeling of engagement. In this sense Gendlin writes (1970, p. 549):

> But unconditional regard really meant appreciating the client as a person regardless of not liking what he is up against in himself (responding to him in his always positive struggle against whatever he is trapped in). It includes our expressions of dismay and even anger, but always in the context of both of us knowing we are seeking to meet each other warmly and honestly as people, exactly at the point at which we each are and feel.

In the context of confrontation, I would like to finish this part by briefly giving some 'confrontation rules' that appear in the client-centered/experiential literature and that I also find important (see, among others, Boukydis, 1979; Carkhuff and Berenson, 1977; Gendlin, 1967, 1968, pp. 220–5, and 1981, pp. 127–44; Kiesler, 1982; Kilborn, 1996; Rogers, 1970, pp. 53–7; van Kessel and Lietaer, 1998).

First of all, there is the importance of timing. In a first session I cannot yet say what I can easily say later on. The relationship should first have acquired sufficient safety and momentum. Moreover, I believe that my impressions and feelings in the first sessions are often still too superficial and insufficiently shaped to bring them in.

It is also important that I clearly communicate my feedback and reactions as something of my own; that is, as a self-revelation without imposition. This gives a more personal touch to the interaction, sustains its non-judgmental character, and implies that I am willing to face my own part in the difficulty. When setting limits, for instance, it is important that I clearly formulate them as coming from myself. When I do so, my client is indeed confronted with *my* reality, but the chance that she will feel rejected is reduced.

I should also try to communicate clearly that my reactions are connected to her concrete behavior and not to her as a person. Therefore, it is important that I provide feedback with as much concrete detail as possible, touching on how this experience has grown in me, and what in her way of interacting has given rise to it. At the same time I ought to have a keen eye for the needs that underlie her behavior. For instance, if I draw a person's attention to the fact that she always smooths the edges, or if I point out to spouses that they are communicating in an indirect way, then it is important that I also focus on the meaning of this behavior. The distinction I am trying to make between person and behavior is, however, not always felt by my client. Sometimes she feels rejected as a person even if this is not the case in my experience.

This leads me to the last 'rule', which includes the basic attitude that inspires all my responses and interventions as a client-centered/experiential therapist: being continuously in touch with the way in which my client experiences the confrontation and responding to that.

POSITIVE REGARD

Alongside an attitude of receptive openness to the experiential world of the client, Positive Regard also belongs to the breeding ground of our therapeutic work. Here we are concerned with a more affective attitude toward the client on the part of the therapist, one in which the following sub-aspects can be distinguished: dedication, affirmation and non-possessive warmth. In the following descriptions of these aspects it will become clear for each that we are here speaking of an optimum, and not a maximum. The communication of this fundamental attitude takes place especially along indirect and non-verbal lines in the context of concrete therapeutic work, although an explicit and verbal communication is not excluded.

Dedication

It is self-evident that the therapist must possess sufficient dedication and an adequate sense of responsibility with regard to the therapies he undertakes. Prior to beginning a new therapy he should ask himself several questions: Do I want to do this? Do I have both time and energy to do it? Am I prepared to work with this particular client? Perhaps this is all rather obvious, yet I am struck by how flippantly one sometimes deals with such conditions: clients are sent to a therapist who several weeks later leaves the area, or a therapist accepts a new client whom he can rarely see because of overwork.

In a research project we conducted — involving 325 sessions from 41 client-centered therapies — it emerged that the enthusiasm felt by the therapists is not always of a high level. In response to the question, 'With what feelings or expectations did you begin this session?', therapists admitted in one of every six sessions that they 'were not in the mood to do therapy'. The reasons they gave included fatigue, illness, an overly busy day, being in a holiday mood, or lack of interest (Lasui, 1988). That this sort of situation occurs once in a while is inevitable, but there are limits: if the level of dedication is consistently inadequate, a therapist should be asking questions. It is important that the therapist realizes that she is not obliged to take on every client that consults her. It appears to us that, where possible, therapy is better not performed on a full-time basis but rather carried out in combination with other less energy-consuming activities.

Clients have a right to our commitment to them, and that includes their right to our availability and to our alert presence and full attention during sessions. These aspects contribute to a safe and energetic (Rice, 1983, p. 46) working relationship in which the therapist becomes someone 'on whom the client can count'. Our dedication must naturally not be taken too far, for then we find ourselves in the position of a 'savior' in which we tend to take the rudder too much into our own hands and fail to nurture the self-agency and self-responsibility of the client.

A confirming attitude and belief in the potentialities of the client

Rogers strongly emphasizes the importance of the affirmation and appreciation of the client as a person in becoming:

> Can I meet this other individual as a person who is in process of becoming, or will I be bound by his past and by my past? If, in my encounter with him, I am dealing with him as an immature child, an ignorant student, a neurotic personality, or a psychopath, each of these concepts of mine limits what he can be in the relationship ... If I accept the other person as something fixed, already diagnosed and classified, already shaped by his past, then I am doing my part to confirm this limited hypothesis. If I accept him as a process of becoming, then I am doing what I can to confirm or make real his potentialities (1961, p. 55).

Further, out of the fear of pinning someone to their past, Rogers is wary of diagnostic labels and 'patient files'. He therefore writes in his introduction to 'A Silent Young Man' that he never consulted the anamnestic data from Jim Brown, for the following reasons:

> I preferred to endeavor to relate to him as he was in the relationship, as he was a person at this moment, not as a configuration of past historical events. It is my conviction that therapy (if it takes place at all) takes place in the immediate moment-by-moment interaction in the relationship (1967, p. 402).

What is at stake here is a therapeutic factor that quite likely constitutes the 'unseen force' of Rogers' therapeutic (and pedagogical) talent. In each contact with a client he is careful to communicate the implicit message: 'You are worthwhile'; 'I take you very seriously'; 'Change is possible, for you too'. Rogers sees such an attitude of 'naïve optimism' as something like a self-fulfilling prophecy, as a 'faith that moves mountains'.

Very much in line with this confirming and validating attitude, Rogers emphasizes his 'gullibility' (Rogers and Wood, 1974, p. 232): he does not listen to the client's tale with suspicion, wondering if the client is trying to conceal something. He is well aware that the client does not always speak 'all of the truth' but he finds that taking seriously what the client is able to say *now* is the best way of inviting him to become more authentic. On the other hand, he does not try to avoid painful experiences. He has the basic confidence that all will eventually be well and declares himself prepared 'to plunge to the depths of fear with this client and trust that they return. I face the unknown in my client and in myself without a complete assurance of, but a trust in, a positive outcome' (Rogers and Wood, 1974, p. 231). This 'unconditional confidence' (Harman, 1990) goes to show that client-centered therapy is not into covering-up: what lives in the client, however painful and anxiety-provoking it may be, is not avoided. 'No unmentionables', as Gendlin puts it:

> I have the choice only whether to leave him alone with it, or keep him interactive company with it . . . Often the patient refers to something which is unmentionable because it 'dare not be', cannot be tolerated — for example, 'that they don't care for me', or 'that I am crazy', or 'that the therapist doesn't care for me,' or 'that I am ugly,' etc. It helps if I speak these out loud. The patient is still here. He has not been shattered. I phrase it with a 'maybe' so we can back out if need be. I say, almost lightly, 'Maybe you're awful scared you really *are* crazy.' Or, 'Maybe I don't care for you at all,' or, 'Maybe you're too ugly for anybody to like.' The result is usually relief. I respect the patient, not the trap he is caught in (Gendlin, 1967, p. 397).

Non-possessive warmth

In a well-functioning therapy there grows a sense of affection and sympathy:

> As therapy goes on, the therapist's feeling of acceptance and respect for the client tends to change to something approaching awe as he sees the valiant and deep struggle of the person to be himself. There is, I think, within the therapist, a profound experience of the underlying commonality — should we say brotherhood — of man. As a result he feels toward the client a warm, positive, affectional reaction (Rogers, 1961, p. 82).

Rogers describes this aspect not in terms of transference and countertransference, but as a component in a good working relationship; this is neither romantic love nor infatuation, but a mutual process of learning to like the other based on the reality of what both therapist and client go through together in the therapeutic process (1961, pp. 81–2). Rogers emphasizes, moreover, that the non-possessive aspect of these feelings refers to the theological term '*agape*':

> His attitude, at its best, is devoid of the quid pro quo aspect of most of the experiences we call love. It is the simple outgoing human feeling of one individual for another, a feeling, it seems to me, which is even more basic than sexual or parental feeling. It is a caring enough about the person that you do not wish to interfere with his development, not to use him for any self-aggrandizing goals of your own. Your satisfaction comes in having set him free to grow in his own fashion (1961, p. 84).

We also find this aspect of the helping relationship put forward by Yalom where he writes of 'need-free' love (1980, pp. 364–73), of the therapeutic eros that is in fact indestructible, and of the therapist as a 'possibilitator'. The therapist is not someone who manipulates, acting out of his own needs, but someone who helps the other to unfold his own unique self: 'The therapist's raison d'être is to be midwife to the birth of the patient's yet unlived life' (Yalom, 1980, p. 408).

Function in the therapeutic process

Perhaps more than other client-oriented authors, Rogers very strongly emphasizes the significance of Positive Regard, and not only as a safety-inducing element of the relational context within which the real therapeutic work is then accomplished, but also as an important curative process in and of itself. Love, in the sense that he gives it here, works in a healing way; it brings about a corrective interpersonal experience. In his commentaries on therapy, Rogers repeatedly refers to this process. He describes the moment when Jim Brown finally 'allows' the warm care of the therapist as a crucial therapeutic event:

> In this relationship there was a moment of real, and I believe irreversible, change. Jim Brown, who sees himself as stubborn, bitter, mistreated, worthless, useless, hopeless, unloved, unlovable, experiences my caring. In that moment his defensive shell cracks wide open, and can never again be quite the same. When someone cares for him, and when he feels and experiences this caring, he becomes a softer person whose years of stored-up hurt come pouring out in anguished sobs. He is not the shell of hardness and bitterness, the stranger to tenderness. He is a person hurt beyond words, and aching for the love and caring which alone can make him human (Rogers, 1967, p. 411).

This theme is also central in the description of the therapeutic process of Mrs Oak: she gradually comes to experience how the therapist actually cares for her and on this basis comes to 'like herself'. Rogers describes this evolution — in a rather poetic manner — as follows:

> Here she arrives, as do so many other clients, at the tentative, slightly apologetic realization that she has come to like, enjoy, appreciate herself. One gets the feeling of a spontaneous relaxed enjoyment, a primitive joie de vivre, perhaps analogous to the lamb frisking about the meadow or the porpoise gracefully leaping in and out of the waves (1961, p. 88).

Perhaps we could see this as a client-centered form of assertiveness training, in the deeper sense of the word. In any case this appears to us to be an important process, one that particularly comes to the fore with clients whose difficulties involve neglect, rejection or abuse within significant relations.

One more remark by way of conclusion with regard to this attitude of Positive Regard. Concepts such as 'affection', 'warmth' or 'sympathy' quickly elicit mixed feelings in psychotherapeutic circles. This makes one mindful of the danger of falling into sentimentality, keeping the client dependent, superficial friendship, excessive closeness, eroticisation, sexual abuse or other forms of interference by the therapist's own needs. We all know that these dangers are not imaginary, thus the great importance — especially in this area of feelings — of congruence on the part of the therapist: his integrity and self-knowledge must aid him in seeing the distinction, both for himself and the client, between the real aspects of a growing working alliance and the irrational aspects that have more to do with own needs and problems. Too little distance can be harmful, but too much distance even more so. Some therapists have a 'warmth phobia', they fear closeness and never dare to show their positive feelings. According to Rogers (1961, p. 52), this often consists of a fear of becoming too much possessed by the client. The consequence may well be that this nonetheless crucial component of the working alliance gets suffocated under a defensive attitude of professional distance.

CONCLUSION

In this chapter we reflected on some theoretical and clinical aspects of Rogers' concept of unconditional positive regard. Although we looked most closely into the dimension of unconditional acceptance, also two other dimensions were reflected upon: non-manipulation under the issue of selective reinforcement or 'verbal conditioning', and positive regard with its aspects of dedication, confirmation and non-possessive warmth.

Research shows that these three dimensions have an important impact on the change process of the client: they are often mentioned as helping factors in client-centered/experiential therapy (Lietaer and Neirinck, 1986; Lietaer, 1992; Greenberg, Elliott and Lietaer, 1994) as well as in other orientations (Orlinsky, Grawe and Parks, 1994). Their ways of impact can be summarized as follows: unconditional positive regard creates a high level of safety which helps to unfreeze blocked areas of experience and to allow painful emotions in a climate of 'holding'; it functions as a medium for interpersonal corrective experiences through which self-acceptance, self-empathy and self-love are fostered (Barrett-Lennard, 1998); it helps the client to become more inner-directed, more trusting his organismic experience as a compass for living and hence to become a better 'therapist for himself'.

REFERENCES

Barrett-Lennard, G.T. (1962). Dimensions of therapist response as causal factors in therapeutic change. *Psychological Monographs,* 76 (43, Whole No 562).

Barrett-Lennard, G.T. (1978). The Relationship Inventory: Later development and adaptations, *JSAS Catalog of Selected Documents in Psychology,* 8.

Barrett-Lennard, G. T. (1997). The recovery of empathy. Toward others and self. In A. C. Bohart and L. S. Greenberg (Eds.), *Empathy reconsidered. New directions in Psychotherapy* (pp. 103–59). Washington, DC.: American Psychological Association.

Barrett-Lennard, G.T. (1998). Carl Rogers' Helping System: Journey and Substance. London: Sage.

Boukydis, K.N. (1979). Caring and confronting. *Voices. The Art and Science of Psychotherapy,* 15, 31–4.

Carkhuff, R.R. and Berenson, B.G. (1977). In search of an honest experience: Confrontation in counseling and life. In R.R. Carkhuff and B.G. Berenson, *Beyond Counseling and Therapy* (pp. 198–213). New York: Holt, Rinehart and Winston.

Gendlin, E.T. (1964). A theory of personality change. In P. Worchel and D. Byrne, *Personality Change* (pp. 100–48). New York: Wiley.

Gendlin, E.T. (1967). Therapeutic procedures in dealing with schizophrenics. In C. Rogers et al. (Eds.), *The Therapeutic Relationship and its Impact: A Study of Psychotherapy with Schizophrenics* (pp. 369–400). Madison: University of Wisconsin Press.

Gendlin, E.T. (1968). The experiential response. In E.F. Hammer (Ed.), *Use of Interpretation in Therapy: Technique and Art* (pp. 208–26). New York: Grune and Stratton.

Gendlin, E.T. (1970). A short summary and some long predictions. In J.T. Hart and T.M. Tomlinson (Eds.), *New Directions in Client-Centered Therapy* (pp. 544–62). Boston: Houghton Mifflin.

Gendlin, E.T. (1974). Client-centered and experiential psychotherapy. In D. Wexler and L. Rice (Eds.), *Innovations in Client-Centered Therapy* (pp. 211–46). New York: Wiley.

Gendlin, E.T. (1981). *Focusing*. New York: Bantam.

Greenberg, L. S., Elliott, R. and Lietaer, G. (1994). Research on experiential psychotherapies. In A. E. Bergin and S. L. Garfield. *Handbook of Psychotherapy and Behavior Change* (pp. 509–39). New York: Wiley.

Greenberg, L. S., Rice, L. N. and Elliott, R. (1993). *Facilitating Emotional Change. The Moment-by-Moment Process.* New York: Guilford.

Gundrum, M., Lietaer, G. and Van Hees-Matthyssen (1999). Carl Rogers' responses in the 17th session with Miss Mun: comments from a process-experiential and psychoanalytic perspective. *British Journal of Guidance and Counselling, 27,*(4), pp. 462–82.

Gurman, A.S. (1977). The patient's perception of the therapeutic relationship. In A. Gurman and A. Razin, *Effective Psychotherapy: A Handbook of Research* (pp. 503–43). New York: Pergamon Press.

Harman, J. I. (1990). Unconditional confidence as a facilitative precondition. In G. Lietaer, J. Rombauts, and R. Van Balen (Eds.), *Client-centered and experiential psychotherapy in the Nineties* (pp. 251–68). Leuven: Leuven University Press.

Jennen, M. (1974). Onvoorwaardelijke positieve gezindheid. Reflectie over de beleving en communicatie van deze therapeutische grondhouding. Unpublished specialization paper, K.U.Leuven.

Kiesler, D. J. (1982). Confronting the client-therapist relationship in psychotherapy. In J. C. Anchin and D. J. Kiesler, *Handbook of Interpersonal Psychotherapy* (pp. 274–95). New York: Pergamon press.

Kilborn, M. (1996). The quality of acceptance. *Person-Centred Practice, 4*(1), pp. 14–23.

Lasui, C. (1988). Gevoelens en verwachtingen van cliënten en therapeuten voor een therapeutische sessie. Een empirische bijdrage. Non-published master's thesis, Katholieke Universiteit Leuven.

Lehmann, B. (1975). Enkele gedachten over afstand en nabijheid in de psychotherapie. *Tijdschrift voor Psychotherapie, 1*, pp. 95–101.

Leijssen, M. (1990). On focusing and the necessary conditions of therapeutic change. In G. Lietaer, J. Rombauts, and R. Van Balen (Eds.), *Client-Centered and Experiential Psychotherapy in the Nineties* (pp. 225–50). Leuven: Leuven University Press.

Lieberman, L.R. (1969a). Reinforcement and non-reinforcement in Rogerian psychotherapy: a critique. *Perception and Motor Skills, 2*8, pp. 559–65.

Lieberman, L.R. (1969b). Reinforcement in Rogerian psychotherapy: rejoinder. *Perception and Motor Skills, 29*, pp. 861–2.

Lietaer, G. (1976). Nederlandstalige revisie van Barrett-Lennard's Relationship Inventory voor individueel-therapeutische relaties. *Psychologica Belgica, 6*, pp. 73–94.

Lietaer, G. (1980). Goals of personal therapy for trainees, considered from a client-centered or existential viewpoint. In W. De Moor and H.R. Wijngaarden (Eds.), *Psychotherapy: research and training. Proceedings of the XIth International Congress of Psychotherapy* (pp. 305–8). Amsterdam: Elsevier/North-Holland Biomedical Press.

Lietaer, G. (1992). Helping and hindering processes in client-centered/experiential psychotherapy. A content analysis of client and therapist post-session perceptions. In S. G. Toukmanian and D. L. Rennie (Eds.), *Psychotherapy Process Research. Paradigmatic and Narrative Approaches* (pp. 134–495). Newbury Park: Sage.

Lietaer, G. (1995). Carl Rogers' verbale interventies in 'On anger and hurt'. Een kwantitatieve en kwalitatieve analyse. In G. Lietaer and M. Van Kalmthout (Eds.), *Praktijkboek gesprekstherapie. Psychopathologie en experiëntiële procesbevordering* (pp. 69–91). Leusden: De Tijdstroom.

Lietaer, G. (1998). From non-directive to experiential: A paradigm unfolding. In B. Thorne and E. Lambers (Eds.), *Person-Centred Therapy. A European Perspective* (pp. 62–73). London: Sage.

Lietaer, G. (2001). Being genuine as a therapist: Congruence and transparency. In G. Wyatt (Ed.), *Rogers' Therapeutic Conditions: Evolution, Theory and Practice. Vol. 1. Congruence* (pp. 36–54). Llangarron, Ross-on-Wye: PCCS Books.

Lietaer, G., and Neirinck, M. (1986). Client and therapist perceptions of helping processes in client-centered/experiential psychotherapy. *Person-Centered Review, 1,* pp. 436–55.

Murray, E.J. (1956). A content-analysis method for studying psychotherapy. *Psychological Monographs, 70* (13, Whole No 420).

Orlinsky, D. E., Grawe, K. and Parks, B. K. (1994). Process and outcome in psychotherapy — Noch einmal. In A. E. Bergin and S. L. Garfield (Eds.), *Handbook of Psychotherapy and Behavior Change* (pp. 270–376). New York: Wiley.

Purton, C. (1998). Unconditional positive regard and its spiritual implications. In B. Thorne and E. Lambers (Eds.), *Person-Centred Therapy. A European Perspective* (pp. 23–37). London: Sage.

Rice, L.N. (1974). The evocative function of the therapist. In D.A. Wexler and L.N. Rice (Eds.), *Innovations in Client-Centered Therapy* (pp. 289–311). New York: Wiley.

Rice, L. N. (1983). The relationship in client-centered therapy. In M. J. Lambert (Ed.), *Psychotherapy and patient relationship.* Homewood: Dow Jones-Irwin.

Rogers, C.R. (1957). The necessary and sufficient conditions of therapeutic personality change. *Journal of Consulting Psychology, 21,* pp. 97–103.

Rogers, C.R. (1959). A theory of therapy, personality and interpersonal relationships, as developed in the client-centered framework. In S. Koch (Ed.), *Psychology: A Study of A Science. Vol. III Formulations of the Person and the Social Context.* New York: Mc Graw Hill.

Rogers, C.R. (1961). *On Becoming a Person.* Boston: Houghton Mifflin.

Rogers, C.R. (1962). The interpersonal relationship: The core of guidance. *Harvard Educational Review, 32,* pp. 416–29.

Rogers, C.R. (1963a). The actualizing tendency in relation to 'motives' and to consciousness. In M. Jones (Ed.), *Nebraska Symposium on Motivation 1963* (pp. 1–24). University of Nebraska Press.

Rogers, C.R. (1963b). The concept of the fully functioning person. *Psychotherapy: Theory, Research and Practice, 1,* pp. 17–26.

Rogers, C.R. (1964). Toward a modern approach to values: The valuing process in the mature person. *Journal of Abnormal and Social Psychology, 68,* pp. 160–7.

Rogers, C.R. (1966). Client-centered therapy. In S. Arieti (Ed.), *American Handbook of Psychiatry* (Vol. 3) (pp. 183–200). New York: Basic Books.

Rogers, C. R. (1967). A silent young man. In C. R. Rogers et al. (Eds.), *The Therapeutic Relationship and its Impact. A study of Psychotherapy with Schizophrenics* (pp. 401–16). Madison: University of Wisconsin Press.

Rogers, C.R. (1970). Can I be a facilitative person in a group. In C.R. Rogers, *On Encounter Groups.* New York: Harper and Row.

Rogers, C.R. (1975a). Client-centered psychotherapy. In A.M. Freedman, H.I. Kaplan and B.J. Sadock (Eds.), *Comprehensive Textbook of Psychiatry* (Vol. 2) (pp. 1831–43). Baltimore: Williams and Wilkins.

Rogers, C.R. (1975b). Empathic: An unappreciated way of being. *The Counseling Psychologist, 5,* pp. 2–10.

Rogers, C.R. (1977). *Carl Rogers on Personal Power.* New York: Delacorte Press.

Rogers, C.R., Gendlin, E. T., Kiesler, D., and Truax, C. (Eds.). (1967a). The *Therapeutic Relationship and its Impact: A Study of Psychotherapy with Schizophrenics.* Madison: University of Wisconsin Press.

Rogers, C.R. et al. (1967b). A dialogue between therapists. In C.R. Rogers et al. (Eds.), *The*

Therapeutic Relationship and its Impact: A Study of Psychotherapy with Schizophrenics (pp. 507–20). Madison: University of Wisconsin Press.

Rogers, C.R. and Skinner, B.F. (1956). Some issues concerning the control of human behavior. *Science, 124*, pp. 1057–66.

Rogers, C.R. and Truax, C.B. (1967). The therapeutic conditions antecendent to change: A theoretical view. In C.R. Rogers et al. (Eds.), *The Therapeutic Relationship and its Impact: A Study of Psychotherapy with Schizophrenics* (pp. 97–108). Madison: University of Wisconsin Press.

Rogers, C.R. and Wood, J.K. (1974). The changing theory of client-centered therapy. In A. Burton (Ed.), *Operational Theories of Personality* (pp. 211–54). New York: Brunner/Mazel.

Schmitt, J.P. (1980). Unconditional positive regard: The hidden paradox. *Psychotherapy: Theory, Research and Practice, 17*, pp. 237–45.

Standal, S.W. (1954). The need for positive regard: A contribution to client-centered theory. Unpublished doctoral dissertation, University of Chicago.

Troemel-Ploetz, S. (1980). I'd come to you for therapy: Interpretation, redefinition and paradox in Rogerian therapy. *Psychotherapy: Theory, Research and Practice, 17*, pp. 246–57.

Truax, C.B. (1966). Reinforcement and nonreinforcement in Rogerian psychotherapy. *Journal of Abnormal Psychology, 71*, pp. 1–9.

Truax, C.B. (1969). Reinforcement and nonreinforcement in Rogerian psychotherapy: 'a reply'. *Perception and Motor Skills, 29*, pp. 701–2.

Truax, C.B. and Carkhuff, R.R. (1967). The client-centered process as viewed by other therapists. In C. Rogers et al. (Eds.), *The Therapeutic Relationship and its Impact: A Study of Psychotherapy with Schizophrenics* (pp. 419–505). Madison: University of Wisconsin Press.

Truax, C.B. and Kiesler, D.J. (1967). A tentative scale for the rating of unconditional positive regard. In C.R. Rogers et al. (Eds.), *The Therapeutic Relationship and its Impact: A Study of Psychotherapy with Schizophrenics* (pp. 569–79). Madison: University of Wisconsin Press.

Truax, C.B. and Mitchell, K.M. (1971). Research on certain therapist interpersonal skills in relation to process and outcome. In A.E. Bergin and S.L. Garfield (Eds.), *Handbook of Psychotherapy and Behavioral Change: An Empirical Analysis* (pp. 299–344). New York: Wiley.

Van Balen, R. (1990). The therapeutic relationship according to Carl Rogers: A climate? A dialogue? Or both? In G. Lietaer, J. Rombauts, and R. Van Balen (Eds.), *Client-Centered and Experiential Psychotherapy in the Nineties* (pp. 65–85). Leuven: Leuven University Press.

Vandevelde, V. (1977). Het koncept onvoorwaardelijke positieve gezindheíd ín de client-centered terapie. Unpublished masters' thesis, K.U.Leuven.

van Kessel, W. and Lietaer, G. (1998). Interpersonal processes. In L. S. Greenberg, J. C. Watson, and G. Lietaer (Eds.), *Handbook of Experiential Psychotherapy* (pp. 155–77). New York: Guilford.

Wachtel, P.L. (1979). Contingent and non-contingent therapist response. *Psychotherapy: Theory, Research and Practice, 16*, pp. 30–5.

Wexler, D.A. and Rice, L.N. (Eds.). (1974). *Innovations in Client-centered Therapy*. New York: Wiley.

Wilkins, P. (2000). Unconditional positive regard reconsidered. *British Journal of Guidance and Counselling, 28*, 23–36.

Yalom, I. D. (1980). *Existential Psychotherapy*. New York: Basic Books.

Unconditional Positive Regard: Constituent activities

James R. Iberg

In this chapter, I consider Unconditional Positive Regard (UPR) first as it was described by Carl R. Rogers and then examine how some subsequent theorists and writers have studied and elaborated it. I then place my emphasis on activities especially pertinent to the momentary enactment of Unconditional Positive Regard, because as it is one of many possible modes of regarding, we need to know how to enter this particular mode. In the end, I hope to have helped answer questions a student therapist might have such as 'What can I *do* to develop my capacity to have Unconditional Positive Regard for clients?'

THEORY OF CARL R. ROGERS

Unconditional Positive Regard is a central concept in the theories of Carl R. Rogers, both for psychotherapy and for interpersonal relations. A universal need for positive regard by others appears at about the same time a person begins to experience awareness of self (Rogers, 1959). In therapy, UPR is a quality of the therapist's experience toward the client (p. 239). Rogers' writing sheds light on various aspects of this construct:

Unconditional
> One experiencing UPR holds 'no *conditions* of acceptance . . . It is at the opposite pole from a selective evaluating attitude.' (p. 225).

Positive
> One offers 'warm acceptance . . . a "prizing" of the person, as Dewey has used that term . . . It means a caring for the client . . . ' (p. 225).

Regard
> One regards 'each aspect of the client's experience as being part of that client . . . It means a caring for the client, but not in a possessive way or in such a way as simply to satisfy the therapist's own needs. It means caring for the client as a *separate* person, with permission to have his [or her] own feelings, his [or her] own experiences' (p. 225).

Rogers acknowledged an undesirable connotation of his term 'unconditional positive regard' (p. 225, footnote): it suggests an all-or-nothing condition. However, for the effective therapist, Rogers said it probably occurs sometimes ('at many moments') and not at other times, and to varying degrees.

Theoretically, the importance of UPR lies in its power to build up or restore the recipient's unconditional positive self-regard. To understand this as Rogers did, I will review a few other related terms: conditions of worth, self-concept, organismic valuing, and incongruence.

Rogers postulated that the human infant equates organismic experiencing with reality. Experiences perceived as enhancing or maintaining the organism are valued positively, and those experiences perceived as negating maintenance or failing to enhance the organism are valued negatively.

As the person develops, the further differentiation natural to the actualizing tendency results in some parts of experiencing being symbolized in an awareness of being, an awareness of functioning (ibid. pp. 244–5). This partial awareness of experiencing gets elaborated into a concept of self.

When significant others communicate to a person that his/her positive regard depends on certain behaviors or certain experiences, the part of the person identified with the self-concept has incentives to include some behaviors and experiences and to resist, deny, or distort other behaviors and experiences. These incentives are powerful because of the 'pervasive and persistent' need for positive regard from significant others. Rogers says 'the expression of positive regard by a significant social other can become more compelling than the *organismic valuing process*, and the individual becomes more [oriented] to the *positive regard* of such others than toward experiences which are of positive value in *actualizing* the organism' (ibid. pp. 245–6).

Rogers describes the development of incongruence between self and experience as follows:

> Experiences which run contrary to the *conditions of worth* are *perceived* selectively and distortedly as if in accord with the *condition of worth*, or are in part or whole *denied to awareness* . . . Thus from the time of the first selective *perception* in terms of *conditions of worth*, the states of *incongruence between self* and *experience*, of *psychological maladjustment* and of *vulnerability*, exist to some degree (ibid. p. 247).

Moving toward less defensiveness and healthier adjustment requires a decrease in conditions of worth and an increase in unconditional self-regard, and the communicated UPR of a significant other is one way of achieving these things (ibid. p. 249). This is a very interactional notion of how things intrapsychic (incongruence, psychological maladjustment) can change. An environment of empathy and UPR, when perceived by the person, weakens existing conditions of worth, or dissolves them. Positive self-regard increases. Threat is reduced, and the process of defense is reversed, so that experiences customarily threatening can be accurately symbolized and integrated into the self-concept (p. 249).

Thus, a central theoretical issue bearing on UPR is the self-concept and how that can feel threatened by experiences inconsistent with conditions of worth. There is a kind of resistance to or looking away from some parts of experience. Conditions of worth foster a basic me/not-me division in experiencing and reinforce a sense of self limited to parts acceptable to significant others. Rogers argued that this problem resolves when one experiences empathy and UPR so that the self-concept can be expanded or opened up to be more inclusive of all of one's diverse experiences and qualities of experiencing.

An example from a therapy client of the effects of conditions of worth, and the struggle to undo their damage, may make these matters more tangible and clear (names and certain facts have been changed to protect the client's identity).

After more than two years of therapy in which he has made good progress, Mr K. is now more aware of some of his tendencies, and he has changed many old patterns. He has described how he was treated by his older siblings (their father was absent): several of them would consistently get angry at and critical of him if he presented a situation involving what they construed as a mess, or if he required some special attention. He has often said tearfully 'the only safe thing for me to do was to keep quiet and not make any trouble.' He has made a great deal of progress toward being more assertive and self-expressive and is building a sense that he has every right to have his needs attended to with respect and caring. But he is not yet in a position where he can always operate out of this new sense of more positive regard for himself. A recent incident illustrates both his progress and the continuing struggle to escape the constraints of conditions of worth: at a holiday gathering at his sister's house, he went into the bathroom to find the toilet backed up and in danger of overflowing if it were to be flushed again. He anticipated people criticizing him and embarrassing him by saying 'Oh, what did you do, Pete?' A year ago, he probably would have just kept quiet about it. This time he told his sister of the problem. As he was waiting for her to locate a plunger, he saw someone else go into the bathroom. He felt anxious and became unsure if it was his sister or someone else who went in there (he said to me that at some level he knew it wasn't her — it was a male friend of the family). In that moment, he couldn't be sure. (He believes this perceptual distortion happened so that he wouldn't have to draw attention to the situation and himself, risking mockery and embarrassment, but he was extremely frustrated about allowing himself to get confused like this.) Then his sister appeared, and he said 'Oh, someone went in there. I thought it might be you.' Before she finished saying 'tell him not to flush,' Pete was already yelling this to him.

This example shows how therapy enables living differently in a relevant life situation. It also shows the very real limits in the extension of these benefits. At this point in his therapy, when reflecting on a situation, Pete is readily aware of much complexity and nuance in his emotional reactions and implicit thinking. Many things he wouldn't have been able to admit to himself before, he easily acknowledges now. Nevertheless, in the situation with the significant others who were and still are sources of conditional regard, the same effects squelching certain aspects of his experiencing (in this case confusing his perception of what he saw) take hold and tend to dominate. He seems determined to eventually free himself of such squelching effects even in this powerful family social context. We should not minimize the importance of the change Pete has experienced already: within this most challenging situation with the purveyors of conditions of worth, self-assertive behavior is sprouting in spite of the likelihood of derision from significant others. This development is consistent with Rogers' theoretical claims

111

that empathy and UPR in the therapy relationship bolster the client's capacity for unconditional positive self-regard.

FROM A RELATIONSHIP CHARACTERISTIC TO ACTIVITIES

More than 40 years ago, Barrett-Lennard (1959) became interested in researching the conditions Rogers had postulated to be necessary and sufficient for personality change (Rogers, 1957), among them UPR. He wanted to be able to assess the degree to which a therapy relationship provided these conditions, so that Rogers' theory could be put to empirical test. The instrument he developed, the Relationship Inventory (RI), now has a long history of psychometric development and use in a wide range of studies of psychotherapy. About the above clinical vignette, he might have asked, 'how can we measure the extent to which the therapy relationship includes UPR, and relate that to measures of the client's progress in therapy and improvement in living?'

Barrett-Lennard defined the conditions as features of a relationship, less enduring than personality traits, rather 'a sphere and axis of experienced response in a particular relationship, at the present juncture . . . but not with reference to the immediate moment or a very brief episode in that relationship' (Barrett-Lennard, 1986, p. 440). Thus he framed the relationship conditions as lasting over time, more than just a momentary occurrence, but also not so lasting that they were like therapist personality traits. As he construes them, they are not even a permanent feature of any given relationship. The items he uses to operationalize the concepts reflect this way of thinking. For example, 'She respects me as a person and 'she cares for me' are items indicating Level of Regard.

Separating Conditionality from Level of Regard

Very early in the development of his instrument, Level of Regard and Conditionality were separated to differentiate and simplify the 'operationally awkward concept of unconditional positive regard' (Barrett-Lennard, 1986, p. 440). The Relationship Inventory is designed to scale quantitative degrees of these two components of UPR (as well as other relationship conditions).

The axis of 'Level of regard' is seen as ranging from certain negative affects to certain positive affects (not the full spectrum of affects on either the positive or negative extensions of the axis). He says,

> On the positive side it is concerned in various ways with warmth, liking/caring, and 'being drawn toward', all in the context of responsive feelings for the other as another self like oneself. It does not encompass very close, passionate feeling (as of romantic love), or attitudes which do not imply interactive relationships . . . On the negative side, feelings of extreme aversion (except for contempt) or of anger to the point of rage, are not encompassed. No item points to feelings that allude to fear of the other (1986, pp. 440–1).

The unconditionality component of UPR for Barrett-Lennard,

> . . . was interpreted literally . . . with the focus being on *conditional* variation of regard . . . more precisely, regard is conditional to the extent that it is contingent

on, or triggered by, particular behaviors, attitudes, or (perceived) qualities of the regarded person . . . Regard (whether generally high or low in level) that is strongly unconditional is stable, in the sense that it is not experienced as varying with or otherwise dependently linked to particular attributes of the person being regarded (p. 443).

Barrett-Lennard's measures have been influential on the course of exploration of Rogers' hypotheses. They made it possible to launch the empirical examination of Rogers' theoretical predictions.

Factor analytic studies of the Relationship Inventory seemed to confirm that there were indeed meaningfully distinct relationship conditions useful to characterize therapeutic relationships. Other studies showed these conditions to be generally positively associated with therapeutic outcome. Gurman (1977) concluded:

Barrett-Lennard's (1962) stress on the two distinct aspects of regard — the level of regard and the unconditionality of regard — appears to be justified in light of the nine studies reviewed . . .[and] *it appears that the RI is tapping dimensions that are quite consistent with Barrett-Lennard's original work on the inventory* (p. 513) . . . *there exists substantial, if not overwhelming, evidence in support of the hypothesized relationship between patient-perceived therapeutic conditions and outcome in individual psychotherapy and counseling.* (p. 523, italics in the original).

Distinguishing regard as activity from unconditionality and positivity

The Relationship Inventory makes no distinction between the *activity* which is the first meaning in the American Heritage Dictionary for 'regard' ('to look at attentively; observe closely') and the valence associated with the regard (Lewin, 1935). I want to distinguish the activity of regarding, the act of 'looking at attentively', from its attributes: positive or negative, conditional or unconditional. Just as a skier has modes of skiing with different attributes (racing to maximize speed vs. cruising down the hill for sightseeing, for example), with their respective activity subsets (different positions over the skis, different types of turning), there are different modes of regarding. My goal is to further clarify the activity subset inherent to the mode of regarding which can be unconditional and positive.

Lietaer, who did some of the factor analytic work referred to above, later wrote a chapter on UPR (Lietaer, 1984). Some of his comments are suggestive of activities essential to this kind of regarding:

. . . congruence and acceptance are thought to be closely related to one another; they are parts of a more basic attitude of 'openness' (Truax and Carkhuff, [1967] p. 504): Openness toward myself (congruence) and openness toward the other (unconditional acceptance). The more I accept myself and am able to be present in a comfortable way with everything that bubbles up in me, without fear or defense, the more I can be receptive to everything that lives in my client (p. 44).

Thus achieving openness to oneself and to the other is one activity we need to understand.

113

Lietaer also makes the distinction between client experience and client behavior, which is useful when congruence seems to conflict with UPR. He says unconditionality is to the client's *experience,* the acceptance and understanding of which is necessary to enable the client to 'explore the deeper needs underlying this experience'. Elaborating further, he says,

> It remains important that [the client] can express and discuss everything that she experiences with respect to me, without my becoming reluctant or rejecting her as a person; but with regard to her behavior, I do confront her with my limits. *'Unconditionality,' then, means that I keep on valuing the deeper core of the person, what she basically is and can become* (ibid. p. 47).

Two more interrelated regarding activities are involved here: one is to manage my reactions which sometimes arise while interacting with a client (like the need to keep my limits, or the impulse to withdraw or strike back when hurt) so as to avoid rejecting or abandoning the client. The other is maintaining a broad sense of and respect and caring for the whole client as a person even when an aspect of the client's presentation is something I disagree with or which challenges me personally.

THE OBJECT OF UNCONDITIONAL POSITIVE REGARD

This invites first a clarification of what it is in another person (or ourselves) which we can regard in an unconditionally positive way: what is meant by the 'deeper core' or 'deeper underlying needs' that could have a positive valence for the therapist even when conflicts or value differences may exist between client and therapist?

Wilkins (2000) reiterated that what we regard unconditionally must be very inclusive: we must accept *all* the parts of the client's feelings and experiencing, including *even the part(s) that may be uninterested in changing* (p. 27).

Wilkins also cites Bozarth as one who considers UPR to be 'the curative factor of (person-centred) theory' (p. 29). Rogers' theory of pathology emphasizes UPR's capacity to restore the even more basic (but thwarted) actualizing tendency inherent in the client (Bozarth, 2001a).

Bozarth (2001b) says the healing that he has witnessed in people he has worked with came not from his *doing* anything in particular as therapist, nor from the clients looking deeply into their experiencing, but from the clients pursuing their own unique steps of growth, which varied greatly from client to client. He points to the trustworthiness of something originating in the client that moves them to constructive action. However, we must be cautious about assuming people will act constructively. This could be mistaken if a person were emotionally upset and acting out of only certain parts of experience without the benefit of reflection and therapeutic interaction. As Bozarth's examples illustrate, the trustworthy thing that moves the client to constructive action happens in the context of (or as the result of) a relationship providing UPR and empathy so that the client finds that particular urge to act that has enough subtlety and nuance to take into account the various parts and perspectives comprising the client's experiencing.

Interactive processes rather than thing-like objects

Part of the challenge in enacting UPR is to correct for our tendency to 'see' things as fixed entities. The idea of a 'self-concept' invites an image of a relatively consistent identity. UPR conceived as a relationship characteristic similarly emphasizes sameness over time. 'Incongruence' readily invokes a notion of established contents of experience which are perceived with distortion to maintain a fixed self-concept. In a human being, very little is actually so fixed and unchanging.

Gendlin's philosophical work (Gendlin, 2000) and its practical counterparts are enormously helpful for thinking about human processes that involve interaction and change. Theories are built on a foundation of basic (often unexamined) assumptions. One common assumption is that there is an empty three-dimensional space that can be marked off in equal units of measurement within which reality exists. Similarly, for many theories, time with equal intervals is taken as a given fact. It is within this geometric space and time that events and phenomena are thought to take place and be observed. This starting point powerfully promotes our tendency to construe reality as composed of separate objects with parts that can be disassembled and reassembled and that work together mechanically. A disadvantage which comes with thinking this way is that it makes it more difficult to see and understand phenomena that aren't naturally so thing-like. Although we might very well be able to understand how to build bridges and computers with concepts like these, human feelings and interactions are not so amenable to understanding with concepts that suggest they are like atoms or bricks: fixed units that can be combined into larger units to make other things, or broken down into component parts. Part of the difficulty in identifying the object of UPR is that such philosophical assumptions get us looking for a relatively static, thing-like object. But if we really look clearly at the client, what we see is not thing-like.

Gendlin starts instead with living interaction processes as the basic given (linear time and geometric space are derived later in his theory as special case by-products of living interactions, so he does not lose the advantages of those ideas). From this different starting point he develops ideas early in his theory that are much more naturally suited to the life processes we as therapists and students of human behavior would like to understand. I cannot give a serious treatment of his theory in the context of this paper, but the interested reader will find it beneficial to read *A Process Model* (Gendlin, 2000) carefully.

A few key ideas may help the reader gain appreciation of Gendlin's way of thinking and help us answer the question at hand. An important feature of many life processes is that they are cyclical. An example is eating, which includes locating food, preparing it, chewing, digesting, absorbing water and nutrients, and eliminating wastes. This sequence repeats again and again. Such cycles are called 'functional cycles'. The elements of the cycle working together serve an essential function in maintaining the living process.

Each step in such a cycle implies the next step, and all the others, in an intricate order that cannot be rearranged arbitrarily if the function of the cycle is to be served. The status of the body at a given step in the sequence is such that

115

immediate felt sensory experience implies the next step in the sequence. In the functional cycle of breathing, for example, lungs after inhaling produce a very specific set of sensations which imply exhalation.

When an aspect of environment needed to further a functional cycle is missing, the process is 'stopped' in that regard. The body carries such a stoppage with it in how the remaining (not stopped) processes go on differently because of the stopped one. A starving person walks in and looks at the environment differently than a satiated one. In this way the body itself 'knows' what is needed: what isn't right and what would resolve the dilemma is implied in the sensations of the tissues of all the ongoing interrelated processes, by how they are changed by the stoppage. This 'implying' of the body is a central concept in Gendlin's model.

Bodily implying is very intricately determined by many interwoven processes and only certain things will allow the stopped process to proceed properly. And yet what will allow the process to proceed is open-ended in many ways, so that numerous variations in the environment could carry the stopped process forward. When it happens, any one of these variations is a special occurrence which changes the bodily implying in just the way it needs to be changed for the functional cycle to be served. Other occurrences, although they may affect the body, fail to enable the process to properly proceed, and the implying remains active in the body. When the special events occur which change the process as it implied itself changed, the process is said to be 'carried forward'. Note that this carrying forward of a process that was stopped requires no mental reflection or cognition.

The bodily felt sense

Much later in Gendlin's development of terms, when he has built up to the level of the conscious human being, the person who attends (with unconditional positive self-regard) to the bodily implying of a stopped process is said to be focusing on his or her 'bodily felt sense'. It is the bodily felt sense which can be trusted to move the client to do things that are in the direction of healthy, satisfying further living. Thus, bodily felt sense is Gendlin's carefully fashioned term closely related to, but more specific than the actualizing tendency with its long history in client-centered thought. You might notice immediately that even the basic words suggest a subtle difference: the actualizing tendency connotes a general thrust of the organism toward furthering its ends and capacities. The bodily felt sense refers to the body's remarkable capacity, on a given occasion, under specific circumstances, to register as one holistic sense all relevant considerations and influences from the personal past and the external circumstances which comprise the meaning of the situation.

For the purpose of this article on UPR, I offer the bodily felt sense as something to which we can hold an attitude of unconditional positive regard. The bodily felt sense is implicitly complex, not always present to the client's awareness, and may take some time working in special circumstances (UPR and empathy) to form. It hearkens to other places and people and times in its associated emotions and thoughts. It tends to keep changing.

116

When a bodily felt sense forms, it is a trustworthy source of constructive action from within the client. Prior to the formation of a bodily felt sense, the person may be under the influence of some parts of experiencing and lack the balanced perspective that takes all relevant considerations into account. Action in that condition is not so trustworthy. A bodily felt sense is not something simply physical inside the person: it is not less than the person, but is rather the person's fullest sensitivity to everything that matters about the situation to the person, with the person in a centered relationship to this complexity.

The formation of a felt sense is coincident with the person developing a certain attitude toward his or her experiencing in all its facets. We can say the formation of a felt sense involves the person having a certain relationship to the manifold of emotions, thoughts, physical sensations, etc. involved at that moment. Now we proceed to clarify the kind of relationship to self-experience which helps form and carry forward a bodily felt sense.

RELATING TO EXPERIENCING IN UNCONDITIONAL POSITIVE REGARD

How does one open to one's experiencing and then manage what one finds in the openness?

The empirical results already cited support the utility of construing relationship conditions as Barrett-Lennard did: as phenomena of intermediate duration, neither momentary events nor personality traits of the therapist. Thus we can think of level of positive regard as a variable useful for scaling relationships for their differing amounts of this quality. Therapists and types of therapy can also be compared with each other on such a variable.

But this is not the level we need for thinking about how to improve the level of UPR in a given relationship, nor to think about how to improve a given therapist's capacity to have UPR for clients. All relationships, whether high or low on their typical levels of positive regard, would have some moments in which they are not at their respective maxima. As noted earlier, Rogers recognized variability in unconditional positive regard as part of how things are for effective therapists, and that the idea that an effective therapist never wavers from full positive regard was misleading. What can help us think about how one makes the momentary move into the mode of unconditional positive regard?

Momentary enactments of unconditional positive regard

To answer this question, we need to focus our attention on momentary events rather than the typical or average levels which the RI is designed to assess.

The question is obviously pertinent to novice therapists who would like to become more skilful. But even for seasoned therapists it is relevant, as one may on some occasions find what a client is saying more difficult to accept than usual. It may be that the relationships with more unconditionality of positive regard at the level assessed by the Relationship Inventory are in fact those in which the participant(s) are especially adept at this movement, able to recover quickly from the loss of positive regard, or to quickly arrive at positive regard from neutrality

117

or from having one's attention elsewhere. Without ways to turn on or recover positive regard when it is absent or lost, one would have no way to improve one's average level of positive regard in a relationship. Momentary movements from lower to higher levels of positive regard are also necessary for transitions from the activities of other modes of regard (such as giving instructions, or diagnosing) into the mode which can be unconditionally positive.

When the movement from less to more positive regard occurs, it is something that happens in interaction with a specific person presenting specific life experiences, thoughts and feelings on a specific occasion. Thus, following Gendlin's way of thinking, positive regarding and its communication are therapist activities responsive to the client's bodily felt sense which have special power to carry forward stopped process aspects. [1]

Many writers cited above have suggested that the therapist's capacity for unconditional self-regard is a factor limiting the therapist's capacity to provide UPR for clients. And a goal of providing a client with UPR is to build the client's capacity for unconditional self-regard. So let's start by asking how, for oneself, one moves into the mode of unconditional positive regard. In the study of Focusing (Gendlin, 1969, 1981, 1996), much has been written related to this question. Focusing is Gendlin's practical method for carrying forward one's bodily felt sense. The ways one acts toward and reacts to one's experiencing are essential to how one does this.

Focusing attitudes and activities

In his early writing about focusing, Gendlin (1978) described several common tendencies to relate to experiencing which seem to be less than optimal for carrying it forward. Some of these are 'belittling the problem', 'analyzing', '"facing down" the feeling', 'lecturing yourself', and 'drowning in the feeling'. These activities were described to clarify what *not* to do. The focusing instructions offered alternatives: one was to quietly wait and sense what came in experiencing. Another thing that was emphasized was that when a feeling begins to come 'DO NOT GO INSIDE IT. Stand back, say "Yes, that's there. I can feel that, there."' (1978, p. 48). If the feeling, when focused on, begins to change, one is instructed to follow the feeling and pay attention to it. Much emphasis is placed on going gently and easily with oneself, and on patiently seeking fresh, new words and pictures for what one is experiencing, rather than accepting familiar or commonplace explanations and interpretations that may come to mind very quickly. A key emphasis is placed on finding words or pictures expressive of experiencing which 'make some fresh difference' and on letting 'words and pictures change until they feel just right in capturing your feeling' (ibid. p. 49).

In discussing how the therapist can work with her own experiencing of a therapy interaction to keep it genuine and fresh, Gendlin described a move from minor incongruence to congruence:

---

1. Iberg (2001) has been developing post-session instruments to measure the relationship to experiencing which occurred during a single therapy session. These measures, especially the 'opening' and the 'focusing attitude' sub scales, are more appropriate than the RI for assessing momentary enactments of unconditional positive self-regard by the client.

One is usually turned away from such feelings [of being confused and pained, thrown off stride, put in a spot without a good way out], and in the habit of ignoring them. I have gradually learned to turn toward any such sense of embarrassment, stuckness, puzzledness or insincerity which I may feel. By 'turn toward it', I mean that I don't let it simply be the way I feel, but I make it into something I am looking at, from which I can get information about this moment (Gendlin, 1968, p. 223).

Cornell (1996) suggested a term for one key part of what Gendlin described, which is 'disidentification.' She says of this move,

> The essence of disidentification is to …move from 'I am [this feeling]' to 'I have [this feeling]'. In most cases, disidentification can be facilitated simply with empathic listening or reflection, in which the therapist adds phrases like 'a part of you' or 'a place in you' or 'something in you' (p. 4).

Wiltschko (1995) has discussed the same idea in terms of the 'I' which is distinct from all contents of experiencing.

Cornell (1996) also articulates three other 'inner relationship' techniques: 'acknowledging' what's there, 'resonating', and 'sensing from its point of view'. These three distil out essential features of what Gendlin described in detail in the movements intended to guide someone through a focusing process (Gendlin, 1981).

Acknowledging what is there involves just that: acknowledging without evaluating or selecting (note how this is a refrain of the quote from Rogers at the beginning of this paper for the 'unconditional' part of UPR). In addition to noticing each aspect of your experience, Cornell adds emphasis on *making some gesture of acknowledgment*, like 'saying hello' or saying, 'I know you are there' to each aspect of your feelings. Cornell has also discussed this in terms of 'Presence':

> Presence is what we call that state of non-judgmental awareness which can give company to any part of us . . . we reserve the word 'I' for Presence, as in 'I'm sensing something in me that wants to tell him to go to hell' . . .
>
> Most of the time, all you need to move into Presence is to acknowledge both [or all] parts using Presence language: 'I'm sensing that something in me wants to tell him to go to hell, and another part of me that's not so sure about that.' 'I'm acknowledging the part of me that's wanting to go back to school and the part of me that feels like it's a big change.' 'I'm aware of the part of me that wants to find the right person and the part of me that feels like giving up.'
>
> Presence needs to be maintained through the whole process; it's not just something you can attend to once and forget about. So if you find yourself judging or taking sides or trying to determine who is 'right', you have lost Presence and you need to find it again (Cornell, 2000).

Resonating 'is checking whether a word, or other symbol, or a larger unit of meaning, fits how the felt sense feels . . . in order to do it, the Focuser must be in direct contact with the felt sense, with a neutral observer (i.e. non-victim) perspective' (Cornell, 1996, p. 4).

Sensing from its point of view:

> . . . is a powerful and empowering move, when the client is able to shift from

her point of view (which may be 'overwhelmed' or 'victim') to the felt sense's point of view. This brings in the possibility of empathy and compassion. The aspect of self which has the capacity for empathy and compassion is not a victim (p. 5).

Collecting activities productive of unconditional positive regard

The foregoing includes a strong emphasis on the importance of moving from identified to disidentified. Cornell, a linguist, helps us see how language can be chosen carefully to elicit and support this move. She also sharpens activity-oriented terminology for acknowledging what's there, resonating, and sensing from its point of view. Another important point Cornell makes is that these things require ongoing maintenance during the time we wish to be unconditionally positive in our regard.

In another paper (Iberg, 1996), I abstracted six variables involved in the range of possible focusing experiences (Table 2, p. 28). These variables cover much of the same ground (and a bit more), and they suggest prompts for activities which may help at the times in which one finds it difficult to 'disidentify' from some aspects of experiencing, or when one has been unable to find action that is carrying forward.

1. *Seek enough safety to be able to feel things in your body:* The situation in which one does therapy must feel safe enough to allow the formation of a bodily sense of experiencing, which has a certain vulnerability to it. When a bodily felt sense forms, one leaves the everyday mental realm of the familiar, clearly known, and enters a more murky, unclear, unknown but pregnant-with-personal-meaning inner territory. What makes a situation safe enough includes your internal requirements from personal history, your preferences, the pressures you put on yourself, as well as the external environment, which may be too loud, judgmental, too bright, smelly, crowded, or in other ways unsatisfactory to you.

Activity prompt: You could check and see if things are arranged okay for you in the room. Do we need to make some adjustments to make you feel comfortable and safe?

Another prompt: You could notice if there is anything making you feel unsafe.

2. *Make complexity explicit:* One may need to further articulate the complexity, internal or external, in one's situation. Until all important intricacies of one's experiencing have been acknowledged, it may not be possible to disidentify. Unnoticed or ignored parts can keep us off balance until they get noticed.

Activity prompt: You might ask yourself if there is something more to this that is feeling left out or neglected.

3. *Seek congruence between words and experiencing:* Sometimes we have internalized rules for what it is okay to feel and think. We may not immediately notice the filtering effect of such rules on what we can readily acknowledge in our feelings.

Activity prompt: Please check and see if there is any nervousness about what you might discover or reveal about yourself.

We may also simply be sloppy at times about the accuracy of words for our feelings.

Activity prompt: You might take a moment to see if in any way you feel dissatisfied with what we've said so far.

4. *Find the witnessing perspective:* This refers to the same idea as disidentification. The alternative to witnessing is being identified with some part of our experience.

Activity prompt: Please check and see if you are able to observe what you feel with non-evaluative interest. Notice and acknowledge any evaluative reactions you are having to the things you feel and have talked about.

5. *Let go of rigid control:* There is a natural tendency to cling to the things we are used to, especially ways of thinking and being that have served us well. But to open to experiencing we need to surrender a degree of control, so what is fresh and new can accurately emerge and not be fit only roughly into old symbols (Gendlin, 1981, 1996; Campbell and McMahon, 1985, especially the chapter 'Humor, Playfulness, and Surprise').

Activity prompt: You might check to see if there is anything in you that needs reassurance that we won't go too fast or be reckless.

6. *Transcend your personal stake in the issue:* The detachment from one's personal rewards and interests that Rogers spoke of (see 'Regard' on page 2) is a generous perspective. It lacks pride and possessiveness. It involves viewing a person as a complicated human being worthy of honor and respect. A certain humility about the extent of one's knowing fosters openness to experiencing. In contrast, self-assuredness and self-centeredness tend to be defensive and threatening to the other and to parts of ourselves. Opening to one's experiencing is facilitated when one's attachments and ego-interests become part of what one senses from the witnessing position, rather than those being the perspective with which one is identified.

Activity prompt: Notice if any part of you feels disdain or contempt for someone else in the situation you are working on.

Another prompt: Notice if any part of you feels oppressed by someone else.

Another prompt: Notice if you feel any need to protect your interests from attack.

Self as the beholder of bodily intelligence

One theme we see running through all the preceding is that we seek to foster an expansive, inclusive experience of self, open to experiencing without distortion. In focusing, we observe how becoming open to experiencing involves a qualitative change in the experience of the body: when one is able to have an attitude of presence toward a bodily felt sense, one's physical body seems to 'open up' almost like a delicate flower blossom. One's sensitivity increases so that one can feel and think about many interconnected emotions and meanings with ease and without bias for some feelings in favor of others. When this qualitative change occurs, the

121

implying body reveals much wisdom to the person.

Part of what resolves with this qualitative shift is the *identification with any set self-concept*. By a disciplined practice of mindfully (Santorelli, 1999) examining experience from a disidentified distance, one learns over time that one is more than any symbolized part of awareness, and that one can rest in the witnessing process, rather than in the contents of experiences, patterns of behavior, or in familiar ways of understanding oneself (self-images, personae). The witnessing process can give a respectful, friendly hearing to *all* the various parts of one's experience, even when they conflict with each other. One can find security in this content-free form of continuity. The security grows as, over time, one accumulates experiences which demonstrate one's organismic wisdom at dealing with situations that are highly complex and difficult from the perspective of the 'me'.

What we can regard in an unconditionally positive way is the person situated in the witnessing position in relation to the whole complex interwoven set of processes his or her implying-body is. Out of this intrapersonal relationship (which almost always happens more easily in an empathic interpersonal situation), we repeatedly see healthy forward living emerge. This emergence of forward living is not mainly conceptual, nor does it require psychological sophistication in terms of introspective insight (although that often comes as a welcome bonus). When an interaction helps one find a step that carries forward, it is likely to be taken, conceptual insight or not.

CODA: 'ENJOYABLE BEAUTY' AS A MODEL FOR UNCONDITIONAL POSITIVE REGARD

I will close by likening UPR to the experience of enjoyable beauty. I do this in hopes of giving the reader an experiential referent with which to grasp and organize the preceding complexity. All of us have experienced enjoyable beauty.

Mortimer Adler (Adler, 1981) distinguished 'enjoyable beauty' from 'admirable beauty', the latter of which requires expertise to fully appreciate. In contrast, any person can experience enjoyable beauty. He wrote a separate chapter for each kind of beauty. I find what Adler has to say about enjoyable beauty remarkably relevant to UPR.

Adler starts with a definition articulated by Thomas Aquinas in the 1200s: 'The beautiful is that which pleases us upon being seen', Adler further specifies several aspects of the meaning of this definition.

Beauty pleases us — in enjoyable beauty this refers to the obvious way, when our desires or appetites are met, we *feel satisfied*. It is a direct experience of satisfaction, not dependent on reasons or justifications. This pleasure can be quite strong or intense: we might say we are 'moved'. For example, when I saw the ice dance performance by Torvil and Dean televised in the 1984 Olympics, I could detect no clumsy movements, and they seemed perfectly coordinated with each other and the music. When, again precisely in time with the music, on the last note they fell gracefully but forcefully to the ice to end their routine, I was moved to cry, stand and cheer, and applaud. My emotions and body were quite literally and directly moved without requiring expertise on my part regarding the fine points of ice dancing.

Adler goes on to say the pleasure of experiencing enjoyable beauty involves simply *seeing* the object — the kind of pleasure which is non-possessive and non-controlling. This is in contrast to the pleasure involved in eating, drinking, buying something, or having health or wealth, which all please us when we *consume* them, *possess* them, or *control* them. Rather, the pleasure of enjoyable beauty is 'disinterested' in that we are content to contemplate or behold the object, rather than needing to possess or control it. For example, being pleased by the beauty of a picture in an art museum does not require the acquisition of the painting or any control over or alteration of it. This clearly echoes the comments of Rogers and many other writers about the attitude of a person experiencing UPR.

Adler notes that perceiving enjoyable beauty involves seeing in more than a visual way — we can easily grasp that it involves more than the visual sense. It involves beholding, or apprehending with the mind as well. As in the example of a near perfect execution of an athletic or musical performance, the visual sense is much involved, but we certainly use more of our capacities to perceive the beauty. It may involve timing and coordination of movement, the musicality of the object, and a sense of the whole of the performance as a gestalt. The mind brings together apprehension of a range of possibilities and input from various senses within the context of which we 'see' the current one.

Another example of non-visual apprehending is when we perceive that the course of action persons take requires the courage of their convictions: in spite of risking costly personal consequences, they decide to do what they consider to be morally right. What we apprehend is more than what we can see in their immediate behavior or statements. An inspiring source of examples of this kind of beautiful living is the film *Weapons of the Spirit* by Pierre Sauvage, which is about the residents of a small village in France who sheltered 5000 Jewish children during World War II with full knowledge of the fact that neighboring villages had been burned to the ground when suspected of doing similar things. The mind provides a context of relevant experiences within which the beauty of what we see comes into relief.

How the mind is involved — Adler insists that a further qualification deserves emphasis in this kind of 'seeing', since we normally associate the mind with concepts and thinking. But the kind of mental apprehending involved in enjoyable beauty is *devoid of concepts* in the way they are usually used. Enjoyable beauty does *not* involve regarding the object as an example of a 'kind' or 'type' or member of a category. Rather, the object is regarded as a unique individual, for and in itself alone, appreciated in its rich, individual detail. The similarity to the openness that has been described as essential for UPR, requiring acceptance of all the parts of a person's experiencing, is striking. Acceptance is, in large part, looking in an open, non-categorizing way.

I believe these features of the experience of enjoyable beauty apply nearly completely to the activity subset for the mode of unconditional positive regard. The one additional element that we had not already seen in the discussion of UPR is the idea that there is a personally moving kind of satisfaction in perceiving enjoyable beauty. From my personal experience in working as a therapist, and in personal relationships where I have been able to be present with UPR, I have often experienced being moved by a sense of the beauty before me. Santorelli has also noted this somewhat paradoxical fact: when we stay closely and non-judgmentally with someone exploring pain, we find beauty in the midst of the 'ruins' (Santorelli, 1999).

To witness someone carry feelings and actions forward on a matter about which the person has been troubled is, for me, a moving experience: one witnesses intricate complexity of motives, reasoning, and emotions which, when fully taken into account, make perfect sense of the person's reactions and dilemma. We see emerge in the midst of this complexity the person's genuine 'positive strivings' (Gendlin, 1968): perhaps an intense desire to be a good parent or partner or child, or a moral or ethical sense of the right thing to do. We might witness the person rise above a previously egocentric perspective on an interpersonal matter and become more empathic to the perspective of the other, as the result of more fully honoring the complex mesh of his or her own experiencing. To glimpse these things in another person is often for me, and I suspect for many, an experience of enjoyable beauty. This is a partial answer to a question often asked of therapists: 'how can you stand to listen to people's problems all day?'

Thus, here is my simpler answer to the question of how to *do* the activities of UPR: seek the enjoyable beauty in the person you regard. To do this, (1) do not attempt to control or change the person; (2) use all your senses plus your conceptual grasp of the full range of possibilities to understand; (3) maintain a non-categorizing mentality, attending to the full rich detail rather than thinking of categories into which to fit things, and (4) allow yourself to be moved by what you behold.

Persons we regard for their beauty in this way are likely to welcome our help to find the witnessing position from which they can tap the wisdom in their complex bodily senses of situations. This promises to lead to their discovery of exactly what is needed to bring them into fuller and better living.

REFERENCES

Adler, M. (1981). *Six Great Ideas*. New York: Macmillan.

Barrett-Lennard, G. T. (1959). *Dimensions of Perceived Therapist Response Related to Therapeutic Change*. Unpublished Doctoral Dissertation, University of Chicago.

Barrett-Lennard, G. T. (1962). Dimensions of therapist response as causal factors in therapeutic change. *Psychological Monographs, 76*, (43, Whole No. 562).

Barrett-Lennard, G. T. (1986). The Relationship Inventory Now: Issues and Advances in Theory, Method, and Use. In L. Greenberg and W. Pinsof (Eds.), *The Psychotherapeutic Process: A Research Handbook*. New York: Guilford.

Bozarth, J. D. (2001a). Personal communication, July, 2001.

Bozarth, J. D. (2001b). Forty years of dialogue with the Rogerian hypothesis. Available at http://personcentered.com/dialogue.htm.

Campbell, P. A. and McMahon, E.M. (1985). *Bio-Spirituality: Focusing as a Way to Grow*, Chicago: Loyola University Press.

Cornell, A. W. (2000). Monday, August 21, 4:25 pm on Focusing-discuss@focusing.org

Cornell, A. W. (1996). Relationship = Distance + Connection: A comparison of Inner Relationship Techniques to Finding Distance Techniques in Focusing. *The Folio: a Journal for Focusing and Experiential Therapy, 15*, 1, pp. 1–8.

Gendlin, E.T. (2000). *A Process Model.* Available at http://www.focusing.org/philosophy.

Gendlin, E.T. (1996). *Focusing-Oriented Psychotherapy: A Manual of the Experiential Method.* New York: The Guilford Press.

Gendlin, E.T. (1981). *Focusing (2nd Ed.).* New York: Bantam.

Gendlin, E.T. (1978). *Focusing.* New York: Everest House.

Gendlin, E.T. (1969). Focusing. *Psychotherapy: Theory, Research, and Practice,* 6, pp. 4–15.

Gendlin, E.T. (1968). The experiential response. In E. Hammer (Ed.). *Use of Interpretation in Treatment.* New York: Grune and Stratton.

Gurman, A. S. (1977). The Patient's Perception of the Therapeutic Relationship, in A. S. Gurman and A. M. Razin (Eds.), *Effective Psychotherapy: A Handbook of Research.* Pergamon Press: New York.

Iberg, J.R. (2001). Focusing-Oriented Session Report. Available at <http://www.experiential-researchers.org/instruments/iberg/fsr.html>.

Iberg, J.R. (1996). Finding the body's next step: Ingredients and hindrances. *The Folio: a Journal for Focusing and Experiential Therapy,* 15, 1, pp. 13–42.

Lewin, K. (1935). *A Dynamic Theory of Personality: Selected Papers.* New York: McGraw-Hill.

Lietaer, G. (1984). Unconditional positive regard: A controversial basic attitude in client-centered therapy. In R. Levant and J. Shlien (Eds.) *Client-Centered Therapy and the Person-Centered Approach: New Directions in Theory , Research, and Practice.* New York: Praeger.

Rogers, C.R. (1957). The necessary and sufficient conditions of therapeutic personality change. *Journal of Consulting Psychology,* 21, p. 95–103.

Rogers, C.R. (1959). A theory of therapy, personality, and interpersonal relationships as developed in the client-centered framework. Reprinted in H. Kirschenbaum and V. Henderson (Eds.) *The Carl Rogers Reader* (1989). Boston: Houghton Mifflin.

Santorelli, S. (1999). *Heal thy Self: Lessons on Mindfulness in Medicine.* New York: Bell Tower.

Truax, C. and Carkhuff, R. (1967). The client-centered process as viewed by other therapists. In C.R. Rogers, E.T. Gendlin, D.J. Kiesler, and C. B. Truax (Eds.), *The Therapeutic Relationship and its Impact: A Study of Psychotherapy with Schizophrenics.* Madison: University of Wisconsin Press.

Wilkins, P. (2000). Unconditional positive regard reconsidered. *British Journal of Guidance and Counselling,* 28, 1, pp. 23–36.

Wiltschko, J. (1995). Focusing therapy. *Focusing Bibliothek* special issue. Würtzburg, Germany: Deutsches Ausbildungsinstitut für Focusing und Focusing-therapie.

Appreciation

I appreciate the Monday Vasavada group I attend in many ways, but in particular because when I was writing this paper I became identified with a notion that I was responsible for what to say about Unconditional Positive Regard. This got me stuck. The group helped me disidentify from this notion, and the writing then flowed better. Thanks to Fred Schenck, Sally Iberg, Jan Doleys, and Jerold Bozarth for their very helpful comments on earlier versions of the manuscript. I also feel grateful to Drs. Eugene Gendlin and Arwind Vasavada for their guidance, inspiration, and abundant supplies of Unconditional Positive Regard even though they also responded often and strongly in other modes. Finally and fundamentally, I am grateful to Bob and Irene Iberg, my parents, for their consistently positive regard as they nurtured and supported me into adulthood.

11 An Experiential Version of Unconditional Positive Regard

Marion H. Hendricks[1]

My client is an elderly gentleman in his seventies. He has been talking about how good he felt on his vacation, which he would like to keep. It is unusual for him to feel good, rather than depressed, fearful and angry. I feel pleased and then disappointed. I fall into a very un-client-centered exchange.

C: *What was so special about being at the retreat center, is I had a number of people who said to me in one way or another, 'John, you are of some value'.*

T: *So that good feeling has to do with being in relation with other people who feel you as valuable.*

C: *(angrily) Well, that's a dead end.*

T: *No, don't do that. Don't collapse.*

C: *There is nothing here (in New York) for me . . . not relationships.*

T: *(impatiently) If that's what you need, then the next thing is to sense how do you get that for yourself?*

C: *(Silence) Well, I guess I see it as just some kind of lovely vacation away from my usual self.*

My client's good feeling disappears into an angry, hopeless emotion. He does not now let a felt sense form in his body of relating with others who find him valuable. He only knows that such relating *did* feel good during his vacation. He short-circuits letting his body feel that now, because he doesn't see any concrete way it could happen now in his life. He does not know that staying with a felt sense of what would be right opens situations and some step may then form or become possible. He predefines any positive step as impossible. I feel frustrated that he continually creates 'dead ends'.

He goes on to tell me why he can't pursue what he needs. He says he can't be sure that any move he might make would work out.

T: *Right, there is no guarantee, but that doesn't mean you don't pursue where you feel openings for your life.*

C: *(Sigh) To do that you have to be interested in your life.*

T: *Right.*

C: *You have to care for yourself. I think I am quite deficient there.*

1. I thank my colleague Dr Akira Ikemi, Kobe University, Japan for his initial collaboration and on-going comments.

He sounds resigned, angry. Again, no sense forms in him of what he might do from here, or how he might work with this. He has defined this inability to care about his life as his central problem many times. The manner in which he does this makes it another 'dead end'.

He feels angry and depressed and I feel frustrated and angry too. I am firing directives at him: 'Don't do that. Do this.' This is certainly not an interaction characterized by Unconditional Positive Regard (UPR)! My client is attacking himself, and I am attacking him. He insists that he has no capacity for change. We are both angry. I definitely don't feel prizing and warm towards him. I wish to change him so that he will care for himself.

As client-centered therapists, we all know how we want to feel towards our clients — prizing, valuing without any conditions. '. . . a warm, positive and acceptant attitude toward what is in the client . . .' 'not simply accept the client when he is behaving in certain ways and disapprove of him when he behaves in other ways . . . outgoing positive feelings without reservations, without evaluations' (Rogers, 1961 p. 62). We all wish to feel this way. But how does it come about that one does so? UPR isn't something we can simply 'decide' to feel.

FIRST PROBLEM: UPR AS A 'POSITION'

How do I prize and feel warmly towards someone who is repetitively angry, stuck, depressed, cannot process his feelings and attacks me for not changing him? I can deny 'negative' feelings, in order to feel only prizing and warmly towards my client. I can 'have' UPR but not be congruent or I can be congruent and not prize my client. This is the tension between therapist congruence and therapist UPR, which has been discussed for years.

In practice, we have ways to meet this problem which may seem to be UPR, but are not. We may commit ourselves to the *position* that we value our client no matter what. We do this by remaining unaffected by clients in any upsetting way. We 'value' them 'no matter what', as if who they are or what they do doesn't affect us. We maintain our even-toned 'care'. We say to ourselves, 'My client is doing the best she can.' Or, 'I care about you, but I don't like your behavior.' We may 'remain empathic' in order to move away from our negative emotions, putting us in an incongruent state. We try not to become disturbed, angry or feel disgusted.

On the other hand, in our close life relationships, we often feel anger, fear, disgust. We wish our spouse or our children would change, so that they or we will feel better or so they will better fit our needs. Experiencing the 'otherness' of close people is terribly annoying. Because they are the way they are, we don't get what we need. The cat cries and wakes me up at night. My husband likes the temperature boiling hot, whereas I can't sleep unless the room is cool. I am frightened and furious that my teenage daughter likes to go to Manhattan night- clubs.

We don't often have 'negative' feelings with our clients, partly because what they do or experience does not impact so strongly on our own lives. We go home after the hour; maybe we think of them and feel concern, but they are not centrally important to our sense of well-being. But the definition of UPR cannot rest on this relative distance of their lives from ours. *It will be one thesis of this paper that UPR is not a prizing that depends on this distance.* If UPR depended on distance, we could never have such an interaction with our close people. Something we are not capable of with our loved ones, cannot be what UPR means with our clients. There is a more genuine, deeper kind of UPR that doesn't depend on this insulated, 'hothouse' effect.

We need a definition of UPR that encompasses the whole range of feelings. *There is a kind of UPR in which I might well feel anger, disgust, disapproval towards my clients.* This sounds impossible by definition, but I will develop a concept of UPR in which we needn't constrict the range of our response to the client. This may help solve the problem of the contradiction between UPR and congruence.

SECOND PROBLEM: I CARE ABOUT YOU BUT I DON'T KNOW YOU

My mother loves me. She always will, no matter what I might do. She would do anything she could to help me. She has provided unwavering stability in the background of my life. This sounds like UPR. Her care is unconditional. However, I do not feel prized by my mother.

Positive regard is not something we feel without really knowing a particular person. My mother does not know who I am. My mother has 'UPR' for 'her daughter', no matter who that might be. UPR is not a permanent positive feeling for 'my clients', apart from a particular person actually in interaction with me at a given moment.

UPR arises in a particular interaction and it is not well understood as a pre-defined 'attitude' on the part of the therapist. The problem is when the care arises from an abstraction, rather than out of really knowing the client. Holding any predefined position interferes with knowing the actual person. 'In order to accept a person you must clearly know him or her. Therefore, accurate empathy can be seen as the main vehicle for building acceptance and positive regard . . . Now that I really know you, I can also accept you' (Braaten 1998).

While empathy is a way we really know someone, I distinguish the warmth within an empathic interaction from UPR. In empathy, we experience how it is to be the client, as though we were she. In a sense, we put ourselves aside, except to allow the client's experience to register in us, as it is for her. We feel the sense that the client's experience makes, as well as feelings of care. Even if the contents being dealt with are painful, angry, sad, this manner of process feels good in the client and therapist. In an empathic interaction we do not form judgments, and thus rarely feel negative emotions. There is a large sense of warmth and connection. Perhaps Rogers meant this warmth as being UPR. But I believe equating the warm feeling in empathy with UPR gives rise to the seeming contradiction between congruence and UPR. In a UPR interaction, we do not put ourselves aside, and we may feel negative emotions.

THIRD PROBLEM: I WANT MY CLIENT TO CHANGE

Most clients come to us because they want change. We all wish change for a person who is suffering, so she will suffer less. And yet, our concept of UPR seems to require that we look away from our wish for change. The concept of UPR I will develop can encompass our wish that change would happen, rather than forcing us to pretend that we don't want this.

To summarize these three problems:
- UPR seems to contradict congruence when we have 'negative' emotions in response to the client.
- 'Valuing' clients may come from a formula or definition rather than arising in an interaction.
- We have to pretend that we do not want change for our clients.

I will develop an experiential version of UPR that will help with these problems.

THINKING AT THE EDGE (TAE)[1]

The TAE procedure for experiential theory-building can be found on the Focusing website (www.focusing.org). It has 14 steps, some of which I will show here. In experiential theory-building we start from what we 'know' in experience and cannot yet say. We go beyond preconceived ideas and begin freshly from our unique felt sense of what we know. I will use the TAE process to articulate my felt sense of UPR. I have many years of experience as a client-centered therapist from which to speak. Using this method, I will make new distinctions that should give us more ways to speak about UPR and to have UPR interactions.

Let a felt sense form

Rather than starting with what other people have written or said about UPR, I bring my attention into my body and ask inside, 'What do *I* know about this whole thing about UPR?' I wait and let a sense form in my body of all that I know about UPR. This is bodily felt and does not yet have words. This is a felt sense.

Then the TAE procedure asks me to write a rough first sentence that says my felt sense of UPR. I let words emerge directly from my felt sense.

UPR is an interaction in which I feel that I and the other person are perfect, exactly as we are, and I have no wish to change myself or the other.

You can notice that my felt sense seems to exclude negative emotions (the first problem), relates to the unique person, rather than to a role (the second problem), and involves no wish to change myself or the client (the third problem).

Next I collect an example of when I actually experienced this sense of UPR. I felt UPR for my daughter recently. She said to me, 'This is just the way I am — joyful, anxious, smart, obsessive, crazy. This isn't caused by some hidden trauma, which, if I found it, would make everything fine. This is just who I am.' I felt upset. I focused on why I was upset. It seemed to me, by calling herself 'obsessive' and 'crazy', she was defining herself in boxes/concepts. This puts her out of touch with who she really is. As I articulated this, I realized *I* was defining her, through what she said, and that I didn't need to, because, for me, there is no such thing as boxes. Then I felt that she is completely perfect exactly as she is and that I could

---

1. See appendix A

129

never wish to change her in any way.

Now we have my beginning sentence about UPR and an example of it. If you would like to, you could find your own particular sense of UPR, write a sentence and find an example.

No words fit; any words fit

A next step in TAE is to find what exceeds logic in your 'knowing' and cannot be said in the usual terms. Then you write a paradoxical sentence that captures this illogic.

> UPR is an interaction in which I feel that I and my client are perfect in our imperfection, right now.

The TAE method rests on a certain relationship between language and a felt sense. If we look at the public meaning of the words we are using, we can see that we don't mean exactly what they say. We experience, 'That's not what I mean!' Then we must return to our unique felt sense and further articulate what we do mean. By 'perfect', I don't mean the dictionary definition of living up to some ideal standard. So I must return to my felt sense and say, 'Well then what do I mean?' Now a new phrase comes from my felt sense. I mean that a person is inherently a kind of '*flow or motion*'.

Now we again see if we mean the usual definition of this second phase. By motion I don't mean moving from one location to the other. I mean a kind of openness that *exceeds any definition*. But by that I don't mean formless or vague. The openness I mean is a feeling that I can take in the other person without any barriers. There are *no obstructions*. I feel in a *joyful thickness* with the other person.

Now we have an expanded sentence about UPR:

> UPR is an interaction in which I and my client are perfect, in motion, exceeding definitions, no obstructions . . . and I feel in a joyful thickness and don't wish to change her or myself in any way.

We already begin to have more language with which to speak about UPR.

Expanding what each word means by writing fresh, linguistically unusual sentences

The point in this first phase of TAE is to generate fresh language that cannot be understood in old concepts. Since we are trying to say something from our own particular knowing, which can never be identical to someone else's knowing, we need a fresh use of language. The usual meanings of words are not likely to convey our new knowing. These steps are fun to do. A great richness comes.

I go further into my felt sense of my knowing about UPR. I go back to each phrase or word I used above and let it now bring out from my felt sense, new and odd sentences, which can surprise even me, but which feel like what I 'mean' by UPR. I find I want to say: by 'exceeding definitions', I mean that a person is a *vast textured aliveness*, always *inherently untwisting*.

Now I have a new phrase, 'inherently untwisting', This is not a phrase that has a public meaning. It probably cannot be understood, but at least it will not be taken to mean some commonly defined idea. Now I can continue to ask into my felt sense what I mean by 'inherently untwisting'.

By 'inherently untwisting' I mean a *spiral movement of turning backwards into itself in such a way that it comes back out in its own forward motion*. Then there is no obstruction.

By 'unobstructed' I mean there are no *discrete shapes* (definitions) between which there would be gaps which can't be gotten over. There is *no gap or hole* in existence.

Again, these sentences do not make much sense in the public language. Just because they don't, they can begin to bring a new intricacy from my knowing of UPR. Each of these sentences checks out with my body felt sense: 'Yes, that is what I mean.'

By 'not defined' (discrete shapes) I mean not trapping our clients in a concept. Definitions hold you suspended within themselves, *stopping growth*. By defining, I mean *standing at a distance* from myself or another and imposing a concept, a fixed shape or pattern. I make the client into an instance of a concept and then *relate to the 'meanings' of that concept*. I proceed from the concept, rather than remaining in the interaction. I *'empty out'* the person and end up with a set of meanings. *Definitions twist people into shapes that constrain inherently untwisting.*

Collect facets

The next step is to collect facets. Facets include anything that relates to the felt sense of the 'knowing' you are tracking. They include times when it came up, what someone said that related to it, any incidents that relate to it, even if we cannot tell ourselves why they are relevant. One reason we collect facets is because any instance is superior to a higher order generalization. When you have a generalization there is nothing further inside it. An instance has specificity. Any real life event has complex structure. It can answer a question.

Here are two facets that have in them the experience of what I 'know' UPR to be:

- Another client says that he is struggling to let himself be as depressed as he feels right now in the session, rather than covering it up to himself or to me, in order to be acceptable. He says that he wants to be as he is rather than performing. I notice how welcoming I feel towards both his 'depressed' experience and his struggle to let himself be seen by me. I have an image of my husband and his 'depressed' moods. I have always had difficulty with them. Suddenly I feel an overwhelming love for him, exactly as he is. I love him *in his depressedness.* I feel that if he had been different, even by one iota, the universe would have suffered an irreparable loss. A life is such a big thing, a mystery, that one can only feel awed. This was a moment of what I mean by UPR.
- I have a client who has what I mean by UPR for herself and others. She says, '*I don't have to do anything.* I don't have to know what is next. *I don't need to erect boundaries to protect myself.*' She doesn't manipulate her own or anyone else's experience.

These are two facets of my 'knowing' about UPR.

Some terms in which to talk about UPR

After some more TAE steps, not shown here, I end up with terms that are logically and inherently linked in a sentence. Each of my main words and phrases has been linked with all the others. By the processes of logic, I can then substitute any one term for another and generate sentences, some of which will say more about UPR than I started with in my felt sense.

You can see in the Table below my main terms for talking about UPR — *Inherently Untwisting, Definitions (fixed shapes), and Not Protecting* — and some of the detail that is built into each term. The first two sentences are examples of linking sentences between my terms, which define a UPR interaction.

CENTRAL SENTENCES GENERATED BY INTERLOCKED AND INHERENTLY CONNECTED TERMS

*When I don't **define** myself or my client, our interaction is **inherently untwisting**.*
　　Terms: definitions and inherently untwisting.

*When I am **not protecting** myself, the interaction is **inherently untwisting***
　　Terms: not protecting and inherently untwisting

OTHER PHRASES LINKED INTO THE TERMS

INHERENTLY UNTWISTING INVOLVES:

　　turning back into itself to come out with its own forward movement
　　joyful-thickness
　　a vast expanse of textured aliveness
　　sadness, anger, hate ... untwisting by themselves
　　unobstructed existence (no gaps between fixed shapes)

DEFINITIONS (FIXED SHAPES) INVOLVE:

　　standing at a distance and imposing a fixed pattern
　　trying to change myself or another by rearranging the person from the
　　　　outside
　　disconnecting us from ourselves and the other person
　　twisting people by putting them into fixed patterns
　　making people into categories and sets of meanings
　　a person is inherently not contacted from a distance

NOT PROTECTING INVOLVES:

　　not doing
　　not standing at a distance
　　untwisting happening by itself
　　crossing, interaffecting, being changed by each other
　　felt sensing; connecting to the flow of experience

MY EXPERIENTIAL VERSION OF UPR

Now we can use these experientially derived and logically linked terms to talk about UPR.

UPR is an interaction in which people inherently untwist by not protecting themselves with definitions. They exceed definitions, and participate in a joyful, thick, textured aliveness.

Definitions block UPR

As I said earlier, defining means that we stand at a distance from our client and relate to a concept. We drop out the person. As client-centered therapists we know the violence it is to a person to be considered an instance of a category, whether it is diagnostic or interpretive. When we define someone, we trap them and ourselves in a discrete explicit entity or form.

Let us return to the session with which we began this chapter. This is a few minutes later. Both my client and I are still angry and stuck.

C: *Well, I felt at the retreat center that people were kind to me. I don't feel that here, in the city. (Sigh) I don't know how to get out of this thing. To have lived with my mother for so many years. To have been totally ignored, in a way that YOU (angry) have never understood. As Tony said to me, 'your mother did the worst possible thing. She didn't hate you, she made you hate yourself.'*

He and I have been here many times. He does not differentiate further from this point. If I respond to this content about his mother in any way — reflecting, asking about it, being receptively silent, trying to empathically feel what that must have been like, he gets agitated and depressed. After such a session, he may not sleep well for several days and will take medication to calm himself. This is another dead end. Feeling exasperated, I think to myself, 'You lived with the lady for 17 years and without her for 58 years! Can't we get on from here!'

Why am I angry at my client? What has happened in our interaction? *He has defined himself and I have accepted his definition of himself:* 'I am a person who will always hate myself.' He is standing at a distance from his experience and defining himself in terms of a pattern, rather than sensing his whole situation, which included a new openness he felt during his vacation. I feel thrown out of interaction with him by this definition. If he is only a pattern, how can I care for him? I feel as if there is no one there to relate to. In a UPR interaction, I would not feel his self-hating as a fixed shape. In a UPR interaction, I would prize the 'him' that is also partly *in his self-hating.* I was not able to do this.

I joined him in looking at himself from a distance. He disconnected from his experience, and I disconnected from his experience. We are both seeing him through a pattern. I have also become disconnected from my own on-going experience of him. He became static and flat *to me.*

My client is also standing at a distance from me. I feel unvalued by him. He is angry at me because I have not changed him, and because I have not understood his experience. It is true that I don't know how to change him and that I don't understand his experience. He is defining me as someone who should understand

and should know how to change him. He has often said to me, '*I* don't know how to change my self-hate. *You* should know how to change that. Isn't that what being a therapist means?' *He has put me into a definition,* '*the therapist who should but does not help him*'. When he does this, he is not in interaction with me. I feel wiped out as a person.

Trapped in definitions, my client and I want to control and change each other. I want him to stop short-circuiting his untwisting by always claiming, 'Because of my mother, I cannot change.' He wants me to be a 'better therapist' and change him! We are not in interaction. We are each relating to our definitions of the other.

UPR is a particular interaction, not an unchanging attitude

Our usual definition of UPR seems to say that we should not feel positively sometimes and negatively sometimes in response to our clients. This variation is commonly called 'conditions of worth'. If I feel positively about a client when she is discussing B, but disturbed when she discusses A, my regard is said to be 'conditional'. The 'positive' side of this response is not the 'positive' that Rogers intended in UPR, because it is to only certain client traits or behavior. The intended meaning of UPR is that 'positive' regard does not depend on *any* definable way the client is being. I am trying to show a way that this becomes possible. UPR involves staying with the flow of experience, even if we see things which we would define negatively or positively. To stay with the flow of experience, rather than patterns, is to remain in interaction.

UPR is not a trait which a therapist 'has'

UPR is a particular kind of interaction which does not always happen. Interaction *means* not standing at a distance, not categorizing or judging the client. Judging is an assignment of fixed shapes and takes us out of interaction. Because UPR is a kind of interaction, rather than a property of the therapist, it is sometimes present and sometimes not, depending on the particular interaction. If I demand UPR from myself as an automatic trait, then I am standing at a distance, outside of myself. I am trapped in my definition that a therapist should experience UPR. I put away my experience, thereby becoming unavailable for the kind of interaction I am defining as being really UPR. It is empirical whether UPR will arise in any particular interaction or not. It becomes important to ask how a UPR interaction arises.

If we stay in the flow of experience, we don't need to protect ourselves

When we lose the flow of experience and have only a definition, then we need to protect ourselves from the meanings of the definition. When my daughter said, 'I am obsessive,' I took that as defining her. I felt scared. I disconnected from her and felt only the *meanings of the definition*. The meanings scared me. I 'emptied her out' by relating to meanings instead of a person. I am standing at a distance, unavailable for interaction. I am enclosed in the definition and the definition generates emotions in me. Definitions can generate positive emotions as well as negative ones. These also are not a UPR interaction. When we don't lose the flow of experience, then we don't need to protect ourselves from the meanings of definitions and we become available to interact in a UPR manner.

Not defining is not just an absence. How do we not define? Or how do we let go of definitions we have made? We can directly refer to the on-going flow of experience at any moment by bringing our attention into the body and sensing, 'how is this whole thing for me right now?' By this simple move we stop defining our experience. We directly enter a sense of intricacy and complexity, which does not yet even have words. By asking internally into this complexity the body stirs, responds and moves. This movement is life inherently untwisting. After many experiences of this untwisting, a bodily knowledge develops that definitions and emotions need not be taken as opaque entities like stones. When we move from the empty pattern to our sense of the texture in the pattern, then we experience that it is in the nature of patterns, taken as texture, to arise and untwist. *It is because a felt sense exceeds definitions and emotions, that a UPR interaction can include definitions and emotions.*

The capacity to perceive definitional patterns is a unique human power. Patterns are involved in all typically human acts and productions and are inherent in any experience. The felt sense comes after this capacity, not before it. The vast texture does not wipe away any definition, but always exceeds any definition and also any emotion. It is because a felt sense exceeds definitions and emotions, that a UPR interaction can include definitions and emotions.

Emotions untwist by themselves in a UPR interaction

What is twisted, stuck, painful has implicit movement. There is even a sense in which the twisted gives rise to untwisting. Untwisting inheres in twistedness. From inside the vast texture, emotions like sadness, anger, fear are simply part of the person being perfect exactly as she is right now. If it were possible to displace these painful emotions, other than by untwisting, the untwisting that inheres in them would be lost and there would be a loss or a hole in creation.

When I felt UPR for my husband, it wasn't that I no longer saw or had reactions to his depressed moods. In the moment of UPR, I felt them quite clearly, and still didn't like them, but I loved him exactly as he is — which includes his depressed moods. We can't, and would not wish to parcel out what we will include as being *this* person.

However, to say that a person is perfect in her painful emotions, does not mean that we white-wash suffering. It is always right to alleviate suffering. I remember my daughter saying to me when she was about 12 years old, 'Mommy, it used to be if I were scared you could make it all go away. Now you can't anymore.' It was right to 'make it all go away' when I could. In our early interaction, her fears untwisted and her body relaxed. Later, her body knew when some different way of dealing with her painful feelings became right.

When a person is outside of a UPR interaction, emotional pain seems to be a fixed shape. Within a UPR interaction, we experience that painful emotions come and go on their own, as part of the vast texture of aliveness. This inherent untwisting is 'wiser' than any manipulation from the outside.

A UPR interaction is in the texture of aliveness

What happens if we don't define ourselves or our clients? That which is more than definitions appears. This 'more' is a vast texture of aliveness which, without exception, exceeds any definition at any point. It includes verbal exchange and even definitions, but it is a vast, inexhaustible texture. It is not that we are lost in this vast texture. It is rather that *the vast texture is this person.* This person is irreplaceably different than any other person, not because of any content. *The content is different because it is generated by her texture.* So even if we say the exact same words, or both feel the same emotions, as soon as we go further we are immediately different. I am also a vast texture. The crossing[2] of two 'more than defined' people, from both sides, generates possibilities that cannot ever be predefined.

I am here deriving the non-directiveness of client-centered therapy. I can offer an additional understanding of what non-directiveness actually is. It is not that we never suggest something to a client or answer a question. The content of a specific UPR interaction can never be prescribed. To hold to any particular form of behavior (e.g. reflecting, not answering a question) on the basis of theory is to define, rather than to be in the vast texture. *Rather than being a particular behavior, non-directiveness is our deep bodily recognition that anything we can know (define) about the client does not limit what can happen.*

THE PHILOSOPHY OF THE IMPLICIT: A NEW KIND OF CONCEPT

Shifting to a philosophical level, I will point to a new kind of concept that is being used here. The TAE process I used to build an experiential theory of UPR is the process which was used to generate 'A Process Model' and other writings on the 'Philosophy of The Implicit' (Gendlin, www.focusing.org). This kind of concept-making was entwined in Rogers' re-formulation of client-centered therapy. (Rogers, 1959, 1961, pp. 183–99). Client-centered therapy has been difficult to convey to colleagues because its basic approach to therapy and people is so different and there are not commonly understood concepts with which to explain it. It has been accused of being simple, but, on the contrary, it expresses a new more complex paradigm badly needed today. We can use concepts from 'A Process Model' to communicate and further articulate client-centered therapy. I will briefly discuss one relevant concept.

Interaction-first concepts

Interaction-first concepts start with the assumption that, in some sense, body and environment are one.

---

2. ' . . . you affect me and with me you are not just yourself as usual either. You and I happening together make us immediately different than we usually are. Just as my foot cannot be the locking kind of foot pressure in water. We occur differently when we are the environments of each other. How you are when you affect me is already affected by me and not by me as I usually am, but by me as I occur with you' (Gendlin, 1997 p.33).

> Body and environment are one event, one process. It is air-coming-into-lungs.
> We can view this event as air (coming in) or as lungs (a coming into). Either
> way it is one event, viewed as environment or as body. Here we are not calling
> it 'environment' because it is all around, but because it participates within the
> life process. And, 'body' is not just the lungs, but the lungs expanding. Air
> coming in and lungs expanding cannot be separate. We need not split between
> the lungs and air' (Gendlin, 1997, p. 1).

Even though lungs and air do not look alike, internal to the behavior of breathing,
they are one.

In this philosophy any defined entity or anything fixed is the product of a
process. It takes a special kind of process to keep something the same over and
over. This reverses the order in which we usually think. We usually start from
separated entities and then see them acting upon each other.

Breathing is an example at a most basic, physiological level. At a more complex
level, the body and the situation/environment are one in behavior.

> When an animal hears a noise, many situations and behaviors will be implicit
> in its sense of the noise, places to run to, types of predators, careful steps,
> soundless moves, turning to fight, many whole sequences of behavior (Gendlin,
> 1997, p. 7).

When we come to the human level, our body-situation interaction includes
language, emotions, cultural routines, other people, the past, the future and vastly
more. Even our breathing is affected by our 'situational', not just our physical
environment. Humans have a capacity to form a 'bodily felt sense' of our
situations. We can become able to refer directly to this sense, in which our bodies
and our situations are one process.

I used an interaction-first concept when I said that UPR is not an attitude
inside the therapist; it is, rather, an interaction. To say UPR is an attitude in the
therapist, which the client may or may not perceive, assumes that we first have
two separated entities: a therapist, inside of whom there is an 'attitude', and in a
different location a client who may or may not 'perceive' this attitude. Then we
have the problem of getting these separated entities in contact with each other.
I reversed this when i defined UPR as a new kind of interaction which makes
new participants. A UPR relationship can make for therapeutic change because
it is a process, not a trait of the therapist. This interaction re-creates the two
individuals. Because both people are involved in a *single* interaction, the quality
of the process necessarily changes how the client experiences herself. She now
experiences herself as she is with the therapist who is experiencing her.

To say that the client might not perceive the therapist's UPR or prizing attitude
assumes that these prizing feelings are entities inside the therapist, rather than a
kind of interaction. *This implies that the client's experience of the therapist is not
part of the therapist's UPR.* Rather than thinking of the therapist attitude as a
content in the therapist and rather than thinking of the client's feelings as
'contents' which the therapist has warm feelings about, we can clarify the
situation. 'Warm feelings' are interactions. In a UPR interaction the vast texture
determines the feeling quality beyond the fixed contents.

137

REFERENCES

Braaten, L. (1989). A person-centred perspective on leadership and team-building. In Thorne, B. and Lambers, E. (Eds.) *Person-Centred Therapy: A European Perspective*, London: Sage.

Gendlin, E.T. (1981). *Focusing* (second edition. New revised instructions). New York: Bantam Books.

Gendlin, E.T. (1996). *Focusing-Oriented Psychotherapy. A Manual of the Experiential Method*. New York: Guilford.

Gendlin, E.T. (1997). *A Process Model*, Spring Valley: The Focusing Institute. www.focusing.org

Gendlin, E.T. (2001). An introduction to thinking at the edge, www.focusing.org

Hendricks, M. (2001). Focusing-Oriented/Experiential Psychotherapy: Research and Practice in Cain, D. and Seeman, J. (Eds.) *Handbook of Research and Practice in Humanistic Psychotherapies*, Washington D.C.: American Psychological Association.

Rogers, C.R. 1959 A theory of therapy, personality and interpersonal relationships as developed in client-centered framework in S. Koch, (Ed.) *Psychology: A Study of a Science, Vol. 3. Formulations of the Person and the Social Context*. New York: McGraw-Hill Book Company.

Rogers, C.R. (1961). *On Becoming A Person*. Boston: Houghton Mifflin.

Weiser Cornell, A. (1996). *The Power of Focusing*. Oakland, California: New Harbinger Publications.

APPENDIX 1

TAE STEPS	HOW TO DO THE TAE STEPS
Steps 1–5 Words from the felt sense	**Steps 1–5 Words from the felt sense**
1 Let a felt sense form • Choose something you 'know' and cannot yet say, that wants to be said. Write it down in a few paragraphs in a very rough way.	*1 Let a felt sense form* • Choose something you care about, something you are tracking but cannot well say. It needs to be in a field in which you are knowledgeable and experienced. Do not start with a question, but with something that you 'know.'
• **Have this knowing as a distinct felt sense to which you can always return.** Write that in one sentence, even though the sentence doesn't really say it. Underline one key word or phrase in the sentence.	• Let yourself form the whole felt sense of this. What in this do you 'know' and wish to articulate? Sense what is live **for you** in it. And within this, again, what is the live point **for you** in it? When you sense this central crux, write a single rough sentence.
• Think of one instance, example, or time when it actually happened. Write that instance down.	• You need a specific example, an event that actually happened, which exemplifies your felt sense of knowing.
2 Non-logical • Be particularly attentive to anything that does not make the usual logical sense.	*2 Non-logical* • What is new about something can seem quite illogical. This may be the most valuable part. Please assure yourself that you are not dropping this out.

• If it helps, write a paradox .

• To help you to hold on to what seems illogical, you can write a paradoxical sentence, for example something is 'x' and also not 'x'. If this is not helpful, skip this step.

3 No words fit

• Take out the key word from your sentence in Step 1. Write the usual (dictionary) definition of the word and notice that it is not what you meant.

• Return to your felt sense and let another word come to say what you mean. Write the usual definition of the second word.

• Return to your felt sense and let a third word come. Write the usual definition of the third word.

• **Accept the fact that there is no established word or phrase for that knowing.**

3 No words fit

• Building theory is partly to communicate. Therefore we consider the public meanings of the words. If you are saying something new, none of the words in their usual meanings will say it exactly.

• Take the underlined key word (or phrase) which carries your central meaning. Think of its usual public meaning. Look it up in the dictionary if you like. You recognize, 'that's not what I meant'.

• Let a second word come from the felt sense to say what you do mean. Make sure it is not just a synonym, but a word with a somewhat different meaning.

• When you consider its public meaning, you see that the second word does not fit either.

• Let a third word come from the felt sense. Again its public meaning is not what you meant.

• Now you have written down the three words and their ordinary definitions.

• No word fits. None should, if this is new.

4 Any word fits

• **Now let the first word speak from your felt sense after all. Let yourself feel THIS in your sentence.**

• Do this with the second word. Do this with the third word.

• Write a sentence that articulates exactly what the first word pulls out from your felt sense (which the other two do not).

• Do this with the second and third word.

4 Any word fits

• You are now keenly aware that these three words do not say what you mean. Take the first word and insist that in this sentence it does speak from your felt sense. The sentence can make the word change. This time, do not give up your sense. Do not let the word say what it usually says. **Wait until you feel this whole sentence speaking from your felt sense, in a way,** even though most people might not understand it so.

• Go back and forth between your meaning and the usual meaning, until both have become familiar to you.

• So far all this was private, just inside you.

• Now for each word write a sentence to say what that word means in this sentence when it speaks from your felt sense.

• Now you have three sentences, one for what each of the three words means when it speaks from your felt sense.

5. Expanding what each word brings out by writing fresh linguistically unusual sentences

• For each of the three, write a fresh, somewhat wild sentence which expands what you mean. Phrase the sentence so that it makes no sense unless it means what you mean. Then it cannot be misunderstood.

• Underline the new details which each of the three sentences brings out.

• Now string all three sets of details into the slot in your original sentence.

5. Expanding what each word brings out by writing fresh linguistically unusual sentences

• Check your three sentences from Step 4. If you already have fresh new phrases, very different from a usual use of words, you can skip this step.

• Check whether you used any major public words. If so make fresh phrases to replace those.

• Let your felt sense express itself into fresh language. Use sentences that make no sense unless they are understood as you mean them. If you let your felt sense speak directly, something linguistically unusual can come.

• Here are examples of linguistically unusual sentences: 'Knowing the rules is a container from which new ways open'. 'Definitions stop cellular growth'. 'Behavior shows something it has'.

• Each item says something from your original felt sense.

• Make one long string of these three meanings of the three words (omitting the words themselves). Fit this long string in where the underlined key word appeared in your original sentence.

• Play with the grammar and order, and eliminate excess words until you have a sentence you like. Now you have a sentence with more elaboration to say what you are tracking.

Steps 6–8 Facets

6. Collect Facets

• Collect facets (incidents, any kind of examples).

• Choose three facets and write them. Include the details which relate to your felt sense.

• Also copy your original facet from step one here.

Steps 6–8 Facets

6. Collect Facets

• A facet does not need to illustrate all of your felt sense. Include anything that relates to the felt sense of the 'knowing' you are tracking. Include times when it came up, what someone said that related to it, any incidents that relate to it, even if you cannot tell yourself why they are relevant. Do not omit odd or private things such as 'the time the dentist said . . .'

• Do not include general ideas or metaphors. (It isn't an actual example to say 'it's like heating something to agitate it'. It could be an example, if you say 'that time when I heated the . . .') Write three instances that actually happened.

• Any instance is superior to a higher order generalization When you have a generalization, you only have it. An instance has specificity. Any real life event has complex structure. It can answer a question.

7. Each facet contributes more detailed structure
• In each of the four facets, underline a specific pattern which this facet contributes.
• Using this pattern, write an odd sentence about each facet.
• Now underline the structural detail in each of the odd sentences.

8. Crossing the facets
• If it can help, 'cross' your facets. You ask: 'What does looking from the second facet let me see in the first facet, that I could not see just from within the first facet?'
• If crossing gave you new details, write sentences to capture each.

7. Each facet contributes more detailed structure
• Ask yourself in what way the facet is an example of what you are trying to articulate. All real events have 'structural details' that don't appear when we generalize. In an actual experience the relationships you are tracking have specific characteristics. Let each facet give you one new elaboration, a specific pattern which you did not have before. The 'structural detail' need not be central to your felt sense, but don't adopt anything that somehow lessens your felt sense.

8 Crossing the facets
• You might already have done this. 'Crossing' means trying out whether you can attribute to one what is true of the other. When the facets do not contain the whole central thing, looking at each through the other may expand them and give you what is additional structure for your central thing. Look at each through the other.

Steps 9–14 Theory

9. Write freely
• Freely write what you are now thinking, that comes out of this process.

10. Choose three terms and logically link them
• Choose three words or phrases other than your three original words to be your **main terms**. Decide which will be 'A', 'B' and 'C'. Put the three terms in a box.

• Now define A in terms of B, and also in terms of C. A = B. A = C. First write each

Steps 9–14 Theory

9. Write freely
• This is a free space to write anything you want.

10. Choose three terms and logically link them
• These three terms are your major notions. A term can be one word or a whole phrase. Each should bring a whole cluster along with it. Choose from among all the new entities you have differentiated.
• If you imagine a triangle connecting the three terms, **is your felt sense somewhere within the triangle?**
• Any other important things you may have thought of on the way, can wait until a later step. This step concerns only the central nucleus. Later you will expand it to cover more and more.
• If you are using a phrase as a term, keep the phrase the same for every occurrence

equation as an empty formula. You don't yet know what it might mean.

• Rewrite the sentence A=B, replacing the = sign with the word 'is'. Now consult your felt sense. Find the smallest change you can make on one or both sides of this sentence, so that the 'is' becomes true. (Always insure that you keep the crux of your felt sense.)

• **Do this also with the second sentence.**

11. Inherency
INHERENCY:
•Rewrite the 'A is B' sentence, adding the word 'inherently' after the word 'is' 'A is inherently B.'
• You do not as yet know what this might mean.
• Dip into the intricacy of the felt sense to find out why these two things are inherently connected. What is the very nature of 'A', such that it has to be 'B'?
• Do this also with the 'A = C' sentence.

• Reorder or change your two sentences to take account of the inherency and/or the reversal.

of that term from now on.
• Now define 'A' by using the second term, 'B', to tell about 'A'. This is a formula: A = B. Also define 'A' by using 'C': A = C. Write each equation out as a formula, even though you don't yet know what it might mean.
• The = sign means 'is' or 'are'. In a new sentence, where the = sign appears, write the word 'is' or 'are'. It means that you are saying that what is on the left side is (amounts to, can actually be) what is on the right side.
• If the sentence is grammatical and true, and speaks from your felt sense, let it stand. If not, keep the word 'is' (or 'are') and add or change whatever you need on either side, so that the assertion is true and also speaks from your felt sense. If it seems too inclusive, you can say 'some,' 'one kind' 'is at least'.
• You will need to return to your felt sense to find what you need to do to the sentence to make it true.
• If you added something to 'A' in the first sentence, you need to keep that in 'A' also in the second sentence.
• Now you have one true sentence that connects 'A' and 'B', and one that connects 'A' and 'C'.

11. Inherency
INHERENCY:
• Since 'A' and 'B' came from one felt sense, it will be the case that 'A' is inherently 'B', not only that it happens to be 'B'.
• This requires entering into the felt sense behind the two terms, so that you discover what each inherently is, so that it is already the other. Be sure that the illogical crux remains in the connections between the two. There has to be an 'Aha' about this. Of course! 'A' always was nothing but the sort of thing that has to be 'B'.
• Example 'A' (Free people) are 'B' (creative). This may be observably so. But, how is it inherently so? Human nature is inherently the sort of thing that is creative (changes the environment, makes new things), and to be free is to develop in accord with one's own nature. So, of course, being free inherently involves being creative.
• Rewrite your main 'A' is 'B' and 'A' is 'C' sentences, reordering or reorganizing them so that they take account of the inherency and/or the reversal.

12. The nucleus of your theory generates sentences

• Reword your A, B and C terms so that the inherency you developed in Step 11 is in the A term and in your sentences that connect A, B and C. Re-write your A=B, A=C and B=C sentences using the new A, B and C terms. From all the details you have so far, select those which are within or between the three main terms. Put your two sentences and your details in a box.

• Next take some of your further key words or phrases (for example what you under-lined in Steps 5 and 7) and define each one in relation to A, B or C. So you are setting up sentences like D=A, E=A, F=B, G=C. Wait each time, to see what sense the new sentence might make. Only then fix it to make it true. Be sure that the change you make keeps the crux of your felt sense.

• Now logically substitute terms to generate new sentences, which may surprise you and extend your theory in ways you did not initially have. These 'substitution' sentences are generated in the following way: If D=A and A=B, then D=B. The sentence D=B is new. Another example is: if F=B and B=C, then F=C.

12. The nucleus of your theory generates sentences

• Connect your main terms. Leave other details for later. You might have five kinds of details: Within 'A'. Within 'B'. Within 'C'. Between 'A' and 'B'.

• By substituting a detail in for a main term, you can generate a very large number of new sentences. Pick the details that seem most important to you, and put one of them into one of your two sentences instead of the term 'A', of 'B', or 'C', to generate a new sentence.

• When a new sentence seems quite wild or false, stay with it and pinpoint what is wrong with it, so that you can change the sentence to make it true without losing what was new and wild about it. Apply inherency where possible.

• For example, it may seem both ungrammatical and false to say that some detail from a very odd instance 'is' 'B'. But it can be exciting to rethink the nature of 'B'. Might 'B' have this odd patterning? How might that be true of 'B'? Then — aha! — it might suddenly emerge for you that this is indeed so! It might tell us more about the nature of 'B' than we knew before.

• By substituting you can make a great many logically correct new sentences which you can adjust according to the felt sense underneath them You become able to say more and more.

13. Large applications

• The odd structure of your terms can now serve as a 'model' for anything else. Your terms can bring their structure into any large area such as art, religion, education, art, metaphor.

• Choose either your AB or your AC sentence from inside the box at Step 12. Write it down with a blank in place of one of the terms.

• Choose any area outside your field. Substitute it into the blank in your sentence.

• Now wait for something about the topic to leap up, which makes it truly like that. Freely write what you are now thinking.

• You might want to choose something specific from that area to put in the blank, rather than the whole area.

13. Large applications

• What would come, if we apply **just your pattern** (not what it is about) to human nature, society, the state, groups, interpersonal relations, the physical sciences, truth, beauty, ethics, writing, sexuality, language, — any large idea?

• We know that the pattern you have articulated can happen in human experience. The pattern probably does not yet exist in the common language of our society. One tends to think about these Big Things with very poor simplistic spatial patterns. Therefore it is likely that your new pattern can bring out something important from such Big Things. These large things are unclear accumulations of much meaning and experience. The usual concepts about them are much poorer. Looking at a large thing through your theory, surely some

143

aspect of it will cross and reveal some way in which the large thing truly has, or should have, the pattern of your theory.

• Do not let fixed definitions or old ways of thinking limit what can be said about these large things. By applying your model, something new and further can leap out at you from all that you know of such a large thing. Although it can say something true, this is largely a playful move unless you happen to be an expert on the given topic. Then you could develop it.

14. Elaborate your theory in your original area of interest

• Stay within your field and apply your theory to any topics close to yours. Your theory is located near other matters in your field. List some of these related topics.

• As you bring up each related topic, let your theory restructure that. Let yourself have a felt sense of what is right or important in the related topic and cross it with (look at it through) one of your terms. Assert that A (the new topic) is structured like, or a special case of B (Your term). Write sentences about the sense in which this is true. You are **deriving** concepts for the related topics from your initial concepts.

• You can also go further into the felt sense under any term in your theory, and ask what are different kinds of A or different ways in which A happens.

14. Elaborate your theory in your original area of interest

• You can build the structure of your theory into any topic in your field. This is the serious development of your theory. It may continue for years. You can derive one or more new terms for the topic when it acquires the specificity that the rest of your theory can give it. In this way the theory can develop and elaborate itself indefinitely within your field.

• If you logically derive a sentence which does not seem true, go more deeply into your felt sense so that you can modify the assertion until it seems true. Introduce additional distinctions.

• Also if you add new distinctions to your theory where it keeps wanting them, then you may realize that you have derived certain topics in your field.

• People sometimes don't value their theory because they feel that it 'must be' what some older existing theory 'really means', if correctly understood. But the old theory alone does not give people this precise way. You are redefining its old terms with your precise concepts to give them this new precision.

• Your theory can be entirely new. We do not need to be afraid of new theories. We need them.

• The function of a theory is social. Being able to speak **precisely** about something lets us build it into the world in which we live.

Thinking At The Edge Eugene Gendlin, Ph.D.

12 Unconditional Positive Regard: The distinctive feature of Client-centred Therapy.

Elizabeth Freire

Rogers' theory of therapy and personality change states clearly that unconditional positive regard is the primary therapeutic healing agent (Rogers, 1959; Standal, 1954; Bozarth, 1998). This assertion strongly sets client-centered therapy as a unique and revolutionary approach in the field of psychotherapy. The other therapist's conditions postulated by Rogers, empathic understanding and genuineness, have been to some extent assimilated and incorporated by other therapeutic approaches. However, *the attitude of unconditional positive regard is the distinctive feature of client-centered therapy.* No other approach has assimilated nor understood the paradox posited by this attitude. The paradox of unconditional positive regard in Rogers' theory of personality is that a person must accept herself in order to change (Rogers, 1995). That is, the person must acquire unconditional positive self-regard: she must accept her basic organismic experiences to fulfil her growth potential (Bozarth, 2001; Rogers, 1959). This assumption underpins Rogers' theory of therapy that states that the therapist has to accept the client in order that the client may change. This relationship between 'accepting' and 'change' seems so illogical to most views that it begets strong resistance and negative reactions from the mainstream approaches. Common sense suggests that if a person wants to change himself, first of all he must strive to change. This common sense begets the common 'therapeutic sense' which assumes that *it is the therapist's task to do something in order to promote the client's change.* The therapist is supposed to join efforts with the client in his attempt to change. This assumption underpins the therapist's need for assessment and diagnosis. The therapist wants to evaluate and diagnose the client in order to know 'what' to change and 'how' to change the client's personality or behavior. The therapist is considered, within the conventional therapeutic model, to be the expert in psychological change. She has the power, the knowledge, the tools, the techniques, in short, the *expertise* that will afford the client to change.

In the face of this common and mostly invisible assumption, the client-centered approach emerges as a distinguishable and unique approach in the psychotherapeutic field. In opposition to the mainstream paradigm, the client-centered approach postulates that the therapist must unconditionally accept the person of the client. Therefore the client-centered therapist does not try to change the client. There is no goal to change the client. Client-centered therapy is not a problem-centered therapy (Bozarth, 1999). This assumption has been largely incomprehensible, misunderstood and unaccepted by other therapeutic approaches. Therefore, this paper aims to clarify and unfold this central axiom of client-centered therapy. The following client/therapist interaction is presented for this purpose.

A CLIENT-CENTERED INTERACTION: RITA

Rita was a 45 year-old housewife. She entered therapy because she had a fear of water. She would no longer drink water nor wash her head when taking a shower. Whenever doing so she had panic feelings as though she was going to die. Most therapists other than client-centered therapists would first diagnose her 'disease' as phobia and would make strategies to diminish the 'symptoms'. The therapist would take charge of the task of changing her behavior or 'symptoms'. The therapist would feel responsible for her behavioral change and would make efforts to promote her change. This is what is expected from 'common sense'. But I, as a client-centered therapist, did not try to change her. Quite the opposite, I accepted her unconditionally and this included acceptance of her behavior of water panic. When she came to therapy she was desperate and frightened. She blamed herself for not being able to control her fear and behavior. She was depressed and felt so powerless to change herself. She desperately wanted me to give her a magical response, which would discontinue her fear of water. She viewed me as a surgeon who could remove a tumor. She wanted me to resolve her problem for her. As a client-centered therapist I was with her in her desperation, guilt, depression and feeling of being powerless. I accepted all of these feelings. My acceptance was communicated by typical empathic understanding responses. I only 'walked' with her, following her self-direction, going with her at her own pace. I trusted her self-determination. I did not try to diminish her desperation, fear or powerless feelings. To the extent that I was fully present with her as she experienced these feelings, I accepted her feelings. It was never my intention to change her or her feelings. I was fully present with Rita in her personal struggle to grow. To me, her panic, her desperation and depression were acceptable parts of her.

After three sessions, Rita's behavior completely changed. Her panic and fear of water disappeared. However, she was then very depressed. She started to view herself in a quite different way. She questioned the way she previously dealt with her feelings. She realized that during her whole life she had been struggling to view herself as a very strong woman with no feelings of vulnerability nor fear. In this struggle, she realized that she had been denying her true feelings and emotions. She said that her 45 years of life were a 'total lie' to the extent that she had denied her own feelings of pain, hurt, vulnerability and dependency. Then, for about three months into our therapeutic sessions, she chose to explore these 'hidden' feelings of vulnerability and pain. It was indeed a difficult, painful and threatening experience. She would explore those feelings slowly and cautiously. She was afraid of losing control. I did not try to hurry, push or lead her to such self-exploration. I followed her at her own pace and direction through my empathic understanding responses.

After four months of therapy, she decided that she was ready to stop. She had deeply changed her personality. She opened herself to feelings of fear and vulnerability and discontinued to force herself to be so powerful and strong. Thereby, she became more open to others and improved the quality of her interpersonal relationships. Also, she reached the conclusion that she had 'transferred' her fear of painful feelings to the water. It was amazing that she decided this entirely by herself without any such discussion from me. She found her own answer by her own way.

What is important to note here is that I was able to accept her desperation and panic behavior because I trusted her. I trusted her actualizing tendency. *This primary trust in the actualizing tendency is critical since it underpins the therapist's attitude of unconditional positive regard towards the client. It is only with such trust that the therapist can experience unconditional positive regard towards the client.* This is discussed next.

TRUSTING AND ACCEPTING

The therapist's trust in the actualizing tendency underpins her experience of unconditional positive regard towards the client. The actualizing tendency is the foundation block of the client-centered approach (Bozarth and Brodley, 1991; Bozarth, 1998; Brodley, 1999; Rogers, 1963, 1980). It is the 'directional tendency inherent in the human organism — a tendency to grow, to develop, to realize its full potential' (Rogers, 1986, p. 127). Rogers' theory of personality posits that psychological maladjustment occurs when this organismic tendency is thwarted by introjected conditions of worth (Rogers, 1959). When unconditional positive self-regard replaces the introjected conditions of worth the actualizing tendency is released driving the individual towards positive, constructive and healthy directions. Thereby the client-centered therapist's commitment is to provide the therapeutic atmosphere that releases the client's actualizing tendency. It is not the therapist's intention to resolve immediate problems of the client's life. The therapist is committed to the promotion of the client's growth force. This assumption makes the unconditional acceptance of the client's experience the therapist's sole aim in client-centered therapy.

The therapist's trust in the client's self-direction and self-determination fosters her unconditional acceptance of the client's experience. The therapist's trust in the positive directional drive in each human being affords her to unconditionally accept the most painful, disrupted and dreadful client's experiences. *The greater the extent the therapist trusts the client's actualizing tendency, the greater her capacity to experience unconditional positive regard towards the client.*

The therapist does not easily attain this unfaltering trust of the client's growth-forces and self-determination. Most often therapists (even experienced client-centered therapists) tend to feel threatened by certain experiences of the client and thereby become conditional in their acceptance of the client. The therapist's conditional acceptance may be expressed through several attitudes according to the therapist's unique way of being. The two most common ways of being conditional is by taking the lead and providing support to the client. These are considered in the next section.

BEING CONDITIONAL

In order to clarify how a therapist may experience unconditional positive regard towards the client, one should consider the most common ways through which the therapist expresses *conditional positive regard* to the client.

Taking the lead

Whenever the therapist takes the lead in the therapist-client relationship, she is expressing that she does not accept the client's lead. The therapist may wish to take the lead for various reasons — mostly because she does not trust enough in the client's self-direction or because she is not willing to relinquish the locus of control in the relationship. When the therapist takes the lead, the client has the experience of not being unconditionally accepted. An example may illustrate this statement:

> *A therapist reported to me a therapeutic session with an 11 year-old boy. He told me that the 'problem' with the boy was that he was too timid and did not have friends. He showed me a picture drawn by the boy. It was a boat surrounded by water with four persons on it. The therapist told me that the boy had drawn only one person on the boat but the therapist asked him 'Is that guy alone?' The boy answered: 'No!' and proceeded to draw three more individuals on the boat. He reported that the new figures were the father, the mother and the brother of the individual in the first drawing. I asked the therapist why he questioned the boy in this way. He responded that since loneliness was a 'problem' to the boy, he wanted to help the boy explore this feeling.*

When the therapist asked the boy about the loneliness of the person in the picture, the boy experienced the question as disapproval. He perceived the therapist as not accepting the loneliness of the person in the picture. The fact is that the therapist was not accepting the boy's loneliness. It is likely that the boy did perceive the therapist's question as communicating his loneliness as not being an acceptable experience. In short, with this simple question, the therapist communicated a conditional positive regard towards the client.

Usually the therapist takes the lead through questioning the client from the therapist's own frame of reference as in this example. Most often, the questions that come from the therapist's frame of reference intend to lead the client's self-exploration to 'appropriate' directions selected by the therapist. Whenever selecting and suggesting directions to the client, the therapist is not trusting and accepting the client's own direction. This is one reason that non-directivity is considered a logical consequence and necessary corollary of person-centered theory (Bozarth, 2000; Brodley, 1999; Patterson, 2000).

Providing support

When the therapist does not trust the client's actualizing tendency, she may assume the responsibility for the client's growth. So, in face of any intense painful client's experience as dread, desperation and confusion, the therapist may not be able to maintain her unconditional acceptance of the client's experience. Even experienced client-centered therapists may feel their confidence threatened by intense client experiences and be led to provide support to him. Thereby it is not unusual for a therapist to be tempted to encourage a client who is quite frightened, or to give suggestions and explanations to a confused client, or to comfort a desperate client. However, such tutelary attitudes do express a therapist's conditional acceptance of the client's experience. Whenever the therapist encourages a client, she is not accepting the client's fear. Whenever the therapist enlightens, she is not accepting the client's confusion. Whenever the therapist comforts, she is not accepting the client's desperation.

THE THERAPIST'S UNCONDITIONAL POSITIVE SELF-REGARD

The therapist experiences unconditional positive regard towards the client to the extent that she experiences such unconditionality towards herself (Rogers, 1959). A therapist who is defensive, who is not open to her organismic experiencing is likely to feel threatened by certain client's experiences. The therapist's introjected conditions of worth cause her to be selective in her acceptance of the client. That is, the therapist's defensiveness prevents her from being fully open to the client's experience and thereby prevents her from experiencing unconditional positive regard towards the client.

Bozarth points out the inseparable relationship between the therapist's unconditional positive self-regard and the other therapeutic conditions:

> The relationship among the conditions results in a 'conditions loop' that manifests unconditional positive self-regard (UPSR) of the therapist. It is the therapist's UPSR that fosters congruence, unconditional positive regard and empathic understanding of the client's frame of reference. The therapeutic conditions are manifestations of the therapist's UPSR (Bozarth, 2001).

PUTTING THE THERAPIST'S SELF ASIDE

In order to be able to unconditionally accept the client's experience, the therapist must put her self aside. The therapist's self has values, needs, biases and expectations. All of these comprise the therapist's frame of reference and it must be put aside so that the therapist may be fully open to the client's frame of reference. The self acts like a filter selecting what is worthy and acceptable in the other individual's experience. Therefore, the therapist must take her self out of the client's way so that her values, needs, biases and expectations might not lead her to experience conditional acceptance of the client's experience (Rogers, 1951).

One of the most efficient ways for the therapist to keep her self aside is through the empathic understanding response process (Brodley, 1977, 1998). Empathic understanding responses help the therapist to keep her own frame of reference from interfering with the client's way. Such responses, therefore, facilitate the therapist to attain the attitude of unconditional positive regard towards the client.

BEING PRESENT

Rogers defined unconditional positive regard as a 'warm acceptance of each aspect of the client's experience as being part of that client' (Rogers, 1957, p. 98). It is worthwhile to analyze what 'warm' means here. It is likely that Rogers aimed to distinguish 'warm' acceptance from a 'cold' one. A cold acceptance would be a sort of indifference or neutral passivity. One may be led to think that when a therapist lays her self aside what would be left would be just a dead shell or a puppet without life. So, there must be something else in the therapist's attitude that provides such warm quality to her unconditional acceptance.

It is my thesis that the warmth expressed in the therapist's unconditional positive regard is the manifestation of the therapist's *presence*. I assert that as the therapist lays her self aside in her experiencing unconditional positive regard, she furthermore offers her *presence* to the client (Freire, 2000). Hence, it is the therapist's willingness to be present in the client's private world, going with the client, which distinguishes an unconditional warm acceptance from a mere cold indifference. That is, the therapist's *presence* into the client's world turns unconditional regard into unconditional *positive* regard:

> Yet the therapist's presence is not imposed. It is not that the therapist's self imposes itself into the relationship . . . The presence of the therapist comes through the *surrender*, through the therapist's dedication to the client's unique being (Freire, 2000, p. 51).

Similarly, Bozarth states that 'the essence of person-centered therapy is the therapist's dedication to going with the client's direction, at the client's pace, and in accordance with the client's unique way of being' (Bozarth, 1998, pp. 8–9). Hence, unconditional positive regard may be considered as the essence of person-centered therapy. The following vignette may illustrate the meaning of this kind of therapist's presence within the client-therapist relationship:

Diana

Her pediatrician referred Diana to psychotherapy. Her mother forwarded me a paper in which he wrote her diagnosis: 'hyperactivity'. Her mother claimed that Diana's behavior was unbearable since she was so extremely agitated. 'She does not stop!' were her words to describe Diana. Fortunately, the pediatrician did not prescribe psychiatric drugs to her. We met for therapy once a week for seven months. The first five months she acted similarly during the sessions. She took all of the small paint containers on the shelf and made a mess. Instead of painting, she mostly mixed the paint up, dirtying the table, the floor, her hands and clothes. Most often she even dirtied her face and hair. Unintentionally she would drop the paint's pot on the table or would lean her hair on the paint or lean her dirty hands on her clothes. In the beginning of each session, she would often say to me that she would not paint because her grandmother did not want her to dirty her clothes (Diana's grandmother was the person who took care of her while her mother was at work). But Diana always ended up painting and creating a great mess. She also left the room many times during the sessions. She would go to the bathroom in order to wash her hands or to wash the pots or cleaning-cloth or she would leave the room just to talk briefly with her grandmother who was in the waiting-room. She would say: 'Look grandma what I'm doing!' and show her a paper covered with paint or a paint pot full of water.

What was my experience with her during those sessions? First at all, I never looked at her agitated and awkward behavior as a 'symptom' of 'hyperactivity'. Actually I never looked at her as a 'hyperactive' child. I did not view her behavior as a 'problem' that I would have to resolve. I did not have the intention to change her or her behavior. Quite the opposite: my intention was 'only' to be with her. So, I accepted her behavior. The first time that she left the room, I was rather anxious that she might do something 'wrong'. But I remember that at this moment I told myself: 'I need to trust her'. Then, I kept myself calm while waiting for her to return to the room. In fact, she never did anything wrong. She just washed things in the bathroom. She demonstrated that she was a trustworthy person. In addition to accepting her behavior, I offered something else to her. I wished to communicate to her that I was indeed present with her. The way I found to communicate my presence was most often by repeating her words. It was not actually a typical 'empathic understanding response' or 'reflection of feelings'. I was not reflecting her feelings or meanings but I was just concretely repeating her words. For instance, when she would say: 'I emptied the yellow pot' or 'my cousin Ana beat me' or 'I won't paint today', I would repeat 'You emptied the yellow pot', 'your cousin Ana beat you' and 'you won't paint today'. I felt a need to repeat her words as a way to show her that I was fully available to her, and that she might take me and use me in whatever way she wished. Repeating her words also helped me to not interfere with my own frame of reference.

During the last two months, her behavior started to change. She would seldom play with the paints and would seldom leave the room. She most often would play with clay. She would spend the whole time of the session concentrating on the clay. Also, she would organize small blocks of wood within a larger box. It was quite amazing to observe her radical change from the awkward and agitated behavior to the quiet concentrated behavior. In my last interview with her mother, she reported that Diana's behavior changed in the same way at home and in the school.

My interaction with Diana illustrates how unconditional positive regard is a powerful experience in the promotion of the actualizing tendency. The therapist's unconditional positive regard was communicated through an unconditional acceptance of the client's behavior and through the therapist's willingness to be present with the client in the client's world.

UNCONDITIONAL POSITIVE REGARD AS EMPATHIC EXPERIENCE

In a 1975 paper entitled *Empathic: An Unappreciated Way of Being*, Rogers revisited his earlier 1959 conceptualization of empathy. After his intensive experience with encounter groups and with individuals institutionalized in psychiatric hospitals, he proposed a broader definition for empathy. He described the empathic way of being as comprised of 'several facets' (Rogers, 1975). In another investigation, I identified three distinct facets in this last Rogers' definition of empathy. These are: (1) empathic experience, (2) empathic understanding and (3) empathic understanding response (Freire, 2000). *Empathic experience* was identified as the experience of entering another's private world without judgments whereas *empathic understanding* was identified as the knowledge of the meanings and feelings that are being experienced by another individual. *Empathic understanding response*, as previously defined by Brodley (1977, 1998), corresponds to a specific mode of communication within a relationship. Rogers viewed these three facets as comprising a sole phenomena: the *empathic way of being*. These terms were used interchangeably by Rogers as synonyms to represent empathy. Nonetheless, it is suggested that these three facets exist separately. An empathic experience may or may not be followed by empathic understanding and it is also true that empathic understanding may or may not be followed by an empathic experience. From that viewpoint, empathic experience corresponds to the facet of empathy described by Rogers in his 1975 definition as:

> entering the private perceptual world of the other and becoming thoroughly at home in it . . . Temporarily living in his/her life, moving about in it delicately without making judgements . . . for the time being you lay aside the views and values you hold for yourself in order to enter another's world without prejudice. In some sense it means that you lay aside your self . . . (Rogers, 1975, p. 4).

This description leads us inevitably to the conclusion that empathic experience and unconditional positive regard are ultimately the sole and same experience. With unconditional positive regard, the therapist accepts every aspect of the client's experience as she offers her *presence* to the client. With empathic experience, the therapist accepts every aspect of the client's frame of reference as she enters into the client's world. Being *present* with unconditional acceptance and 'entering in the client's world laying her self aside' are ultimately the same experience. Bozarth (1998) also states that 'the empathic and unconditional acceptance of the therapist is, in essence, the same experience' (p. 58). *This experience is the essence of client-centered therapy.*

SUMMARY

Unconditional positive regard is the revolutionary feature of the person-centered approach. It has not been assimilated by the other psychotherapeutic approaches since it presents the paradox: that a person must accept herself in order to change. Several features of client-centered therapy are presented as important in relation to unconditional positive regard:

First, the client-centered therapist does not try to change the client. Client-centered therapy is not a problem-centered therapy. The unconditional acceptance of the client's experience is the therapist's sole aim in client-centered therapy.

Second, the therapist's trust in the actualizing tendency underpins the experience of unconditional positive regard. The greater the extent the therapist trusts the client's actualizing tendency, the greater her capacity to experience unconditional positive regard towards the client.

Third, the therapist experiences unconditional positive regard towards the client to the extent that she experiences unconditional positive self-regard.

In order to experience unconditional positive regard the therapist must put her self aside while offering her *presence* to the client. This presence comes through the surrender, through the therapist's dedication to the client's unique way of being.

The experience of unconditional positive regard and the empathic experience are ultimately the sole experience that is the essence of the client-centered approach. This essence is presented in the following poem:

The Validity of the Moment

I know not what you will do or become
At this moment or beyond
I know not what I will do except stay with you
At this moment
And be mother, father, sister, brother, friend, child, and lover
At this moment;
I exist for you and with you
At this moment;
I give you all of me
At this moment;
I am you
At this moment;
Take me and use me
At this moment
To be whatever you can become
At this moment and beyond (Bozarth, 1998, p. iii).

REFERENCES

Bozarth, J. D. (1998). *Person-Centered Therapy: a Revolutionary Paradigm*. Ross-on-Wye: PCCS Books.

Bozarth, J. D. (1999). Forty years of dialogue with the Rogerian hypothesis. Paper presented at the 14th Annual Meeting of the Association for the Development of The Person-Centered Approach. Ruston, Louisiana.

Bozarth, J. D. (2000). Non-directiveness in client-centered therapy: a vexed concept. Paper presented at the Eastern Psychological Association. Baltimore.

Bozarth, J. D. (2001). Congruence: the Freedom to Be. In G. Wyatt (Ed.) *Rogers' Therapeutic Conditions: Volume 1: Congruence*. Ross-on-Wye: PCCS Books.

Bozarth, J.D. and Brodley, B.T. (1991). Actualization: a functional concept in client-centered psychotherapy. *Journal of Social Behavior and Personality*, 6, pp. 45–59.

Brodley, B.T. (1977). The empathic understanding response. Unpublished manuscript. University of Chicago.

Brodley, B.T. (1998). Criteria for making empathic responses in client-centered therapy. *The Person-Centered Journal*, 5, pp. 20–8

Brodley, B.T. (1999). The actualizing tendency concept in client-centered theory. *The Person-Centered Journal*, 6, pp. 108–20.

Freire, E. (2000). A implementação das atitudes facilitadoras na relação terapêutica centrada no cliente. Unpublished masters dissertation. Pontifica Universidade Católica de Campinas.

Patterson, C.H. (2000). *Understanding Psychotherapy: fifty years of client-centred theory and practice.* Ross-on-Wye: PCCS Books.

Prouty, G. (1994). *Theoretical Evolutions in Person-Centered/Experiential Therapy: applications to schizophrenic and retarded psychoses.* Westport, Conn: Praeger.

Prouty, G. (1999). Carl Rogers and experiential therapies: a dissonance? *Person-Centred Practice,* 7, pp. 4–11.

Rogers, C.R. (1951). *Client-Centered Therapy.* Boston: HoughtonMifflin.

Rogers, C.R. (1957). The necessary and sufficient conditions of therapeutic personality change. *Journal of Consulting Psychology,* 21, pp. 95–103.

Rogers, C.R. (1959). A theory of therapy, personality, and interpersonal relationships as developed in the client-centered framework. In S. Koch (Ed.), *Psychology: a study of science: vol. 3, Formulation of the person and the social context* (pp. 184–256). New York: McGraw Hill.

Rogers, C.R. (1963). The actualizing tendency in relation to 'motives' and to consciousness. In M. Jones (Ed.) *Nebraska Symposium on Motivation.* Lincoln: University of Nebraska Press.

Rogers, C.R. (1975). Empathic: An Unappreciated Way of Being. *The Counseling Psychologist,* 5, pp. 2–10.

Rogers, C.R. (1980). *A Way of Being.* Boston: Houghton Mifflin.

Rogers, C.R. (1986). A client-centered/person-centered approach to therapy. In I. Kutash and A. Wolfe (Eds.) *Psychotherapists' Casebook* (pp. 197–208). Jossey-Bass.

Rogers, C.R. (1995). What understanding and acceptance mean to me. *Journal of Humanistic Psychology,* 35, pp. 7–22.

Standal, S.W. (1954). *The need for positive regard: a contribution to client-centered theory.* Doctoral dissertation. University of Chicago.

Valenstein, E. (1998). *Blaming the Brain: the truth about drugs and mental health.* New York: Free Press.

13 Unconditional Positive Regard as Communicated Through Verbal Behavior in Client-centered Therapy

Barbara Temaner Brodley and Carolyn Schneider

Any experienced client-centered/person-centered therapist will testify that unconditional positive regard (UPR) is usually communicated by implication when the therapist is engaged in empathic understanding response process (Temaner, 1977). As Bozarth (2000, personal communication on e-mail) has stated:

> The consistency of empathic understanding response communicates the acceptance of the client's frame of reference to the extent that acceptance of the client is clearly implied.

Acceptance of the client is communicated indirectly through the therapist's impartial, expressed whole understandings of the client as well as through the therapist's syntax, choice of words and general manner of communication. During speech it is also conveyed through the therapist's tone of voice, intonation and body language when making empathic responses. It is also implicitly communicated by the *absence* of certain kinds of communications from the therapist's frame of reference, including certain kinds of communications commonly found in other therapy approaches (Tomlinson and Whitney, 1969) such as interpretations, leading questions, confrontations, and suggestions.

This paper aims to illustrate how unconditional positive regard (UPR) is communicated through the verbal interactions of client-centered therapy (CCT), as examined in transcripts. Our method employs transcript segments of client-centered interviews conducted by Carl Rogers. Auditory and visual features of therapist behavior are crucial aspects of the communication of UPR, but a written paper aiming to illustrate limits one to the study of the verbal features of interaction. Such an examination, nevertheless, reveals much about how the acceptant attitude gets across to the client.

Rogers (1957, 1959a) stated in his therapy theory that therapeutic impact requires that 'the therapist is experiencing unconditional positive regard toward the client' and 'the client perceives, at least to a minimal degree' (p. 213) the therapist's unconditional positive regard and empathic understanding. Lietaer (1984) distinguishes the concept of unconditional positive regard (UPR) into three parts: positive regard, nondirectivity and unconditionality. These three parts function together, along with the empathic attitude, within the therapist, affecting his or her communications while relating to clients.

Bozarth (1998) and Wilkins (2000) recognize UPR as the fundamental therapist-cause of change in the client on the basis of Rogers' theories of personality development and the processes of its distortion (1959a). Many writers (e.g. Bozarth, 1998; Brodley, 1998; Haugh, 1998; Merry, 1999; Wilkins, 2000; Wyatt, 2000) interpret congruence as the underpinning for empathic understanding and UPR. Most client/person-centered therapists view the therapist's empathic understandings as the prominent, although not exclusive, vehicle for communicating UPR in their therapy.

The primary difficulty in the practice of UPR is the reality of therapists' judgmental and evaluative reactions to their clients' experiences, desires and behaviors. One of the client-centered (CC) therapists' tasks is to put aside their personal opinions and morality when attempting to experience acceptant empathic understanding in relation to clients. There is no leeway for any kind of prejudice in consistently effective client-centered work. UPR, however, involves putting aside approving reactions as well as criticisms. It is an attitude of acceptance of the person that includes feelings of warmth, caring and compassion toward the client but not approval of, or agreement with, the client's beliefs, choices or predilections.

The CC therapist who maintains UPR tends to convey steady evaluative neutrality in relation to clients' behaviors and narrative contents along with warmth (Merry, 1999) towards the client. The practical difficulty is most often perceived in terms of therapist's negative reactions, but there is a lesser although not insignificant difficulty in maintaining warm neutrality rather than telegraphing endorsement of clients' feelings and behaviors. A therapist may find it difficult to maintain an unconditionally acceptant attitude towards a client when he or she discloses or shows experiences, or desires, or behaviors that are repugnant or morally unacceptable to the therapist. Under certain circumstances the therapist may find it equally difficult not to experience or display pleasure, appreciation or approval in reaction to the manner in which the client is presenting self. There may be, of course, exceptions to the therapist's evaluation-neutral presence, which have been explained elsewhere (Brodley, 1999). There are no absolutes in the method.

Client-centered therapists consciously cultivate a capacity for unconditional acceptance towards clients regardless of the client's values, desires and behaviors. The UPR capacity involves the ability to maintain a warm, caring, compassionate attitude and to experience those feelings towards a client regardless of their flaws, crimes, or their moral differences from oneself. UPR, however, is almost never a deliberate communication in CCT. A statement such as 'I accept everything you tell me with a sympathetic or compassionate feeling and I never feel critical towards you' is not an impossible, honest comment in client-centered therapy work. If something of that kind is honestly expressed, it is most likely in response to a direct question from the client.

For the most part, UPR is communicated by certain qualities in the therapist's presence (Baldwin (interview of Rogers), 1987; Brodley, 2000) and by the absence of certain other qualities such as annoyance, criticism. These UPR qualities are the result of a philosophical orientation and learned disciplines. The most fundamental attitudes in client-centered work are attitudes of respect and trust in relation to clients. They are theoretically interpreted to follow from the therapist's belief in the actualization tendency principle, and from the ubiquitous nondirective attitude (Raskin, 1947; Brodley, 1997) that is inherent in client-centered therapy. The latter attitude carries the therapist's intention to protect the client's self-determination, autonomy and sense of self, thus contributing to the absence of certain kinds of counter-therapeutic responses to clients. These basic attitudes are consistent with and contribute to the therapist's unconditional positive regard. The qualities communicated are the therapist's consistent acceptant understanding of the client's experienced and communicated internal frame of reference, the therapist's consistency in expression of warm interest in the client, and the therapist's consistent attention to the client's self-representations. Unconditional positive regard is also communicated by the *absence* of communications that display challenge, confrontation, interventions, criticisms, unsolicited guidance or directive reassurance or support. Whether it is intended or not, all of these omitted types of communication, if expressed, are likely to be perceived as the therapist's expression of conditional approval or explicit disapproval.

The therapist's UPR is a fundamental attitude that colors the therapist's entire behavior in relation to the client. This behavior includes conversations that deal with arrangements for the therapy, responses to clients' questions and any statements the therapist may initiate from his or her own frame of reference, as well as the therapist's empathic understanding responses. The therapist's UPR is likely to be experienced by the therapist and felt by the client as the therapist's *acceptance* of the client. *Acceptance* is also implied in the therapist's empathic understanding r*esponsiveness* that may be contrasted to a benign inexpressiveness that clients often perceive as disinterest. Regardless of the client's attitudes and feelings that are manifest in his or her narrative, the CC therapist attempts to internally experience what the client appears to intend to communicate, and tries to understand that material from the perspective the client is giving to it. This *empathic orientation* to the client means the therapist understands and is receptive to whatever the client is feeling or however the client is construing experiences. Empathic orientation includes accepting the client's shifts in point of view, his or her atypical interpretations of commonly consensual perceptions, ambivalence, inconsistencies or contradictions and it also includes psychotic experiences — delusions, hallucinations and blatant distortions in perception.

The first transcript segment will show a typical client-centered interaction with a voluntary, self-disclosing client. It is an example of client-centered empathic understanding response process (Temaner, 1977), as it appears midway into the seventeenth session conducted by Rogers (circa 1955).

Illustration I

> C38: *Of course I know that she isn't able to be that way any longer . . . but for a minute I thought 'well, I really miss her and I sort of need a mother at this point, and yet it's impossible'.*
>
> T38: *Even though it's factually impossible, the feeling was 'gee, I miss her, I wish*

she were here to take care of me and look after me'.

C39: *Uh um. Yet at the same time I felt, well a little later I thought, 'Maybe that wasn't what I needed, maybe it was a more adult sort of . . . companionship in some way, rather than a mother'. But I needed something, or somebody.*

T39: *You really didn't feel sure in yourself whether what you wanted was someone to really give you close mothering . . . or whether you wanted some more grown-up kind of relationship.*

C40: *And then in another sense I felt (sighs) well, maybe it's just something I have to go through alone.*

T40: *Maybe it's just hopeless to wish that that could really be in a relationship with anybody . . . Maybe I have to be alone.*

C41: *Uh um . . . the thing that's sort of thrown me this week is that . . . well, I feel better about the physical condition compared to last week. I talked to my doctor and I sort of made friends with him, which makes me feel a little better (laughs). So we're not sort of quietly fighting without saying anything, and I think I have more confidence in him. I read an article about this and it said it's very hard to diagnose so I don't hold that against him any longer. But he feels he has to be sure that this is what it is, and so they're giving me X-rays and I'm frightened because I kind of feel they're having to be sure that it isn't cancer and that really frightens me terribly.*

T41: *Uh um. Uh um . . . It's, 'If it's really something like that, then it just feels so alone'.*

C42: *And it's really a frightening kind of loneliness because I don't know who could be with you in that.*

T42: *Is this what you're saying? 'Could anyone be with you in a fear or in a loneliness like that?'*

C43: *(Cries).*

T43: *It just really cuts so deep.*

C44: *I don't know what it would feel like if there was somebody around that I could feel as though I did have someone to lean on. I don't know whether that would make me feel better or not. I kind of think this is something that you just have to grow within yourself, to stand it. It will take two weeks I guess before they know. Would it help to have somebody else around? Or is it just something that you just have to really be intensely alone in? I just felt that way this week, just dreadfully, dreadfully all by myself.*

T44: *Uh um . . . Is the feeling as though you're so terribly alone, in the universe almost, and whether . . .*

C45: *Uh um.*

T45: *Whether it even, whether anyone could help, whether it would help if you did have someone to lean on or not, you don't know.*

C46: *I guess sort of, basically, that would be a problem you would have to do alone. I mean you just couldn't maybe do it with anybody, you just couldn't take anybody along with some of the feelings, and yet it would be sort of a comfort, I guess, not to be alone.*

T46: *It surely would be nice if you could take someone with you a good deal of the way into your feelings of aloneness and fear.*

C47: *I guess I just have.*

T47: Maybe that's what you're feeling right this minute.

In this segment the client moves from wishing for the comfort of her deceased mother, through her questioning whether it would help her deal with her fear if she were not alone in facing a diagnosis of cancer, to the immediate sense that Rogers has been a companion. Throughout the process Rogers has empathically followed the client without expressing an opinion, without giving explicit support, and without giving any promise of accommodating her wishes. Without the visuals and soundtrack, which give more vivid evidence of Rogers' emotional attunement and compassion, his wording communicates his intention to closely understand her feelings. In his responses he includes her tentativeness and indecisiveness in his empathic understanding responses (T38, 40, 44, 45, 47). The client's comment in C47 expresses her feeling that Rogers has been a supportive presence.

Another example of empathic understanding process to illustrate UPR is a segment near the end of an interview conducted by Rogers (1983). This session took place 30 years after the first segment. Rogers is with a client who has expressed fears about relationships.

Illustration II

C62: I think two things, in being caught up in a relationship. I know it could take me in a lot of new directions, really new uncharted courses could be very exciting . . . and I guess I'm a bit afraid about where that might lead me. It might lead me to very new, very unknown things, but . . . something that excites me, that idea, 'cause I know it would only be positive I think. But I think I'm afraid of being led, being swept away, and being led to where I don't want to go and not feeling control to pull away.

T62: Your whole face lights up with the idea of a close relationship that might open up new and uncharted possibilities, but wow, that's also scary.

C63: Yeah, the feeling of getting . . . tied down.

T63: You might lose control again or might be controlled.

C64: Not lose control but be controlled, yeah. Being tied up . . . just the image I have is like an octopus, holding me, you know. I just can't get loose.

T64: Uhm hm.

C65: Being taken where I don't want to go, where I'm not ready to go.

T65: That's one picture you have of a relationship . . . is of an octopus. Many tentacles that would just hold you tight.

C66: Yeah, just can't get free. See, that was really exactly the relationship with my mother. And now I think that's why I've got to have complete distance with her because if I let one tentacle touch, it's too much (laughs).

T66: You're so super-sensitized to that, that one touch of that tentacle — one of those tentacles — is more than you can take.

C67: Yeah. Well the one tentacle I could take but the others I couldn't and I know that you don't get one without getting all eight (laughs). It's . . . Yeah, that's very much — that very much captures the relationship with my mother.

T67: You're in the grip of an octopus.

C68: Yeah. And you just can't get close at all. But — I have a tendency, particularly I think with women to see them as all potential octopuses . . .

T68: It really does make it hard to see women any other way than that.

C69: Yeah. It's not a conscious thing, but . . .

T69: Sort of some deep thing in you that feels, 'Look out, this might be another octopus'.

C70: Uhm hm. Yeah. Well, I'm not really conscious of that. But I know that's the feeling there. Yeah, I'd just be . . . pounced upon if I let myself — you know — and then, I mean further than I want . . . I mean maybe I want just four tentacles and not all eight (laughs). Yeah. I like that image.

T70: You wouldn't mind a few but not the whole eight.

C71: Yeah . . . taking it in small doses. What I'm capable of handling. Make it in proportion to what I want; what I'm ready for.

T71: Sounds like you might like to be held, but not gripped.

C72: Yeah, yeah. And then be able just to say, 'OK, that's enough now.' Just, you know . . .

T72: Shed the tentacles.

This client expresses his sense that he would have exciting benefits from being open to a relationship but is afraid of being controlled. He then realizes his fearful response to relationships comes out of his experience of his mother whom he pictures as an octopus whose eight tentacles will grip him if he allows a single one. He then continues with his wish to have only some tentacles, a metaphor for some degree of attachment, and to be released when it is too much for him. Rogers, again, stays close to his client's expressed meanings. The material is provocative and might be perceived by some therapists as an opportunity to support the client's more daring feelings. Rogers' acceptance is implied many ways including by the absence of reassurances, suggestions or interpretations and by his use of the client's metaphor in his empathic responses (T65, 66, 67, 69, 70 and 72).

Interactions with clients who are critical of the therapist's methods, or who express anger at the therapist, or who make responses indicating they are not being accurately understood may be experienced as difficult and undermine the therapist's unconditional positive regard. The following interview (circa 1982) took place at a training conference with a voluntary demonstration client who was not comfortable with the nondirective approach or with Rogers. The segment starts at the beginning of the interview.

Illustration III

C1: I began to realize how frightened I am of the nonstructured nature of this interaction. (Pause) And I have to ask myself why. It's easy for me to come up with a problem; I have no trouble talking. In fact I use talking as a way of controlling situations. I think the nondirectiveness of your approach is very frightening to me.

T1: Sounds as though the fear of not knowing where this might go . . . and the fact of your being in charge of the direction. Both of those things are really scary.

C2: *That's right. It's like I would like you to take over now and ask me lots of questions . . . and I don't want to have to do much work. In fact, the fantasy was . . . I would rather have volunteered for a hypnotist (laugh) than for you. (T: Mhm) So it's saying something about my not wanting to be as active as I probably will have to be with you.*

T2: *It really does say something about the deep fear you have of initiating something entirely on your own.*

C3: *Yes . . . It's very contradictory. Because if you look at my life, the one thing that would be most apparent is my independence and my initiative. So it's a contradiction. (T: Uhm hm) But down deep I am very frightened of non-structure, and yet resist structure when it's imposed.*

T3: *Mhm. How do you understand that? That in dealing with the external world you're quite willing to take initiative and organize things and so on, but when it comes to revealing your internal self, then that becomes much more frightening.*

C4: *Yes. (Pause) I should tell you that I'm a behavior therapist.*

T4: *(Laughs) I did know that.*

C5: *You did know that (laughs). I prefer to work directively. So coming here was an experiment (T: Uhm hm) for me, and I've been very uncomfortable with the nondirective aspects of the workshop and the interview . . . It just highlights this problem.*

T5: *So when I said it was a risk, that's an understatement.*

C6: *It's a real risk . . .*

The client responds, explaining some facts about her background including the dissolution of her marriage, having to raise her children alone and support her family. She expresses the feeling of being gypped in her life. Then she continues:

C7: *There's a feeling of being lost without a structure, a structure of family, a husband, somebody to come to every night after work (T: Uhm hm). Someone who is just there.*

T7: *That does bring a real sense of loss even to think about that.*

C8: *That's right. That's right. So I guess having to structure this interview is like more of the same. I just don't feel comfortable in sitting and letting things happen. 'Cause when they happen, they haven't turned out so positively.*

T8: *So this interview is part of the whole sense of being lost.*

C9: *Yes. Yes. I feel very lost in my life.*

T9: *And the same carries over to the interview a little bit.*

Rogers responds empathically throughout the client's expression of feelings and views that are challenging to his method in the same neutral and understanding manner as he has done about external material in the previous segments. A bit further on, there is a long pause and the client complains:

C10: *I feel that you're waiting for me to say something else (small laugh). I have trouble with silences.*

T10: *Uhm hm. (Pause) I don't have that trouble. I'm perfectly willing to wait until you know what you wish to say.*

C11: *(Pause) I'm just feeling very hot — my cheeks are burning. And I'm not sure that I know what I want to say.*

T11: *Uhm, hm. I wonder if you aren't sort of experiencing that sense of being lost right now . . . 'What the hell do I do?'*

C12: *That's right, exactly.*

Although Rogers does not accommodate the client by helping her to find a topic, his T10 is responsive in the form of a self-disclosure acknowledging his difference with her feelings and then a response that is a combination of a reassurance and letting her know the direction remains with her. His T11 is an empathic guess based on her previous expression of feeling lost and in a first-person form. It is an intense response about her predicament. Rogers reveals no impatience with her, no sense of feeling discomfort or disapproval of her condition throughout the interaction. Then the client reflects further on herself:

C13: *I just have trouble just sitting quietly. (Long pause)*

T13: *I think I see in your eyes a sense of 'please, please guide this!'*

C14: *Do something (laughing), that's right.*

T14: *'Do something'.*

C15: *Do something. Uh (pause) yes, I've had a hard time with you this workshop. My feelings for you have, uhm, been on a roller coaster. (T: Uhm hm) Uhm, I wondered, I had curiosity about how you could just sit there and just . . . what did you do while all this was going on with yourself because . . . there was so much going on and I kept wanting something to happen. I was very angry at you for not realizing how many people were in pain, or not creating a plan. Uhm, uhm, at one point, if I could have been more active, I would have just ranted and raved at you and I was in a fury. I didn't do that. Uhm, and I think it was partly the group, but then it's very hard for me to be angry with someone who sits there so benignly. Uhm, and, uh, wants things to sort of be nice and good and, then it became harder for me to be angry at you when you said . . . were nice to me or uhm, started making contact . . . So I really had a hard time with you. Uhm, I keep wanting more of a response than you give.*

T15: *So you've been very angry with me in the workshop . . . Perhaps not expressed, but nevertheless the feelings have been there . . . (C: Yes) Being very angry toward me . . . 'Why the hell don't you do something, why the hell don't you see what's going on?' (C: Yes) And part of that anger carries over right here.*

C16: *That's right, right now . . .*

T16: *'Why the hell don't you do something?'*

C17: **Do** *Something. Uhm, (pause) yeah, do something, be . . . don't just let people sit and struggle (pause and sigh).*

T17: *And it isn't only 'Why do you let people sit and struggle', it's 'why do you let me sit and struggle?'*

C18: *Yeah. Why are you letting me sit and struggle like this? You set up this interview, interview me! Uhm, it's a contradiction that I have with . . . in terms of my feelings with you. And then I say, 'What's the use'. I mean you are who*

you are, this is the way you are and I have a hard time dealing with it, so what's the point of even expressing the anger since it's not going to do any good. Nothing will change, nothing will change.
T18: *It's hopeless, you can't change our relationship.*
C19: *That's right, if I yell and scream at you it's not going to change.*

In this segment Rogers obviously accepts her anger and vigorously acknowledges it in first-person-form empathic responses (T15, 16, 17). Rogers does not defend himself or his method, he simply continues to try to understand her feelings. In a segment not quoted the client continues to complain that Rogers has not provided supportive arrangements in the workshop. She goes on:

C20: *I'm not feeling the rage I felt . . . At one point I was furious . . . What I'm feeling now is . . . Obviously, my problems with you really relate to my problems in dealing with my father who was not a responsive person. (Pause) And one of the problems that I have is that you are very different than my father in that you would accept whatever choices I made. And my father doesn't respond . . . hardly ever responds, but when he does respond, it's with disapproval — 'I don't like what you're doing' (pause).*
T20: *So you really are, in a sense, dealing with your father in dealing with me, and yet it's with a different father who is more willing to accept.*
C21: *And it's confusing. It's confusing (pause).*
T21: *It makes it very hard to know how the hell to relate to me.*
C22: *That's right. Exactly.*

Rogers' response (T20) represents her interpretation that she is responding in part to Rogers out of her history of experiences with her father with his usual neutrality. He then expresses the intensity and anger aspect of her confusion by using 'how the hell' in his next empathic response (T21). As may be observed in this segment Rogers does not side-step to his client's anger, even when it is directed at him. A study by Bradburn (1996) of Rogers' affect demonstrated that Rogers consistently responds to client's anger with acceptance and affective empathic responses.

The following illustration of UPR is in a session with a client who is a patient in a psychiatric hospital (Rogers, 1958) who has been diagnosed with a paranoid schizophrenic disorder. There are several instances during the interview when the client perceived Rogers as not understanding her, and Rogers' responses express his unperturbed acceptance of the corrections and of the client.

Illustration IV

C11: *I think it means working all day in the laundry, too, and I'm not quite ready for that . . . I asked the doctor [before] if he would move me so I could go to work in the laundry. (T: Uhm hm) And the transfer came today. I didn't ask to be transferred, though, at this time.*
T12: *It troubles you as to whether you're really ready to face some of the things that would be involved.*

C12: I don't know, there isn't much to face. It's kind of confusing, I think.
T13: I see. It's more a question of facing the uncertainties, is that what you mean?
C13: I don't know what I mean (little laugh). I just know that . . .
T14: Right now you feel kind of mixed up?

Rogers' responses (T12 and T13) were probably too abstract for the client, given her mental condition, and thus were poor attunements to her in these instances. Consequently, he may have stimulated her confusion (C12 and C13). He continues to follow, however, going to the client's more immediate and concrete level in T14. The client continues, explaining a nurse's ambiguous behavior. Rogers responds to her:

T17: The explanation was doctor's orders and all that, but you can't help but feel, 'Is she really trustworthy?' 'Cause here she seemed to . . .
C18: No, I don't trust people anyway, anymore. (T: Uhm hm) That's why I don't want them to trust me. I either believe in them or I don't believe in them.
T18: Uhm hm. And all or none.
C19: And I don't think I believe in her very much.
T19: Uhm hm. And really with most people you feel, 'I don't think I trust 'em'.
C20: That's the truth, I don't trust 'em. Either believe 'em or I don't believe 'em or I don't . . . I'm not quite certain whether I believe them yet or not. (T: Uhm hm) But I don't believe in trust anymore.
T20: Uhm hm. That's one thing that you feel has really dropped out for you, that's just to trust people. Not for you.
C21: No, I don't trust 'em. You can get hurt much too easily by trusting people.
T21: Uhm hm. If you really believe in someone, and let your trust go out to them, then . . .
C22: I don't have any trust. That's why I can't let any out to 'em!
T22: Uhm hm. But evidently your feeling is that when that has happened in the past . . .
C23: You just get hurt by it.
T23: That's the way you can get hurt.
C24: That's the way I have been hurt.
T24: That's the way you have been hurt.

The client apparently needs precise and relatively concrete responses in order to feel understood. In T21 Rogers expresses a hypothetical that implies the trust the client states she does not experience. When corrected (C22), Rogers makes a reconciling response by referring to the past (T22). In the segment Rogers errs in understanding several times (C12, 12, 21, 23), but each time he accepts the correction and tries to understand exactly what she means. The audiotape of his voice supports the patience and sincerity in Rogers' attitude toward the client that is suggested by his words.

In another illustration, Rogers (circa 1977) interacts with a client who feels afraid of emotional risks in relationships, and the experience of that fear occurs in the therapy encounter.

164

Illustration V

C7: I think I'm keeping myself in a kind of no-win situation where I'm really lonely and yet it's kind of like I'm keeping myself there because I've got a guard around me, and I'd kind of like to break out of that.

T7: It's as though you're in some way sort of responsible for your loneliness.

C8: Yes, I know that . . .

T8: And that something you'd like to break out of that shell, or that safeguard that you've been hiding behind.

C9: Part of me does.

T9: Part of you does, OK, OK.

C10: Part of me says 'noo way'.

T10: So it really is a very ambivalent, two-way thing.

The client then explains some history of her withdrawal and fear of getting hurt and continues:

C13: I've been aware of this for a long time too, but I never go beyond the awareness level.

T13: So that the knowledge isn't new, it is the question of what you do about it.

C14: That's right, that's right. How can one stay safe and still be open?

T14: The way you shake your head makes me feel, 'I don't see any way'.

The client explains her caution in friendships and that she requires friendship before she would feel love or have a sexual relationship. Then she refers to her immediate relationship with Rogers:

C21: We've gotten to the point where I won't go beyond.

T21: Uh-huh. That's what I was sort of thinking, you've thought your way this far, but then where do you . . .

C22: I've laid the cards out and that's all I want to play.

T22: So that, in this relationship it's like in your other relationships.

C23: That's right.

T23: 'It goes so far and then let's stop. That's as far as I want to go.' If you go any further, there's a risk, isn't it?

C24: Yes, it is.

T24: And I think your eyes tell me you're feeling that risk right now.

C25: (Pause) So here I am. (Pause) I feel like saying to myself, 'Well, you got this far, it's not so bad (laughs). It's all right; I make the best of it.'

T25: It's all right up to this point.

C26: Yeah, right.

T26: So let's laugh it off.

C27: Yeah, make a joke, talk about something else.

T27: Could . . . very easy to run away from yourself.

But the client doesn't do that, she re-engages in her personal exploration. Rogers' acceptance of her reluctance to go on (C21, T22, 23, 24), and ambivalence (C10,

T10), leaves the choices to her. But Rogers also doesn't shy away from subtle expressions of anger (Illustration III, C15, T15, T16) or states expressed as nervous laughter (C25, T26).

The next illustration is a segment from an interview Rogers (1959b) conducted with a teenage girl in a psychiatric hospital. The interview is not very coherent. The client is quite difficult to understand, but it illustrates Rogers' attempt to relate to the young woman regardless of the difficulty, and reveals his patience that is a form of acceptance of her. It begins with Rogers initiating contact and expressing his interest in her.

Illustration VI

T1a: I've seen [around the hospital] you twice now. (C: Uhm hm.) I just thought that I would like to talk with you. I would be interested if you would tell me about yourself and your situation.
C1: *Well, my situation is tough.*
T1: *Your situation is tough. (C: Yeah) Do you want to tell me a little about it?*
C2: *Well, it's mostly home and with my parents except when other people . . . I don't know exactly what happened . . .*
T2: *You're confused why it's so disruptive.*
C3: *Yes, it is.*
T3: *But it's hard to tell about.*
C4: *Yes it is. (T: Uhm hm) I think to drop it is an answer. Just drop it, or something.*
T4: *That's one possibility is to just drop it. Uhm hm.*
C5: *Just forget about it.*
T5: *Ah . . . if you could just put it out of mind. (C: Yeah.) Uhm hm. And then sometimes that seems like . . .*
C6: *The only possible thing to do.*
T6: *The only possible thing to do. You might like to forget it and drop it. But . . .*
C7: *Once you get away with murder, once you get more away with other . . .*
T7: *Is. Uh, that . . . and this is your parents you're speaking of? (C: Yes) That when they get away with . . .*
C8: *Or anyone.*
T8: *Or anyone. (C: Yes) That 'When they get away with murder once, why, boy, then they try it again'.*
C9: *Yeah. Yeah.*
Observer: Do you feel that's true with your parents?
C10: *No, not naturally, 'cause (inaudible) when she got beat up . . . She's been meddling in other peoples' affairs.*
T10: *Uhm hm. And I guess you don't like her when . . . (C: No, I don't) . . .she meddles in other peoples' affairs. That makes you . . .*
C11: *Pretty disgusted.*
T11: *Disgusted. Uhm hm, Uhm, hm. (Pause) Could you tell me any more about that?*
C12: *Well, it would incriminate me quite a bit.*
T12: *I see. If you really told, that would . . . It would kind of incriminate you.*
C13: *Yes. It would.*

T13: *Kind of put you in a bad light if you really . . . (C: Yes it would) told about it.*
C14: *Except my mother and father.*
T14: *I see. So you feel you would hardly um, dare tell your side of it because it might incriminate you. You'd rather leave it up to your folks.*
C15: *Yes. (T: Uhm hm, Uhm hm) Does that settle that?*
T15: *Well, there might be . . . the thing is that, uh; I guess that settles part of it. But I was thinking that if there was anything that you were willing to tell me that would help me to know you better.*
C16: *Well, my heritage for one thing.*
T16: *About your heritage.*
C17: *I feel incriminated myself.*
T17: *You feel incriminated yourself.*
C18: *You see (inaudible) my son was in it?*
T18: *You're son was in it.*
C19: *Yeah (T: Uhm, hm) my grandmother told me my history and that . . . (T: Hmm) She wants me to know her son's history. (Inaudible)*
T19: *Uhm hm. She brings in her son's history and your parents bring in your history? Hmm? And that's pretty rough.*
C20: *Yes it is.*
T20: *I'm not sure I quite understand that.*
C21: *Mine isn't any better than his.*
T21: *Yours isn't any better than his. (C: No) So that, in a sense, both histories sort of incriminate each other. (C: Yes) Uhm hm. Hmm. I guess what you're saying is that if the truth came out, or your parents told the whole story, it would make it look pretty bad for you. Is that . . . ?*
C22: *Yes that would (inaudible).*
T22: *So you feel that if the (C: History) story came out . . .*
C23: *That would (inaudible).*
T23: *If the (inaudible).*
C24: *(Inaudible)*
T24: *Uhm hm. Uhm hm. But it does seem as though, if the true story came out, you're afraid that, that you'd be put away for life. (C: Uhm hm) Hmm, You must feel that the true story is pretty bad.*
C25: *The true story is . . . (Inaudible) and he gets away with everything (inaudible) 'cause I won't have anything to do with it.*
T25: *I see. So that when he gets out, you're going to have to sort of face up to the truth. (C: Inaudible) You won't have anything to do with it.*
C26: *No. I won't.*
T26: *So I guess it sounds like you did have something with him in the past. But not in the future you won't.*
C27: *No, not in the past, present or future, no. (T: Uhm hm.) There's nothing to look forward to.*
T27: *You really feel there's nothing to look forward to.*

Rogers has been encouraging the client to disclose about herself and she appears to be generally willing. She lets it be known she would prefer not to go further into a certain topic (C15) and Rogers accepts (T15). This is another example of his acceptance, his respect for the person and of his commitment to following the client:

> C42: *I do want to stop fighting so my father can (inaudible).*
> T42: *Uhm hm, Uhm hm. That's one of the things you'd like.*
> C43: *Yes I do. And all the way up to my friend's house. (T: Uhm hm.) Up to the house and let me clean up. That's what I wanted to do.*
> T43: *The other thing you wanted to do was to clean it up as far as the road.*
> C44: *There will be a highway. (Inaudible) It would be better not to talk about it. (T: Uhm hm) That's good.*
> T44: *Are there other things you could tell me to help me know you a little better? 'Cause I don't know anything of your record or . . .*
> C45: *You probably already know.*
> T45: *No. I really don't.*
> C46: *You really don't know me.*
> T46: *No. I really don't know you. Just what you've told me now is what I know of you.*
> C47: *Mhm. It takes lots of expense and money (inaudible).*
> T47: *It takes lots of expense and money to . . .*
> C48: *To carry on such a performance.*
> T48: *Now there I'm not quite sure. You carry on such a performance . . . ?*
> C49: *Well this is awfully embarrassing. (T: Hmm.) 'Cause my father is connected to it too. I wouldn't want to say anything to . . . (inaudible).*
> T49: *But really, there is something that troubles you and all, but you don't like to bring it out because it may affect other people and you feel it might do them . . .*
> C50: *More harm and no good. More harm as far as my father's mom. (Inaudible) I can't do anything about it. My name and his name (inaudible) (T: Uhm hm) When we went through this as far as the performance, that settled me.*
> T50: *So that you think you've settled.*
> C51: *Yeah. At least I hope it is. 'Cause I know my dad wouldn't make a habit of it.*

The session continues for the most part with intelligible remarks that Rogers responds to with empathic understanding responses. Rogers hears and understands more information in the client's remarks than are audible on the audiotape. The tape took many reviews to get to the present level because the client speaks very fast and with a rural dialect. But Rogers is also dealing with very unclear meanings and the client's idiosyncratic manner of speech even when she can be heard. It requires some guesswork and occasional admission to her that he has not understood.

Whatever Rogers is doing — trying to stimulate more conversation, making empathic responses, making guesses, or admitting he doesn't understand — he does it with a steady, respectful and acceptant responsiveness, as best he can, and he always accepts the limits the client puts on specific topics. This fifth illustration is not typical client-centered work, but neither is it unusual for its context. It is an example of a type of session involving incompletely coherent client statements requiring extreme patience and attentiveness. It is a type of session that occurs frequently when the therapist is working in a psychiatric hospital and initiates the relationship, and when the patient's illness makes clear or totally comprehensible communication difficult or impossible.

The final illustrative segment is from an interview (Rogers, 1986) that took place as a demonstration in front of a training group. The client initially expressed her problem as difficulty in stopping her habit of smoking. A short way into the session, her legs and body began to twitch, or involuntarily jerk, and that became the focus of the interaction. After starting to discuss her smoking, the client felt distracted by the group of observers. She then calmed herself with a deliberate breathing exercise.

Illustration VII

C26: I can feel you have that calmness too. It's fine. (T: Uhm hm) I guess, I can be with me and with you without interrupting that feeling.

T26: Uhm, hm. We can be calm together and calm separately. (C: Uhm hm) And, each of us breathing okay.

(Pause 40 seconds)

C27: I'm aware of my body trembling, and my legs.

T27: Uhm hm. There is a nervousness there and your legs are just . . .

C28: Uhm, hm. The breathing's okay.

T28: The breathing's okay.

(Pause 40 seconds)

C29: Jerkin' here. (T: Hmm?) My body jerked right here. (T: Uhm, hm. Uh, huh. Uh huh) Do you want to see that (smiles)?

T29: Whatever you want to bring up is what I want to hear. (Pause) It was important to you that your body jerked at that point.

C30: (Laughs) I don't know why. (Pause 13 seconds) (She makes a fluttering gesture close to her body).

T30: You feel fluttering? (Fluttering gesture.)

C31: Uhm hm. A jerk here. (She points to her midriff, her body jerks, she shakes her head.)

T31: Uhm hm. Another jerk. (Pause 10 seconds) Can you say what those jerks mean to you?

C32: (She shakes her head in negative) It's a very uncomfortable feeling.

T32: Your body is just doing something that's out of your control.

C33: Hmm. (Nods) Well, I could control it (T: Yeah) but if I go with the process (T: Yeah) then . . .

T33: But it just happens without your knowing why.

C34: Uhm hm. In the encounter group we had earlier this week, this happened. (T: Uhm hm) And I still don't know why. (Her body jerks.)

T34: Uhm hm. Uhm, hm. You don't quite understand what happens when your body is, (inaudible) goes . . .

C35: And I feel it just races around . . . (inaudible). (She gestures toward her forehead.)

T35: Yeah. Can you say some of the things that are racing around up there? (Gesturing towards his head.)

C36: 'What is this about?' 'This looks stupid.' You know, 'What are you doing?'

You know, uh, I've seen people who have seizures, you know?
(T: Uh, huh. Uh huh.) And that's my experience of what my body's doing. And it's . . .
T36: *Uh, huh. So, you are being stupid or having a seizure or 'what in the world is going on?' You keep asking yourself.*
C37: *Yeah.*
T37: *Sort of critical of yourself.*
C38: *Hmm. Part of me is judging it as wrong and the other part is saying, 'Shut up. Whatever this is, just go with it and be . . .'*
T38: *Uhm hm. Part of you is saying, 'Now stop it, it's stupid. This is ridiculous.' And another part of you is saying, 'Wait a minute. My body is doing something, if I can go with it, maybe I can learn something.'*
C39: *Right.*

Rogers remains empathic throughout this unusual interview although he was probably surprised by the turn of events. Verbally, most of his responses are of the empathic understanding, following-type responses (T 26, 27, 28, half of 29, 30 in the form of a question for clarification, half of T31, T33, 34, 36, 37 and 38). Other responses are attitudinally consistent but of a different type. In T29 he first addresses the client's question and immediately follows that with an empathic understanding response. In T31 he first empathically follows and then asks the client if she can verbalize the meaning of the movements. In this he is pursuing more empathic understanding of her experience through a leading question. T32 is an empathically intended guess about what is happening. His following response (T33) accepts the client's clarification (C33). Rogers' T35 is similar to T31, it pursues understanding of the client's experience employing a leading question based on the client's gesture. There is nothing obviously evaluative in Rogers' remarks and nothing in his manner or tone of voice (seen and heard on the videotape) suggesting conditional acceptance or disapproval of the client. He tries to stay with the client and pursues empathic understanding of her communications and the behaviors she is attending to in the interaction.

CONCLUSION

The seven illustrative segments reveal Rogers responded with empathic understanding or other explicit following responses (such as questions for clarification and parroting-type responses) in 97 (84.3%) of all responses. He gave answers or an explanation in response to explicit or implied questions on five occasions. He made comments that were observations of clients' expressive appearance on six occasions. He requested that his client (only in Illustration VI) tell him something more about herself four times — twice after she stated she was finished with particular topics that he did not attempt to pursue.

In the illustrations he verbalized two leading questions (only to the client in Illustration VII). These were specifically about the meaning the client might be attributing to her involuntary behavior in order to better understand her phenomenology in the situation. He made one explicit statement of not understanding the client (in Illustration VI). These make a total of 18 responses that we are not classifying as empathic understanding or other type of following responses. This total is slightly less than 16% of the 115 therapist responses in the illustrations. It seems to us on the face of it, it would be difficult to successfully argue that any of these particular responses, all expressed from the therapist's frame of reference, had a likelihood of stimulating a sense of disapproval or conditional approval in these clients. Although we must admit we cannot be certain of our conclusion, having no way of assessing the clients' perceptions in the transcripts.

This paper has presented very typical and masterful examples of client-centered therapy by Carl Rogers to illustrate unconditional positive regard in the therapist's verbal behavior. It aimed to illustrate UPR in good implementations of Rogers' theory of therapy with clients who are able to be in contact, who are able to some considerable extent represent themselves, and who are able to narrate about their experience. These are features of most clients, even psychotic clients, participating in psychotherapy. The paper shows how the UPR attitude appears to come across — depending for evidence only on the verbal aspects of the communication — as unqualified acceptance of the person and with an absence of judgments or conditional acceptance.

Bozarth (2000, personal communication on e-mail) has theorized:

> Empathic understanding is the total acceptance of the client's frame of reference at any given moment, and unconditional positive regard is the total acceptance of the individual as an individual at any given moment. In that sense, empathic understanding is a subset of unconditional positive regard.

This formulation appears to be supported by the observations we have made of the seven transcripts. The impact of Rogers' consistency in acceptance, as it is primarily expressed in empathic responses throughout the dialogues, as well as in his other forms of response, comes across as a total acceptance of the client.

REFERENCES

Bozarth, J. D. (1996). A theoretical reconsideration of the necessary and sufficient conditions for therapeutic personality change. *The Person-Centered Journal*. 3 (1), 44–51. Also adapted as: A reconceptualization of the necessary and sufficient conditions for therapeutic personality change (1998) in *Person-Centered Therapy: A Revolutionary Paradigm*. Ross-on-Wye: PCCS Books, pp. 43–50.

Bozarth, J. D. (1998). *Person-Centered Therapy: A Revolutionary Paradigm*. Ross-on-Wye: PCCS Books.

Bradburn, W. M. (1996). Did Carl Rogers' positive view of human nature bias his psychotherapy? An empirical investigation. Unpublished doctoral dissertation. Illinois School of Professional Psychology, Chicago, IL.

Brodley, B. T. (1997). The nondirective attitude in client-centered therapy. *The Person-Centered Journal*, 4 (1), pp. 61–74.

Brodley, B. T. (1998). Congruence and its relation to communication in client-centered therapy. *The Person-Centered Journal*, 5(2), pp. 83–116.

Brodley, B. T. (1999). Reasons for responses expressing the therapist's frame of reference in client-centered therapy. *The Person-Centered Journal*, 6(1), pp. 4–27.

Haugh, S. (1998). Congruence: A confusion of language. *Person-Centred Practice*, 6 (1), pp. 44–50.

Lietaer, G. (1984). Unconditional positive regard: A controversial basic attitude in client-centered therapy. In R.F. Levant and J.M. Shlien (Eds.) *Client-Centered Therapy and the*

Person Centered Approach. New York: Praeger, pp. 41–58.

Merry, T. (1999). *Learning and Being in Person-Centred Counseling.* Ross-on-Wye: PCCS Books.

Raskin, N. J. (1947). The nondirective attitude. Unpublished paper.

Raskin, N. J. (1948). The development of nondirective therapy. *Journal of Consulting Psychology,* 12 (94), pp. 92–110.

Rogers, C.R. (circa 1955). Transcript of Rogers' interview with 'Miss M'. The Carl R. Rogers Archive. Congressional Archives. Washington, D.C. Also in The Carl Rogers Memorial Library, Center of the Studies of the Person, La Jolla, CA.

Rogers, C. R. (1957). The necessary and sufficient conditions of therapeutic personality change. *Journal of Consulting Psychology,* 21, 95–103. Also in H. Kirschenbaum and V. L. Henderson (1989). (Eds.) *The Carl Rogers Reader.* Boston: Houghton Mifflin. pp. 219–35.

Rogers, C.R. (1958). Transcript of Rogers' interview with Loretta. *Archives of The American Academy of Psychotherapy.* Also in The Carl R. Rogers Archive. Congressional Archives, Washington, D.C.

Rogers, C. R. (1959a). A theory of therapy, personality and interpersonal relationships, as developed in the client-centered framework. In S. Koch (Ed.), *Psychology: A Study of a Science. Vol. 3. Formulations of the Person and the Social Context.* New York: McGraw-Hill. pp. 184–256.

Rogers, C.R. (1959b). Transcript of Rogers' interview with 'Elaine'. The Carl R. Rogers Archive. Congressional Archives, Washington, D.C. Also in The Carl Rogers Library. Center for the Studies of the Person, La Jolla, CA.

Rogers, C.R. (circa 1977). Transcript of Rogers' interview with 'Ms K'. In E.L. Shostrom (Producer). Three approaches to psychotherapy II. Part 2: Carl Rogers [Film]. Corona del Mar, CA: Psychological and Educational Films. Also in The Carl R. Rogers Archive. Congressional Archives, Washington, D.C.

Rogers, C.R. (1983). Transcript of Rogers' interview with 'Daniel'. The Carl R. Rogers Archive. Congressional Archives, Washington, D.C. Also in The Carl Rogers Memorial Library, Center for the Studies of the Person, La Jolla, CA.

Rogers, C. R (1984). Transcript of Rogers' interview with 'Vivian'. The Carl R. Rogers Archive. Congressional Archives, Washington, D.C. Also in The Carl Rogers Memorial Library, Center for the Studies of the Person, La Jolla, CA.

Rogers, C. R. (1986). Transcript of Rogers' interview with 'Lydia'. The Carl R. Rogers Archive. Congressional Archives, Washington, D.C. Also in The Carl Rogers Memorial Library, Center for the Studies of the Person, La Jolla, CA.

Temaner, B.T. (1977). The empathic understanding response process. *Counseling Center Discussion Papers.* Chicago Counseling and Psychotherapy Center.

Tomlinson, T. M., and Whitney, R. E. (1970). Values and strategy in client-centered therapy: a means to an end. In J. T. Hart and T. M. Tomlinson (Eds.) *New Directions in Client-Centered Therapy.* Boston: Houghton Mifflin, pp. 433–67.

Wilkins, P. (2000). Unconditional positive regard reconsidered. *British Journal of Guidance and Counselling,* 28 (1), pp. 23–36.

Wyatt, G. (2000). The multifaceted nature of congruence. *The Person-Centered Journal.* 7 (1), pp. 52–68.

14   A Reconceptualization of the Necessary and Sufficient Conditions for Therapeutic Personality Change

Jerold D. Bozarth

In this chapter, I suggest a reconceptualization of Rogers' hypothesis of the necessary and sufficient conditions for therapeutic personality change. A conceptual model entailing the relationship of the three conditions of therapist genuineness, empathic understanding and unconditional positive regard to each other is proposed. It is suggested that these conditions continue to be necessary and sufficient but that their relationship can be reconceptualized in a way that will emphasize their unique conceptual contributions. Genuineness and empathic understanding are viewed as two contextual attitudes for the primary condition of change; i.e. unconditional positive regard. My conclusions come primarily from a re-examination of Rogers' two major theoretical statements (1957, 1959). The first of these statements in 1957 generated a wealth of research in the realm of psychotherapy. However, the theoretical statement of Rogers in 1959 is the most disciplined statement of his theory of psychotherapy, personality and interpersonal relationships. It is the 1959 statement that provides the basis for the view that unconditional positive regard is the primary change agent in client-centered therapy.

REVIEW OF PERSON-CENTERED THEORY

The foundation block of person-centered therapy is the concept of the actualizing tendency. The implications of this concept is that the therapist can trust the tendency of the client and, hence, the therapist is liberated to concentrate on the role of creating an interpersonal climate that promotes the individual's actualizing tendency (Bozarth and Brodley, 1986; Bozarth, 1998a). The rationale for person-centered theory in interpersonal relationships rests on the actualizing tendency as the foundation block of the theory (Bozarth and Brodley, 1991; Rogers, 1980; Bozarth, 1998b). The actualizing tendency is promoted by the attitudinal conditions held by the therapist and noted by Rogers as the necessary and sufficient conditions for therapeutic personality change.

Originally published as: A theoretical reconsideration of the neccesary and sufficient conditions for therapeutic personality change. In *The Person Centered Journal*, Vol. 3, No. 1, pp .44–51. Adapted and republished by kind permission of the PCJ editor, in *Person-Centred Therapy: A Revolutionary Paradigm*, Bozarth, J.D. 1998, published by PCCS Books, pp. 43–50.

THE 'IF - THEN' DELINEATION

Rogers' most disciplined and rigorous presentation of his theory is an 'if - then' format (Rogers, 1959). That is, he postulates that, if certain conditions exist, a certain process in the client will follow, and if that process occurs in therapy, then there is a certain outcome in personality and behavior. It is important, however, to note this is not an instruction but an observation of what happens and a hypothesis of the process. Thus, there is not intent 'to make' such processes occur. Among other things, the process includes certain occurrences in the client. These occurrences include the following:

1. That the client is freer in expressing feelings;
2. That the client's ' . . . expressed feelings increasingly have reference to the self, rather than nonself' (Rogers, 1959, cited in Kirschenbaum and Henderson, 1989, p. 239);
3. That the client's ' . . . experiences are more accurately symbolized' (ibid., p. 239);
4. That the client has increasingly more reference to incongruity between certain experiences and concept of self;
5. That the client is more able to experience the threat of incongruence;
6. That the client experiences in awareness feelings which have been denied or distorted in the past;
7. That the client has the concept of self reorganized to include previously distorted or denied experiences;
8. That the client's concept of self becomes congruent with experiences; including those which would have been too threatening in the past;
9. That the client ' . . . becomes increasingly able to experience, without a feeling of threat, the therapist's unconditional positive regard' (ibid., p. 239)
10. That the client ' . . . feels an unconditional positive self regard' (ibid., p. 239);
11. That the ' . . . client experiences self as the locus of evaluation' (ibid., p. 239);
12. That the client ' . . . reacts to experience less in terms of his conditions of worth and more in terms of an organismic valuing process' (ibid., p. 239).

The outcomes of therapy include the client becoming:

1. More congruent and open to experience;
2. More realistic and objective in perceptions;
3. More effective in problem solving; this suggests more enhanced psychological adjustment, increased degree of positive self-regard, more acceptance of others, and behavior being perceived as more social and mature by others.

Rogers' statement concerning the person's capacity to experience the threat of incongruence (point 5) is especially appropriate. He quite specifically states: 'The experience of threat is possible only because of the continued unconditional positive regard of the therapist, which is extended to incongruence as much as to congruence, to anxiety as much as to absence of anxiety' (ibid., p. 239). Point 12 is also especially relevant to this chapter; i.e. that the individual reacts to experience less in terms of conditions of worth and more in terms of the organismic valuing process. This occurs as the individual experiences unconditional positive regard. In short, the increasing experience of worth (or unconditional positive regard) promotes the organismic valuing process (or the actualizing tendency).

THE THEORETICAL STATEMENT OF ANXIETY

Rogers' theoretical statement of anxiety further clarifies unconditional positive regard as being the fundamental component for personality change in the theory. He states that anxiety exists because of ' . . . the threat that if the experience were accurately symbolized in awareness, the self-concept would no longer be a consistent gestalt, the conditions of worth would be violated, and the need for self-regard would be frustrated. A state of anxiety would exist' (ibid., p. 247). The crux of Rogers' theory is summarized in his statement on the process of integration of an individual moving in the direction of congruence between self and experience: for threatening experiences to be accurately symbolized in awareness and assimilated into the self-structure, there must be a decrease in conditions of worth and an increase in unconditional *self*-regard. The communication of unconditional positive regard by a significant other is one way to achieve the above conditions. In order for unconditional positive regard to be communicated, it must exist in a context of empathic understanding. When the individual perceives such unconditional positive regard, conditions of worth are weakened and unconditional positive self-regard is strengthened (ibid., p. 249). The consequences of threatening experiences being assimilated into the self-structure and unconditional positive regard being perceived:

> . . .are that the individual is less likely to encounter threatening experiences; the process of defense is less frequent and its consequences reduced; self and experience are more congruent; self-regard is increased; positive regard for others is increased; psychological adjustment is increased; the organismic valuing process becomes increasingly the basis of regulating behavior; the individual becomes nearly fully functioning (ibid., p. 249).

Rogers is also explicit about the role of unconditional positive regard when discussing his ultimate hypothetical actualized person. In essence, he says that the individual has two tendencies which are (1) an inherent tendency toward actualizing his or her organism and (2) the capacity and tendency to symbolize experiences accurately in awareness; or, in other words, to keep the self-concept congruent with one's experience. The individual needs positive regard and positive self- regard. The first two tendencies are most fully realized when the second two needs are met. Rogers further states that the first two tendencies tend to be most fully realized when:

1. The individual experiences unconditional positive regard from significant others.
2. The pervasiveness of this unconditional positive regard is made evident through relationships marked by a complete and communicated empathic understanding of the individual's frame of reference.

It is significant that although Rogers' writings about empathic understanding included reference to the importance of understanding and clarification of meaning of the person's frame of reference that these writings always included reference to unconditional positive regard or acceptance in one way or another; and that in his formal theoretical statement, unconditional positive regard is the fundamental concept affecting change (Rogers, 1951, 1959, 1980). Although some individuals discuss extrapolations of Rogers' view of therapy, the fundamental base of the theory remains in the 1959 statement (Van Balen, 1990; Van Belle, 1980). Rogers never revised his theory statement to include thoughts that just his presence could be healing (Baldwin, 1987; Rogers, 1959).

THEORETICAL RELATIONSHIP OF THE ATTITUDINAL CONDITIONS

Given that unconditional positive regard is the attitudinal condition that is the primary change agent, the attitudes of genuineness and empathic understanding are integrally interrelated. However, the focus on unconditional positive regard as the primary change agent suggests to me that the theoretical relationship of the three necessary and sufficient attitudinal qualities can be viewed in a different way. It is, thus, proposed that the following reconceptualization be considered.

Genuineness is a therapist trait that must exist. It is contextual; that is, this condition is an attitudinal development that enables the therapist to be more able to experience empathic understanding and unconditional positive regard towards the client. It is, for the therapist, a way to prepare him- or herself as a maximally receptive therapist. In both the 1957 and 1959 hypothesis statements, congruence (or genuineness) is stated by Rogers as a therapist quality in the relationship but unlike the other two attitudinal qualities it is neither related directly to the client nor viewed as an attitude to be perceived by the client.

Empathy is also contextual. Empathy is the 'vessel' by which the therapist communicates unconditional positive regard in the most pure way. I interpret this to mean that Rogers thought that the therapist's frame of reference tends to contaminate the purity of the therapist's experience of unconditional positive regard. Empathic understanding of the client's internal frame of reference is one of the two attitudinal qualities which needs to be perceived by the client. It is, however, the only attitudinal action on the part of the therapist. The action of understanding the momentary frame of reference of the client is an ultimate confirmation of the person by the therapist; hence, representing the purity of the therapist's experience of unconditional positive regard towards the client.

Unconditional positive regard is the primary theoretical condition of client change in person-centered therapy. Although there may be other ways that unconditional positive regard is communicated and/or perceived by the client, the underlying premise of the theory is unconditional positive regard in which therapist congruence and empathic understanding of the client's frame of reference is embedded. This attitudinal quality is the unconditional acceptance of the person's momentary frame of reference and all that entails (e.g. feelings and perceptions).

In summary, this reconceptualization of the necessary and sufficient conditions for therapeutic personality change entails (1) genuineness (or congruency) being viewed as a therapist state of readiness that enables the therapist to better experience the client with empathic understanding of the client's internal frame of reference and experience unconditional positive regard towards the client; (2) empathic understanding of the client's frame of reference being viewed as the action state of the therapist in which the client's world is accepted as he or she is experiencing it at any given moment. This is the most optimal way for the client to experiencing unconditional positive regard; and (3) unconditional positive regard being viewed as the primary change agent in which the client's needs for positive regard and positive self-regard are met, resulting in congruence between his or her experience and self-concept and promotion of the actualizing tendency.

PRACTICAL IMPLICATIONS

The attitudinal conditions of genuineness, empathic understanding and unconditional positive regard have been considered as skills (Truax and Mitchell, 1971). They have been considered to be preconditions for other actions (Gendlin, 1990; Tausch, 1990), and they have been considered to be attitudinal qualities (Bozarth and Brodley, 1986; 1991; Heppner, Rogers, and Lee, 1984; Rogers, 1951; 1957, 1959, 1980, 1986). They have rarely (if ever) been viewed in a logical theoretical relationship to each other or to the general theory of personality and behavior change posited by Rogers.

An examination of these conceptualizations in relation to Rogers' theory of psychotherapy, personality theory and interpersonal relationships, suggests that the quality of genuineness is a therapist preparatory attitude and enabler, i.e., for the therapist to be more able to experience empathic understanding of the client's frame of reference and unconditional positive regard toward the client. This view of the concept of genuineness suggests that therapists participate in activities that help them to become more genuine or more able to be more '. . . freely and deeply him (her) self, with his or her actual experience accurately represented by his awareness of himself' (Rogers, 1959, cited in Kirschenbaum and Henderson, 1989, p. 224). Such activities as individual therapy, encounter groups, person-centered community groups might be some ways in which therapists can develop this attitudinal quality.

Empathic understanding of the client's frame of reference is, thus, more aptly experienced by the therapist in a natural way. The view that the attitudinal quality of empathic understanding is the vessel for maximizing the probability of the therapist experiencing unconditional positive regard toward the client, and for the client to perceive unconditional positive regard of the therapist has several pragmatic implications.

First, the idea that understanding by the client of his or her world view is of utmost importance for change is a questionable assumption. The therapist can concentrate on the therapist's intention to understand the client's frame of reference and not be concerned about whether or not the client understands. Second, this could suggest that the intention of the therapist to understand might be as potent as the understanding in and of itself. Third, Rogers' references to his presence as a person in therapy and the use of self as a therapist being, perhaps,

177

more important than providing the attitudinal conditions might be explained within the framework of this reconceptualization (Baldwin, 1987). That is, the presence of total attending to another individual is apt to be perceived by clients as unconditional positive regard. Unconditional positive regard as the fundamental change agent may have greater significance for the focus on 'being' person-centered versus 'doing' person-centered communication. This has implications even more contradictory to the concepts of intervening, directing, controlling and confronting the client's own process than generally associated with person-centered theory. This conceptualization renews the importance of nondirectivity in the framework of person-centered theory. When the client perceives that ' . . . the therapist is experiencing a positive, nonjudgmental, accepting attitude toward whatever the client is at that moment, therapeutic change is more likely' (Rogers, 1986, p. 198). This involves ' . . . the therapist's willingness for the client to be whatever immediate feeling is going on — confusion, resentment, fear, anger, courage, love, or pride' (p. 198). Unconditional positive regard of the therapist for the client is the acceptance of the client's totality of experience, feelings, cognitions at any given moment. As stated by Van Belle (1980):

> . . . we are only actualized by others and ourselves at the regard level, if/when the regard that others show us, and which consequently we show ourselves, is unconditionally positive, that is, if/when it is such that personality development can be interpersonally assimilated (p. 90).

The following comments from an interview with a participant in a person-centered community workshop exemplifies the meaning of unconditional positive regard (Stubbs, 1992):

> And in a moment . . . there was a pressure on me to speak more about something . . . the whole group made a pressure on me. Speak, speak, and I was in a tension. And in that moment the facilitator said, 'Well you know, if you don't want to speak, it's perfectly okay.' And it was the very first moment that made me good, made me feel well. And it made me feel safer. That was very, very fine . . . and the change in me was that, uh (begins to cry), the great point of that change was that I felt my mother (the facilitator) accepts me with all my mistakes, all my wrong qualities . . . Because I was not accepted by my own mother, long ago in my childhood . . . that moment or when that change had a big influence on my work or in my job, and I don't know why, because I was very happy or very satisfied with that experience, and I, uh, tried very hard to be a member of this community. I wanted to go on to continue in this process but in my counseling work, in my job, I, uh . . . uh, became a little bit more directive (laughs) or maybe freer to be directive after that experience, which is a paradox (p. 88).

Although this statement is not necessarily one of empathic understanding, the impact of the perceived unconditional positive regard of his facilitator, whom he viewed as similar to his mother, is clear.

My reconceptualization of the necessary and sufficient conditions for therapeutic personality change is, perhaps, reflected in a statement that I heard Rogers make several times more to himself than to others. He stated: 'If I can be

178

all that I am, then that is good enough.' I would add, 'If the individual can be affirmed in being who he or she is at the moment, then that is good enough.'

REFERENCES

Baldwin, M. (1987). Interview with Carl Rogers on the use of the self in therapy. In M. Baldwin and V. Satir (Eds.) *The Use of Self in Therapy*. New York: The Haworth Press, pp. 45–52.

Bozarth, J. D. (1998a). The core-condition is us: implications for critical mass consciousness. Paper presentation at the Association for the Development of the Person-Centered Approach, Wheaton College, Massachusetts, USA.

Bozarth, J. D. (1998b). Person-Centred Therapy: A Revolutionary Paradigm. Ross-on-Wye: PCCS Books.

Bozarth, J. D. and Brodley, B. T. (1986). Client-Centered Psychotherapy: A Statement. *Person-Centered Review*, 1 (3), pp. 262–71.

Bozarth, J. D. and Brodley, B. T. (1991). Actualization: A functional concept in client-centered psychotherapy: a statement. *Journal of Social Behavior and Personality*, 6, (5), pp. 45–59. Adapted and reprinted in Bozarth, 1998.

Gendlin, E. T. (1990). The small steps of the therapy process. How they come and how to help them come. In G. Lietaer, J. Rombauts and R.Van Balen (Eds.) *Client-Centered and Experiential Psychotherapy in the Nineties*. Leuven: Leuven University Press, pp. 205–24.

Heppner, P. P., Rogers, M. E. and Lee, L. A. (1984). Carl Rogers: Reflections on his life. *Journal of Counseling and Development*, 63, pp. 14–63.

Kirschenbaum, H. and Henderson, V. (Eds.) (1989). *The Carl Rogers Reader*. Boston: Houghton Mifflin Company.

Rogers, C. R. (1951). *Client-Centered Therapy*. Boston: Houghton Mifflin.

Rogers, C. R. (1957). The necessary and sufficient conditions of therapeutic personality change. *Journal of Consulting Psychology*, 21, pp. 95–103.

Rogers, C. R. (1959). A theory of therapy, personality, and interpersonal relationships as developed in the client-centered framework. In S. Koch (Ed.) *Psychology: A study of science: Vol. 3. Formulation of the person and the social context*. New York: McGraw Hill, pp. 184–256.

Rogers, C. R. (1980). *A Way of Being*. Boston: Houghton Mifflin.

Rogers, C. R. (1986). A client-centered/person-centered approach to therapy. In I. Kutash and A. Wolfe (Eds.) *Psychotherapists' Casebook*. Jossey-Bass, pp. 197–208.

Stubbs, J. P. (1992). Individual experiencing in person-centered community workshops: a cross-cultural study. Unpublished doctoral dissertation, University of Georgia.

Tausch, R. (1990). The supplementation of client-centered communication therapy with other valid therapeutic methods. In G. Lietaer and R. Van Balen (Eds.) *Client-Centered and Experiential Psychotherapy in the Nineties*. Leuven: Leuven University Press, pp. 65–85.

Truax, C. B. and Mitchell, K. M. (1971). Research on certain interpersonal skills in relation to process and outcome. In A. E. Bergin and S. L. Garfield (Eds.) *Handbook of Psychotherapy and Behavior Change*. New York: Wiley, pp. 299–344.

Van Balen, R. (1990). The therapeutic relationship according to Carl Rogers: Only a climate? A dialogue? or both? In G. Lietaer, J. Rombauts and R. Van Balen (eds.) *Client-Centered and Experiential Psychotherapy in the Nineties*. Leuven: Leuven University Press, pp. 65–86.

Van Belle, H. A. (1980). *Basic Intent and Therapeutic Approach of Carl R. Rogers*. Amcaster, Ontario, Canada: Wedge Publishing.

15   Potentiating Growth: An examination of the research on unconditional positive regard

Jeanne C. Watson and Patricia Steckley

INTRODUCTION

Acceptance, a touchstone of unconditional positive regard, is fundamental to survival from the moment of conception. Without wanting and accepting her pregnancy, a mother is unlikely to nurture the life within her. This is just as true after the child is born. Acceptance and warmth, together with caregiver responsiveness, facilitates the physical, emotional and social development of the young infant and child (Bowlby, 1969, 1973; Bradley, 2000; Rogers, 1959; Schore, 1994; Sullivan, 1956). In addition to providing a sense of physical safety and protection, both of which are necessary for secure attachment, the sense of being accepted, prized, and cherished is fundamental to how we view ourselves. In the absence of these feelings we may feel defective and unlovable, and may spend the rest of our lives seeking to belong, fearing rejection. In contrast, if we are accepted, we feel a sense of belonging that allows us to grow, explore and mature into socially responsible adults.

Acceptance by another is an ontological affirmation of our own existence and fosters a sense of belonging and participation in an interconnected world. It allows us to accept our experience. The development of our cognitive-affective functioning is closely linked to our ability to apprehend our experience, become aware of it, label it in consciousness and reflect and evaluate it as a guide to future action. Acceptance of our experience by others facilitates our ability to be aware of our experience and to process it in ways that can be optimally life enhancing. Unconditional positive regard enables us to see our experience for what it is in the moment so that we might move forward into the next with greater freedom of choice.

In this chapter we will first find a theoretical grounding in Rogers' concept of unconditional positive regard and its place in client-centered theory so that we can better evaluate the research that followed from his conceptualization. We will then review the existing research on unconditional positive regard and conclude with a discussion of the future directions that research needs to take to move us forward to a more comprehensive understanding of unconditional positive regard.

THE CONCEPT OF UNCONDITIONAL POSITIVE REGARD

Therapist provision of unconditional positive regard and its role in client functioning

Unconditional positive regard is a pivotal concept in client-centered theory. It refers to an attitude of warmth, respect and openness towards another and his/her experience. Rogers stated that unconditional positive regard is an overriding need in human beings and is crucial for the development of a fully functioning self. Client-centered theory argues that it is through the perception of unconditional positive regard from others that an individual integrates his or her own experiences into the self and self-concept (Biermann-Ratjen, 1998). For example, if parents or caretakers are able to mirror their children's experience of emotion and convey that their feelings are acceptable and can be guided in constructive ways, then these children will be able to accept their own experiences as part of themselves, without developing complicated reactions or defenses around their emotions. In addition to accepting their experiences, these children will also view themselves with regard and worth. In contrast, when individuals receive conditional regard, they introject the perceived values of others into their self-concepts rather than what is true to their own experience. This sets up a dynamic of conditional self-worth, whereby individuals defend against self-experience that threatens the introjected aspects of their self-concepts upon which they have built their sense of worth. For example, if a parent responds with rejection when the child shows anger, the message that may be introjected is that the experience of anger is bad (i.e. if I am angry, I am unworthy of regard). Consequently, these feelings may be cut off from awareness. In this way individuals lose contact with their inner referents as they begin to invalidate and distort their inner experience setting the stage for the development of cognitive-affective difficulties and a view of the self as unworthy, bad or possibly untrustworthy (Kennedy-Moore and Watson, 1999; Rogers, 1959; Van Kalmthout, 1998). Thus, unconditional positive regard is essential for the development of adaptive cognitive-affective processing and functioning and a healthy view of self.

In client-centered theory, personality change is thought to occur when individuals experience a relationship characterized by conditions, such as acceptance and empathy, that promote positive self-regard and a sense of safety. These relationship conditions free a person to explore feelings and ways of functioning and develop new ways of being without having to deal with the other (i.e. therapist) as a threat. Rogers (1957) argues that to help facilitate personality change in the client, therapists must experience unconditional positive regard for the client in themselves as well as communicate it to the client. The therapist is experiencing unconditional positive regard, 'to the extent that the therapist finds himself experiencing a warm acceptance of each aspect of the client's experience as being a part of that client' (Rogers 1957, p. 829).

Rogers describes acceptance of the client as a prizing of and a caring for the client in a non-possessive way that is not driven by the therapist's needs. He writes, ' it means a caring for the client as a separate person, with permission to have his own feelings, his own experiences' (Rogers, 1957, p. 829). This qualifier of being able to see the client as a separate person is very important for the experience and communication of unconditional positive regard. To provide unconditional care, therapists must be congruent. This means that they must be aware of their own experiencing, accept it and be responsible for it, in order that they are able to see and relate to clients for who they are, in their own right, separate from themselves. This is essential to the client's process of individuation and the development of autonomy; otherwise the client is viewed through the filters of the therapist's own needs and projections. As Wilkins (2000) writes, the therapist's ability to provide unconditional positive regard 'depends on the attitude individuals hold towards themselves' (p. 33). If therapists are blind to the ways in which they cut off parts of their own experience, they will not be able to relate without some kind of defense to these aspects in their clients. Acceptance cannot be conditional on the therapists' needs, expectations, projections or desires — clients' experiences need to be accepted 'as is'.

Acceptance of the client's experience does not mean that the therapist evaluates it as good. Rather, it is a type of acknowledgment that this is what the client is experiencing in the moment — acceptance is 'to be as close to the client's experiencing as possible, not allying with their thoughts and feelings' (Wilkins, 2000, p. 29). Sensing therapists' unconditional acceptance of their experience, clients lose their preoccupation with the other (therapist) and their energy becomes available to turn inward and contact their own experience (Pearson, 1974). The therapist's steadfast interest in, and acceptance of, the client and his or her experience affords the client the opportunity to turn inward to investigate what life is like on the inside, and to be open to this experience and own it as part of the self. Rogers believed that we cannot change until we accept what we are experiencing in the moment. Rogers (1961) wrote:

> . . . the curious paradox is that when I accept myself as I am, then I change. I believe that I have learned this from my clients as well as within my own experience — that we cannot change, we cannot move away from what we are, until we thoroughly accept what we are. Then change seems to come about almost unnoticed (Rogers, 1961, p. 17).

It is as if when we accept what is true in the moment that all the energy that has been bound up in defending against it is released and becomes available for forward movement towards one's own organismic potential (Pearson, 1974). As we can see, unconditional positive regard is an essential ingredient if a therapeutic relationship is to be a corrective relational experience. It is through the therapists' acceptance of clients and their experiences that the latter can begin to feel safe enough to explore the nature of their cognitive-affective difficulties and begin to develop new ways of processing experience and relating to the self.

Unconditional positive regard's relationship to the actualization tendency

Therapists who are truly accepting believe that clients have the innate potential to change. The growth and movement that occurs in an individual is what Rogers' termed 'the actualizing tendency'. This actualizing tendency is the intelligence that is present in all living organisms and is the foundation of client-centered therapy (Rogers, 1977). The connection between unconditional positive regard and the actualization tendency is important to understand. The unconditional positive regard of their therapists fosters clients' abilities to accept what is true for them in the moment. This kind of acceptance facilitates the flow of clients' innate actualizing tendencies.

Bozarth and Brodley (1991) argue that the actualization tendency is the motive for growth and change and the therapist's unconditional positive regard is based on the belief that this is so. With trust and belief in the actualization tendency the therapist regards the client as 'doing the best that he/she can under the particular existing inner and outer circumstances' (Bozarth and Brodley, 1991, p. 53). Regarding the client in this way facilitates the therapist's nonjudgmental attitude towards the client and his/her experience. The therapist's ability to acknowledge the client's experience without judgment sets up the space for the client to come to know and accept his/her own experience. Clients then become observers of their own experience — they can be aware of what arises in them instead of cutting themselves off from their experiences and come to see the links between their thoughts, feelings, needs, behaviours and situations. This type of awareness allows clients the opportunity to acquire some distance from their experience, which frees them to make more life-enhancing choices because they are no longer trapped in unconscious modes of reacting.

Unconditional positive regard from the therapist acts like a steady and unchanging backdrop against which the client's states of mind and conditional ways of relating to the self come into vivid relief. With the awareness that one is treating oneself conditionally and that this is a cause of suffering, there awakens the possibility of developing unconditional positive self-regard. This kind of self regard is a way of relating to the self and its experiences that eases suffering because identification with protracted parts of experience or self occurs less often allowing a spectrum of experience to flow unhindered. In this way we see that the therapist's unconditional positive regard and trust in the client facilitates the client's self regard and potential to unfold and actualize.

Is unconditional positive regard feasible?

Several issues have been raised in the literature critiquing unconditional positive regard's feasibility. Schmidt (1980) has argued that unconditional positive regard is a paradox and impossible to achieve because one cannot separate self from behaviour. He argues that a therapist cannot and should not regard all behaviours 'positively', particularly negative behaviours (i.e. violence) because people need to learn what behaviours are not acceptable in society. He argues that because self and behaviour are causally linked, if some behaviour is regarded as unacceptable then it necessarily follows that the source of this behaviour (the self) is conditionally regarded. This argument seems based on the assumption that unconditional positive regard is a positive evaluation of clients and their behaviours. However, unconditional positive regard is a non-evaluative stance (neither positive nor negative) towards the client's experience. This kind of stance creates the space for the client to discover what is appropriate instead of the therapist assuming an expert role and dictating what is appropriate. Wilkins (2000) states that:

> while it is neither ethical nor appropriate for a therapist to condone antisocial or harmful behaviour or to collude in its perpetuation, there is a real risk that in attempting to hold the attitude 'I disapprove of what you do but I accept you', the therapist will fail to offer unconditional positive regard, and the client's experience is then one of censure and perhaps rejection . . . the attitude of unconditional positive regard requires that, while the therapist does not collude with harmful or antisocial behaviour, it is neither condoned nor opposed (p. 30).

Purton (1998) argues that it is necessary to go beyond viewing a person as a limited self, identifying them solely with their behaviours. To foster our ability to have unconditional positive regard towards people, we must see their essential natures, their essential selves. Purton (1998) writes:

> . . . I would say that we need to see people as being wholly respect-worthy irrespective of what they empirically are (this is precisely the attitude of unconditional respect), and that it helps us to do this if we picture them as having, now an 'essential self' to which our respect may be directed. But this 'essential self' is not an empirical reality, a real unchanging entity. Empirically, the self is a flux, but that is not the whole truth for anyone who adopts an attitude of unconditional respect towards a person. The remainder of the truth is not empirical at all — it is a matter of faith, of hope, of the spiritual imagination (p. 35).

In other words, Purton is arguing that we need to understand unconditional positive regard in spiritual terms. This concept of an essential self is similar to Rogers' conceptualizaton that each person embodies an actualization tendency which is common to and connects all living beings. Thus it seems that therapists can develop unconditional positive regard by acknowledging that both they and their clients are part of and participate in something larger than themselves, something universal. It is the belief in a fundamental principle of nature geared towards growth that allows the therapist and the client to trust in the client's ability to know how to proceed. It is the therapist's job to help facilitate the client's turning inward to connect to this inner wisdom.

In summary, we see that Roger's conceptualization of therapist's unconditional positive regard plays an important role in establishing trust and safety in the therapeutic relationship. It also functions to facilitate clients' self-acceptance, autonomy, exploration and cognitive-affective functioning. Unconditional positive regard is crucial to one's unfolding, not only as a psychological being, but also as a spiritual being who participates in a larger system of inter-relationships. Keeping these ideas in mind we now turn to a discussion of the existing research.

RESEARCH ON UNCONDITIONAL POSITIVE REGARD

The role of the facilitative conditions of unconditional positive regard, empathy, and congruence in promoting change received much attention in the research literature after Rogers posited that they were the necessary and sufficient conditions of psychotherapeutic change. The findings have generated much debate and heated discussion with respect to the efficacy of these three conditions with numerous researchers either supporting or discrediting Roger's position. However, since the late seventies there has been a decline in research that has looked at the role of unconditional positive regard, empathy and congruence. The decline in research examining the role of unconditional positive regard has been attributed to a number of factors, including the difficulty with defining the construct, poor research tools, and increased interest in the working alliance (Barkham and Shapiro, 1986; Gurman, 1977; Lambert, De Julio and Stein, 1978; Orlinsky and Howard, 1978; Orlinsky, Grawe and Parks, 1994; Parloff, Waskow and Wolfe, 1978; Patterson, 1983; Sexton and Whiston, 1994). In this section we will discuss how the concept of unconditional positive regard has been defined and measured, and evaluate its role in treatment.

Measures of unconditional positive regard

After Rogers' initial hypothesis the two most commonly used measures that were developed to measure unconditional positive regard in psychotherapy were the Non-Possessive Warmth Scale (NPW) (Truax and Carkhuff, 1967) and the Barrett-Lennard Relationship Inventory (BLRI) (Barrett-Lennard, 1962). The NPW Scale (Truax and Carkhuff, 1967) is applied by independent raters to evaluate therapist responses on a five-point scale in terms of the degree to which they communicate non-possessive warmth to their clients. Truax and Carkhuff (1967) define non-possessive warmth as acceptance of the other person that involves,

> . . . a non-possessive caring for him as a separate person and, thus a willingness to share equally his joys and aspirations or his depressions and failures. It involves valuing the patient as a person, separate from any evaluation of his behaviour and thoughts. Thus a person can evaluate the patient's behaviour or thoughts but still rate high on warmth if it is quite clear that his valuing of the individual as a person is uncontaminated and unconditional. At its highest level, unconditional warmth involves a non-possessive caring for the patient as a separate person who is allowed to have his own feelings and experiences — a prizing of the patient regardless of his behaviour (pp. 60–1).

At low ends of the NPW scale, therapists are seen to give advice and clearly communicate negative regard. At mid levels, therapists are seen as showing positive caring, however, it is somewhat possessive. While at the highest levels of the scale, therapists are seen as prizing and their behaviour is uncontaminated by evaluations. Initial studies reported difficulty establishing inter-rater reliability with this scale causing some of Rogers' colleagues to express skepticism as to its usefulness (Barrett-Lennard, 1962; Beutler, Johnson, Neville, Workman and Elkins, 1973). Shapiro (1973) also reported low inter-rater reliability in his study in which

185

he sought to determine whether there were cultural differences between British and American raters in the application of Truax and Carkhuff's (1967) scales measuring the facilitative conditions. However, subsequent studies have reported inter-rater reliabilities from .88 to .94 for non-possessive warmth (Barrow, 1977; McWhirter, 1973).

Another way of measuring therapists' levels of unconditional positive regard is from the clients' perspective using the BLRI (Barrett-Lennard, 1962). This is a self-report measure that asks clients to rate their therapists on a seven-point scale on the extent to which they experience their therapists as empathic, congruent, prizing and accepting. The short form (40 items) of the BLRI (Barrett-Lennard, 1962, 1978) assesses the relationship between outcome and the working alliance. The instrument has 10 items in each subscale yielding 40 items in total. There are two forms of the BLRI, therapist and client. The items in the therapist form of the BLRI are the same as in the client form, except pronouns referring to the therapist are in the first person. Clients and therapists respond to the BLRI by assigning a value from +3 to -3 to each item. A response of +3 signifies strong agreement, whereas a response of -3 indicates strong disagreement with the item. The BLRI has been shown to have split-half reliability with coefficients from the client data for the four scales ranging from .82 to .96. The corresponding reliability coefficients for the therapist data range from .88 to .96. The BLRI has been shown to have good predictive and factorial validity (Barrett-Lennard, 1986; Cramer, 1986; Lietaer, 1974). However, there is a poor correlation between therapist and client ratings. Therapists often rate themselves more highly than do their clients. However, this discrepancy appears to be a function of when the ratings are made as both sets of ratings seem to converge at the end of therapy (Barrett-Lennard, 1998). It may be that therapists feel more warmly towards their clients than the latter is able to perceive initially. This may be either because clients feel negatively about themselves at the beginning of therapy or because liking and warmth are covert processes and may not be readily discernible in initial therapy sessions.

Problems with the measurement of unconditional positive regard

An examination of the research on the role of unconditional positive regard in psychotherapy reveals numerous methodological difficulties and highlights the inherent difficulty in trying to measure a dynamic and interpersonal phenomenon (Barrett-Lennard, 1998). The majority of studies find no relationship between Truax and Carkhuff's NPW scale and Barrett-Lennard's level of regard and unconditionality of regard scales (Caracena and Vicory, 1969; Carkhuff and Burstein, 1970; Fish, 1970; Hill, 1974; Kurtz and Grummon, 1972; Lambert, de Julio and Stein, 1978; McWhirter, 1973; Mitchell, Bozarth and Krauft, 1977; Truax, 1966; Van der Veen, 1967). In the few studies that do, the relationship is moderate to low (Bozarth and Grace, 1970; Kiesler, Mathieu and Klein, 1965; Rogers et al., 1967).

A number of reasons have been posited to account for these anomalous findings. One is that there are problems with the way in which the construct of unconditional positive regard has been operationalized. Shapiro (1976) noted that the NPW scale was difficult to interpret and could not be used reliably by raters in Britain. One of the problems is that the scales for RI and NPW are not anchored to behavioural indices. Truax and Carkhuff (1967) do specify evaluative statements as not showing warmth and acceptance, however, the scale is not very specific for other levels of the scale. It would be useful to have other more concrete criteria for ratings by external judges. Given the way in which the measures have been operationalized it seems likely that clients and therapists use different criteria to make their judgments (Barrett-Lennard, 1962). The RI asks clients to comment on their own subjective sense of the presence of the conditions whereas raters using the Truax and Carkhuff scales are attending to the external cues communicated by therapists. Moreover raters are typically limited to audio-recordings and thus are not able to apprise themselves of therapists' non-verbal behaviours as a means of communicating unconditional positive regard (McWhirter, 1973). Thus clients and raters do not have access to the exact same data to make their evaluations.

As noted by numerous reviewers it is ironic that, despite Rogers' emphasis on the clients' experiencing the relationship conditions, researchers continue to use external evaluations to assess unconditional positive regard (Beutler, Crago and Arizmendi, 1986; Bozarth and Grace, 1970; Gurman, 1977; Mitchell et al., 1977; Orlinsky and Howard, 1976; Parloff, Waskow and Wolfe, 1978). The questionable validity of using observer's ratings is further underscored by the finding that ratings of the facilitative conditions can be made independently of client responses (Orlinsky and Howard, 1986). The rationale for not using clients as raters of the facilitative conditions is that they were likely to be unreliable and inclined to distort or incorrectly perceive their therapists' behaviour (Gurman, 1977). This conclusion reveals a clash between certain research assumptions based in a positivist research paradigm, and assumptions of pathology that are at odds with the underlying assumptions of client-centered therapy (Barrett-Lennard, 1998; Bohart and Tallman, 1997; Parloff, Waskow and Wolfe, 1978; Watson and Rennie, 1994). Client-centered theory views the client's experience as primary and it is not to be invalidated; the client's experience is viewed as important information within the therapeutic context that should be heeded and addressed.

Problems with design and sampling

Another criticism of research that has examined the role of the facilitative conditions in therapy, is that it suffers from the assumption of uniformity. Sampling methods may distort findings (Barkham and Shapiro, 1986; Lambert, De Julio and Stein, 1978; Gurman, 1977; Kiesler, Klein and Mathieu, 1965). Samples of therapist behaviour are usually only three minutes in length, taken from the middle third or middle of the final third of the session (Beutler et al., 1973; Lambert et al., 1978; Lockhart, 1984; Parloff et al., 1978). Brief segments do not provide an adequate sense of the relationship over time and there may be differences in early versus later sessions (Rice, 1965) as well as within sessions (Kiesler, Klein and Mathieu, 1965).

It is assumed that conditions are stable within the session across therapy, and with all clients. Numerous studies have found that the time of assessment is an important variable and that judges' and clients' ratings can change depending on when the assessment is made (Cartwright and Lerner, 1965; Patterson, 1983;

Rice, 1965). Cartwright and Lerner (1965) found that therapists' views of clients were more accurate at the end of therapy than at the beginning but only with 'good outcome' clients. It is possible that certain responses or specific levels of the facilitative conditions may be more helpful at certain times than at others. Carkhuff (1969) noted that perhaps it was more important for the conditions to be present at the beginning of therapy rather than later. Barrett-Lennard (1962) noted that client and therapist ratings changed over time so that their ratings merged towards the end of therapy.

The unilinear approach to causation does not take into account the dynamic interactive nature of the therapeutic interaction (Barrett-Lennard, 1998). Therapists and clients mutually influence each other so that therapists are not necessarily the same across different clients (Beutler et al., 1973; Martin, 1990; Mitchell et al., 1977). Therapists' levels of functioning may have implications for their behaviour during therapy. Carkhuff and Alexik (1967) found that high- and low-functioning therapists are affected differently by their client's level of processing in a session. Low-functioning therapists are more likely to reduce their levels of unconditional positive regard, empathy and congruence with clients who are processing at more superficial levels, whereas high-functioning therapists remain at the same high levels or increase them when working with clients who are functioning at lower levels. Clients also have different preferences depending on their personality. Kolb (in Orlinsky and Howard, 1986) found that highly sensitive, suspicious and moody clients do poorly with very empathic, involved and accepting therapists.

Studies of unconditional positive regard have been criticised for a number of other problems including the absence of true experimental designs (Cramer, 1988) and the absence of control groups. Most of the studies employ quasi-experimental, correlational designs. Thus it is difficult to hold the level of facilitative conditions constant, and the criteria that were employed to distinguish high-functioning therapists from low-functioning therapists have not always been clearly specified (Beutler et al., 1986; Mitchell et al., 1977). Moreover, clients' problems at the beginning of therapy and their rate of improvement prior to a rating of the level of therapist-offered facilitative conditions is not controlled for in the statistical analyses. Several writers have questioned the adequacy of the statistical analyses reported in a number of the studies (Beutler et al., 1986; Marshall, 1977; Parloff et al., 1978). It has been suggested that the positive views expressed by clients are the result of a halo effect that may be more related to the success of treatment and the use of other interventions than the presence of the facilitative conditions per se. Notwithstanding, as we will see when we look at the relationship between unconditional positive regard and outcome, the presence of these behaviours is consistently associated with good outcome whilst the opposite is related to poor outcome.

The relationship between unconditional positive regard and outcome

There have been numerous studies to determine whether the three conditions of empathy, congruence and unconditional positive regard are related to good outcome in therapy (Barrett-Lennard, 1962; Barrow, 1977; Bent, Putnam, Kiesler and Nowicki, 1976; Carkhuff and Alexik, 1967; Cramer and Takens, 1992; Halkides, 1958; Hlasny and McCarrey, 1980; Lessler, 1961; Peschken and , 1997; Truax, 1970; Truax and Carkhuff, 1967; Truax and Mitchell, 1971; Truax, Wargo, Frank, Imber, Battle, Hoehn-Saric, Nash and Stone, 1966). Overall, there is a preponderance of evidence to suggest that therapists' unconditional positive regard is indeed a crucial variable in psychotherapy, notwithstanding those studies that have failed to find significant relationships (Bergin, 1966; Gurman, 1977; Patterson, 1983; Luborsky, Crits-Christoph, Mintz and Auerbach, 1988; Orlinsky, Grawe and Parks, 1994). Recently Greenberg, Elliott and Lietaer (1994), in their review of humanistic psychotherapy, note that a meta-analysis of studies that looked at the relationship between therapist facilitativeness and outcome showed that r = .43. This strong association is supported historically. In 1971 Mitchell et al. noted that out of 26 studies conducted, 20 had a positive relationship with outcome, three were mixed but supportive and three failed to show any relationship. Orlinsky and Howard (1978), in their review of studies observed that two-thirds of the studies showed a positive association with outcome while the remaining one-third were not significant. The one exception was the study by Truax et al. (1966) which showed a negative correlation between warmth and outcome. Further corroboration for the relationship between unconditional positive regard and outcome comes from Orlinsky and Howard's second review in 1986. They noted that, out of 47 studies with 94 findings, only two out of the 94 showed a negative relationship with outcome. The predominant absence of negative findings, along with the large number of studies that have found a relationship between the presence of the therapists' level of facilitative conditions and the very few that have found a negative relationship, speak to the importance of their presence in therapy. Moreover as Patterson (1983) argues cogently, the methodological limitations of the studies would in fact mitigate against finding significant differences rather than allow for their detection.

Other studies, in which clients have been interviewed, have consistently found that an important factor is the opportunity to talk with an understanding, warm, and involved person (Cross, Sheehan and Khan, 1982; Feifel and Eels, 1963; Lietaer, 1990; Strupp, Fox and Lessler, 1969; Watson and Rennie, 1994). Lietaer (1974) and Gurman (1977) in their factor analyses of the components of empathy found that it included six and five factors respectively. Other components of empathy included respect, unconditional positive regard, transparency, directivity, and congruence. In order to experience another as empathic it is not sufficient to feel that the other cognitively understands you, but in addition there must be some sense that the other is involved and receptive to your concerns.

The importance of unconditional positive regard in therapy is supported by Bent et al. (1976) who found that satisfied patients see their therapists as warmer than dissatisfied ones. Furthermore, Hlasny and McCarrey (1980) found that therapists who were rated as warm were seen as more effective and active. Similarly Caligon (1976) in looking at attrition data found that clients in the low attrition groups viewed their therapists as more accepting, secure and affectionate and more able to understand their concerns than subjects in the high attrition group. Orlinsky and Howard (1978) observed that clients appreciate therapists who encourage independence, and who are personally involved, warm, close and intimate as opposed to domineering and confrontational .

This view finds support in a number of studies that have looked at therapist and client interactions using the Structural Analysis of Social Behaviour (Benjamin, 1974). These studies found that therapists in good outcome cases were supportive, affirming, openly receptive, involved, nurturing and stimulating with their clients. In contrast, therapists in poor outcome cases were more likely to be controlling, critical and hostile with their clients (Henry, Schacht and Strupp, 1986; Lorr, 1965; Watson, Enright and Kalogerakos, 1998). Interestingly, therapists in the poor outcome cases were also affirming, supportive, nurturing and stimulating. However, the presence of only a small proportion of hostile, critical behaviour was associated with poor outcome. This underscores the need to carefully examine the level of the therapist conditions during a session and over the course of therapy. Cahoon (1968) and Tosi (1970) both found that dogmatic counsellors as determined by the Rokeach Scale, were seen by their clients to provide a relatively unfavourable therapeutic climate. Therapists' trust in their clients has been found to be positively related to therapists rating themselves highly on the facilitative conditions (Peschken and Johnson, 1997) and clients' ratings of their therapists' level of positive regard was positively related to their sense of trust in their therapists. Other studies have shown a relationship between unconditional positive regard and good process in therapy. Beutler et al. (1973) found that clients' depth of exploration was positively related to the presence of the facilitative conditions.

There are physiological concomitants to the presence and absence of unconditional positive regard. Dittes (1957), using a Galvanic Skin Response rating, found that clients' levels of anxiety change as a function of therapists' levels of unconditional positive regard, with clients showing less anxiety with higher rather than lower levels. The relationship conditions of empathy, congruence and unconditional positive regard may also lead to a 'corrective biological experience'. Evidence is sketchy, but some studies have suggested that the physiology of the therapist and client attune to one another (Levenson and Ruef, 1997). Lewis, Amini and Lannon (2000) have suggested, based on evidence from a variety of sources, the concept of 'limbic resonance. .They have suggested that limbic resonance between mother and child is a significant factor in the child's social development, and that limbic resonance between therapist and client can correct for childhood deficits. Wickramasekera (in Bohart, Elliott, Greenberg and Watson, in press) has speculated that empathy may impact on vagal tone. Low cardiac arousal (Levenson and Ruef, 1997) and high vagal tone (Wickramasekera, 1998) have been found to be associated with greater alertness, i.e. with the potential for more effective information-processing. At present, research in this area is sketchy, but the possibility that unconditional positive regard and empathy may have a direct physiological impact is worth further investigation.

Evidence for the potency of unconditional positive regard outside therapy

Research on the factors that mediate the relationship between physicians and their patients support the importance of empathy and unconditional positive regard in the treatment of physical disorders. Studies have found that physicians who try to understand their patients' concerns, treat them as equals, and are warm and caring are more likely to obtain higher levels of self-disclosure from their patients, continuity in treatment and greater adherence to treatment regimens (Bohart et al., in press). Patients also report higher levels of satisfaction with the care they have received from physicians conveying unconditional positive regard and empathy than patients of physicians who are less so. Other studies have found that physicians who listen to patients' concerns, offer them choices and support their autonomy vis-à-vis their treatment elicit better treatment adherence by patients. Patients also tend to be more trusting of physicians who are warm, understanding, and autonomy-granting than those who are more task-focused and thorough (Bohart et al., in press).

The positive effects of unconditional positive regard have also been noted in a teaching context. Stoffer (1970), in a study with children with difficulties at school, found that when the children were paired with female volunteers who were unconditionally warm and supportive, the children's reading and school performance improved. Cramer (1988, 1990, 1994) has attempted to redress the weaknesses of previous studies by looking at the role of unconditional positive regard in relationships (non-therapeutic) in a systematic and controlled way. He has consistently found that self-esteem is positively related to the presence of unconditionality of acceptance in a current close relationship. The importance of the relationship between unconditional positive regard from a significant other and self-esteem was highlighted in a recent study by Betz, Wohlgemuth, Serling, Harshbarger and Klein (1995). These authors found that the self-regard of female students was positively related to the unconditional positive regard they reported receiving from their mothers. Medinnus (1965) reported similar findings; adolescents high in self-acceptance and adjustment perceived their parents as loving and not neglectful or rejecting.

Functions of unconditional positive regard

A review of the studies that have looked at unconditional positive regard suggest that it has three important functions. First, it increases people's self-regard; second, it helps people feel safe in relationships with others; and third, it facilitates the work of therapy to the extent that clients self-disclose more and explore their experiences more deeply. Experiencing the relationship conditions in therapy provides a 'corrective relational experience'. Theoretically, a relationship characterized by empathy, congruence and unconditional positive regard may help strengthen the self and reduce a clients' sense of isolation. It may also help clients learn that they are worthy of respect and are worth listening to. In addition it may help clients view talking about feelings as positive and appropriate (Bohart, et al., in press). Qualitative studies, although sparse, (Bachelor, 1988) generally support these hypotheses. They find that clients who feel understood and accepted also experience self-validation, and find it safe to self-disclose.

Acceptance and belonging are fundamental human needs and they are the foundation for human growth and survival. Not surprisingly the characteristics of therapists who provide the facilitative conditions including being autonomy-granting, accepting, involved, and warm, are very similar to those qualities found in highly functional families and the characteristics most likely to promote healthy growth and differentiation in children and adolescents. Moreover, controlling and critical behaviours are associated with relapse in schizophrenics and contribute to depression and other difficulties in functioning (Vaughn and Leff, 1976; Greenberg, Rice and Elliott, 1993; Kennedy-Moore and Watson, 1999).

CONCLUSION

A review of the research studies on unconditional positive regard demonstrates both its importance and its validity. Many of the theoretical functions discussed earlier in the chapter have been studied and supported while other aspects have not yet been explored. There is a need for more systematic and controlled studies and greater attention needs to be paid to how we measure and operationalize the construct. The BLRI has proven to be a reliable and valid measure, however, it is limited by the fact that it is rated from a third-party perspective. It would be helpful if external, behavioural indices of unconditional positive regard could be identified to increase reliability and to strengthen the relationship between client and therapist ratings. To date, few attempts have been made to validate the scales with other measures tapping similar constructs. It might be fruitful to validate each scale with other measures of interpersonal behaviour, for example, Benjamin's (1974) Structural Analysis of Social Behaviour. This process measure provides a number of more specific criteria for evaluating interactions as hostile or friendly and laissez-faire or controlling, using external judges.

Although current operationalizations and measures of unconditional positive regard have helped us explore certain aspects of its nature and importance, they do not adequately allow us to study the interactive processes between the client and therapist. In addition to experimental and quasi-experimental designs there is a need for more qualitative and process-oriented research that can better illuminate the intersubjective and participatory nature of unconditional positive regard. As discussed earlier in this chapter, the summoning of unconditional positive regard towards another is not merely an exercise of the therapist's intellect but rather a surrendering to a larger system of interrelationships. As Berman (1981) argues, the intellect is a subsystem of a larger system and,

> ... as a result, the common perception of my skin as a sharp boundary between myself and the rest of the world begins to weaken, but without my becoming a schizophrenic or a preconscious infant. A science that attends to such relationships rather than to so-called discrete entities would be a science of what has been called 'participant observation', and it is this type of holistic thinking which might hold the key to future human evolution (pp. 140–1).

The exploration of unconditional positive regard would greatly benefit by employing this kind of science.

This view reflects similar arguments that have been put forth in the client-centered literature. Bozarth (1985) argued that client-centered theory is a new paradigm less in keeping with linear Cartesian logic (cause and effect) and more akin to systems theory characterized by (a) relationships rather than isolated parts, (b) inherent dynamics of relationships, (c) process thinking (d) holistic thinking (e) subjectivity, and (f) autonomy. Few qualitative studies have been conducted to date but this type of methodology is essential to help investigate the participatory nature of unconditional positive regard and the transformations in self processes that are associated with this kind of acceptance because quantitative methods fail to capture non- linear relationships. Qualitative research would be necessary for exploring the following aspects of unconditional positive regard as outlined in the first part of this chapter: the relationship between therapists' trust and belief in the actualizing tendency and their ability to embody acceptance; the spiritual nature of unconditional positive regard; and the ways that therapists can develop unconditional positive regard towards themselves and be present in the moment with their clients (Geller, 2001; Greenberg and Geller, 2001).

In conclusion, while there is a wealth of information that points to the potency of unconditional positive regard as well as the other relationship conditions in promoting healthy development and growth, the area would benefit from renewed interest focused both on more rigorous and systematic quantitative research as well as in-depth qualitative exploration.

REFERENCES

Bachelor, A. (1988). How clients perceive therapist empathy: A content analysis of received empathy. *Psychotherapy, 26,* 372–9.

Barkham, M. and Shapiro, D. (1986). Counselor verbal response modes and experienced empathy. *Journal of Counseling Psychology, 33,* 3–10.

Barrett-Lennard, G. T. (1962). Dimensions of therapist response as causal factors in therapeutic change. In N. L. Munn (Ed.), *Psychological Monographs: General and Applied, 76*(43), (pp. 1–36). American Psychological Association.

Barrett-Lennard, G.T. (1978). The relationship inventory: Later development and adaptations. *JSAS Catalog of Selected Documents in Psychology, 8,* 68 (MS1732).

Barrett-Lennard, G.T. (1986). The Relationship Inventory now: issues and advances in theory, method and use. In L.S. Greenberg and W.M. Pinsof (Eds.). *The Psychotherapeutic Process: A Research Handbook* (pp. 439–76). New York: Guilford Press.

Barrett-Lennard, G. T. (1998). *Carl Rogers' Helping System: Journey and Substance.* Thousand Oaks, CA: Sage Publications Ltd.

Barrow, J. C. (1977). Interdependence of scales for the facilitative conditions: Three types of correlational data. *Journal of Consulting and Clinical Psychology, 45*(4), pp. 654–9.

Benjamin, L. S. (1974). Structural analysis of social behaviour. *Psychological Review, 81,* pp. 392–425.

Bent, R.J., Putnam, D.G. and Kiesler, D.J. (1976). Correlates of successful and unsuccessful psychotherapy. *Journal of Consulting and Clinical Psychology, 44,* 149.

Berman, M. (1981). *The re-enchantment of the world.* Ithaca, N.Y.: Cornell University Press.

Bergin, A. E. (1966). Some implications of psychotherapy research for therapeutic practice. *Journal of Abnormal Psychology, 77,* pp. 235–46.

Betz, N. E., Wohlgemuth, E., Serling, D., Harshbarger, J. and Klein, K. (1995). Evaluation of a measure of self-esteem based on the concept of unconditional self-regard. *Journal of Counseling and Development, 74,* 76–83.

Beutler, L.E., Crago, M. and Arizmendi, T.G. (1986). Therapist variables in psychotherapy: Process and Outcome. In S.R. Garfield and A.E. Bergin (Eds.) *Handbook of Psychotherapy and Behaviour Change.* (3rd ed.). (pp. 257–310). New York: Wiley.

Beutler, L. E., Johnson, D. T., Neville, C. W., Jr., Workman, S. N. and Elkins, D. (1973). The A-B therapy-type distinction, accurate empathy, nonpossessive warmth, and therapist genuineness in psychotherapy. *Journal of Abnormal Psychology, 82*(2), pp. 273–7.

Biermann-Ratjen, E. (1998). Incongruence and Psychopathology. In B. Thorne and E. Lambers (Eds.), *Person-Centred Therapy: A European Perspective* (pp. 119–30). Thousand Oaks: Sage Publications.

Bohart, A., Elliott, R., Greenberg, L.S. and Watson, J.C. (in press). Empathy Redux. In J. Norcoss (Ed.) *A Guide to Psychotherapy Relationships that Work*. Washington: APA.

Bohart, A. and Tallman, K. (1997). Empathy and the active client: An integrative cognitive-experiential approach. In A. Bohart and L.S. Greenberg (Eds.). *Empathy Reconsidered*. Washington: APA Books.

Bowlby, J. (1969). *Attachment and Loss: Vol. 1. Attachment*. New York: Basic Books.

Bowlby, J. (1973). *Attachment and Loss: Vol. 2. Separation: Anxiety and Anger*. New York: Basic Books.

Bozarth, J.D. (1985). Quantum Theory and the Person-Centered Approach. *Journal of Counseling and Development, 64*, pp. 179–82.

Bozarth, J.D. and Brodley, B.T. (1991). Actualization: A functional concept in client-centered therapy. *Journal of Social Behavior and Personality, 6 (5)*, pp. 45–59.

Bozarth, J. D. and Grace, D. P. (1970). Objective ratings and client perception of therapeutic conditions with university counseling center clients. *Journal of Clinical Psychology, 26*, pp. 117–18.

Bozarth, J.D. and Rubin, S.E. (1977). Empirical observations of rehabilitation counselor performance and outcome: Some implications. *Rehabilitation Counseling Bulletin. Vol 19*,(1), pp. 294–8.

Bradley, S. J. (2000). *Affect Regulation and the Development of Psychopathology*. New York: Guilford Press.

Cahoon, R.A. *Some counselor attitudes and characteristics related to the counseling relationship*, Unpublished doctoral dissertation, Ohio State University, 1968.

Caracena, P. F. and Vicory, J. R. (1969). Correlates of phenomenological and judged empathy. *Journal of Counseling Psychology, 16*, pp. 510–15.

Carkhuff, R.R. (1969). *Helping and Human Relations*. New York: Holt, Rinehart and Winston. 2 volumes.

Carkhuff, R. R., and Alexik, M. (1967). Effect of client depth of self-exploration upon high- and low-functioning counselors. *Journal of Counseling Psychology, 14*(4) pp. 350–5.

Carkhuff, R. R. and Burstein, J. W. (1970). Objective therapist and client ratings of therapist offered facilitative conditions of moderate to low functioning therapists. *Journal of Clinical Psychology, 26*, pp. 394–5.

Cartwright, R. D. and Lerner, B. (1965). Empathy, need to change, and improvement in psychotherapy. *Journal of Consulting Psychology, 27*, pp. 138–44.

Cramer, D. (1986). An item factor analysis of the revised Barrett-Lennard relationship inventory. *British Journal of Guidance and Counselling, 14(3)*, pp. 314–25.

Cramer, D. (1988). Self-esteem and facilitative close relationships: A cross-lagged panel correlation analysis. *British Journal of Social Psychology, 27*, pp. 115–26.

Cramer, D. (1990). Self-esteem and close relationships: A statistical refinement. *British Journal of Social Psychology, 29*, pp. 189–91.

Cramer, D. (1994). Self-esteem and Rogers' core conditions in close friends: A latent variable path analysis of panel data. *Counselling Psychology Quarterly, 7(3)*, pp. 327–37.

Cramer, D. and Takens, R. J. (1992). Therapeutic relationship and progress in the first six sessions of individual psychotherapy: A panel analysis. *Counselling Psychology, 5(1)*, pp. 25–36.

Cross, D.G., Sheehan, P.W. and Khan, J.A. (1982). Short- and long-term follow-up of clients receiving insight-oriented therapy and behavior therapy. *Journal of Consulting and Clinical Psychology, 50*, pp. 103–12.

Dittes, J.E. (1957). Galvanic skin response as a measure of patient's reaction to therapists' permissiveness. *Journal of Abnormal Social Psychology, 55*, pp. 295–303.

Feifel, H. and Eels, J. (1963). Same psychotherapy. *Journal of Consulting Psychology, 27*(4), pp. 310–18.

Fish, J. M. (1970). Empathy and the reported emotional experiences of beginning psychotherapists. *Journal of Consulting and Clinical Psychology, 35*, pp. 64–9.

Geller, S.M. (2001). Therapist presence: The development of a model and measure.

Unpublished doctoral dissertation, York University.

Greenberg, L.S., Elliott, R. and Lietaer, G. (1994) Research on experiential psychotherapies. In A.E. Bergin and S.L. Garfield (Eds.), *Handbook of Psychotherapy and Behavior Change* (pp. 509–39). New York: Wiley. Fourth Edition.

Greenberg, L.S. and Geller, S.M. (2001). Congruence and therapeutic presence. In G. Wyatt (Ed.). *Rogers' Therapeutic Conditions: Evolution, Theory and Practice. Vol. 1. Congruence.* Ross-on-Wye: PCCS books.

Greenberg, L.S., Rice, L.N. and Elliott, R. (1993). *Facilitating Emotional Change.* New York: Guilford.

Gurman, A.S. (1973) Effects of therapist and patient mood on the therapeutic functioning of high- and low-facilitative therapists. *Journal of Consulting and Clinical Psychology, 40,* pp. 48–58.

Gurman, A.S. (1977). The patient's perception of the therapeutic relationship. In A.S. Gurman and A.M. Razin (eds). *Effective psychotherapy: A handbook of research.* New York, NY: Pergamon Press.

Halkides, G. (1958). An experimental study of four conditions necessary for therapeutic change. Unpublished doctoral dissertation, University of Chicago.

Henry, Schacht and Strupp (1986). Structural analysis of social behaviour: Application to a study of interpersonal process in differential psychotherapeutic outcome. *Journal of Consulting and Clinical Psychology, 54,* 1, pp. 27–31.

Hill, C. (1974). A comparison of the perceptions of a therapy session by clients, therapists, and objective judges. *JSAS Catalog of Selected Documents in Psychology, 4,* 16, (Ms. No. 564).

Hlasny, R. G. and McCarrey, M. W. (1980). Similarity of values and warmth effects on clients' trust and perceived therapist's effectiveness. *Psychological Reports, 46,* pp. 111–18.

Kennedy-Moore, E. and Watson, J.C. (1999). *Expressing Emotional Myths, Realities, and Therapeutic Strategies.* New York: Guilford Press.

Kiesler, D.J., Klein, M. H. and Mathieu, P. L. (1965). Sampling from the recorded therapy interview: The problem of segment location. *Journal of Consulting Psychology, 29, (4),* pp. 337–44.

Kurtz, R. R. and Grummon, D. L. (1972). Different approaches to the measurement of therapist empathy and their relationship to therapy outcomes. *Journal of Consulting and Clinical Psychology, 39,* pp. 106–15.

Lambert, M. J., De Julio, S. S. and Stein, D. M. (1978). Therapist interpersonal skills: Process, outcome, methodological considerations, and recommendations for future research. *Psychological Bulletin, 85,* pp. 467–89.

Lessler, W.M. (1961). The relation between counselling progress and empathic understanding. *Journal of Counselling Psychology, Vol. 8,* pp. 30–6.

Levenson, R.W. and Ruef, A.M. (1997). Physiological aspects of emotional knowledge and rapport. In W. Ickes (Ed.). *Empathic Accuracy.* (pp. 44–72). New York: Guilford.

Lewis, T., Amini, F. and Lannon, R. (2000). *A general theory of love.* New York: Random House.

Lietaer, G. (1974). 'Nederlandstalige Revisie van Barrett-Lennard's Relationsip Inventory: Een Faktoranalytische Benadering van de Student-Ouderrelatie (Dutch Revision of Barrett-Leannard's relationship Inventory: A Factor Anlytic Approach to the Student-Parent Relationship)'. *Nederlands Tijdschrift voor de Psychologie, Volume 29,* 1974, pp. 191–212.

Lietaer, G. (1990). The client-centered approach after the Wisconsin Project: A personal view of its evolution. In G. Lietaer, J. Rombauts and R.Van Balen, (Eds.). *Client-centered and Experiential Therapy in the Nineties.* (pp. 19–46). Leuven, Belgium: Leuven University Press.

Lockhart, W. H. (1984). Rogers' 'Necessary and sufficient conditions' revisited. *British Journal of Guidance and Counselling, 12(2),* pp. 113–23.

Lorr, M. (1965). Client perceptions of therapists: A study of the therapeutic relation. *Journal of Consulting Psychology, 29(2),* pp. 146–9.

Luborsky, L., Crits-Christoph, P., Mintz, J. and Auerbach, A. (1988). Who will benefit from psychotherapy? *Predicting Therapeutic Outcomes.* New York: Basic Books.

Marshall, K. A. (1977). Empathy, genuineness, and regard: Determinants of successful therapy with schizophrenics? A critical review. *Psychotherapy: Theory, Research and Practice, 14(1),* pp. 57–64.

Martin, J. (1990). Individual differences in client reactions to counseling and psychotherapy: A challenge for research. *Counselling Psychology Quarterly, 3(1)*, pp. 67–83.

McWhirter, J. J. (1973). Two measures of the facilitative conditions: A correlation study. *Journal of Counseling Psychology, 20(4)*, pp. 317–20.

Medinnus, G. R. (1965). Adolescents' self-acceptance and perceptions of their parents. *Journal of Consulting Psychology, 29(2)*, pp. 150–4.

Mitchell, K.M., Bozarth, J.D. and Krauft, C.C. (1977). A reappraisal of the therapeutic effectiveness of accurate empathy, nonpossessive warmth and genuineness. In A.S. Gurman and A.M. Razin (eds). *Effective Psychotherapy: A Handbook of Research*. New York, NY: Pergamon Press.

Orlinsky, D., Grawe, K. and Parks, B. K. (1994). Process and outcome in psychotherapy — Noch einmal. In A. Bergin and S. Garfield (Eds.). *Handbook of Psychotherapy and Behavior Change*. (pp. 270–376). New York: John Wiley and Sons, Inc.

Orlinsky, D. E., and Howard, K. I. (1978). The relation of process and outcome in psychotherapy. In S. Garfield and A. Bergin (Eds.). *Handbook of Psychotherapy and Behavior Change*. New York: Wiley and Sons.

Orlinsky, D. E., and Howard, K. I. (1986). Process and outcome in psychotherapy. In S. Garfield and A. Bergin (Eds.). *Handbook of Psychotherapy and Behavior Change* (pp. 283–330). New York: Wiley and Sons.

Parloff, M., Waskow, I., and Wolfe, B. (1978). Research on therapist variables in relation to process and outcome. In S. L. Garfield and A. E. Bergin (Eds.). *Handbook of Psychotherapy and Behavior Change*. New York: Wiley and Sons.

Patterson, C. H. (1983). Empathy, warmth, and genuineness in psychotherapy: A review of reviews. *Psychotherapy, 21*, pp. 431–8.

Pearson, P. (1974). Conceptualizing and measuring openness to experience in the context of psychotherapy. In D. Wexler and L. Rice (Eds.), *Innovations in Client-Centered Therapy* (pp. 139–70). New York: John Wiley and Sons.

Peschken, W. E. and Johnson, M. E. (1997). Therapist and client trust in the therapeutic relationship. *Psychotherapy Research, 7(4)*, pp. 439–47.

Purton, C. (1998). Unconditional positive regard and its spiritual implications. In B. Thorne and E. Lambers (Eds.) *Person-Centred Therapy: A European Perspective* (pp. 23–37). Thousand Oaks: Sage Publications.

Rice, L. N. (1965). Therapist's style of participation and case outcome. *Journal of Consulting Psychology, 29*, pp. 155–60.

Rogers, C.R. (1951). *Client-Centered Therapy*. Boston: Houghton Mifflin.

Rogers, C.R. (1957). The necessary and sufficient conditions of therapeutic personality change, *Journal of Consulting Psychology, 21*, 95–103.

Rogers, C.R. (1959). A theory of therapy, personality and interpersonal relationships, as developed in the client-centered framework. In S. Koch (Ed.) *Psychology: A Study of a Science, Vol. 3: Formulations of the Person and the Social Context* (pp. 184–256). New York and Boston: McGraw-Hill.

Rogers, C.R. (1961). *On Becoming a Person*. Boston: Houghton Mifflin.

Rogers, C. R. (1967). (Ed.) *The Therapeutic Relationship and its Impact: A Study of Psychotherapy with Schizophrenics*. Madison: University of Wisconsin Press.

Rogers, C.R. (1977). (Ed.) *Carl Rogers On Personal Power: Inner Strength and Its Revolutionary Impact*. New York: Delacorte Press.

Schmidt, J.P. (1980). Unconditional positive regard: The hidden paradox. *Psychotherapy: Theory, Research and Practice, 17*. No. 3, pp. 237–45.

Schore, A.N. (1994). *Affect Regulation and the Origin of the Self*. New Jersey: Lawrence Erlbaum Assoc. Inc.

Sexton, T. L., and Whiston, S. C. (1994). The status of the counseling relationship: An empirical review, theoretical implications, and research directions. *The Counseling Psychologist, 22*, pp. 6–78.

Shapiro, D. A. (1973). Naïve British judgements of therapeutic conditions. *British Journal of Social and Clinical Psychology, 12*, pp. 289–94.

Shapiro, D. A. (1976). The effects of therapeutic conditions: Positive results revisited. *British*

Journal of Medical Psychology, 49, pp. 315–23.

Stoffer, E. L. (1970). Investigation of positive behavioral change as a function of genuineness, nonpossessive warmth, and empathic understanding. *The Journal of Educational Research, 63*(5), pp. 225–8.

Strupp, H.H., Fox, R.E. and Lessler, K. (1969). *Patients View Their Psychotherapy*. Baltimore: John Hopkins University Press.

Sullivan, H.S. (1956). *Clinical Studies in Psychiatry*. New York: W.W. Norton.

Tosi, D. J. (1970). Dogmatism within the counselor-client dyad. *Journal of Counseling Psychology, 17*, pp. 284–8.

Truax, C. B. (1966). Therapist empathy, warmth, and genuineness and patient personality change in group psychotherapy: A comparison between interaction unit measures, time sample measures, and patient perception measures. *Journal of Consulting and Clinical Psychology, 22*, pp. 225–9.

Traux, C. B. (1970). Effects of client-centered psychotherapy with schizophrenic patients: Nine years pre therapy and nine years post therapy hospitalization. *Journal of Consulting and Clinical Psychology, 35*(3), pp. 417–22.

Truax, C. B. and Carkhuff, R. R. (1967). *Toward Effective Counseling and Psychotherapy: Training and Practice*. Chicago, IL: Aldine Publishing Co.

Truax, C.B. and Mitchell, K.M. (1971). Research on certain therapist interpersonal skills in relation to process and outcome. In A.E. Bergin and S.L. Garfield (eds.), *Handbook of Psychotherapy and Behaviour Change*. New York: Wiley.

Truax, C. B., Wargo, D. G., Frank, J. D., Imber, S. D., Battle, C. C., Hoehn-Saric, R., Nash, E. H. and Stone, A. R. (1966). Therapist empathy, genuineness and warmth and patient therapeutic outcome. *Journal of Clinical Psychology, 30*, pp. 395–401.

Van der Veen, F. (1967). Basic elements in the process of psychotherapy: Research study. *Journal of Consulting Psychology, 31*, pp. 295–303.

Van Kalmthout, M. (1998). Personality Change and the Concept of the Self. In B. Thorne and E. Lambers (Eds.), *Person-Centred Therapy: A European Perspective* (pp. 53–61). Thousand Oaks: Sage Publications.

Vaughn, C.E. and Leff, J.P. (1976). The measurement of expressed emotion in the families of psychiatric patients. *British Journal of Clinical Psychology, 15*, pp. 157–65.

Watson, J.C., Enright, C. and Kalogerakos, F. (1998 June) The impact of therapist variables in facilitating change. Paper Presented at the annual meeting of the Society for Psychotherapy. Snowbird, Utah.

Watson, J. C. and Rennie, D. (1994). A qualitative analysis of clients' reports of their subjective experience while exploring problematic reactions in therapy. *Journal of Counseling Psychology, 41*, pp. 500–9.

Wickramasekera, I. (1998). Secrets kept from the mind but not from the body or behaviour: The unsolved problems of identity and treating somatization and psychophysiological disease. *Advances in Mind and Body Medicine, 14*, pp. 81–132.

Wilkins, P. (2000). Unconditional positive regard reconsidered. *British Journal of Guidance and Counselling*, Vol. 28, No. 1, pp. 23–36.

16   Acceptance of the Truth of the Present Moment as a Trustworthy Foundation for Unconditional Positive Regard

Judy Moore

INTRODUCTION

This chapter is concerned with a level of experiencing that I have found very difficult to make sense of, yet I know that it is where the deepest change takes place. I know that it is arrived at through acceptance of what is happening in the body at an experiential level, that I recognise it as something quite distinct from other layers of experiencing, and I am beginning to understand something of the process by which it is reached. I also know that it is from this place that we, as human beings, are capable of offering the purest form of unconditional positive regard.

What I present here is my current intellectual understanding of an inner journey that has finally enabled me to make sense of a section of Carl Rogers' writing that puzzled me for years. It is the section in *A Way of Being* (1980) where Rogers (by then nearing the end of his life) describes what happens in a helping relationship when he is closest to his 'inner, intuitive self':

> . . . when I am somehow in touch with the unknown in me, when perhaps I am in a slightly altered state of consciousness, then whatever I do seems to be full of healing. Then, simply my *presence* is releasing and helpful to the other. There is nothing I can do to force this experience, but when I can relax and be close to the transcendental core of me . . . it seems that my inner spirit has reached out and touched the inner spirit of the other. Our relationship transcends itself and becomes a part of something larger. Profound growth and healing and energy are present (p. 129, original emphasis).

This seemed to me for many years an impossible and incomprehensible ideal and as far removed from my clumsy and partially successful endeavours to 'accept' the client, as I was from Carl Rogers himself. How on earth *was* I to 'relax and be close to the transcendental core of me'? How *does* a relationship 'transcend itself and become part of something larger'?

Eventually I gave up on this ideal and just got on with the painstaking work of tracking the client and trying to deepen my capacity to stay with the complexities of my own inner experiencing. Then, several years after I had first encountered Rogers' statement, a session with a very long-standing client took an unexpected turn and I found myself experiencing the very phenomenon that had so puzzled and eluded me. In that session, as 'I' disappeared and the boundaries between myself and the client seemed to dissolve, our relationship did indeed 'transcend . . . itself and become . . . a part of something larger' and, unmistakably, there was 'profound growth and healing and energy' present. It was a transformational moment for both of us, which I describe more fully below, but what is clear to me in retrospect is that it was reached at the very moment the client accepted a final truth that had hitherto held her to a constricted sense of self. It was a moment born of much hard inner work.

Since that time (six years ago), moments of such experiencing have come to me again, sometimes in groups, sometimes in the presence of another person, sometimes alone, but always as if by accident, when I and whoever else is present are undefended and without expectation of anything unusual happening. Rogers talks about the quality of his own experiencing of this phenomenon, but does not explain how he got there himself, so in order to understand the process more fully and to prove that we are *all* capable at times of living from and working beyond the constraints of our limited selves, I have had to go beyond his writings and ultimately beyond the Person-Centred Approach. The work of Eugene Gendlin, of André Rochais and the Pérsonnalité et Rélations Humaines (PRH) Organization, as well as the teachings of Soto Zen Buddhism, have been significant milestones in this search. All stress the need for acceptance of the truth of inner experiencing as vital for human growth, but take it further than Rogers.

The importance of staying with and listening to inner experiencing without distortion is nevertheless present in the theory of the Person-Centred Approach from its earliest stages. Rogers writes in 1951:

> 'You must let your own experience tell you its own meaning' — when that sentence is deeply understood we will, in the writer's estimation, know much of what we wish to know in regard to psychotherapy. What is the usual alternative? It is to try to distort the many items of experience so that they fit in with the concepts we have already formed (p. 97).

Unfortunately, the profundity of this statement has got lost, not least, I am convinced, in partial consequence of Rogers' endeavours to establish a school of psychotherapy that admitted 'the construct of self':

> The self has for many years been an unpopular concept in psychology, and those doing therapeutic work from a client-centred orientation certainly had no initial leanings toward using the self as an explanatory construct. Yet so much of the verbal interchange of therapy had to do with the self that attention was forcibly turned in this direction. The client felt he was not being his real self, often felt he did not know what his real self was, and felt satisfaction when he had become more truly himself. Clinically these trends could not be overlooked (ibid., p.136).

Over the years much has been written within the Person-Centred Approach about 'the self', not least Dave Mearns' recent and very helpful work on 'configurations of the self' (Mearns and Thorne, 2000), but I would suggest that wholeheartedly letting 'your own experience tell you its own meaning' takes us not only into looking at the many aspects of the self, but also beyond the self into more profound territory from which excessive focus on the self can only divert us.

'AN EXTRAORDINARY LETTING-GO'

Much of the material of this section is taken from a presentation on our experience of the counselling process that my client, Lucy, then a student in her mid-twenties, and I made to a group of counsellors-in-training several months after Lucy's counselling had ended. We both wrote a separate account of our work together based on a list of dates of our meetings and our own memories. I also had notes that I had made after every session throughout the counselling. The session in question is the penultimate session of a total of 47, spread over three and a half years. The first 38 of these sessions took place weekly during term-time but after that we met only occasionally while Lucy did group counselling and also undertook an intensive person-centred self-development programme (the Associates' Programme) that we ran at the university at that time.

I had not seen Lucy for several months because she had taken a break from her studies and gone travelling. She returned to counselling because, although many areas of her life had radically improved and she felt much better about herself, she was having real difficulty with her academic work. This was surprising because, when we first met, academic work had been the one area of her life where she had no problems.

One particular session Lucy described how she feared beginning to write an analysis of a poem in case it should be 'sneered at'. We looked at how this fear derived from her experience of being bullied at school for being 'clever' and how she had hidden herself since then. The session seemed quite helpful at the time and I was very surprised when Lucy didn't turn up the following week. This is her account of what had happened for her and what happened next:

> *My overwhelming feeling was embarrassment at having 'gone on' about school. I 'overslept' and missed the next appointment, but decided I had to go to the next session and be honest about my reasons for missing the previous one. My expectation was that we would then move on, that it would simply be a matter of honestly apologising, then the real session would start. But my embarrassment became the focus, and I realised that I still felt I should be in control of my emotions, not 'weak'. The distance in time between what we were talking about and the present seemed to suddenly collapse, and we were looking at and feeling my present emotions and perceptions. Judy mentioned that I was still seeing 'being all right' as a fixed state that I was yet to arrive at, and sparks began to fly in my mind as connections were made. All my counselling with Judy, the experience of the Associates' Programme, some of my academic work on changing perceptions of the self, so much of my experience, seemed to suddenly be pulled together and then flip into a whole, a calm fundamental change in perception. My perception of myself and others radically shifted. Rather than seeing those that had arrived and those that hadn't, I felt all as moving, changing. I suddenly felt that I could be OK now, with all my anxieties, fears and embarrassments, rather than looking to a future point where they just didn't happen to me! I felt this physically—at the*

> *end of the session I felt as if my body had been pummelled all over, rather like a very thorough massage. When I walked out of the counselling centre I felt a qualitative change in everything...*
>
> *We were both aware that what had happened was so significant and fundamental. I really feel it is amazing and wonderful that we were able to share perceptions so closely in the session that it could lead me into such an enormous shift.*
>
> *Above all I would say that I am now able to accept myself — such a small phrase to cover such an enormous shift. I can now accept my pleasure, anger, tensions and still feel that I am human, that I am of value ... Judy's acceptance of me and willingness to be with me and to share my fear of letting-go for so long was so important, and led to the extraordinary letting-go in the second-to-last session.*

This is my own memory of the session, written at around the same time as Lucy's account:

> *Lucy said that she felt she 'should' be OK now, having done the Associates' Programme. It occurred to me at this point that she was seeing growth in terms of 'arrival' at a fixed point rather than as a constantly-changing process and I said this. I remember Lucy dissolving as if she was completely overwhelmed by the revelation. I can remember but can't begin to do justice to the strength of the emotion that took over the session ... It seemed as if she was allowing herself to be the process that she had hitherto understood to be a desirable state and I became swept up in that process.*

I can still remember, even at a distance of six years, that I 'dissolved' as Lucy 'dissolved' and that we were *both* being whatever it was that was happening. It was as if I had challenged us *both* by bringing in the idea of letting-go as opposed to being in a fixed state. We *both* had to let go — into whatever it was (I would now probably not use the word 'emotion': it was something that could be felt but not defined as anything specific). Although when everything began to dissolve I felt a momentary stab of anxiety (*'Why* did I say that?!') it was clear that, however incomprehensible, what was happening was profoundly good and trustworthy.

I cannot claim that it was the quality of my 'presence' that brought about this letting-go, but we did have a very close and trusting relationship and when Lucy 'let go' I instinctively 'let go' as well. Whatever was healing in that interaction was nothing to do with either of us: it was something that was beyond our limited selves. It fascinates me now to read Lucy's account and how it is clear that she *knew* that we were *both* experiencing 'her *present* emotions and perceptions' and her experiencing of 'all as moving, changing'. We were both capable for that short time of being together in the present moment without defences and this opened the way for 'something larger' (Rogers, 1980, p. 129) to come in.

'EXPERIENCING IS ... *IMPLICITLY* MEANINGFUL'

The sticking-point for Lucy had been the particular configuration of self that had seen 'growth' as she had seen academic work: as something to be reached, a fixed point of 'success', like a degree classification. Having done so much work on herself she felt she 'should' be more 'advanced' than to be bothered with what had happened at school many years ago. In the moment of losing that final 'should' she lost all sense of 'having' to be anything in particular. Growth didn't have to be struggled towards or clung on to: it was (and is) there right now as a palpable living process.

Lucy and I arrived at that moment as two human beings who had worked hard over years to contact the truth of our own experiencing, but the deep shift that came about was nothing to do with either of our limited self-concepts. So where did the 'growth and healing and energy' (Rogers, 1980, p. 129) come from? How might access to this level of experiencing be brought more fully into everyday life?

Jerold Bozarth sees the actualizing tendency as being 'the fundamental curative factor' in the person rather than unconditional positive regard:

> The basic curative factor lies in the client's normal motivational drive of actualization. It is this tendency that is the fundamental curative factor lying within the person. The reference to unconditional positive regard as the curative factor assumes the thwarting of the natural tendency; hence, making it necessary that the client become more directly connected with the actualizing tendency through unconditional positive self-regard (1998, p. 83)

The experience of the penultimate session with Lucy might be described as a direct encounter with the actualizing tendency, a pure experiencing of the living force within us all. It was also something that brought a deeper level of acceptance and affirmation that everything was all right as it was: it was, in effect, deep unconditional positive regard.

The intrinsic value of listening within at a bodily 'felt sense' level is stressed throughout the work of Eugene Gendlin. His commentary on Rogers' theory in *Experiencing and the Creation of Meaning* (1962, re-published 1997) reinforces Rogers' own point about the importance of allowing meaning to emerge from within rather than be taken in from the outside:

> People have always fallen into the trap of interpreting their experience only through stereotyped concepts whereby the actual stream of experience is largely missed (1997, p. 17).

Gendlin, however, makes a significant distinction between 'experience' and 'experiencing':

> 'Experience' is constituted of *contents* that are posited in the individual. These contents are the same in nature, whether they are in awareness or denied to awareness. In either case, the nature of experience is that of explicit conceptual contents . . .
>
> '*Experiencing*', on the other hand, is a present, felt *implicitly* meaningful datum . . . It is capable of many different conceptualizations . . . conceptualizations of it can be accurate or inaccurate, yet the felt datum itself will still be directly present. It will still be something other than any of its conceptualized aspects. Experiencing is thus *implicitly* meaningful. It is something present, directly referred to and *felt* (1997, pp. 242–3, original emphasis).

This takes Rogers' statement 'You must let your experience tell you its own meaning' a stage further. Within what can be felt at any given moment is something which we may interpret ('explicit conceptual contents') or simply experience *without* explicit meaning. Yet this moment of pure experiencing has its own intrinsic value.

It is this notion of simply experiencing that underlies the practice of focusing, the practical implementation of Gendlin's thinking as set out in *Focusing* (1978; revised 1981) and *Focusing-Oriented Psychotherapy* (1996). This is how he explains the process:

> Usually a felt sense must first be allowed to come; it is not already there . . . [It] is not [for example] the scared feeling — though the scared feeling is part of it, as is every other aspect of the whole problem. It is not the heart pounding, not the memories, not the desire to approach, not the anger about your inability. If attention is put in the middle of the body, the felt sense can be allowed to come. It comes, so to speak, 'around' or 'under' the anger or 'along with' the heart pounding or as the physical quality that the memory brings with it . . .
>
> With the emergence of such a single bodily sense comes relief, as if the body is grateful for being allowed to form its way of being as a whole. The bodily sense becomes something in and of itself, a fact, a datum, something that is there . . . It is something you *have*, but not something you are. Now you are the new living that is ongoing . . .
>
> When a step comes from a felt sense, it transforms the whole constellation . . . Such a change or 'shift' is experienced unmistakably in the body. One has a sense of continuity, the sensed whole is altering, and one senses this altering directly and physically.
>
> In such a step or shift one senses oneself differently. There is more to be shown about what 'self' means in this kind of experiential step. Such a step is a (perhaps small) development of the centred whole of the person.
>
> As one comes to have a sense of this whole as an object there comes to be a difference between oneself and that sense. 'It is there. I am here.' There is a concrete disidentification . . . 'Oh . . . I am *not* that!' A felt sense lets one discover that one is not the felt sense. When one has a felt sense, one becomes more deeply oneself . . .
>
> . . . when a person's central core or inward self expands . . . strengthens and develops . . . The person — I mean that which looks out from behind the eyes — comes more into its own (pp. 20–1).

Gendlin is clear that this physically based experiencing of a shift within has implications not only for the question or the situation that was the original focus but for the whole sense of the person. The radical questioning implied in his choice of the term 'that which looks out from behind the eyes' to define 'person' permeates his work and raises many questions about who or what we are. 'I' am not this 'scared feeling' or this 'anger'; 'I' am not the 'bodily sense' of the whole situation, but rather 'I' / 'the person' / 'that which looks out from behind the eyes' am / is 'the new living that is ongoing'. Deep, bodily acceptance of what is there leads to a 'concrete disidentification' and a sense that is akin to Lucy's sudden experiencing of 'all as moving, changing', arrived at by a different method, but equally involving accepting the truth of what is there and then letting go into something deeper.

'THE PRINCIPAL PIVOTAL CENTRE OF THE PERSON'

Focusing may or may not take place within a therapeutic context. It can be done with or without a 'guide'. It can be learnt as a method to bring about creative shifts in thinking as well as feeling. It can be learnt by anyone:

> With some commitment of time it seems that any type of person can learn to isolate the felt sense, from hospitalized persons labeled 'psychotic' to college students, children, and creative artists — seemingly anyone (Gendlin, 1996, p. 20).

There is a living force within us that can be tapped as a resource, but this resource is not the 'I' who thinks nor the 'I' who feels. It is a deeper aspect of self than the configurations from which we habitually operate and in which we can get stuck — both in and out of therapy.

In parallel to the work of Gendlin and his colleagues and, indeed, in parallel to the development of the Person-Centred Approach over the past few decades, has been the deepening understanding of human growth to have found expression in the work of André Rochais and his colleagues within the PRH Organization. The PRH (Pérsonnalité et Rélations Humaines) Organization was founded in 1970 by the Frenchman André Rochais (1921–1990). Rochais was a priest as well as a teacher and devoted his life to researching and developing education programmes in human growth, programmes still taught and actively evolving around the world under the auspices of PRH-International. Rochais' work and the PRH programmes are based on painstaking observation and analysis of Rochais, and his colleagues' internal processes. Like focusing, the PRH method is not aimed at specialists: it can be learnt by anyone from any walk of life willing to undertake one of the many training programmes that exist.

Rochais was influenced, particularly in the early years of his work with adults, by the view of the person put forward by Carl Rogers in *On Becoming a Person,* but he subsequently evolved with his colleagues a model of the person that is more refined than any to be encountered within the Person-Centred Approach. I have found the PRH model invaluable in furthering my understanding of what are termed the 'pivotal centres of the person'. In the diagram overleaf I regard the 'growth dynamism of the being' as the same as the actualizing tendency of person-centred theory.

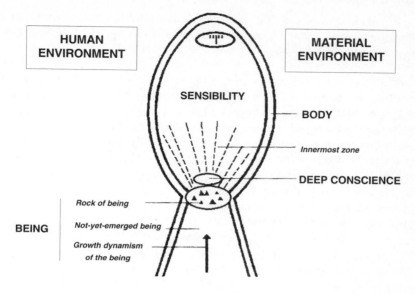

Note: This very refined diagram is intended to highlight the existence of the different pivotal centres of the person. It is not intended to represent persons in their entirety, nor in the complexity of their psychological life.

Figure 1. The pivotal centres of the person (1985). *Persons and their Growth,* p. 53

I began my first PRH programme with what I now consider to be an excessive regard for the 'sensibility' (the area which encompasses feelings and emotions) — a regard that I know was encouraged by my years within the counselling world. I had only a hazy understanding of how far my thinking (the main function of what is termed the 'I' in PRH terms) could generate suffering for myself. In the course of this and subsequent programmes I came to a clearer understanding of the pivotal centres and also learnt, both experientially and in clear conceptual terms, the value of paying more attention to what is called in PRH the 'being'— the deepest part of ourselves from which growth occurs. The being is defined by the PRH Organization as follows:

> The being is a dynamic and positive pivotal centre, located in the inner depths of the person. It makes up the nucleus of one's personality. In the PRH explanatory system, the being is considered to be the principal pivotal centre of the person as seen from the perspective of one's growth . . .
>
> — the other pivotal centres of the person are [ideally] subordinated to the being and at the service of its fulfilment. In fact, actions prompted by the needs of those other pivotal centres must be in harmony with the being if they are to contribute to the growth of the overall person;
>
> — this is the level at which one can experience the most fundamental joys of existence, whereas the satisfactions and pleasures linked to the functioning of the other pivotal centres are not as intense, durable, fulfilling or stimulating.

> In other words, *'it is the most important place'* for the personalization, the growth and therefore the happiness of the human being (PRH, 1997, p. 56, original emphasis).

This account of the importance of the being is accompanied by a very clear description of how it can be accessed. Like the sensations in focusing, it can be accessed *only* through direct experiencing in the body:

> Reflection, readings, action or the reflection of others can be paths of approach and awakening for knowledge of the being. However, if one wishes to account for the reality of this pivotal centre in all of its profundity, flavour and dynamism, such knowledge can only be experiential . . . the being reveals itself in the form of sensations which emanate from the very depths of self . . .
>
> The other pivotal centres of the person are able to participate in this approach to the being. This can happen:
>
> — when the 'I' emerges from ideas, images or worries which preoccupy it, when it becomes attentive to this level of the person and puts itself in a receptive state, suitable to capture sensations coming from that locus;
>
> — when the sensibility is peaceful, relieved of painful or agitated sensations which can encumber it, or also when it is free from any defense mechanisms which anaesthetize or harden it;
>
> — when the body is relaxed (PRH, 1997, p. 67).

In other words, the being can be accessed only when the other pivotal centres will let it be heard. When the 'I' and the sensibility can let go of their preoccupations and defences this creates space for the being. It may be heard through subtle sensations or through a more dramatic realisation such as happened when Lucy let go of her 'hardened' construct around growth. It can only be reached by acceptance of inner truth.

PRH goes beyond the theory of the Person-Centred Approach in its categorization of the pivotal centres and also in the explicitness with which it encompasses the transcendental as part of its system:

> . . . the being [also] has a capacity for openness to a 'Transcendency'. Everyone can experience in their own intimate selves the presence of realities which are of the same nature as their being, but are also experienced as infinite, absolute and permanent realities, non-reducible to what persons are, to what they do, nor to what is in their consciousness . . .
>
> It is through contact with this recognized and identified Transcendency that human beings discover the deep meaning of their existence and the strength to advance toward their fulfilment. Personality development, in the fullness to which individuals can reach . . . requires an openness to that which transcends them (available to all human beings), and eventually to a relationship with that Transcendency (PRH,1997, pp. 60–1).

PRH is a means of helping the actualizing tendency to manifest in the person free from the distortions that can arise through thinking and feeling. That pure manifestation of growth is at the 'edge' of who we are — not our thoughts, not our feelings, not the particular configurations of the self-concept that drive us in any particular situation — but something more. That something has an openness to that which transcends us — and, while it may be accessed in the presence of another, it can also be accessed by each of us alone — simply by listening within, accepting what is there and continuing to listen ever more deeply.

LOSING THE SELF

It is no accident that Eugene Gendlin in the US and André Rochais in France should have arrived at a means of promoting growth that is so strikingly similar as both have, through painstaking observation, accessed basic truths about the human condition that transcend time and place. As far as I am aware, neither has been influenced by the other, yet both take Carl Rogers' fundamentally optimistic view of persons and their growth as their starting-point and, in effect, major in one of the core conditions, unconditional positive regard, turning it very clearly *within* to become acceptance of what is happening in the present moment, not only in terms of thoughts and feelings but also at the level of bodily sensation. That simple acceptance of what is there, according to the PRH system, eventually opens the person to the pure unconditional positive regard of a transcendent reality.

While what the focusing movement and PRH have done is ground-breaking in terms of the relatively new science of psychology, both have, knowingly or unknowingly, tapped into the wisdom of ancient traditions. PRH is very explicit about the broad human truth of 'the being':

> This notion of the being as a central and fundamentally positive reality of the person can be found in many anthropologies. The soul for Christians, the hara for people of the Far East, the innermost self for Carl Rogers,[1] the being for Abraham Maslow, Graf Durckeim, Erich Fromm, etc. are among the approaches that present analogies with this reality observed at PRH (PRH, 1997, p. 56).

In our culture we are inclined to look outwards for solutions rather than to look within. Yet looking within is at the heart of contemplative prayer within the Christian tradition and also at the heart of Soto Zen meditation.

I have been practising Soto Zen (Serene Reflection Meditation) for about seven years and have found within it a sense of direction that is far more trustworthy than any that can be accessed by thoughts or feelings alone. Focusing and PRH have helped me to listen for bodily sensations beneath thoughts and feelings, but it is through the repeated practice of going within, accessing whatever is there and being willing to let go of it, that, at times, I have experienced an opening-up to an inner reality that transcends all thought, feeling and sensation. When I am in touch with this inner reality then a trustworthy sense of direction emerges. I find it difficult to get there, even more difficult to stay there, but at least I know that this is a place to which I can return. Different aspects of Buddhist teaching support this practice, but it is the meditation, in my experience, that has brought about real change, an opening-up to another, broader, more compassionate view

---

1. Rogers describes the prerequisite for a relational-based opening-up to 'profound growth and healing and energy' to be his capacity to be 'closest to [his] inner, intuitive self' (1980, p. 129; see above, p. 155).

of life that I could never have reached through the counselling/therapy world alone.

Soto Zen Buddhism was founded in the thirteenth century by Great Master Dogen (1200–53) and brought to Britain in the late twentieth century largely through the efforts of the Japanese master Keido Chisan Koho Zenji[2] and his disciple, an Englishwoman, Reverend Master Jiyu-Kennett[3].

In an introduction to Soto Zen, written specifically for westerners and first published in 1960, Koho Zenji points to the importance of moving from thinking into direct experiencing in the body:

> . . . as long as one plays with mental discriminations of good and bad, right and wrong, as intellectual ideas, it will be impossible to find the True Way of the Buddha. Dogen said, 'Attainment of the Way can only be achieved with one's body' (Perry, 2000, p. 61).

Dogen's 'Rules for Meditation', recited daily in temples of the Soto Zen tradition, make this very clear:

> . . . The Ancestors were very diligent and there is no reason why we people of the present day cannot understand. All you have to do is cease from erudition, withdraw within and reflect upon yourself . . .
>
> . . . Understand clearly that the Truth appears naturally and then your mind will be free from doubts and vacillation . . . It is no more possible to understand natural activity with the judgmental mind than it is possible to understand the signs of enlightenment . . . Already you are in possession of the vital attributes of a human being — do not waste time with this and that — *you* can possess the authority of Buddha . . . (Jiyu-Kennett, 1990, pp. 98–9, original emphasis).

Written in the thirteenth century this is a clear message that 'the Truth' is to be found within *all* of us if we are prepared to 'withdraw within' to find it. Such knowledge is not confined to the historical figure of Shakyamuni Buddha, but, it is made clear, '*you* can possess the authority of Buddha'.

The universality of this message seems to me very important. The truth of inner experiencing (however deep we may want to go with that) is open to all of us. The quality of 'presence' is something that we can *all* access, not through striving to be like Carl Rogers or by looking outside of ourselves, but through simple acceptance of what is there within us right now.

The self is where we begin, but not necessarily where we end. Dogen also wrote:

> When one studies Buddhism one studies oneself; when one studies oneself, one forgets oneself; when one forgets oneself one is enlightened by everything and this very enlightenment breaks the bonds of clinging to both body and mind not only for oneself but for all beings as well (Jiyu-Kennett, 1999, p. 206).

The inner path leads us through the innermost recesses of the self into something which, ultimately, transcends the self and opens the way for that within us that is

---

2. Keido Chisan Koho Zenji (1879–1967) was Chief Abbot of Sojiji Temple in Japan.
3. P.T.N.H. Jiyu-Kennett (1924–1996), founder of the Order of Buddhist Contemplatives.

way beyond what we may strive for with our conscious, but limited, mind.

CONCLUSION

I have here tried to present something of my efforts towards understanding how it is possible to reach the edge where a relationship — including one's inner relationship with the different parts of the self — 'transcends itself and becomes a part of something larger' (see p. 198 above). I have briefly described some different means of accessing an inner path towards an edge where definition ceases. I think that it is at that point — where definition ceases and the sense of self collapses — that compassion enters and true unconditional positive regard begins.

As a helper I can do only a small amount from the limitations of my thinking or feeling pivotal centres, however much these aspects — or configurations — of self may shift and change. Ironically, it seems that the success of Rogers' efforts to establish a school of psychotherapy that admitted 'the construct of self' has led to an excessive focus on the self and hence to a kind of stuckness in our way of working and in our ability to conceptualize our practice. Even if I begin to think that 'I' am helpful and rest — even for a moment — complacently in that thought, I lose touch with the flow of inner experiencing and so limit my capacity for deeper understanding.

I am convinced that if we are to release within ourselves our full capacity for unconditional positive regard we must be prepared to risk moving beyond thinking and beyond feeling into the territory of pure experiencing and letting-go.

REFERENCES

Bozarth, J. (1998). *Person-Centered Therapy: A Revolutionary Paradigm.* Ross-on-Wye: PCCS Books.

Gendlin, E. (1981). *Focusing.* New York: Bantam Books.

Gendlin, E. (1996). *Focusing-Oriented Psychotherapy: A Manual of the Experiential Method.* New York: Guilford Press.

Gendlin, E. (1997). *Experiencing and the Creation of Meaning: A Philosophical and Psychological Approach to the Subjective.* Evanston: Northwestern University Press.

Jiyu-Kennett, P.T.N.H.(1990). *The Liturgy of the Order of Buddhist Contemplatives for the Laity.* Mt. Shasta: Shasta Abbey Press.

Jiyu-Kennett, P.T.N.H. (1999). *Zen is Eternal Life.* Mt. Shasta: Shasta Abbey Press.

Mearns, D. and Thorne, B. (2000). *Person-Centred Therapy Today: New Frontiers in Theory and Practice.* London: Sage.

Perry, J. (Ed.) (2000). *Soto Zen: An Introduction to the Thought of the Serene Reflection Meditation School of Buddhism by the Very Reverend Keido Chisan Koho Zenji.* Mt. Shasta: Shasta Abbey Press.

PRH-International (1997). *Persons and their Growth: The Anthropological and Psychological Foundations of PRH Education.* Poitiers: PRH.

Rogers, C. (1951). *Client-Centered Therapy.* London: Constable.

Rogers, C. (1980). *A Way of Being.* Boston: Houghton Mifflin.

An Interpretation of
Unconditional Positive Regard from the
Standpoint of Buddhist-based Psychology

Toru Kuno

INTRODUCTION

Dave Mearns of Scotland compared the characteristics of the person-oriented approaches typical of England and the United States. He found that while the American school placed an emphasis on empathy among the list of 'necessary and sufficient conditions', the English school focused primarily on congruence (Morotomi, 2000). In contrast, the Japanese school tended to place the greatest importance on the concept of unconditional positive regard (UPR) — from the relatively early stage after the introduction of Rogers into Japan.

The focus herein will be on UPR centering around the following two points. The first is to examine the conceptual framework in regards to UPR from the standpoint of a Buddhist-based psychological approach. Buddhist culture has been an overriding culture force in Japan for over 1,500 years. Any examination of why UPR has become the central theme in the Rogerian school in Japan absolutely requires that Buddhism, as this overriding cultural force in Japan, be investigated. This chapter will demonstrate how what Rogers called UPR is at the core of Buddhism.

The second point shall be to disclose the strong possibility that UPR is an essential concept for the person-centered school in forwarding the philosophical legacy of Carl Rogers. As was foreseen by the American international political scientist, Samuel Huntington, the world community is groping for a new global order. After the Cold War was declared over at the end of the twentieth century, there were also the outbreaks of ethnic disputes and wars. These were identified as 'The Clash of Civilizations' by Huntington and were considered highly unlikely to dissipate as we enter the twenty-first century (Huntington, 1966). We suggest that the alleviation or even avoidance of this clash of civilizations will start only when each and every individual in all parties to these disputes adopt an attitude of 'Unconditional Positive Regard'.

THE CHRISTIAN INTERPRETATION OF THE 'NECESSARY AND SUFFICIENT CONDITIONS'

Before examining a Buddhist interpretation of UPR, the Christian interpretation of the 'necessary and sufficient conditions' should be considered. This process will clarify the areas where Christianity and Buddhism are the same in their understanding and where they differ.

Dr Logan Fox was a minister of the Church of Christ who first introduced Carl Rogers to Japan in the aftermath of the Second World War. Fox felt in his contracts with Rogers, who had strayed from Christianity, that Rogers still embodied within himself, and within his philosophy, elements that deeply corresponded to the best of religious spirituality (Fox, 1968). However, the issue of religion in Rogers' work was not considered in early research conducted in Japan. Critical examinations into Rogers' philosophy and methods began in the 1970s and debate since that time has centered around the influence of Christianity on the life and work of Carl Rogers. Takao Murase and Toru Hosaka have stated that the approach which is embodied in Rogers' 'necessary and sufficient conditions' is equivalent to the Christian concept of 'love'. This sparked a debate in Japan over the intrinsic connection between the clinical approach of Rogers and Christianity (Murase and Hosaka, 1990). However, Murase and Hosaka did not adequately address exactly what Christian 'love' is considered to be and in what way it can be equated with the 'necessary and sufficient conditions'. In my thesis I demonstrated that the Christian concept 'love' is part of the 'necessary and sufficient conditions' required to bring about personality change and that the Christian attitude toward 'love' was deeply inscribed in Rogers' philosophy (Kuno, 1997).

The Christian interpretation of UPR

First these issues should be addressed from the standpoint of UPR. UPR means that both the 'good' and 'bad' of the client are accepted and that the therapist opens his heart to the client as a separate individual (Rogers, 1957). This concept is found in Christianity in the belief that one does not act as God in his judgments of another. An example of UPR in this sense is expressed in the actions of Jesus toward a woman who had committed the crime of adultery as described in Chapter 8 of the Book of John. (*Good News New Testament — Today's English Version/ed. 2*). This woman was brought before him by a teacher of Law and the Pharisees, who were present in a group who had gathered to hear the teachings of Jesus. His response to those who were eager to condemn the woman was, 'Whichever one of you has committed no sin may throw the first stone at her.' After all those assembled, with the exception of Jesus and the accused woman, had left, Jesus asked her, 'Is there no one left to condemn you?' 'No one, sir,' she answered. 'Well, then,' Jesus said, 'I do not condemn you either. Go, but do not sin again.' If a person looks deep into himself, he will understand that he is prone to everything that happens to another. If he has come to this realization, he will become unable to place himself in judgment of others. This is what Jesus meant when he repeatedly admonished people, 'Take the log out of your own eyes.' The image of Jesus telling the woman who committed adultery, 'I do not condemn you either' is the ultimate example of Unconditional Positive Regard.

The Christian interpretation of congruence

Next, let's look at the concept of congruence. Rogers describes congruence as the state where the therapist, 'within the relationship [to the client] he [the therapist] is freely and deeply himself, while his actual experience is accurately represented by his awareness of himself' (Rogers, 1957). Thus, no matter what the circumstances may be, he must be clearly aware of the feelings and emotions residing within his heart. This, in turn, means that he accepts what is in his heart without fear. An ultimate example of congruence is described in Chapter 26 of the Book of Matthew (*Good News New Testament — Today's English Version/ed.2*). The servants of the High Priest Caiaphas told Peter that they had seen him with Jesus and he denied it saying that 'I do not know that man!' After Peter denied knowing Jesus three times, a rooster crowed. It was then that Peter remembered Jesus saying to him, 'Before the rooster crows, you will say three times that you do not know me', and he was overcome with the regret and guilt of what he had done. Even if a person looks straight at his own heart with sincerity, he will have to, after much painful soul-searching, confront the fact that UPR toward another is, in the end, impossible. At the root of congruence is the inevitable conclusion that we cannot love others in the same way that Jesus loved. What makes 'love' impossible is the love of oneself, which was demonstrated by the bereft Peter who had examined the depths of his soul and peered into that hell that was created by love of oneself.

The Christian interpretation of empathy

The third of the conditions proposed by Rogers is empathy. Rogers described empathy as, 'To sense the client's private world as if it were your own, but without ever losing the "as if" quality' (Rogers, 1957). The judging of the other often results from his fear and worry of losing his world when sharing the other's. Conversely, if one moves to share the world of another, he becomes entangled in the emotions of the other and falls into co-dependency. If one does not forsake another, but does not become entangled in the emotions of the other and maintains the precipitous balance of congruence, then one is confronted with the impossibility of UPR. At this point emerges the issue of human 'sin', but this is also when, as has been demonstrated by many theologians, a person first acquires conversion, and achieves confidence that Jesus took it upon himself to atone for all of mankind's sins, and that Jesus indeed was Christ. It was through this understanding that he comes to know the all-encompassing love of God. Only through such an experience does a person come to understand that he cannot live solely by his own will and desires, and that his life is the gift from God. Only once this belief in God is obtained, can a person know true peace.

Paul, who had once made desperate efforts to persecute Christians, and then experienced a sudden conversion, said the humankind who do not hesitate to crucify Jesus shall admit Jesus is God only with the Holy Spirit, the gift from God. He continues that the people are bound into the one body by the same Spirit. As Paul said in the First Letter to the Corinthians, Chapter 12 (*Good News New Testament — Today's English Version/ed. 2*): 'If one part of the body suffers, all the other parts share its happiness. All of you are Christ's body, and each one is a part of it.' Therefore, if another suffers, it becomes your suffering, and if another is happy, it becomes your happiness. This feeling arises because both parties are part of the same body, and underlying this feeling is the recognition that you cannot change places with another. What Rogers characterized as empathy springs out of this situation and the recognition of its implications.

It thus becomes clear from the above that there is a spiritual and theological basis to the 'necessary and sufficient conditions'. These 'necessary and sufficient conditions' only become complete for Rogers when they are placed within the concept of Christian love.

AN INTERPRETATION OF 'UNCONDITIONAL' FROM THE BUDDHIST STANDPOINT

Rogers himself noted that 'It is not necessary (nor is it possible) that the therapist be a paragon who exhibits this degree of integration, of wholeness, in every aspect of his life. It is sufficient that he is accurately himself in this hour of this relationship, that in this basic sense he is what he actually is, in this moment of time' (Rogers, 1957). David Mearns states that:

> Unconditional positive regard is an extremely difficult attitude to develop . . . it involves the counsellor in considerable personal development work to attain a level of personal security and self-acceptance which reduces her need to protect self against others. Unless that extensive personal development work takes place any 'display' of unconditional positive regard on the part of the counsellor tends to be superficial and usually wilts under the challenge of well-developed client self-protective systems (1994).

Such difficulty in achieving the condition of UPR for a client during an hour-long session might be viewed from the perspective of Japanese Buddhism. On the basis of the 1,500-year-old history of Japanese Buddhism, the individual uses his daily life itself as the practice arena for achieving UPR.

How is UPR viewed from the Buddhist standpoint? UPR should first be broken down into the two elements of 'unconditional' and 'positive regard' and examined separately from the standpoint of Buddhist psychology.

First, 'unconditional' means that a person is accepted exactly as he is. Rogers explains 'unconditional' as 'it involves as much feeling of acceptance for the client's expression of negative, "bad", painful, fearful, defensive, abnormal feelings as for his expression of "good", positive, mature, confident, social feeling, as much as acceptance of ways in which he is inconsistent as of ways in which he is consistent' (Rogers, 1957). To approach another in an 'unconditional' state, it goes without saying that the therapist himself must accept his negative feelings in the same manner as he accepts his positive feelings.

How, then, can we achieve an 'unconditional' state in this sense? The teachings of Buddha show that everyone would achieve this state if he could completely understand his Four Noble Truths which Buddha set down after achieving enlightenment (Syinnyo-en, 1998).

This first of these truths is 'the truth that there is affliction'. Buddha teaches us to face the reality that affliction imbues all of our lives. However, affliction is not merely psychological suffering. Buddha explained that: 'Birth, aging, sickness, death, association with what is unpleasant and separation from what is pleasant, not getting what one wants, and the whole process of attachment is affliction'.

The second of these four truths is 'the truth that there is a cause for affliction'. This is the state when a person confronts suffering. The conventional interpretation of this fourth truth is that 'ignorance' is where a person does not understand that the process of living itself involves affliction and suffering. However, David Brazier, a Zen therapist from England, has posited a totally new Buddhist-based psychological interpretation that goes off in a totally different direction. He posits that when a person confronts suffering, emotion corresponding to that state of confronting suffering naturally arises in response (Brazier, 1995). This is the appropriate interpretation from the standpoint of Zen Buddhism.

The third truth is 'the truth that there is an end to suffering'. Building on Brazier's interpretation of the second truth, the logic is: if one does not suppress nor unnecessarily amplify the emotion which arises in the face of suffering, then that emotion, with time, disappears without a trace. However, what typically happens is that we seek to flee from the suffering and the end result is that it only makes the suffering worse. Thus, Buddha teaches us that we should face our suffering calmly, exercise self-control and strive to walk along the path of righteousness in daily life. This is what the fourth truth: 'the truth that there is a path to end suffering', implies (Brazier, 1995).

If one has truly achieved an understanding of the four truths, then no matter what lies in the heart of another, be it an expression of 'good', positive, mature and sincere feelings or be it an expression of 'bad', negative, fearful, defensive or abnormal feelings, the therapist should be able to understand that these feelings will not stagnate in one place. They will eventually dissipate. The premise of this is the notion that the therapist has grasped his own experience and that his own feelings will flow and dissipate in the same manner. Once this level is reached, it is then possible for the therapist to accept 'unconditionally' whatever feelings clients exhibit.

The Five Precepts

How does one face suffering calmly, exercise self-control and strive to walk along the path of righteousness in daily life? While Buddhism offers up many practical ways of living to achieve this goal, the focus herein shall be on the Five Precepts.

The Five Precepts are 'the precept for refraining from killing', 'the precept for refraining from stealing', 'the precept for refraining from sexual misconduct', 'the precept for refraining from lying', and 'the precept for refraining from intoxicants'. The precept for refraining from killing prohibits the taking of the life of a living thing, but at its core is a pledge to refrain from violating another, or using the existence of another for one's own satisfaction. The precept for refraining from stealing prohibits one from coming into the possession of the fruits of another's labor. This precept for refraining from stealing also prohibits one from developing attachment to material goods The precept for refraining from sexual misconduct prohibits falling prey to sexual lust and calls for each person to keep a proper distance from another. The precept for refraining from lying prohibits one from telling falsehoods, because one who lies is cheating himself and polluting his soul in the act.

If one looks at these four precepts discussed above, it can be seen that they are aimed at curbing excesses related to power, money, sex and knowledge. The final precept, prohibiting one from imbibing intoxicants, can be thought of as placing a brake on narcissistic impulses (Kuno et al., 1997). These narcissistic impulses lie at the root of the mindset in which one allows himself to satisfy any of these desires for power, money, sex and knowledge. This mind set is illustrated by those who wish to wield power over others as a matter of course, those who see nothing wrong with sacrificing others in the pursuit of financial gain, those who make sexual slaves out of others to satisfy their sexual desires, those who, like Faust, did not regret selling his soul to the devil to satisfy his intellectual curiosity. To become able to control these desires, daily training is indispensable because these impulses are deeply rooted in the human psyche.

AN INTERPRETATION OF 'POSITIVE REGARD' FROM THE BUDDHIST STANDPOINT

Now let us move on to 'positive regard' from a Buddhist-based psychological approach. Rogers described positive regard as 'a caring for the client, but not in a possessive way or in such a way as simply to satisfy the therapist's own needs. It means a caring for the client as a separate person, with permission to have his own feelings, his own experiences' (Rogers, 1957).

A brief look at the history of Buddhism should be taken first if one wants to consider positive regard from the standpoint of Buddhist philosophy. Historically Buddhism can be divided into two schools, Theravada Buddhism and Mahayana Buddhism. Theravada Buddhism is practised primarily in South-east Asia, while Mahayana Buddhism is practised primarily in North-east Asia in areas such as China, the Korea and Japan. Mahayana Buddhism can be characterized in comparison with Theravada Buddhism as viewing the mission of Buddhism as the salvation of the masses, and that followers of Buddhism should strive to make themselves part of the lives of ordinary individuals. They see the practitioners of Theravada Buddhism ensconcing themselves in monasteries and concentrating on the daily rituals designed to save their own souls in contrast to Mahayana Buddhism which literally is the 'great vehicle' upon which many can ride (Sinnyo-en, 1998). Rogers' positive regard corresponds to the teaching of Mahayana Buddhism in that one should give precedence to the saving of souls of others before saving your own soul. Many Japanese people naturally understand UPR from the viewpoint of Mahayana Buddhism's teaching. In client-centered therapy, the client's feelings and experience takes precedent over the therapist's feelings and experience.

The Four Means of Embracement

The Buddhist scriptures are full of admonitions for believers who offer to save the souls of others. An example of this is the 'Four Means of Embracement' which are to be followed when one is presenting the teachings of Buddha to another. Specifically, these four means of embracement are 'giving', 'kind words', 'altruistic deeds and 'associating with others'. Embracement by 'giving' is achieved by giving another what they are seeking and thus opening the way to the teachings of Buddha. In order to implement this, one must place the satisfaction of another's desires over the satisfaction of your own desires. If one attempts to do this on a daily basis, then their own material (financial) desires shall be held in check. The end result is that the precept of refraining from stealing will be followed.

Embracement by 'kind words' is achieved by selecting those words which are gentle and compassionate. Buddhism teaches that one should choose gentle words that will be accepted by the listener and then the door will open for teaching the way of Buddha. If one interacts with others in such a manner, then the 'precept for refraining from lying' will be honored as a matter of course, because the speaker is careful in the use of those words which will influence the listener.

Embracement by 'altruistic deeds' is achieved by placing the needs of another before your own, and thus opening the way to the teachings of Buddha. This exhorts one to demonstrate the teachings of Buddha through those actions which put the happiness of others above all else. Subsequently, in the course of performing the third means of embracement, the believer will naturally honor the 'precept for refraining from killing' because killing is premised on the notion of seeing others as instruments for the satisfaction of your desires.

Finally, embracement by 'associating with others' is achieved by being there for others and empathizing with their feelings, thus opening the way to the teachings of Buddha. This exhorts one to empathize with the feelings of others, placing oneself at their level. Through this 'association with others', it becomes possible to adhere to the 'precept for refraining from sexual misconduct' because if one is to empathize with the feelings of others, then one must keep an appropriate psychological distance that corresponds to the state of mind of the other. This opens the way for the teachings of Buddha and thus sexual misconduct becomes impossible.

Thus, through the implementation of these four means of embracement, it becomes natural to place the needs of others above oneself, and one naturally follows the 'precept for refraining from intoxicants' and the reins are placed on unchecked narcissism. The process of following the four means of embracement sets out a program for slowly checking narcissistic impulses which are the fundamental source of human desires.

The way to mutual positive regard

As one can see, the teachings of Buddha constitute a superior system for the teaching of the individual. However, one may come to the false conclusion, based on the argument outlined above and earlier in the section on Christianity, that Buddhism is in some way behind Christianity in working at the deeper emotional level in terms of its understanding of the human conditions. Buddhism is not simply the adherence to those precepts that it sets forth. It does not shy away from confronting the transgressions of those who fail to adhere to its precepts.

For example, it states in the Introduction to the Mahaparinirvana Sutra:

> This carnal body is like four vipers. It is continually pecked at by vermin. It is
> bound by greed, so it has a foul odor and is impure. This body is repulsive like

the carcass of a dead dog. The nine orifices of this body exude impurity. The mind of arrogance towers supreme like a castle covered by blood, flesh, muscle, bone and skin. All such defilements are what the World-honored One detests the most, while ignorant and common mortals love and cling to it. This body houses a mind corrupted by greed, anger, and ignorance (Ito, 1993).

This passage illustrates that those who to honor the precepts against killing, stealing, sexual misconduct, lying and imbibing intoxicants are supported in the Buddhist scriptures. Buddhism also recognizes the impossibility of human 'love', and that humans are no more than hungry spirits.

However, Buddhism also offers the following story:

A man asked the King of Hell to provide him with a look into hell. The King ushered him into a room in which there was a long table piled high with a bountiful feast. The room began to fill with dissipated hungry spirits who came for sustenance. However, when they picked up the chopsticks placed in front of them, the chopsticks grew longer and longer, until they grew too long for food to be brought to their mouths. The hungry spirits were thus faced with a sumptuous feast right before their eyes that they could not partake of. This according to the King was hell. Next the man implored the King to show him paradise, and he was ushered into another room. Here again was a long table piled high with a bountiful feast, and once again the hungry spirits were seated around the table to eat. This time when the hungry spirits took up their chopsticks to eat, they used the chopsticks to feed the spirit seated across from them their favorite foods. At the same time, they were fed their favorite foods by the spirit seated across from them. The meal progressed in this spirit of giving. This was paradise.

In this way, Buddhism does not turn its back on transgressors, but instead recognizes them, and strives for a tranquil existence rooted in mutual positive regard.

CONTINUING THE WORK OF CARL ROGERS

The year 2002 will mark the 100th anniversary of the birth of Carl Rogers. At this juncture, as part of the debate over what will be Carl Rogers' philosophical legacy as we live in the twentyfirst century, it would seem appropriate to sit back and consider what kind of conceptual approach Rogers would have adopted today if he were still alive (Kuno et al., 1997).

Rogers first dubbed his clinical approach, 'client-centered', and later, after the emergence of the encounter group movement, he changed it to 'person-centered'. His client-centered approach was developed based on Rogers' antipathy toward psychiatrists and against the backdrop of early twentieth century American society. The client-centered approach reflected the situation where the client and the counselor are ensconced together in an interview room. The person-centered approach reflected his desire to eliminate the furtive activity that went on behind closed doors, go beyond the client and counselor relationship and achieve a meeting of the minds as one individual to another. This approach can be understood when taken together with the sense of loss of purpose that permeated American society in the latter half of the twentieth century, a time during which national pride took a beating as a result of a series of momentous events including the defeat in the Vietnam War, and Watergate.

What term would Rogers use to describe his methodology today if he were still alive? It seems clear that, as a natural extension of Rogers' philosophical development, he would turn his attention to the environmental problems that are facing humankind today. He would conclude that it was a mistake to place the emphasis on people and to see humans as controlling the natural order. Instead it seems reasonable to postulate that Rogers would search for a new path that would go beyond the current paradigm based on the awareness that humans are simply a part of Nature and that Nature lies at the center and controls humankind. The result would be a 'nature-centered approach', and a Buddhist-based psychology could contribute greatly to this new approach.

We must make a further addition to the philosophical legacy of Rogers that should bequeath to the twentyfirst century. In the twilight of his life, it is well known that Rogers, as a promoter of the 'quiet revolution', devoted his energies to the encounter group movement which gathered together those who had been caught up in regional conflicts. The end of the twentieth century was marked by the break-up of the Soviet Union and the end of the Cold War. These events were followed by the emergence of the new world order on a global scale coupled with the outbreak of ethnic conflicts. Samuel Huntington has predicted that the conflicts in the twentyfirst century will involve a 'Clash of Civilizations', and a close examination of the world around us today attests to the validity of this prophecy. This clash of civilizations will involve, in many cases, religious-based conflicts. Religion defines the world view of the peoples of the world, and provides a framework for how each individual should conduct their life while it also tends to make religious conflicts unavoidable. The tolerance that was exemplified by Buddha is the most important factor for those ethnic groups and countries that are most likely to become involved in deep-rooted conflicts among ethnic groups and nations as a result of religious differences. As we move into this new century of international conflict, which shall be characterized by people trying to conquer their mutual mistrust and hate, the acceptance of UPR based in Buddhist philosophy which was discussed in this chapter will become extremely significant as Rogers' methods and philosophy are passed down to future generations.

If we follow Mearns' assertion that the American school of the person-centered approach emphasizes empathy, and the English school focuses on congruence among the list of Rogers' necessary and sufficient conditions, then we can conclude that the Japanese school of the person-centered approach tends to place the greatest importance on UPR. This is explained from the Japanese mindset influenced by the 1,500 year-old history of Buddhist understanding. Buddhism, especially Mahayana Buddhism widely spread in the North-east Asia, claims that the true Buddhist way of living is to give priority to other's happiness instead of satisfying his own desire.

Buddha teaches that human unhappiness originated from the lack of understanding that we are driven by our own desire. If one recognizes that, one will naturally attempt to control one's desire in an appropriate manner. However, the human desire is endless. It is not something one can handle by willpower. That is why Mahayana Buddhism reversed the strategy to control one's desire in a revolutionary manner. This reversal of the strategy guided them to the belief that instead of the attempt to gain happiness for himself, striving to make others happy will eventually lead them to their own happiness. If one gives precedence to other's happiness before his own, he must postpone satisfying his desire. At that moment, satisfaction of his desire will be under control as a result. As one follows this path, altruism, wishing for happiness for others, will be developed in himself.

Many Japanese schools of the person-centered approach understand that in order for the therapist to actualize UPR with his client, he must make every aspect of his life a practice arena for his self-training. These deeply rooted teachings of Mahayana Buddhism in Japanese mentality made Japanese therapists very responsive to UPR among other Rogers' necessary and sufficient conditions. In Buddhism, as an excellent character-building system, 'congruence' and 'empathy' would be part of the process of self-training to achieve UPR.

REFERENCES

Good News New Testament — Today's English Version (ed. 2) (1966,1971,1976,1992). New York: American Bible Society.

Brazier, D. (1995). *Zen Therapy*. London: Constable.

Fox, L. J. (1968). *Rogers and Me*. Tokyo: Iwasaki Gakujutsu Shuppan-sha.

Huntington, S.P. (1966). *Bunmei no Shoototsu [The Clash of Civilizations and the Remarking of World Order]*. (T. Suzuki, Trans.), Tokyo: Shuueisha.

Ito, Shinjo, (1993). *Aiming of Nirvana*. Tokyo: Shinnyo-en.

Kuno, T., Suetake, Y., Hosaka, T. and Morotomi, Y. (1997). *Rojaazu wo Yomu [Interpretation of C. Rogers]*. Tokyo: Iwasaki Gakujutsu Shuppan-sha.

Kuno, T. (1997). Christianity of C. Rogers. *Kokoro no Kagaku*, 74, pp. 34–8, Tokyo: Nihon Hyoron-sha.

Mearns, D. (1994). *Developing Person-Centered Counselling*. London: Sage Publications.

Morotomi, Y. (2000). A Commentary on Person-Centered Counselling in England, in *Paason-sentaado Kaunseringu no Jissai-Rojaazu no Apuroochi no aratana Tenkai [Developing Person-Centered Counselling]* (Y.Morotomi, et. al., Trans.), pp. 223–33 Tokyo: Kosumosu Laiburari.

Murase, T. and Hosaka, T. (1990). Carl Rogers, Rinsho-Shinrigaku Taikei [General Features of Clinical Psychology]. *Rinsho-Shinrigaku no Senkusha-tati [The Pioneers of Clinical Psychology]*, Vol. 16, pp. 77–108, Tokyo: Kaneko-Shobou.

Rogers, C. R. (1957). The Necessary and Sufficient Conditions of Therapeutic Personality Change. *Journal of Consulting Psychology*. Vol. 21, No. 2.

Sinnyo-en, (1998). *A Walk through the Garden-Shinnyoen from Different Perspectives*, Tokyo: The International Affairs Department of Shinnyoen.

18   Unconditional Positive Regard: Towards unravelling the puzzle

Jerold D. Bozarth and Paul Wilkins

Unconditional Positive Regard (UPR) reflects the complexity of client-centered theory. Client-centered theory is a mix of simplicity and depth, offering premises from logical positivistic empiricism, clinical practice, and the expansive optimism of the constructive direction of human kind. As such, interpretations of UPR in this book view UPR variously as a therapist/client interaction, a human encounter, as a concomitant to particular religious premises, as a significant element of any human relationship, and as the curative factor of client-centered therapy.

The authors of the chapters agree that UPR is an essential concept central to client-centered and experiential therapy, and indeed, most of the authors imply that this is true for all psychotherapy. Given this agreement, there are still different perspectives on UPR represented in this book that may affect the direction and practice of client-centered therapy.

FACETS OF INFLUENCE

Differences in the understanding of UPR by the authors in this book revolve around several facets.

First, there is a subtle difference regarding UPR as an attitude that exists to achieve a client action and/or client direction, *versus* that of a therapist attitude that exists without particular behavioral or goal expectations. For example, on the one hand Lietaer's primary goal is ' . . . to get the experiencing process of the client going again, or to help it function in a richer and more flexible way . . .'. Likewise, Hendricks and Iberg concur that UPR is a primary therapeutic interaction that assists with the promotion of the client's experiential process. Hendricks and Lietaer view UPR to be impossible as a *state* of the therapist. Hendricks explicitly presents UPR as an interaction process. Watson and Steckley within their impressive research review suggest that UPR influences cognitive re-structuring and process direction, perhaps implying that the latter conceptualizations are the actual determinants of client change. In a different vein, Prouty identifies UPR as essential for Pre-therapy. The implication for these authors is that UPR is a prerequisite for change rather than the actual change agent. However, other authors suggest that UPR is the actual change agent. Moon, Rice, and Schneider delineate Standal's dissertation as the seminal presentation of UPR. It was Standal's conception that was adopted by Rogers in his classic theory statement (Rogers, 1959), wherein the postulate is that it is the client's *experiencing* of UPR (and of empathic understanding) that accounts for behavior, process, and personality change. Authors who believe or lean more or less toward this position include Brodley and Schneider, Kuno, Sanford, and Schmid. More explicitly, Freire suggests that the empathic and unconditional acceptance of the therapist is the *essence* of client-centered therapy. Bozarth bluntly states that UPR is the *curative factor* in client-centered therapy asserting that must be true to remain consistent with Rogers' 'theory of pathology'. Wilkins also identifies UPR as the curative factor asserting that congruence and empathy lay the groundwork for UPR.

Moore offers another level of understanding by referring to experiencing as 'implicitly meaningful' and by citing Bozarth's clarification of his view of UPR as the curative factor. She reminds us that: 'The reference to unconditional positive regard as the curative factor assumes the thwarting of the natural tendency; hence, making it necessary that the client become more directly connected with the actualizing tendency through unconditional positive self regard' (Bozarth, 1998, p. 83, see chapter 16 by Moore in this book). Moore refers to Gendlin and to Andre Rochais as taking ' . . . one of the core conditions, unconditional positive regard, turning it very clearly *within* to become acceptance of what is happening in the present moment, not only in terms of thoughts and feelings but also at the level of bodily sensation' (see p. 207 in this book).

Second, there are several perceptual stances that appear to affect the beliefs about UPR. The extent to which one leans toward research, clinical practice, or theoretical conceptualization appears to influence views of UPR. For example, those who prefer direction from quantitative research lean toward definitions that are segmented operational definitions. That is, definitions of UPR are divided into operational definitions that refer to 'positive regard', 'nondirectivity', and 'unconditionality' or other segmented variations rather than simply to a more global concept of UPR. Such operational definitions were initially referred to as 'level of regard' and 'unconditionality of regard' by Barrett-Lennard (1962). Rogers, who first used the differentiated definitions in his 1959 article, referred to such definitions as useful but also 'significantly different' from theoretical definitions (Rogers, 1959, 1975, 1980, p. 145).

When writing from a clinical view, several authors emphasize the therapist's communication of the conditions including UPR. For example, Brodley and Schneider using evidence ' . . . only on the verbal aspects of the communication . . .' demonstrate the UPR process in classic empathic understanding response process sessions. Hendricks and Iberg separately provide examples of therapy sessions that demonstrate communications and interactions of therapists operating from experiential therapy. Clinical *assumptions* also affect the views of UPR. Hendricks and Lietaer, for example, do not believe that the therapist can consistently experience UPR and be congruent. To them, UPR is not the consistent reality of the therapist with the client. Their assumption — that the goal is for the client to achieve a certain process necessary for client change — is not shared by others. Brodley and Schneider, for example, do not assume that any particular process is necessary. To them, reasonable consistency of UPR towards and EU of the client's frame of reference is necessary and sufficient.

Those who focus on the theoretical perspective often involve different controversial speculations. Hendricks, Lietaer, and Iberg take a theoretical position that is contrary to other authors who stay with Rogers' delineated theory. Some believe that client-centered therapy has evolved to a more experiential therapy (Lietaer, 1984, see also chapter 9 in this book). Other contributors offer still different theoretical perspectives, Schmid(chapter 6) offers a rich theoretical discussion revolving around human encounter. Bozarth speculates on Rogers' theoretical statements about 'parent' and 'child' in family life to extrapolate to the assertion that the therapist's unconditional positive SELF-regard begets UPR and, in addition, begets the other therapist conditions. Sanford concludes that the presence or absence of UPR ' . . .can have a far-reaching social and political impact in diplomacy and negotiations' and that the 'absence or presence of this way of relating to others determines the tone or tenor of that person's life and its impact' (see p. 75 this volume). Kuno (chapter 17) suggests that Rogers' foundation of UPR leads to a logical evolution to a 'nature-centered approach', and that a Buddhist-based psychology could contribute greatly to this new approach.

Third, there is a question about the communication of UPR. How does one communicate this attitude? Prouty suggests that UPR in 'pre-therapy' can be communicated in a variety of ways, including love, compassion, non-verbal communications, and concrete empathic responding. Schmid identifies the therapist's involvement of self in a true encounter of two individuals. Brodley and Schneider suggest that the empathic understanding response process is generally the most parsimonious way to communicate UPR, but emphasize the importance of the therapist's attitudinal conditions. In chapter 16, Moore sees 'Acceptance of the truth of the present moment as a trustworthy foundation for UPR.' The truth of the present moment would have probably set well with Rogers. However, he had slightly different comments about the communication of UPR. He noted in his theory statement (Rogers, 1959, p. 230) that UPR *must* exist in a context of *empathic* understanding. Bozarth brings Rogers' comments to the forefront with the re-conceptualization of UPR as the curative factor, while Empathic Understanding (EU) is considered to be the vehicle for *communication* of the curative factor, and congruence enables the therapist to be more capable of experiencing EU and UPR. Bozarth contends that this formulation is consistent with the above references by Rogers, and also fits the context of Rogers' 'theory of pathology'. Wilkins offers a practical rationale for the other conditions in relation to UPR when he states that:

> . . .empathy and congruence provide a framework in which UPR is believable
> . . . it is impossible to be truly accepting of another without being open to one's
> inner experience and bring in a personal state of harmony (see p.45 in this
> book).

In other writings, Bozarth (1997, 1998, 2001a, 2001b) suggests that the conditions are ultimately one condition with the conditions emanating from the therapist's Unconditional Positive Self Regard during therapy sessions.

Few would argue with Iberg's answer to the question of how to *do* the activities of UPR when he suggests that it is to:

> Seek the enjoyable beauty in the person you regard. To do this, (1) do not attempt to control or change the person; (2) use all your senses plus your conceptual grasp of the full range of possibilities to understand; (3) maintain a non-categorizing mentality, attending to the full rich detail, rather than thinking of categories into which to fit things, and (4) allow yourself to be moved by what you hear (see p. 124 in this book).

THEORETICAL CONSIDERATIONS OF UPR

All contributors to this volume agree that UPR is related to the necessary and sufficient conditions of congruence and empathic understanding. To examine the interrelationship of the conditions further, it is worth repeating the central axiom of the conditions that facilitate the therapeutic process in client-centered theory. Rogers presents his statement in two contexts. He postulates that the conditions are: (1) basic to all therapy, and (2) central to client-centered theory (Rogers, 1957, 1959), and is discussed in numerous articles summarized elsewhere (Bozarth, 1998). Rogers' 1959 theory delineation is his self-proclaimed magnum opus and is the definitive source for the theories of personality, psychotherapy, and interpersonal relationships of client-centered theory. He offered only a few refining changes to this statement (Rogers, 1963, 1975, 1978), and re-confirmed his conviction in his last publications (Raskin and Rogers, 1989; Rogers, 1986).

Wyatt (2001) identifies several differences between Rogers' two presentations. She points out that Rogers indicated that he actually wrote the integration statement of 1957 *after* writing his theoretical statement published in 1959 (Hart and Tomlinson, 1970). This is somewhat confusing since Rogers' theory statement in 1959 refers to at least one statement associated with the 1957 publication. He refers in 1959 to the sixth condition of the therapist's '*communication*' of the conditions of UPR and EU in 1957 as being dropped although still acceptable. This particular point is discussed below. Bozarth's conclusion is that Rogers is more likely to have written the articles concomitantly, possibly writing the theory statement first and editing it prior to publication. Nevertheless, Wyatt's quote of Rogers' necessary and sufficient conditions statement is from the theory statement of 1959. The differences of wording in 1957 are italicized.

She quotes as follows:

1) That two persons are in (*psychological*) contact.

2) That the first person, whom we shall term the client, is in a state of incongruence, being vulnerable, or anxious.

3) That the second person, whom we shall term the therapist, is congruent (*or integrated*) in the relationship.

4) That the therapist is experiencing unconditional positive regard toward the client.

5) That the therapist is experiencing and empathic understanding of the client's internal frame of reference (*and endeavors to communicate this to the client*).

6) That the client perceives, at least to a minimal degree, conditions 4 and 5, the unconditional positive regard of the therapist for him, and the empathic understanding of the therapist. (*The communication to the client of the*

> *therapist's empathic understanding and unconditional positive regard is to a*
> *minimal degree achieved)* (Rogers, 1957, 1959 cited by Wyatt, 2001, p. iii).

Rogers' intent in these two seminal articles may be an important key to unraveling the role of unconditional positive regard in client-centered theory. His construct of UPR is the same in both articles. He presents it simply in 1957 as the extent to which the therapist is '... experiencing a warm acceptance of each aspect of the client's experience being a part of the client . . .' (Rogers, 1957, cited in Kirschenbaum and Henderson, 1989, p. 225). The 1959 definition is more detailed:

> Unconditional positive regard . . . may be defined in these terms: if the self-experiences of another are perceived by me in such a way that no self-experience can be discriminated as more or less worthy of positive regard than any other, then I am experiencing unconditional positive regard for this individual. To perceive oneself as receiving unconditional positive regard is to perceive that of one's self-experiences none can be discriminated by the other individual as more or less worthy of positive regard. (Rogers, 1959, p. 208)

Again as Wyatt points out, the 1957 paper does not actually precede the 1959 statement. This realization is more than discovering yet another angel dancing on the head of a pin. It further clarifies the view that Rogers had different purposes in his presentation of the necessary and sufficient conditions. Rogers was always interested in what was central to all effective psychotherapy (Bozarth and Fisher, 1990). As he identified more of the salient variables, he laid out a theory around the central axiom of the necessary and sufficient conditions. At the same time, he suggested that these conditions were the core of all therapies and helping systems that intend to result in therapeutic personality change (and that this would be true even when the theory was founded on other concepts).

Ironically, Rogers' 1957 article had a stifling effect on research in client-centered theory (Bozarth, Zimring, and Tausch, 2001). The central curative factor of UPR became increasing lost in the quagmire of the importance of empathic understanding as a communication system. There were several reasons for this development.

First, Rogers' postulates generated a wealth of research on the *therapist* variables of the necessary and sufficient conditions, yet, research on *client-centered therapy* dramatically diminished. In addition, research on the therapist conditions was often mistakenly identified as research on client-centered therapy. Barrett-Lennard (1998) and Stubbs and Bozarth (1996) separately observe this difference: Barrett-Lennard (1998) referred to the 1957 statement as the 'Conditions Therapy' theory, while Stubbs and Bozarth referred to this article as the 'Integration' statement. Most of the published studies as well as many dissertations were actually investigations of the 'Conditions Therapy' theory, and few of the studies in the United States after the 1957 article actually involve client-centered therapists (Bozarth, Zimring, and Tausch, 2001).

Second, Rogers' 1957 article was the stimulant in the United States (Carkhuff, 1969; Truax and Carkhuff, 1967) for developing 'Human Relations Skills' or 'Interpersonal Skills' programs. These programs focused on empathic responses and ultimately lost the pivotal notion of the nondirectivity of client-centered therapy (Bozarth, 1998, 2000). Most counselor training programs implemented 'Counseling Skills' classes often identifying them as 'Client-Centered Listening' courses and reverting the locus of control to the therapist. Such emphasis has expanded to 'Person-Centered' training programs in other countries, often resulting in focus on such ideas as 'therapist interventions' through empathic responses. UPR was relegated further into the background of theory and practice.

Third, Rogers' claimed that any one of the therapist conditions could be communicated by a varying number of techniques. He states:

> Each of these techniques may, however, become a channel for communicating the essential conditions that have been formulated. An interpretation may be given in a way that communicates the unconditional positive regard of the therapist A stream of free association may be listened to in a way that communicates an empathy that the therapist is experiencing. In the handling of the transference an effective therapist often communicates his own wholeness and congruence in the relationship similarly for the other techniques. But just as these techniques *may* communicate the elements that are essential for therapy, so any one of them may communicate attitudes and experiences sharply contradictory to the hypothesized conditions of therapy (Rogers, 1957, Cited in Kirschenbaum and Henderson, p. 234).

Rogers could ' . . . see no *essential* value to therapy of such techniques as interpretation of personality dynamics, free association, analysis of dreams, analysis of the transference, hypnosis, interpretation of life style, suggestions and the like' (p. 233–4 emphasis added). This is a rather striking statement because techniques that are behaviorally antithetical to empathic understanding are viewed as possible vehicles of communication for attending to the client's frame of reference. Evaluative interpretations of personality dynamics could even communicate UPR. Rogers' theory statement of client-centered therapy offers another hint to the meaning of this assertion when he discusses the omission of the phrase that the therapist *communicates* empathic understanding and unconditional positive regard (Rogers, 1959). Although Rogers is clearly receptive to individuals stressing the communication of these conditions to the client, he goes so far as to state: 'It is not essential that the therapist *intend* such communication, since often it is by some casual remark, or involuntary facial expression, that the communication is received' (Rogers, 1959, p. 213). The emerging conclusion is that it is not what the therapist *does* but how the therapist *is* during therapy sessions. It has to do with the integration of the attitudes by the therapist into her 'way of being' as a therapist. This is reflected by several chapters in this book, whether the focus is upon UPR as a therapist attitude, an interactive process, or embedded in the encounter between the therapist and client.

Chapter 3, the 'historical perspective' chapter, reviews the theoretical acknowledgment by Rogers that the therapist's unconditional positive *self regard* is *the* precursor for the presence of the conditions of Congruence, UPR, and Empathic Understanding. More generally, this is reflected by Rogers' title of his book, '*A Way of Being*' (Rogers, 1980). Most of the authors in this book accept the importance of the therapist's 'way of being' and the central assumption of UPR as critical, but to lesser extent than that contained in Bozarth's interpretation of

Rogers' theoretical statement. Lietaer exemplifies one source of the difference when he refers to the intention of 'client-centered/experiential therapy'. He suggests that therapist's are: ' . . . formally directed toward keeping in touch with and expanding the experiential field of the client, and . . . may direct our interventions . . .'. As mentioned earlier, this represents a difference among authors wherein UPR is viewed either as preliminary to a particular therapeutic process or as the critical curative factor. As Lietaer acknowledges, the assumption of expanding the experiential field of the client has conditionality. Others subscribe to the more unconditional position that the essence of client-centered therapy ' . . . is the therapist's dedication to going with the client's direction, at the client's pace and in the client's unique way of being' (Bozarth, 1990, p. 64). It is the full commitment ' . . . to trust in the client's own way of going about dealing with his problems and his life' (Brodley, 1988, p. 15). Nevertheless, it seems that many of the authors would also agree with most of Lietaer's summary of the effect of UPR:

> . . . unconditional positive regard creates a high level of safety which helps to unfreeze blocked areas of experience and to allow painful emotions in a climate of 'holding'; it functions as a medium for interpersonal corrective experiences through which self-acceptance, self-empathy and self-love are fostered (Barrett-Lennard, 1998); it helps the client to become more inner-directed, more trusting his organismic experience as a compass for living and hence to become a better 'therapist for himself' (see p. 105, chapter 9 in this book).

The agreement concerning the effects of UPR is, perhaps, a basis for unraveling the subtle differences of UPR in the practice of client-centered therapy, experiential therapy and other contextual applications of the person-centered approach. Moore's statement that, ' . . . this moment of pure experiencing has its own intrinsic value' (see p.205 in this book) may hold true for therapist and client. This conceptualization might serve as the rapprochement for differences in the views of UPR.

UPR IN CLINICAL PRACTICE

What does it mean from Rogers' perspective of clinical practice: 'That the therapist is *experiencing* unconditional positive regard toward the client' (Rogers, 1959, p. 213)? Assertions are often made that it is impossible to experience UPR toward certain clients or certain client behaviors. This is extensively discussed in several earlier publications (Bozarth, 1998, pp. 83–8; Lietaer, 1984, pp. 41–58). The central notion of one view is that the therapists' congruence includes conditional thoughts about their clients; hence there is a conflict between the offering of UPR and the authentic feelings of the therapist. The opposite notion is that congruence is the correcting factor. Negative views, conditional regard, and projections of one's own problems are negated through the therapist's congruence. This is, perhaps, the reason that congruence has been identified as the most important condition by Rogers (Bozarth, 2001b). Several of the chapters offer clinical examples of therapist/client interactions that deal with therapists' attention to their correction of conditional regard. Such corrections often represent the therapists' display of congruence.

So, if the essence of the differences among authors is whether or not the therapist has goals and intentions for the client to go in particular directions, then the therapist's wish for, and efforts to obtain, such direction in practice appears to us to demonstrate this difference. The theoretical and functional position of Rogers is clear. His goals were for the therapist to be '*experiencing*' the conditions of UPR and EU. As he states in his last public interview, the most effective therapy is: ' . . . when the therapist's goals are limited to the process of therapy and not the outcome (Baldwin, 1987, p. 47). He elaborates on his meaning of the 'process':

> I want to be as present to this person as possible. I want to really listen to what is going on. I want to be real in this relationship' (Baldwin, 1987, p. 47) . . . [these are] . . suitable goals for the therapist (Baldwin, 1987, p. 48).

Clinical practice in client-centered therapy is *not* directed towards a particular process. The process formulation of therapy refers to the general direction the client follows *if* the conditions are present. However, the conditions of UPR and EU along with the therapist's congruence would result in certain *characteristic directions* (Rogers, 1959, p. 216). These directions include process variables such as the client being ' . . . increasingly free in expressing his feelings . . . increasingly differentiat[ing] and discriminat[ing] the objects of his feeling and perceptions, including the environment, other persons, his self, his experiences and the interrelationships of these. . . increasingly feel[ing] an unconditional positive self-regard. . . increasingly experience[ing] himself as the locus of evaluation.' And ' . . . react[ing] to experience less in terms of his conditions of worth and more in terms of an organismic valuing process' (Rogers, 1959, p. 216). These characteristic directions are set in motion when the necessary and sufficient conditions exist and continue. Outcomes in personality and behavioral changes are also suggested from the function of the conditions. Rogers states that these outcomes are not clearly distinguished from the process variables (Rogers, 1959, p. 218). The outcome variables include the client being more congruent, more open to his experience and less defensive. He is more effective in problem solving, more confident and self-directing, more accepting of others, and has a greater degree of positive self-regard. These process and outcome variables are not intervening variables — there are no intervening variables in client-centered theory according to Rogers (1959, p. 220). Process and outcome are determined by the conditions. Rogers' theory, (according to Rogers), does not instruct therapists to *promote* any experiential process. The instructions are for the therapist to *be* a certain way, not *do* a certain thing. It is the therapist's experiencing of UPR and EU that are the therapeutic facilitators according to Rogers. The theory states that if the six conditions exist, then process and outcome will follow. As Rogers stated:

> Putting this [the functional statement] in more general terms, the greater the degree of anxiety in the client, congruence in the relationship in the therapist, acceptance and empathy experienced by the therapist, and recognition by the client of these elements, the deeper will be the process of therapy, and the greater the extent of personality and behavioral change (Rogers, 1959, p. 220).

This statement by Rogers is a concise summary of the relationship between UPR and the client conditions with the exception that he does not refer to the pre-condition of 'contact' between the therapist and client (Condition 1). Rogers viewed psychological contact as the *minimal relationship* necessary for the other five conditions to take place. This relationship refers to the contact ' . . . when each makes a perceived or subceived difference in the experiential field of the other' (Rogers, 1959, p. 207). Prouty provides examples of his work with hospitalized clients in establishing contact. Wilkins' chapter, as well as the introduction and Bozarth's chapters speculate and elaborate further upon the interplay of the conditions.

The focus on the client's process by those who lean towards experiential therapy is viewed either as an evolution and expansion of Rogers' theory or as a deviation from client-centered theory, depending upon individual biases. It is important for future work to consider these differences since they are key to the position of UPR in Rogers' theory.

A PERSONAL NOTE FROM BOZARTH

I have been struggling for some time to understand the position that therapists can not consistently experience UPR with their clients. My observation of myself is that I *always* experience UPR towards a client during the therapy session. When I experience twinges of negativity or conditional positive regard, I have some inconsistency, or loss of trust in the client, *that is in me*. I must then resolve that in myself to experience my own congruence. Sometimes I say something to the client, but generally not. This does not seem inconsistent with the therapeutic interactions described by some of the authors who believe that it is not possible to consistently experience UPR in the therapy session. I seem to differ from them in that I am always comfortable with where the client is at any given moment. This is true even when I am not particularly comfortable myself with the topic or behavior. If I am too uncomfortable and especially if it is affecting my UPR with the client, I deal with my own discomfort in some way. Of course, I prefer for clients to be happy, to improve, to have less pain, and to make progress from my perspective. I feel satisfaction when a client is better able to interact with others, work better, love better and say that they feel helped. I believe, however, that my perception of such progress is not *necessarily* real progress as experienced by my client. I have known too many clients who show few signs of an experiencing process or depth of self exploration, but who clearly make significant outcome changes and personality changes in their lives.

I have talked with colleagues who also believe that they have little difficulty being congruent and experiencing UPR consistently in sessions with their clients. Most of these colleagues are dedicated to empathic understanding as the primary way of interacting. I adhere to the position that the main activity of the client-centered therapist is to enter into the frame of reference of the client but I am not wedded to an empathic understanding response process. I can concur with Greenberg and Geller (2001) when they say:

> . . . the appropriate response arises out of the in the moment interaction of
> person, situation, and experiencing. It requires the therapist being open, empty
> and receptive to this in the moment, then in touch with their own experiencing

from their own self and their experience in relation to the client's experience, therapist's experience and responding from the therapist's authentic center involves trust, in the process, in the therapist's own emerging experience, and in the client's experience, and is the foundation of therapeutic presence . . .(p. 141)

I suspect that my interpretation of this statement may be different from that of others who read it. I think that may be because my understanding of to 'process' is different. I think that the *individual's unique* process is critical, rather than the commonly-held conceptualization of therapeutic process. My experience leads me to a conclusion the therapist's non-judgmental empathic acceptance of the client's world is what is most central and consistent with Rogers' theory of therapy. I think, however, that it is essential that we strive to unravel the meaning of UPR in Rogers' theory of therapy and to identify the sources of difference in the views of UPR that appear to divide practitioners

SUMMARY

This chapter has attempted to ferret out the agreements and differences among the presentations of unconditional positive regard within the context of Rogers' theory.

The substantial agreements among authors are that UPR is a critical variable in client-centered therapy and is integrally related to the whole of the necessary and sufficient conditions. Examples of therapy in several chapters provide rich examples of therapists' functioning with unconditional positive regard.

The disagreements about UPR revolve predominantly around one point. This point is whether or not UPR is a precursor to other goals or is itself the essential curative factor that induces the processes and behaviors associated with the actualizing tendency. Other goals are directed to expanding the experiential field of the client and are mostly views of those who are more associated with 'experiential' therapy or the integration of other theoretical concepts with client-centered therapy.

The implications of Rogers' work, and the role of UPR beyond therapy that are forwarded in several chapters, further suggest the importance for unraveling the complexities of UPR proposed in Rogers' revolutionary theory of therapy.

REFERENCES

Baldwin, M. (1987). Interview with Carl Rogers on the use of self in therapy. In M. Baldwin and V. Satir (Eds.) *The Use of Self in Therapy*. New York: The Haworth Press, pp. 45–52.

Barrett-Lennard, G. T. (1962). Dimensions of therapist response as causal factors in therapeutic change. *Psychological Monographs*, 76 (43. Whole No. 562).

Barrett-Lennard, G. T. (1998). *Carl Rogers' Helping system: Journey and substance*. London: Sage.

Bozarth, J. D. (1990). The essence of client-centered therapy. In G. Lietaer, J. Rombauts, and R. Van Balen (Eds.) *Client-Centered and Experiential Psychotherapy in the Nineties*. Leuven: Leuven University Press, pp. 59–64.

Bozarth, J. D. (1997). Empathy from the framework of client-centered theory and the Rogerian hypothesis. In A. C. Bohart and L. S. Greenburg (Eds.) *Empathy Reconsidered: New Directions in Psychotherapy*. Washington D.C.: American Psychological Association, pp. 81–102.

Bozarth, J. D. (1998). *Person-Centered Therapy : A Revolutionary Paradigm*. Ross-on-Wye, England: PCCS Books.

Bozarth, J. D. (March, 2000). Non-directiveness in client-centered therapy: A vexed concept. Paper presentation at the *Eastern Psychological Association*, Baltimore, Md.

Bozarth, J. D. (2001a). An addendum to Beyond Reflection: Emergent modes of empathy. In S. Haugh and T. Merry (Eds.) *Empathy*. Ross-On Wye: PCCS Books, pp. 144–54.

Bozarth, J. D. (2001b). Congruence: A special way of being. In G. Wyatt (Ed.) *Rogers' Therapeutic Conditions. Evolution, Theory and Practice. Vol. 1: Congruence*. Ross-on-Wye, England: PCCS Books, pp. 184–99.

Bozarth, J. D., and Fischer, R. (1990). Person-centered career counseling. In W. B. Walsh and S. Osdipow (Eds.) *Career Counseling*. Hillsdale, NJ: Erlbaum, pp. 45–78.

Bozarth, J. D., Zimring, F. and Tausch, R. (2002) Client-Centered Therapy: Evolution of a revolution. In D. Cain and J. Seeman (Eds.) *Handbook of Humanistic Psychotherapy: Research and Practice*. Washington D. C.: America Psychological Association, pp. 147–88.

Brodley, B. T. (1988). Carl Rogers therapy. In F. Zimring (Chair), Re-examination of client-centered therapy using Rogers' tapes and films: Symposium conducted at the meeting of the American Psychological Association, Atlanta.

Carkhuff, R. R. (1969). *Helping and Human Relations, vol. l*. New York: Holt, Rinehart, and Winston.

Hart, J. T. and Tomlinson, T. M. (1970). *New directions in client-centered therapy*. Boston: Houghton Mifflin.

Kirschenbaum, H. and Henderson, V. L. (1989). *The Carl Rogers Reader*. Boston: Houghton Mifflin Company.

Lietaer, G. (1984). Unconditional positive regard: A controversial basic attitude in Client-Centered Therapy. In R. Levant and J. Shlien (Eds.) *Client-Centered Therapy and the Person-Centered Approach: New Directions in Theory, Research, and Practice*. New York: Praeger, pp. 41–58.

Raskin, N. J. and Rogers, C. R., (1989) Person-centered therapy. In R. J. Corsini and D. Wedding (Eds.) *Current Psychotherapies* Itasca: F. E. Peacock, pp. 155–94.

Rogers, C. R. (1957). The necessary and sufficient conditions of therapeutic personality change. *Journal of Consulting Psychology, 21*(2) , 95–103.

Rogers, C. R. (1959) A theory of therapy, personality, and interpersonal relationships as developed in the client-centered framework. In S. Koch (Ed.) *Psychology: A Study of Science: Vol. 3 Formulation of the Person and the Social Context*. New York: McGraw Hill, pp. 184–256.

Rogers, C. R., (1963) The actualizing tendency in relation to 'motives' and to consciousness. In M. Jones (Ed.), *Nebraska Symposium on Motivation*. Lincoln: University of Nebraska Press.

Rogers, C. R. (1975) Empathic: An unappreciated way of being. *The Counseling Psychologist, 5*(2), 2–10.

Rogers, C. R. (1978). The formative tendency. *Journal of Humanistic Psychology, 18*(4), 23–6.

Rogers, C. R. (1980). *A way of being*. Boston: Houghton Mifflin.

Rogers, C. R., (1986). A client-centered/person-centered approach to therapy. In I. Kutash and A. Wolfe (Eds.) *Psychotherapists' Casebook*. Jossey-Bass, pp. 197–208.

Stubbs, J. P. and Bozarth, J. D. (1996). The integrative statement of Carl Rogers. In R. Hutterer, G. Pawlowsky, P. Schmid, and R. Stipsits (Eds.) *Client-Centered and Experiential Psychotherapy: A Paradigm in Motion*. New York: Peter Lang, pp. 25–33.

Truax, C. B. and Carkhuff, R. R. (1967). *Toward effective counseling and psychotherapy: Training and practice*. Chicago: Aldine.

Wyatt, G. (2001). *Rogers' Therapeutic Conditions. Evolution, Theory and Practice. Vol. 1: Congruence*. Ross-on-Wye, England: PCCS Books.

Index of Authors

Contributors to this Volume

THE EDITORS

Jerold D. Bozarth, Ph.D is Professor Emeritus of the University of Georgia where his tenure included Chairperson of the Department of Counseling and Counseling Psychology, and Director of the Person-Centered Studies Program. He was Editor of the *Person-Centered Journal* and is currently on the editorial board of numerous journals. Dr. Bozarth has been a consultant with person-centered training programs in England, the Czech Republic, Portugal, and Brazil. He has participated widely in international presentations and written over 300 professional articles and book chapters. His book, *Person-Centered Therapy: A Revolutionary Paradigm*, is in its second printing with PCCS Books.

Paul Wilkins writes: I am an academic and therapist deeply committed to the person-centred approach about which I have written papers, chapters and books. My doctoral study was of what it means to be person-centred and I am currently as much interested in how to be person-centred as a researcher as I am in extending my understanding of person-centred theory and practice. I am passionate about the creativity I see as inherent in the approach and seek to apply this to all areas of my life. When I am not thinking, writing, researching or teaching I like to enjoy the good things the world has to offer, wild places, music, wine and food to name but a few!

CONTRIBUTORS

Barbara Temaner Brodley Ph.D has been a client-centered therapist for many years. She received her Ph.D in clinical psychology and human development at the University of Chicago and was on the staff of the Counseling Center there founded by Carl Rogers for seven years. She is in private practice and is a Core Associate professor and Co-coordinator of the Minor in Client-Centered and Experiential Therapy at the Illinois School of Professional Psychology — Chicago Campus. She is the Training Director at the Chicago Counseling and Psychotherapy Center and teaches client-centered therapy to training groups in Europe. She has written several dozen articles on client-centered theory and practice.

Gerald Bauman is a clinical psychologist who has been in the private practice of psychotherapy for 50 years. His orientation as a person-centered psychotherapist gradually evolved, facilitated in large part by his acquaintance with Carl Rogers and his writings, and by his 'teaming up' with Nat Raskin and Armin Klein in a very close three way friendship. In the 1960s, he was a member of the originating group of the Lincoln Hospital Mental Health Center, where he served as Associate Clinical Professor at the Albert Einstein College of Medicine, director of psychological services and psychotherapy supervisor for psychology interns and psychiatric residents.

Elizabeth Schmitt Freire is a psychologist and person-centered therapist, and is Director of a Person-Centered Training Program in Brazil. She is also a therapist supervisor and has written a book with Newton Tambara, in Portuguese, about the theory and practice of Client-Centered Therapy. She has recently published an article in Brazil entitled 'The therapy is the relationship and the therapist is the client', and has published in the Person-Centered Journal about the challenges of the clinical practice of client-centered therapy.

Marion N. Hendricks Ph.D is the Director of the Focusing Institute, and conducts workshops and lectures on Focusing-Oriented Psychotherapy and 'Thinking At The Edge' world-wide. She runs the Institute's two year post-degree training program for therapists in New York City and has been in private practice for thirty years. She received her Client-Centered training at the University of Chicago. She was one of the founders of CHANGES, a community therapy network and has worked as a psychologist-trainer in the New York State Hospital system. She was a core faculty member at the Illinois School of Professional Psychology in Chicago for ten years, where she established the Experiential/Client-Centered specialization, before moving to New York. She is married to Eugene Gendlin and they have one daughter.

James R. Iberg, Ph.D has been in private psychotherapy practice for over 20 years in Chicago and Evanston, IL, USA. He is Associate Core Faculty at the Illinois School of Professional Psychology, and a Certifying Coordinator for the Focusing Institute. He has taught focusing, empathic listening, and other communication skills in several countries. He conducts process-outcome studies with student and private practice therapists and their clients. He organized and directs a group of therapists serving clients outside of the third party payer system (see Quinpro.com). Therapists in Quinpro collaborate for process-monitoring to track client progress, and process and maintain therapist effectiveness.

Armin Klein is a psychologist in private practice in Rochester, N.Y. He trained with Carl Rogers at the Counseling Center of the University of Chicago in 1950. He developed the Counseling Center of Hampton University and taught at the University of Rochester. He became Assistant Director of the Convalescent Hospital for Children, a community mental health center for children and their families. He is also a member of a famous psychotherapy trio with Nat Raskin and Gerald Bauman.

Toru Kuno: Toru Kuno, M.A. is in charge of business planning of the distance education, and an editor of teaching materials, at SANNO Institute of Business. He also teaches industrial and general psychology at SANNO University and SANNO Junior College. He is a Collaborative Editor of the *Japanese Journal of Clinical Psychology*. He is a member of Employee Assistance Professional Association in U.S. and the President of Healthy Company Association in Japan. He promotes the exchange programs for Person-Centered oriented people from Japan and overseas. He is an author of *Interpretations of Carl Rogers, Rogers and Rogerians in Japan*.

Germain Lietaer studied as a post-doctoral fellow with Carl Rogers at the Center for the Studies of the Person in La Jolla in 1969–70. He is a full professor at the Catholic University of Leuven and teaches client-centred/experiential psychotherapy and process research in psychotherapy. He is also a staff member of a three year part-time postgraduate training programme in client-centred/experiential psychotherapy at the same university. Professor Lietaer has published widely: he is chief editor (with J. Rombauts and R. Van Balen) of *Client-Centered and Experiential Psychotherapy in the Nineties* (Leuven, Belgium: Leuven University Press) and co-editor (with L.S. Greenberg and J. Watson) of the *Handbook of Experiential Psychotherapy* (New York: Guilford, 1998).

Kathryn Moon is a therapist in the client-centered practice group that has devolved from the original Chicago Counseling Center. She has a passion for unfacilitated large group meetings and is intrigued by questions pertaining to family and couples therapy. She received her B.A. at the University of Chicago in 1973, MALS in Library Science in 1976, and her MA in Clinical Psychology at the Illinois School of Professional Psychology in 1989. She is involved in training programs for the Chicago Counseling and Psychotherapy Center and is an adjunct faculty member at the Illinois School of Professional Psychology.

Judy Moore has worked within the person-centred approach since the mid-1980s and has taught for several years on the Diploma in Counselling at the University of East Anglia. She is currently Director of Counselling as well as part-time lecturer in the Centre for Counselling Studies at UEA. She has published several chapters and articles on the person-centred approach and, through her study and practice of Soto Zen and the teachings of the PRH organisation, has become increasingly interested in how we, as human beings, may further our spiritual as well as our emotional and intellectual growth.

Dr. Garry Prouty PhD is a fellow of the Chicago Counseling Center and an Honorary Member of the Chicago Psychological Association. He is author of *Theoretical Evolutions in Person-Centered/Experiential Therapy: Applications to Schizophrenic and Retarded Psychoses* (Praeger). He is also co-author of *Pre-Therapie* (Klett-Cotta, Stuttgart). He is currently serving as an editorial consultant to several international client-centered journals. Also, he has served as a consultant to *Psychotherapy: Theory, research and Practice* and *The International Journal of Mental Imagery.* As the founder of the Pre-Therapy approach, he has toured Europe over the past 16 years, lecturing and providing workshops at universities, clinics and training programs. Currently he is a member of the Pre-Therapy International Network and consults for the *International Pre-Therapy Review.*

Bert Rice left the practice of law in 1996 to pursue learning opportunities in an elementary school classroom. His wife, Kathy Moon, introduced him both to the writings and theories of Carl Rogers and to the joys of the person-centered community as experienced at the annual Association for the Development of the Person Centered Approach (ADPCA) meetings and the workshops in Warm Springs, Georgia. He seeks to apply to education Rogers' idea that the relationship between therapist and client should be based on the profound respect of the former for the self-directing capabilities of the latter.

Ruth Sanford has been a teacher, counselor, administrator, researcher and therapist over her career. She has been a facilitator of learning for individuals ranging from school children to doctoral candidates. For ten years, she worked with Carl Rogers as a co-facilitator and co-faculty in programs in the United States and abroad. These programs included the facilitation of notable workshops in Russia and South Africa with Rogers. She has also published professional papers concerning the theory and practice of the person-centered approach. With colleagues, she developed and implemented the Person-Centered Training Program in New York.

Peter F. Schmid, Univ. Doz. HSProf. Mag. Dr. Born in 1950; Associate Professor at the University of Graz, Styria and teaches at European universities. He is a person–centred psychotherapist, practical theologian and pastoral psychologist, founder of person-centred training and further training in Austria, and co-director of the Academy for Counselling and Psychotherapy of the Austrian 'Institute for Person–Centred Studies (IPS of APG)'. He is a Board Member of both the World Association (WAPCEPC) and the European Network (NEAPCEPC), and has published many books and articles about anthropology and further developments of the Person–Centered Approach.

Carolyn Schneider has practiced as a client-centered therapist since 1987. She was fortunate to proceed directly from graduate school to the Chicago Counseling and Psychotherapy Center's practicum, then internship, and to later join the group and serve as director from 1992 to 2001. She received her B.A. and M.A. from the University of Chicago where she completed research with Dr. Mihalyi Csikzentmihalyi. In addition to a therapy practice, Carolyn now serves as director of psychotherapy services and training supervisor at Horizons Community Services. Carolyn is also a part time trainer for the Chicago Metropolitan Battered Women's Network.

Patricia Steckley, MEd is currently a doctoral student at the Ontario Institute for Studies in Education at the University of Toronto. She has done research on the function of emotion in film viewing as well as research on psychotherapy process in the treatment of depression. Her dissertation pertains to the impact of therapeutic empathy on clients' treatment of themselves. Patricia is currently studying Tibetan Buddhism and exploring meditiation and its impacy on mental and physical well-being.

Jeanne C. Watson, Ph.D is an associate professor in the Department of Adult Education, Community Development and Counselling Psychology at the Ontario Institute for Studies in Education of the University of Toronto. She is co-author (with Eileen Kennedy-Moore) of *Expressing Emotion: Myths, Realities and Therapeutic Strategies* and co-editor (with Leslie Greenberg and Germain Lietaer) of the *Handbook of Experiential Psychotherapy*. In addition Dr. Watson has written numerous articles on psychotherapy process and outcome and maintains a part-time private practice in Toronto.